The
Rape
of the
Taxpayer

The
Rape
of the
Taxpayer

PHILIP M. STERN

Random House
New York

All rights reserved under International and Pan-American Copyright Con-
ventions. Published in the United States by Random House, Inc., New
York, and simultaneously in Canada by Random House of Canada Limited,
Toronto.

Library of Congress Cataloging in Publication Data

Stern, Philip M.
The rape of the taxpayer.
1. Income tax—United States. I. Title.
HJ4652.S783   336.′4′0973   72-11368
ISBN 0-394-46998-4

Manufactured in the United States of America

First Edition

This book is dedicated to my five beloved personal exemptions

Henry
Michael
Holly
David
Eve

each of whom, in his or her special way, has brought joy,
pride and love into my life. No father was ever more blessed.

If income taxes were 99 percent, we'd figure a way.

—W. CLEMENT STONE

Chicago insurance executive who contributed $4 million to President Nixon's 1968 and 1972 election campaigns, making him the "largest known political donor in American history."

If the government cannot collect its taxes, a man is a fool to pay them.

—J. PIERPONT MORGAN

PREFACE

TEN YEARS AGO I WROTE *The Great Treasury Raid,* whose object was "to make the subject of tax loopholes intelligible to my wife." It was published in 1964, and it did well: was on the nether end of several best-seller lists for a number of weeks. But, at the time, tax reform was a little-discussed political issue, and public disgruntlement with the loopholes was virtually imperceptible.

Since then, however, public unrest about the tax system has begun to grow—sparked in large measure, I think, by the 1969 revelation by outgoing Treasury Secretary Joseph Barr that 155 Americans making more than $200,000 were paying no tax whatever.

Accordingly, in the late summer of 1971, as tax reform was becoming much more widely discussed, my friend Art Buchwald suggested that *The Great Treasury Raid* had appeared before its time, and that a revised version of the book would attract far wider public attention. Since most of the loopholes described in *The Great Treasury Raid* have remained pristine and untouched since 1964, I thought at first that revising the earlier edition would merely be a matter of updating the statistics, correcting the text where necessary to reflect those instances, since 1964, where Congress has changed the tax law. Certain portions of *The Great Treasury Raid* lent themselves to such an approach. Those include the chapters on special provisions of the tax law, tailor-made for certain individuals or companies (Chapter 3); capital gains (Chapter 5); marital "income-splitting" (Chapter 6); the oil and mineral industries (Chapter 11); the inevitable proliferation of loopholes (Chapter 14); estate and gift taxation (Chapter 16); some of the

more unexpected moral preachments of the tax laws (Chapter 17);
and "loopholes for the many" (Chapter 18).

But as I began the revisions and delved into the subject once
again, I found there was much more new to say about tax loopholes and tax reform than I had initially thought. For one thing,
while Congress did, in 1969, close or narrow some of the long-
standing loopholes, it has also opened up some gaping new ones
since 1964, especially in the field of corporate and business taxation. For another, there were several important areas I had not
dealt with at all in *The Great Treasury Raid*—that very area of
tax concessions to corporations being prominent among them (see
Chapter 10, " 'Tax Welfare' for the Corporate Giants"). Other
untouched areas included the tangle of laws on the taxation of
American companies' operations abroad (see Chapter 12, "The
World-Wide Game of 'Beat the Tax Collector' "); the favored tax
status of the timber industry (see Chapter 13, "Timber—Ideal for
Your 'Tax Shelter' "); certain of the more exotic forms of "tax
shelters" employed by high-bracket taxpayers who seek to fend
off Internal Revenue (see Chapter 9, "Running for Shelter"); and
the procedure—important and often costly, but virtually unknown
to the general public—by which Internal Revenue and the Treasury Department grant special in-advance-of-the-fact rulings on
tax questions to taxpayers (mostly businesses) that ask for them:
rulings that can mean tens and even hundreds of millions of tax
savings to the companies involved and yet are considered and
issued in secret (see Chapter 15, "Tax Handouts Behind Closed
Doors"). All of those chapters are new to this book.

There were other topics that I had only touched on obliquely
in the earlier book. For example, there are astonishing advantages
that lie in merely *postponing* payment of a tax (see Chapter 8, "A
Dollar Delayed Can Be Many Dollars Saved"). And I had not adequately explained how dollars allowed to leak out of the Treasury
through the loopholes are identical, in their effect upon budgets
and deficits and on taxpayers generally, to dollars appropriated by
Congress and spent directly from the Treasury. Despite that fact,
tens of billions of "tax expenditures" are unbudgeted, unaccounted
for, unreviewed and generally unseen by the public—a subject
important enough to warrant a chapter of its own (see Chapter 7,
"The 'Treasury Papers' Episode"). Nor had I extracted, for

separate cataloging, the sharp contrasts between the tax law's treatment of rich versus poor (or less-rich) as I have sought to do in Chapter 19. Those chapters, too, plus "Portrait of a Non-Tax-payer" (Chapter 2), are entirely new in this book.

The final two chapters—dealing with the obstacles to loophole-closing and with suggestions for tax reform—are also essentially new. I now feel that my previous discussion of both subjects gave far too little weight to the impact on our tax laws of the manner in which we in America finance our political campaigns. Since no American political candidate can finance his election campaign without substantial contributions from the wealthy and powerful, it is not surprising that the tax laws favor those groups and that there is little demand by candidates for ending their tax bene-factions. Because I am convinced that genuine tax reform won't take place until and unless political fund-raising is also reformed, the final chapter proposes a new plan for the financing of campaigns.

Two other factors led to important changes in that final chapter. One is the emerging attention to (and my own new-found interest in) an old subject: the maldistribution of income and wealth in the United States. The second is Senator George McGovern's initial tax-reform proposal that, for the first time in modern American Presidential politics, openly spoke of integrating the tax and wel-fare systems and of using the tax system to attack the maldistribu-tion of income. Both subjects, not touched on in the earlier version, are discussed in Chapter 21.

Finally, since *The Great Treasury Raid* was published in 1964, two new studies of the tax system have appeared. One was a comprehensive study of certain tax preferences conducted by the Treasury Department under the gifted direction of Stanley S. Surrey, to which you will find frequent reference in this book. The other is a remarkable study by Joseph A. Pechman and Benjamin A. Okner, of the Brookings Institution in Washington, that has illuminated more sharply than ever before just "who gets what" from the loopholes in the existing tax laws. That study led to the concept of the outrageous "tax welfare" system described in Chapter 1 ("Uncle Sam's Welfare Program—For the Rich"), the material for which is virtually all new in this book.

And so this book is not *Son of the Great Treasury Raid* or *The Great Treasury Raid Strikes Back*. It is *The Rape of the Taxpayer*.

MY INTEREST in trying to simplify this eye-glazing subject began in the fall of 1951, when a group of political liberals in the United States Senate, led by Minnesota's Hubert Humphrey, made a concerted though thoroughly unavailing assault on tax loopholes. As a research assistant to one member of that group, Senator Paul H. Douglas of Illinois, I peered for the first time into that dark and tangled jungle, the Internal Revenue Code. Sitting in the Senate chamber beside Senator Douglas during the nine days of that remarkable debate, I was introduced to the world of corporate "spin-offs" . . . two-for-one offsets . . . the "one-way street" provision . . . net operating loss carry-backs . . . collapsible corporations.

As I listened, fascinated and bewildered by the jargon, I was struck by the fact that the public must be almost wholly unaware of what was going on in the Senate chamber—unaware that the provisions being considered, and the tax favors being dispensed, involved millions, tens of millions, sometimes hundreds of millions of dollars. (As Harvard law professor Stanley Surrey wrote in 1957, tax decisions "are largely fought out behind [a] technical curtain" that is "impenetrable to the newspapers and other information media.") Not only was the general public screened off from this debate; most of the Senators seemed to have thrown up their hands in helplessness, abdicating tax decisions to the experts on the tax-writing committees.

This was in the period when, it was said, the Senate's tax policy was largely made by two men: Senator Walter George of Georgia and Senator Eugene Millikin of Colorado, each his party's ranking member of the Senate Finance Committee (which handles tax matters), each expert in tax matters—but neither kindly disposed to the Treasury Department's efforts to tighten up tax preferences and prevent the creation of new ones. When they frowned on a Treasury proposal, the Senate frowned too. But when Senator George looked with favor on a provision to grant $2 million of special tax relief to movie magnate Louis B. Mayer (as he did that year—see Chapter 3), there were none to gainsay him. (Even the Humphrey band of tax rebels were unaware that the Mayer provision was nestled in the very bill they were criticizing.)

Since that time, more Senators have sought to interest and educate themselves in the intricacies of taxation. Nonetheless, nowhere is the aphorism "Knowledge Is Power" more apt than in the writing of the tax laws. And because the knowledge is held by so few, so is the power (as you will see in Chapter 20).

Generally speaking, Congress has not responded kindly to proposals to close the loopholes. That is not likely to change, I believe, so long as millions of nonexpert citizens remain unaware of who-gets-what-from-whom—and also who suffers—because of the loopholes. Hence this effort to make the subject intelligible.

A WORD ABOUT the boundaries of the subject matter covered by this book. It is almost exclusively concerned with the Federal income tax applicable to individuals and corporations, and makes no more than passing mention of other forms of taxation (such as excise, sales, property and payroll taxes). It deliberately by-passes the question of whether government spending is too high or too low, and it does not debate the merits or demerits of government deficits or surpluses. Also undebated is the question of whether tax *rates* should be graduated (i.e., higher at higher income levels—which I, personally, strongly favor) or flat—equal for all incomes. Instead, this book takes the view that once Congress decides how much revenue should be raised and adopts a schedule of tax rates to achieve that, those rates should be applied as uniformly as possible to all citizens and corporations.

THOSE WHO WISH to lessen or eliminate their tax burden may do so in two ways. They might practice tax *evasion*, yet this is not only inadvisable (since it is illegal and carries heavy penalties) but quite unnecessary: the same tax reductions can usually be achieved entirely within the law, through what is known as the art of tax *avoidance*. Tax evasion consists of such transgressions as failing to file a tax return, deliberately failing to report certain income, falsely claiming dependents, or any other deliberate falsehood in the preparation of one's tax return. On the other hand, tax avoidance, with which this book is exclusively concerned, consists simply of arranging one's activities or investments so as to take advantage of the provisions of the tax law itself and thereby reduce one's tax burden. (Some have called it "do-it-yourself tax-cutting.")

Tax avoidance sounds more sinister than it is. For example, putting one's money into state or municipal bonds (whose interest payments are tax-free) instead of Federal bonds (interest-taxable) could be considered tax avoidance. So might investing in a no-dividend "growth" stock, in the hope of a large and lightly taxed gain, rather than in a high-dividend but stably priced stock.

Some wonder if there is always a meaningful difference between avoidance and evasion,* but the courts have clearly held that no moral opprobrium should attach to tax avoidance within the law. As Judge Learned Hand once observed:

> . . . there is nothing sinister in so arranging one's affairs as to keep taxes as low as possible. Everybody does so, rich or poor; and all do right. Nobody owes any public duty to pay more than the law demands: taxes are enforced exactions, not voluntary contributions. To demand more in the name of morals is mere cant.

Senator Pat Harrison of Mississippi, former Chairman of the Senate Finance Committee, expressed it simply: "There's nothing that says a man has to take a toll bridge across a river when there's a free bridge nearby."

No criticism is intended in this book of taxpayers who avail themselves of various tax-saving features that Congress has made available. Indeed, being blessed with substantial means, I do so myself. It is at the law itself, and at those who are responsible for writing it, that fingers should be pointed—not at those who follow it.

FOR EXPERTS AND PRACTITIONERS, the field of taxation is already brightly illuminated by a massive amount of technical literature that leaves me both humble and awed, and to which I do not pretend to have added new knowledge. But for the average citizen, this field is as dimly lit as any in the realm of public affairs. This book, like *The Great Treasury Raid*, is addressed to those who may have cursed the darkness.

PHILIP M. STERN

Washington, D.C.
September, 1972

---

* Ex-lawyer David T. Bazelon, in his book *The Paper Economy*, points out that frequently the law is so ill-defined that taxpayers are prompted to try "a whole passel of maneuvers which turn out to be avoidance or evasion only after the fact."

CONTENTS

xvii

The
Rape
of the
Taxpayer

WHAT'S
IN A BILLION?

Throughout this book, you are going to find the word "billion." Invariably, it will be tied to the word "dollars." You'll read, for example, of the ninety *billion* dollars of tax bounty to giant corporations, or of the fourteen *billion* dollars of tax benefits to the select few who enjoy "capital gains."

"Billion." It's a word that is tossed about with increasing non-chalance in the matter of government finance.

But what *is* a billion dollars? How can one comprehend such a stupendous number?

Well . . . ponder this:

If, beginning with the moment Christ was born, you had begun receiving one dollar every minute of every day—twenty-four hours a day, seven days a week, without interruption . . .

. . . by the time of the Battle of Hastings in 1066 A.D.—that is, after more than a thousand years of dollar-a-minute, round-the-clock earning—you would be barely more than halfway toward having collected a billion dollars.

In fact, you would not have amassed your first billion dollars until 2:21 A.M. of April 14, 1901: very nearly two thousand years after the birth of Christ—and after the receipt of your first dollar.

And if, when that magic moment arrived, you wanted to be sure you hadn't been short-changed and began counting your dollar bills at the rate of one per second, eight hours a day, five days a week, with no vacation, it would take you one hundred and thirty-three and a half years to complete the count.

3

I

Uncle Sam's
Welfare Program —
for the Rich

MOST AMERICANS would probably be greatly surprised to find, in their morning newspaper, a story such as this:

Washington, D.C.—Congress completed action today on a revolutionary welfare program that reverses traditional payment policies and awards huge welfare payments to the super-rich while granting only pennies per week to the very poor.

Under the program, welfare payments averaging some $720,000 a year will go to the nation's wealthiest families—those with annual incomes of over a million dollars.

For the poorest families, those earning $3,000 a year or less, the welfare allowance will average $16 a year, or roughly 30 cents a week.

The program, enacted by Congress in a series of laws over a period of years, has come to be called the Rich Welfare Program, after its principal sponsor, Senator Homer A. Rich. In a triumphant news conference, Senator Rich told newsmen that the $720,000 annual welfare allowance would give America's most affluent families an added weekly take-home pay of about $14,000. "Or, to put it another way," the Senator said, "it will provide these families with about $2,000 more spending money every day."

The total cost of the welfare program, the most expensive in the nation's history, amounts to $77.3 billion a year.

Political analysts foresee acute discontent, not only among the poor but also among middle-income families making $10,000 to

$15,000 a year. For them, welfare payments under the Rich plan will amount to just $12.50 a week, markedly less than the $14,000 paid each week to the very rich.

Reporters asked Senator Rich whether wealthy families would be required to work in order to receive their welfare payments, a common eligibility requirement with many welfare programs. Senator Rich seemed puzzled by the question. "The rich? Work?" he asked. "Why, it hadn't occurred to me." Congressional experts advised newsmen that the program contains no work requirement.

THE ABOVE "NEWS STORY" may sound implausible, if not unbelievable. Yet the story is essentially true. The facts and figures are real. Such a system is part of the law of the land. Only the law isn't called a welfare law: it goes by the name of "The Internal Revenue Code of 1954, as Amended"—the basic income tax law of the United States.

Who gets how much of the tax "welfare" payments from the major "tax preferences"—i.e., "the loopholes"? Until recently, one could make, at best, only an educated guess. But now, with the aid of modern computers, making superhuman calculations based on *actual* tax-return information plus other data from economic surveys, the secret is out, and the answers might astound, or even anger, put-upon taxpayers.

On a per-family basis, a breakdown of the average tax savings of Americans—our "tax welfare" program—looks like this: *

If you make:	Your average yearly "tax welfare" payment is:	Your average increase in weekly "take-home pay" is:
Over $1,000,000	$720,490	$13,855.58
$500,000–$1,000,000	$202,751	$3,899.06
$100,000–$500,000	$41,480	$797.69
$50,000–$100,000	$11,912	$229.08
$25,000–$50,000	$3,897	$74.94
$20,000–$25,000	$1,931	$37.13
$15,000–$20,000	$1,181	$22.71
$10,000–$15,000	$651	$12.52
$5,000–$10,000	$339	$6.52
$3,000–$5,000	$148	$2.85
Under $3,000	$16	31 cents

* The source for these figures and other facts throughout this book may be found in the Notes and Sources section, pp. 441–472.

SINCE A TAX LAW takes money *from* people, rather than paying money *to* them, what connection does the tax law have with the topsy-turvy welfare system in the news story? The connection lies in the way Congress has played fast and loose with the Sixteenth Amendment to the Constitution, and with the principle of basing taxes on "ability to pay."

The Sixteenth Amendment, which authorized the first United States income tax, empowered Congress to tax "incomes, *from whatever source derived. . . .*" (Emphasis added.) This expresses the notion that a dollar is a dollar and that, regardless of its source, each dollar endows its lucky recipient with 100 cents of "ability to pay" for food, shoes for the baby, a fraction of a yacht—or taxes. Hence, fairness dictates that all dollars, no matter what their origin, should be taxed uniformly.

But Congress has decreed differently. It has decreed that dollars made in an oil or real-estate venture, in a stock market bonanza, or in interest on a state or local bond, while undeniably capable of buying food, shoes or yachts, are somehow reduced in paying power when it comes to paying taxes—for Congress has exempted such dollars, in whole or in part, from taxation. It has done this via an elaborate network of exemptions, deductions, exclusions, exceptions and special rates that have come to be called "loopholes." And every time Congress enacted one of these preferences, it excused someone from paying what could and would have been collected if Congress had stuck to the Sixteenth Amendment and had taxed "incomes, from whatever source derived."

To give a concrete example, Jean Paul Getty is one of the richest men in the world: he is said to be worth between a billion and a billion and a half dollars, and to have a *daily* income of $300,000. If Congress were to apply to Mr. Jean Paul Getty the standard of the Sixteenth Amendment, and were to tax his entire "income, from whatever source derived" at the current tax rates,* Mr. Getty would, each April 15, write a check to the Internal Revenue Service for roughly $70 million. But Jean Paul Getty is an oilman; and, as is well known, oilmen enjoy a variety of special tax escape routes (see Chapter 11). As a result, according to what President Kennedy told two United States Senators, *Mr. Jean Paul Getty's tax, at least in the early Sixties, amounted to no more than*

---

* These tax rates, of course, rise as a person's affluence grows, on the understandable theory that a person of Mr. Getty's wealth and income is considerably better "able to pay" taxes than, say, an impoverished Kentucky coal miner.

a few thousand dollars. Annual tax saving to Mr. Getty (at 1973 rates): $70 million.

Now, compare the consequences of that $70 million "tax forgiveness" that Congress bestowed on Mr. Getty with the effect if Congress had, instead, voted him a $70 million welfare payment paid to him by check directly from the U.S. Treasury.

Consequences of a $70 Million Direct Welfare Payment to Mr. Getty	*Consequences of a $70 Million "Tax Forgiveness" to Mr. Getty*
1. Mr. Getty is $70 million richer.	1. Mr. Getty is $70 million richer.*
2. The U.S. Treasury is $70 million poorer.	2. The U.S. Treasury is $70 million poorer.†
3. The rest of the U.S. taxpayers have to pay $70 million more taxes to make up the difference.	3. The rest of the U.S. taxpayers have to pay $70 million more taxes to make up the difference.

* Than if he had paid the full tax called for under the Sixteenth Amendment.
† Than it would have been had Mr. Getty paid the full tax.

The fact is there is no real difference, as far as the U.S. Treasury (i.e., you and all the other taxpayers) is concerned, and thus, even though no "tax welfare" checks actually pass hands, all the special gimmicks and escape hatches that Congress has been writing into the tax laws, about which you will read in this book, are *the equivalent of* direct welfare payments to the lucky recipients of the tax favors.

Reduced to its simplest terms, you (and all the rest of the American taxpayers like you) are having to make up for the taxes that Jean Paul Getty and other "loophole" users do not pay. You may make it up in higher taxes or in large Federal deficits. Or you might pay for it in the form of trimmed-down government spending for day-care centers or antipollution, mass transit or housing assistance programs that could be of direct benefit to you— but for which Congress or the President concludes that "the money isn't available." Of course, if the loopholes didn't exist, and the dollars that now leak out through them were collected, the money *would* be "available." One way or another, the cost of the loopholes falls upon those to whom tax escape routes are less available.

In fact, the main point of this book could well be reduced

to one simple sentence that might usefully be embroidered on a sampler and hung on each taxpayer's wall:

WHEN SOMEONE ELSE PAYS LESS
THE REST OF US PAY MORE

Some additional insights into the fairness with which the "tax welfare" payments are distributed among the American people may be drawn from the following figures:

This income group ...	has this many families* ...	and gets this amount of "tax welfare" payments
Under $3,000	6,000,000	$92,000,000
Over $1,000,000	3,000	$2,200,000,000

* See Notes and Sources.

That last line deserves to be put more starkly: more than two *billion* dollars of "tax welfare" is distributed among just three thousand families—the three thousand richest American families. (By happenstance, that two billion is precisely the amount that Congress voted in 1971 to provide food stamps for millions of hungry families throughout the United States.)

For still another appraisal of the tax system's fairness, you might want to identify where you fit into the following picture:

This income group ...	comprises this percent of the population ...	but gets this percent of the "tax welfare" payments
Under $10,000	45.7%	10.0%
Under $15,000	70.6%	24.7%
Over $100,000	0.3%	14.7%

That last statistic comes more to life when you realize that the 14.7 percent that is distributed among the richest three families in every *thousand* comes to a tidy (if that's the proper word) $11,400,000,000 per year. That's $11.4 *billion,* which amounts to:

• thirty-four times what the Federal government is spending on cancer research and seven times proposed U.S. outlays for medical research of all kinds;

• sixty-four times the budget proposals for assuring the purity and safety of all foods and drugs;

• forty-eight times what the United States is spending for all hospital construction;

• sixteen times Federal spending for the training of doctors and nurses;

• ten times U.S. outlays for the school lunch program;

• five times total outlays for crime reduction;

• seven times the budget of the Federal Environmental Protection Agency.

ANOTHER WAY of looking at all this is that $77 billion* worth of wool is being pulled over your eyes. Here's why:

On page 24 of the instructions that come with your income-tax form is a table of tax rates—starting at 14 percent and rising to 70 percent, for the highest-income people—that might lead you to believe, when you sweat over your tax return every spring, that your fellow citizens are called upon to pay taxes in accordance with their "ability to pay." That is, if those tax rates mean what they seem to say, you might find some comfort in the thought that, painful as your own tax might be, rich people are paying a far greater proportion of their incomes to Uncle Sam than you are. After all, it says so, right in the tax-rate table: if a married person's unearned taxable income is more than $200,000, he pays $110,900 plus 70 percent† of everything over $200,000. From the tax-rate table, then, you'd think that people in Jean Paul Getty's income bracket pay well over 60 percent of their colossal incomes to Internal Revenue.

But much of the comfort you may derive from that tax-rate table is unwarranted, for Congress has, in effect, made a sham of it. Here's a comparison of what the rate tables *theoretically* call on people to pay (as a percentage of their incomes) and what in fact

---

* The total of the "tax welfare" payments to individuals.

† Throughout this book, there will be references to people whose top bracket is higher than 50 percent (i.e., between 50 and 70 percent). This is not inconsistent with the 50 percent top-bracket rate, enacted in 1969, which applies solely to *earned* (i.e., salary) income but does *not* apply to so-called *un*earned income (from dividends, interest, stock market profits and the like). So wherever you see references to wealthy people in, say, the 60 or 70 percent bracket, you may assume that they have large amounts of unearned income. (As you will see on p. 27, the stratospherically rich are likely to have huge *un*earned incomes, but minuscule or nonexistent *earned* incomes.)

they *do* pay, after they've taken advantage of all the special loopholes that Congress has written into the tax law:

For a family with this much income* ...	this is the percent of their income* that ...		
	the tax law seems to call on them to pay in taxes	they actually do pay in taxes after using the loopholes	the loopholes save them
$2,000–$3,000	1.9%	0.5%	1.4%
$5,000–$6,000	7.5%	2.8%	4.7%
$10,000–$11,000	12.4%	7.6%	4.8%
$20,000–$25,000	20.8%	12.1%	8.7%
$75,000–$100,000	46.0%	26.8%	19.2%
$200,000–$500,000	58.0%	29.6%	28.4%
$500,000–$1 million	60.5%	30.4%	30.1%
Over $1 million	63.1%	32.1%	31.0%

* These figures are taken from a Brookings Institution computer study, conducted by Joseph A. Pechman and Benjamin A. Okner, which is based on *total* family income.

For those gazing in consternation (or rage) at that third column, it requires no special expertise to realize not only that the loopholes save families a greater *percentage* of their income as they grow richer, but that at the top of the pyramid *this is a greater percentage of an astronomically larger income* than is true at the bottom of the heap. Hence, the dollar savings escalate dramatically. Even though you've seen some of the figures before, they bear repeating in this slightly different form:

If you make:	Your average yearly family income is:	The loopholes save you this much in taxes yearly:
Under $3,000	$1,345	$16
$3,000–$5,000	$4,016	$148
$5,000–$10,000	$7,484	$339
$10,000–$15,000	$12,342	$651
$15,000–$20,000	$17,202	$1,181
$20,000–$25,000	$22,188	$1,931
$25,000–$50,000	$32,015	$3,897
$50,000–$100,000	$65,687	$11,912
$100,000–$500,000	$165,998	$41,840
$500,000–$1,000,000	$673,040	$202,751
Over $1,000,000	$2,316,872	$720,490

Still another way of judging the fairness of the present income tax laws, *including* all the loopholes, is by the amount of "keeping money" various families have left over, after Internal Revenue has taken its toll:

For families in this income range:	The average yearly "keeping money" comes to:	The average weekly "take-home pay" comes to:
Under $3,000	$1,339	$25.75
$3,000–$5,000	$3,947	$75.90
$5,000–$10,000	$7,180	$138.08
$10,000–$15,000	$11,274	$216.81
$15,000–$20,000	$15,375	$295.67
$20,000–$25,000	$19,528	$375.54
$25,000–$50,000	$27,413	$527.17
$50,000–$100,000	$50,334	$967.96
$100,000–$500,000	$117,072	$2,251.38
$500,000–$1,000,000	$468,624	$9,012.00
$1,000,000 and over	$1,574,070*	$30,270.58

* This high average is explained by the fact that the "million and over" income group includes people with incomes of $2 million, $3 million, $5 million, etc.

If you are in either of the lowest two income groups mentioned above—that is, if you are trying to make ends meet on less than $75.92 a week—you might wonder whether *any* family in the United States really needs $1,574,070 a year (or over $30,000 of "take-home pay" each *week*). You might conclude that the present loophole-ridden income tax laws are excessively generous to the super-rich.* And if you feel overburdened by taxes (as who doesn't?), you may be less than overjoyed to learn that for the richest one percent of Americans, their *actual* income tax burden has become markedly lighter in recent years.†

---

* You might also be interested to know that even if there were no loopholes in the tax law, and those over-$1-million-income families had to pay the full 63.1 percent of their incomes that the tax law *seems* to call for, they would still, on the average, have $853,580 of yearly "keeping money." This would give them $16,415 of weekly "take-home pay." This, in turn, might lead to the question of whether the existing top-bracket tax rate of 70 percent, severe as it may at first seem, fully satisfies the concept of "ability to pay." After all, the matter of after-tax "keeping money" is as relevant to "ability to pay" as the before-tax total income.

† Declining from 33 to just 26 percent of their total incomes between 1952 and 1967.

OF ALL THE VARIOUS LOOPHOLES, none contributes so flagrantly or so dramatically to the upside-down "tax welfare" system as the preferential treatment accorded so-called "capital gains"—the profits from the sale of stocks and bonds, buildings, land and other kinds of property—which are taxed at no more than half the rates that apply to other kinds of income. The strange ways in which that provision of the law operates are spelled out in Chapter 5; yet it is worth pausing, at this point, to gaze with wonderment (or anger) at the extent to which a single feature of the tax law can heap Federal largesse upon the well-to-do while it almost totally excludes the "average" taxpayer. Bear in mind, as you examine the following table, that only one taxpayer in ten receives *any* capital gains and the tax benefactions that flow therefrom; nine out of ten Americans have not gained admission to this exclusive club:

If you make:	Your yearly "tax welfare" from capital gains is:
Over $1,000,000	$640,667
$500,000–$1,000,000	$165,000
$100,000–$500,000	$22,630
$50,000–$100,000	$3,795
$25,000–$50,000	$534
$20,000–$25,000	$120
$15,000–$20,000	$55
$10,000–$15,000	$24
$5,000–$10,000	$9
$3,000–$5,000	$1
Under $3,000	—

SO FAR, we've been talking about the tax savings that go to the *average* family in each of the various income groups. But, striking as the averages are, they nonetheless conceal the absolutely extraordinary tax-avoiding achievements of particular families and individuals who managed to fare enormously better than the average. For example, under the tax laws that prevailed throughout the Sixties:

• A rapidly growing number of rich and super-rich families managed to avoid sharing so much as a penny of their huge incomes with the U.S. government—that is, they paid zero taxes. These are the statistics:

Family Income	Number of Families Who Paid No Tax in		
	1960	1967	1969
Over $1 million	11	23	56
Over $500,000	23	63	117
Over $200,000	70	167	301
Over $100,000	104	399	761

• In the late Sixties (before the law applicable to them was changed), four persons* were able to enjoy incomes ranging from $6 million to as high as nearly $11 million in a single year without paying a penny of tax (by diverting what would have been their tax payments to the charities of their choice).

• Still another taxpayer was able to enjoy a total income of about $1,284,718 and escape with paying a tax of just $274— about the amount of taxes payable by a single individual with an income of just $2,400.

• An oil investor was able to shield his entire income of $1,313,811 from the tax collector. Many of his confreres in the oil-investing fraternity managed to avoid paying taxes year in and year out. One such worthy paid no income tax from 1949 to 1962! Another left standing instructions with his tax attorney that should any potentially taxable income appear on his financial horizon, raising the specter that he might have to pay some income tax, the tax attorney should proceed forthwith to "drill it up" (i.e., invest in enough oil-drilling ventures to create tax deductions that would cancel out the offensively taxable income). Some have been reported to have enlisted the aid of computers to calculate pre-

---

* Those four "persons," plus the other taxpayers cited in the next three examples, are *actual* persons cited in a Treasury Department study made public in 1969. Under the law, the Treasury could not publish the names of the taxpayers (or non-taxpayers) involved. The feats described in that study took place before the enactment of the Tax Reform Act of 1969, which made certain types of the avoidance more difficult, but, as you will see, far from impossible.

cisely the amount of tax-deductible drilling required to achieve total tax avoidance with a minimum of "wasted" deductions.

• A real-estate investor paid no tax whatever on an income of $1,433,000.

• Trucking magnate Robert Short managed, with a cash outlay of just $1,000, to purchase the Washington Senators baseball team, and then to exploit the tax laws so as to derive, therefrom, tax advantages totaling $4 million—all on a cash outlay of just $1,000. (For details of this spectacular sports feat, see Notes and Sources.)

• One centenarian lady, Mrs. Horace Dodge (of Dodge auto fame and fortune), was able, before her death in 1970 at age one hundred and three, to amass holdings of state and local bonds amounting to $100 million—which put her in the happy position of being able to receive the grand total of $5 million of income each year, *without even having to file an income tax return!* (You'll learn on page 62 how that feat is possible.)

But all of these tax avoiders, startling as their feats may seem, were rank amateurs compared with one hyper-rich oilman, cited in a 1960 Treasury Department study, who one year had *total income of more than twenty-six million dollars ($26,440,776, to be precise) and yet paid no tax whatever.* (See page 229.)

DURING THE YEARS when these tax-escape exploits were taking place, some 2,200,000 families whose incomes were below the officially designated "poverty line" were obliged to pay some of their meager incomes to the U.S. Treasury (unlike the totally tax-avoiding multimillionaires). And some 20 million families who were struggling to survive on incomes of $100 a week were also compelled to share their incomes with Uncle Sam.

Accordingly, when in January 1969 the outgoing Secretary of the Treasury revealed the existence of the many totally taxless multimillionaires, that news caused considerable grumbling among taxpayers who could not understand why the super-rich should not share the burden of supporting their government. Ripples of unrest reached the Congress of the United States, which responded with what is proudly entitled "The Tax Reform Act of 1969." It was, without question, a tax act; whether it qualified for the title of a "reform" act, you will soon be able to judge for yourself.

As an example of the "reform," Congress enacted a so-called "minimum tax," whose supposed purpose was to put an end to the total tax-escape achievements of the very rich.. Yet, when the dust had cleared, it was evident that Congress had built into even this anti-loophole provision some new escape hatches through which the rich and well-advised could wriggle. For, in the very first year in which this "minimum tax" was in effect:

• three families who had *average* dividend income of $2,450,-000 per family had contrived to pay no tax whatever;

• one hundred twelve families with incomes of more than $200,000 had managed the same feat;

• three hundred ninety-four families taking in more than $100,000 had also been able to protect their entire incomes from Internal Revenue. (The Treasury did not reveal *how* these families were able to avoid the new "minimum tax.")

But this was only the top of the iceberg. Internal Revenue statistics painted a portrait of three groups of super-rich families to whom the new "minimum tax" did apply—that is, families who would have continued to escape wholly tax-free but for the "minimum tax." You can see for yourself, from the following figures, the gentleness of the new tax:

Group	Number of Families	Average Family Income	Percent of That Income Paid in Taxes
1	279	$471,220	3%
2	31	$1,397,420	4.4%
3	8	$1,703,750	4%

In other words, those families were able to keep upward of 95 percent of their ample incomes wholly intact, untouched by the tax collector. Their *average* after-tax "keeping money," respectively, amounted to $457,098 for Group 1; $1,335,678 for Group 2; and $1,636,375 (over $31,000 a *week*) for Group 3.

ALL OF THIS takes on a different perspective when viewed through the eyes of one Ralph Senters, a laborer at the Otis Elevator factory in Cleveland, whose year's work brought him $7,371.72. Of that, he paid Federal income taxes of $1,131.47 —nearly 16 percent, or about one-sixth of his income.

Side by side, the figures look like this:

	Year's Income	Percent of Income Paid in Taxes
Group 3 families	$1,703,750	4%
Ralph Senters	$7,372	16%

The "keeping money" enjoyed *each week* by families in Group 3 was five times Ralph Senters' "keeping money" *for the entire year*.

THE TAX BURDEN borne by Ralph Senters, and taxpayers like him, also stands in sharp contrast to that of many of America's major corporations. For example, in 1970 and 1971, nine corporate giants made a total of $650 million in profits—enough to enable them to pay their shareholders a total of $461 million (nearly a half-*billion* dollars) in dividends—and yet managed to avoid paying a penny of income tax to the U.S. government in either 1970 or 1971.* Here is what analysis of the publicly available information shows:†

Corporation	Net Profits Before Taxes	Dividends Paid to Shareholders	Federal Income Taxes Paid
1971			
Alcoa Aluminum	$50,199,000	$41,300,000	0
Continental Oil	$109,030,000	$76,329,000	0
Gulf & Western	$51,381,000	$15,939,000	0
McDonnell Douglas	$144,613,000	$38,904,000	0
1970			
Bethlehem Steel	$122,071,000	$78,917,000	0
Consolidated Edison	$110,027,000	$108,021,000	0
National Steel	$73,449,000	$41,009,000	0
Republic Steel	$18,264,000	$40,440,000	0
U.S. Steel	$109,491,000	$127,691,000	0

---

* Not only did they pay no tax: they even reported that *refunds* or credits totaling $78,000,000 were due them.

† Corporations' tax returns, like those of individuals, are strictly confidential and not available to the public. As you will learn in Chapter 10, what corporations tell the public (in their annual reports and other public documents) is often very different from what they report to Internal Revenue on their tax returns. Moreover, their public reports are often more confusing than enlightening. The above analysis, like others in this book dealing with individual corporations, represents the best efforts of knowledgeable persons to analyze the publicly available information.

Not all corporations achieved a state of *total* tax avoidance, but many of the very large ones came very close. Their 1971 Federal income tax burden, too, bears comparison with that of laborer Ralph Senters:

	Year's Income*	Percent of Income Paid in Taxes
ITT	$413,858,000	5%
Standard Oil (California)	$855,692,000	1.6%
Texaco	$1,319,468,000	2.3%
Gulf	$1,324,914,000	2.3%
Ralph Senters	$7,372	16%

* Net profit before taxes.

As with the richest individual taxpayers, the tax burden of American corporations has been declining significantly in recent years—thanks in part to two multi-billion-dollar corporate tax breaks enacted by Congress in 1971, about which you will read in Chapter 10. Even before that act of Congressional generosity, however, in the short space of a year (from late 1970 to early 1972), the portion of corporations' income that they paid in taxes declined by 10 percent (how many readers of these words can make the same claim?). As of 1972, according to the conservative New York investment banking firm Goldman Sachs, it was still declining.

HERE ARE SOME other comparisons between Ralph Senters and rich taxpayers such as those in Group 3 above:

Item: Not only was Ralph Senters compelled to pay 16 percent of his income to Internal Revenue, but he never even had the pleasure of seeing and feeling (much less spending) his tax money; it was all whisked away by his employer before he even received his pay check. While Congress has insisted on clamping this wage-withholding system on the likes of Ralph Senters, however, it has, with equal adamance, *refused* to impose a similar withholding system on the dividend and interest income enjoyed in abundance by Group 3 families—even though the failure to do so results in an under-reporting of about four to six billion dollars of dividend and interest income and a consequent underpayment of over a billion in taxes on the part of dividend and interest recipients. Who has to make up for that missing billion? Taxpayers like Ralph Senters.

Item: While Ralph Senters is almost entirely helpless before the tax system—trapped as he is by the wage-withholding scheme—families in Group 3 not only have a variety of escape hatches open to them but can even manipulate the *timing* of their taxes in such a way as to extract, in effect, large interest-free loans from the U.S. Treasury (i.e., from the other taxpayers of the United States). (The financial joys of such manipulations are all spelled out in Chapter 8.)

Item: In the unlikely event that Ralph Senters has a few spare pennies left over after meeting all of his bills, he might put them in a savings account that will net him, say, a 5 percent or at most a 6 percent return. Families in Group 3, however, are besieged with enticing invitations to invest in "tax shelters," which can bring them an *after-tax* return on their money as high as 35 percent! (See page 167.) As you will see, most of these "tax shelters" post a "no trespassing" sign for the likes of Ralph Senters: not only does the minimum "ante" range from $5,000 to upwards of $50,000 to get into the game, but most of the "tax shelter" opportunities explicitly say they are not suitable for or open to persons in Ralph Senters' modest tax bracket. No admittance. Riffraff keep out. (For other sharp differences in the tax law's treatment of the rich versus the poor, see Chapter 19).

Item: Many of these "tax shelter" arrangements are set up in such a way that the top-bracket investors end up with not a penny of their own at risk—that is, with all of the "risk capital" put up by all the other taxpayers of the country. Not that these other taxpayers are consulted in the matter: their dollars are simply drafted. In Chapter 9 you will read about how your dollars were conscripted into a California luxury apartment venture that very few of the involuntary taxpayer-investors could ever dream of living in (one-bedroom apartments start at $470 a month). To make matters worse, while these "other taxpayers" put up all the risk capital, they reap none of the profits. (Some might conclude they were being played for suckers.) The profits all go to the tax-avoiding rich.

Item: The average taxpayer, like Ralph Senters, is excluded from that privileged class of wealthy people who enjoy a variety of special "perquisites." These fringe benefits come to them at the

expense of all other taxpayers, who have no choice but to sit back
and pay the bill. Most Americans, for example, are not part of the
"expense-account culture," in which first-class airplane tickets and
wining-and-dining at the finest restaurants and night clubs and even
$100 ringside seats for The Big Fight can, if properly handled, be
charged in large part to "Uncle Sam" (i.e., the other taxpayers).
Less familiar, perhaps, are the perquisites that often go with the
"tax shelters." For example, those who have $9,000 to invest in a
"Rent-A-Cow" venture, described on page 192, have the privilege
of making a tax-deductible "inspection trip" to Oklahoma to view
their tax-sheltered cows—and to enjoy a free vacation, courtesy the
Rent-A-Cow ranch. (How many readers have $9,000 in spare
cash?) And while most of you who read this book would never
dream of betting thousands of your own dollars on a horse race
(even if you had that much to bet), you will read on page 198 how
the Whitneys and the Fords, with a flick of a finger, bid $200,000
for a yearling that, statistically, hasn't more than a thirty-five-to-
one chance of earning back his purchase price. Why? In part because as much as 70 percent of the dollars they're putting up are,
in effect, *your* dollars.

O N E   N O T A B L E   A S P E C T of the "tax welfare" system,
touched on but briefly in the "news story" that began this chapter,
is its flagrant violation of the Work Ethic that this society so in-
sistently imposes on the recipients of conventional welfare. To
bestow cash welfare payments on the lazy and indolent who do
not "work" to justify society's generosity is widely regarded as
akin to Original Sin. Louisiana Senator Russell Long, chairman of
the Senate's tax-writing committee, for example, has insisted that
"a minimum for people on welfare" ought to be a requirement
that they "do at least some public service work"—such as clean-
ing up their "filthy neighborhoods."

No such Work Ethic applies to the dispensing of "tax welfare."
Generous amounts of tax bounty are available to the very rich in
exchange for no more effort on their part than lifting the telephone
to call their broker to approve the purchase of tax-free bonds (see
pages 62–66) or investment in one or another "tax shelter" (see
Chapter 9). It is not even required that a "tax welfare" recipient
take any risks (personal or financial) in order to "earn" his bene-
faction: the tax-free state and local bonds, for example, are

virtually free of any risk of default (and yet bring billions of "tax welfare" to their lucky owners), and landowners who permit oil drillers to risk money to sink a well on their property share fully in the tax benefits of a "strike," even though they risk nothing.

All of this may seem to you to reflect a strange Congressional double standard. But then, as you will see in Chapter 19, this is far from the only respect in which Congress seems to look at the rich and the poor through two quite different sets of glasses.

It is, basically, the helplessness of the average taxpayer like Ralph Senters that compels analogizing the "tax forgivenesses" to Jean Paul Getty and the super-rich families in Group 3 to "tax welfare" payments to those fortunate tax avoiders.

Now, there are some who insist that such a comparison is tantamount to saying that "all income basically belongs to the government."* In my view, that is a red herring. There is a very large and easily discernible difference between saying (a) that a man owes all his income to the U.S. government and (b) that a man should pay his fair share of taxes *on a uniform basis with all other taxpayers.*† Neither I nor anyone else of my acquaintance argues that a person should pay all his income to the government.

This brings us, though, to the question, What *is* a "loophole"? Many regard the oil depletion allowances as a loophole, but rest assured that the oil industry and Texas oil millionaires and billionaires do not. To the Eisenhower Administration, tax relief for dividend recipients enacted in 1954 (but later repealed) was a long-needed reform; but to the succeeding administration of John F. Kennedy that same provision was a "discriminatory and inequitable" tax concession. The National Tax Equality Association is certain that farm (and other) cooperatives enjoy a loophole, but the Cooperative League of the U.S.A. is equally sure no loophole exists. Is a loophole, then, simply a provision that a particular person doesn't happen to approve of (or doesn't happen to be able to put to use for his own benefit)?

---

* See, for example, *Newsweek* columnist Henry Wallich on April 24, 1972, p. 78.

† Notice, please, that I am careful to say a "uniform" basis and not an "equal" basis. The latter might imply that everyone should pay taxes at equal rates, no matter how great his wealth. I am an undisguised advocate of the graduated income tax rate, which is the only way, in my view, to express fairly and effectively the principle of "ability to pay."

And what about such a universally applauded tax provision as the tax deduction for charitable contributions which, despite its almost unanimous popular support, costs the Treasury (i.e., all the taxpayers who aren't able or willing, for one reason or another, to make charitable gifts), three billion dollars each year? Is *it* a loophole?

Because of these shortcomings, some may feel the word "loophole" should be sentenced to live within quotation marks, and to defer to the term "tax preference." In this book preferences are viewed from the lowly and unhappy position of the most unpreferenced and helpless taxpayers in America: the 15,815,752 unmarried taxpayers whose personal deductions were so small as to make it unprofitable for them to itemize their deductions (so that the only differences between their total incomes and their taxable incomes were their single $750 personal exemption and their $1,300 minimum standard deduction.* As a group, those hapless individuals came closest, in 1970, to paying the rates set forth in Section 1(a) of the Internal Revenue Code (and published in the instructions to the Form 1040), and there is little or nothing they can do about it.

A thumbnail sketch of the typical unmarried "preference-less" taxpayer† will show why:

His average income: $3,933.75.

Occupation: wage earner (or salaried worker), with virtually no income outside what he earns on the job—no dividends, no interest, no capital gains. He probably doesn't own his own home; if he does, he gets no tax advantage from his mortgage interest payments—*or* his medical expenses *or* his weekly contributions to his church, for that matter—since he does not itemize his tax deductions. Instead, he contents himself with the $1,300 minimum standard deduction ("low-income allowance"). But, aside from this and the $750 personal exemption, he pays the taxes an unen-

---

* Now known, technically, as the "low-income allowance."

† Based on the latest available statistics, which are for 1969. Since then, the personal exemption and the standard deduction have changed, so the up-to-date numbers might be slightly different from those that will appear here.

lightened visitor would expect, looking at the tax rates found with the Form 1040 instructions. Being unmarried, he is, of course, denied the more favorable tax rates that come with filing a joint return (see Chapter 6).

When April 15 rolls around, no amount of fancy pencil work or burning of the midnight oil can help him. He can't even capitalize on the frailty of human memory in forgetting to report those little odds and ends of dividend or interest income that dribbled in through the year: his income has long since been reported and his taxes withheld from his pay check, week by week —spirited away without his ever even seeing the money. (Chances are, in fact, that too much was spirited away, and he must depend on a government refund to set matters right.)

Thus, as he and the other 15,815,571 like him see it, everything other than the personal exemption and the minimum standard deduction is a "tax preference," and will be considered such in this book. Even the personal exemption, as currently written, will come in for some close questioning (see page 350). Yet, although our unmarried "preference-less" taxpayer derives comparatively little advantage from our tax system, even he is not wholly unprivileged. He may receive some income he doesn't even have to report on his tax return, such as his Social Security, veterans' or other such benefits from the government, or fringe benefits from his employer.

THIS BOOK CONCERNS itself solely with the Federal income tax. But that, of course, is only part of the burden that every American must bear, and the "other taxes" everyone must pay—payroll taxes, for Social Security and the like, and state and local property taxes and sales taxes—are steadily mounting.

The burden of these "other taxes" falls far more harshly on those with low and moderate incomes than on the wealthy, in that they take a larger *share* of the incomes of the less well-to-do. In that proportional sense, the burden of many of these taxes is *eight times* as severe on the lowest income groups, compared with their effect on the highest income groups studied. These are the figures, as shown in a recent study made by two Census Bureau officials:

Percent of Total 1968 Income Paid in

Total Family Income	Social Security Tax*	State and Local Taxes		
		State	*Property*	*Total*
Under $2,000	7.6%	6.6%	16.2%	27.2%
$2,000–$4,000	6.5%	4.9%	7.5%	15.7%
$4,000–$6,000	6.7%	4.1%	4.8%	12.1%
$6,000–$8,000	6.8%	3.6%	3.8%	10.7%
$8,000–$10,000	6.2%	3.3%	3.6%	10.1%
$10,000–$15,000	5.8%	2.9%	3.6%	9.9%
$15,000–$25,000	4.6%	2.4%	3.6%	9.4%
$25,000–$50,000	2.5%	1.8%	2.7%	7.8%
Over $50,000	1.0%	1.1%	2.0%	6.7%

* This includes half of the employer's share (as well as all of the employee's share) of the Social Security tax, on the assumption that at least this much of the employer's share falls on the worker in the form of lower wages and/or fringe benefits. To allocate only half of the employer's share to the worker may be a conservative assumption. Tax expert Joseph A. Pechman states that "most economists believe that the [entire] burden of the employer tax . . . falls eventually on the workers (either by substituting for larger wage increases or inflating prices)."

What is more, these harshest-on-the-poor taxes have been increasing markedly in the last two decades. Payroll taxes, for example, *quadrupled* from 1958 to 1969. They have been raised seven times since the beginning of 1960. Property taxes and sales and excise taxes more than doubled in that same period although property taxes for the well-to-do seem to have declined slightly in recent years. According to the Census officials' study, these are the increases between 1952 and 1968 in the average "other taxes" paid:

Income Group	Social Security Tax		
	1962	*1968*	*Percent Inc.*
Under $2,000	$50	$74	+48%
$2,000–$4,000	$120	$192	+60%
$4,000–$6,000	$283	$389	+37%
$6,000–$8,000	$421	$592	+41%
$8,000–$10,000	$547	$698	+28%
Over $25,000	$1,017	$1,240	+22%

	Sales Tax		
Income Group	*1962*	*1968*	*Percent Inc.*
Under $2,000	$51	$65	+27%
$2,000–$4,000	$113	$147	+30%
$4,000–$6,000	$186	$236	+27%
$6,000–$8,000	$243	$313	+29%
$8,000–$10,000	$283	$366	+29%
Over $25,000	$774	$976	+26%

	Property Tax		
Income Group	*1962*	*1968*	*Percent Inc.*
Under $2,000	$108	$158	+46%
$2,000–$4,000	$171	$222	+30%
$4,000–$6,000	$252	$277	+10%
$6,000–$8,000	$339	$334	−2%
$8,000–$10,000	$425	$406	−5%
Over $25,000	$1,661	$1,563	−6%

The combined effect of all taxes at all levels is astounding. For, according to the Census officials, in 1968 people with total earned incomes* of less than $2,000—that is, less than $40 a *week—were paying half of that meager privately earned income in taxes of all kinds.*† It is difficult to perceive much justice in an overall tax system that places such a crushing load on the poorest and most helpless of citizens, especially since this load is, proportionately speaking, heavier than that borne by the wealthiest of the groups studied (as the following figures show) :

Income Group	*Percent of Privately Earned Income* Paid in Taxes of All Kinds*
Under $2,000	50.0%
$2,000–$4,000	34.6%
$4,000–$6,000	31.0%
$6,000–$8,000	30.1%
$8,000–$10,000	29.2%
$10,000–$15,000	29.8%
$15,000–$25,000	30.0%
$25,000–$50,000	32.8%
Over $50,000	45.0%

* Exclusive of government benefit payments.
† In the aggregate, people in this lowest-income group received govern-

ONE FACET OF THE ABOVE "profile" of the most un-preferenced taxpayer deserves to be highlighted:

"Occupation: wage earner (or salaried worker), with virtually no income outside what he earns on the job. . . ."

For it is the wage and salary earners of America who bear the brunt of the tax burden. Every dollar they take in, earned by the sweat of their brow or by dint of their individual wit or initiative and hard work, is fully subject to the tax rates contained in Section 1(a) of the law (softened, it is true, to the extent of personal tax deductions—but for those at the bottom of the economic heap, these are likely to be few).

By contrast, the taxpayers cited in the Treasury study (see page 14) who were able, during the Sixties, to escape with paying little or no tax, had little or no *earned* income:

Taxpayer 1

Income from wages and salaries: 0
Income from corporation dividends: $10,806,947[1]
Total income: $10,829,028

Total taxes paid: 0[2]

Taxpayer 2

Income from wages and salaries: $20,000
Capital gains: $1,210,426
Total income: $1,284,718

Total taxes paid: $274[3]

---

ment Social Security and welfare payments that outweighed the taxes they paid. But this does not alter the fact that half of their privately earned income went in taxes of all kinds.

[1] This indicates holdings of corporate stocks worth well over $300 million.

[2] As a result of unlimited charitable deduction (repealed in 1969).

[3] As a result of large itemized deductions. These were almost entirely deductions for interest expenses, on which the 1969 tax law placed a limit.

Taxpayer 3

Oil and gas income: $1,469,179
Total income: $1,313,811[4]

Total taxes paid: 0[5]

EACH TAX PREFERENCE comes complete with its own built-in justification. Suggestions for the tightening or (God forbid) the outright repeal of any given loophole evoke anguished assurances that the tax concession is *urgently* required in the national interest—perhaps to stimulate the economy, or to create an "incentive" for (or perhaps remove a deterrent from) some publicly beneficial activity, such as exploring for oil or building houses or giving to charity. (One wonders how the society managed to survive before the enactment of these various loopholes.) Some preferences are justified as relieving a "hardship" (as when coal royalty contracts unforesightedly failed to allow for rising coal prices [see page 300]). Others are said to be needed to correct an "inequity"—but, as you will discover in the chapter "Old Loopholes Never Die, They Just Get Bigger," equity in taxes, as Congress sees it, is "the privilege of paying as little as somebody else."

Often, tax preferences are defended as compensating for some "extraordinary" risk, such as in oil or real estate. But is real estate, for example, inherently more risky, or less, than other industries? A solid answer is hard to come by, since what reliable or precise measuring stick is there for determining "riskiness"? What's more, can the tax system effectively compensate for risk? Is that its proper function? If so, to be fair to all it should seek to accommodate risk, not just for each industry but for each profession and, indeed, each individual within it. (Doesn't a young lawyer or doctor face great risks when he first hangs out his shingle and seeks to establish himself in practice? What about the struggling, unknown artist? And what of the risks of a layoff that hang over most factory and construction workers?)

---

[4] This is less than the oil and gas income because of certain farm "loss" deductions.

[5] Mainly as a result of oil and gas deductions and farm "loss" deductions (Chapter 11 and pp. 187–199).

Whether a given loophole is justified as an "incentive" or a "hardship reliever" or a "risk compensator," these rationales usually serve to becloud the real result (if not the real purpose) of the preference: namely, to lessen the tax burden of a select and favored group of taxpayers. Taken as a whole, the loopholes represent an oblique assault on the graduated rate schedule of Section 1(a) of the tax law. On the face of it, Congress has maintained high tax rates on the rich; yet, as the table on page 11 eloquently shows, behind the façade of the apparent rates, Congress has softened the blow for all taxpayers—but especially for the rich and the super-rich. It has done so, however, *in ways the public cannot readily see and understand.*

IN SOME CIRCLES, it may not be thought polite to talk about taxes as a vulgar clash of groups or classes; or to mention the fact that one man's loophole is another man's cross; or that when A pays less, B must pay more. Yet this is the essence of the matter. As the late Louis Eisenstein felicitously observed in his gifted book *The Ideologies of Taxation*, taxes "are a changing product of the earnest efforts to have others pay them."

In other words, taxation comes down to a question of

WHO PAYS WHAT?

IN 1895, defending the constitutionality of the income tax before the Supreme Court, Attorney James C. Carter put it this way:

In every community those who feel the burdens of taxation are naturally prone to relieve themselves from it if they can . . . . One class struggles to throw the burden off its own shoulders. If they succeed, of course, it must fall upon others. They also, in their turn, labor to get rid of it, and finally the load falls upon those who will not, or cannot, make a successful effort for relief.

He then went on to say:

This is, in general, a one-sided struggle, in which the rich only engage, and . . . in which the poor always go to the wall.

Whether Carter, speaking nearly eighty years ago, was prophetically correct, you are invited to judge for yourself through the pages that follow.

Portrait of a Non-Taxpayer

ONCE UPON A TIME there was a taxpayer. . . .

No. That's not the correct way to begin this story.

Once upon a time there was a *non*-taxpayer—that is, a person who paid no taxes. He was distinctly different from the millions of other American non-taxpayers, who are excused from paying taxes by reason of their poverty.

But no one could conceivably claim that the non-taxpayer with whom we are concerned here was poor. On the contrary, this particular non-taxpayer, whom we'll call Mr. NTP, was very, very rich. Over a seven-year period, Mr. NTP's huge shareholdings brought in dividends totaling about $1,800,000.* Oil ventures brought in another $1,400,000. And profits on stock sales still another $1,800,000. All in all, over those seven years, Mr. NTP enjoyed no less than $5,000,000 of income—an average of more than $700,000 a year.

And yet, year in and year out, Mr. NTP managed to be an NTP —a non-taxpayer. He paid no taxes. Not a dime.

Except for one year. One year he did pay taxes. How much? $4,509.83. But that wasn't too bad: over the seven years, it amounted to just one-tenth of one percent of his $5 million income.

And in the other six years he was a non-taxpayer.

---

* This would indicate that his stockholdings were worth about $7,500,000.

ALL OF THE ABOVE are true-to-life, accurate facts about a real person. What sort of man was he? What kind of life did he lead?

For openers, he lived in a $280,000 home.

It was amply staffed with servants.

Mrs. NTP drove a Cadillac; Mr. NTP and their son, NTP, Jr., were more modest: they had mere Oldsmobiles.*

Whether or not the NTP family had a chauffeur, I do not know; but I know they did have a $12,000-a-year pilot to fly them around in their $100,000 airplane.

One year, Mr. NTP spent $5,000 flying his prize horse to a show in the Far West. He was able to compel all the Americans who *do* pay taxes to foot part of that bill, for he listed the $5,000 as a tax-deductible business expense.†

He also obliged the taxpayers to pay part of the bill for the expensive cigars that he and his son smoked. How? By wrapping the cigars in bands imprinted with the name of his ranch or his prize show horse, and claiming the cigars as a tax-deductible advertising expense for the ranch.

In similar fashion, Mr. NTP was able to saddle the taxpayers with part of the astounding sum of $3,000 which he spent on his Christmas cards. The cards pictured *all* the members of the NTP family—including the cherished show horse—so Mr. NTP claimed the $3,000 Christmas card outlay as a deductible ranch-promotion expense. Similarly listed were some $3,000 worth of smoked turkeys and hams sent to friends, relatives and neighbors at the Christmas season.

Clearly, this was a highly expensive, if not outright profligate ranching operation. In fact, according to Mr. NTP's tax returns, the ranch showed a seven-year *loss* of just under $2,000,000 (which was the key to Mr. NTP's total taxlessness), and at the end of that period an Internal Revenue agent found that the ranch losses were increasing, rather than diminishing.‡ The agent could

---

* Mr. NTP claimed depreciation deductions on all three cars on his tax return, apparently on the ground that all three cars were used for business reasons.

† Doing so reduced his taxable income by $5,000, which reduced his tax and thus added to the tax burden that had to be borne by those who *do* pay taxes.

‡ Since these events took place, the tax law has been changed so that deductions for consistently losing operations such as this one might not be allowable today.

not help but be skeptical about Mr. NTP's "business motives" in operating the ranch. "How many prudent businessmen would operate a business with a record of losses year after year?" he wondered in a report to his superiors. Would a man out to make a profit furnish his foremen with air-conditioned Oldsmobiles rather than the pickup trucks that more frugal and profit-minded ranchers might choose?

It could not, however, be said that Mr. NTP was a selfish man, for he believed in the nonpayment of taxes by his employees as well as himself. For example, when he decided that more compensation was due his loyal accountant (who had been dutifully recording all the above-mentioned tax-deductible expenditures), Mr. NTP suggested that in lieu of a higher salary (which would result in a higher tax to the accountant) he, Mr. NTP, would pay the rent on the accountant's home so that there would be no *visible* added flow of dollars to the accountant (and hence, reasoned Mr. NTP, no added tax). This notion was less than appealing to the tax-wise accountant, who knew that his failure to report this would be illegal and might subject him to very severe consequences.

DESPITE THE "once upon a time" beginning, every detail of the above may be found in a report to a superior in the Internal Revenue Service (IRS) by an outraged IRS agent who spent many months scrutinizing the multifarious tax-avoidance activities of the NTP family. At the end of that time, the agent wrote to his superior as follows:

[This family's tax] returns reflect one of the best examples of the large inequities in our tax laws today. . . . These people have more money than they know what to do with; yet they pay less tax to the Federal Government than some of the taxpayers whose income would qualify them under the [Federal] poverty program.

It is a necessity that you [the IRS superior] and I and every other employee have an automobile to go to and from our place of employment in order to earn a living for our families. Yet we cannot deduct this expense on our tax return. We look at these taxpayers who drive Cadillac automobiles and fly all over the United States to attend horse races, rodeos, cutting horse contests and other functions and if they can show that this is related in any way to their so-called business, then it is deductible and they never pay taxes.

I don't believe that anyone can look at these returns and the reports showing the type of income and expense that they do, then look me in the eye and tell me that they don't think that it is a shame that a taxpayer of this nature can legally escape taxation as these taxpayers have done.

3

How Would You Like a Special Tax Law, All Your Own?

WHEN, ON OCTOBER 31, 1969, the Senate Finance Committee approved a massive 585-page tax bill, there was no reason for any Senator or member of the public to take note of a proposed new Section 49 (b) (10) of the tax law or, in particular, thirty-seven words tucked into the middle of a sentence on page 420 of the bill. On the surface, those thirty-seven words seemed no different from all the other opaquely worded provisions in the bill. And, to every taxpayer in the United States, save one, they *were* no different. But to that one taxpayer those thirty-seven words were highly precious, *for they spelled a tax saving of about $3,000,000.* (That comes to about $81,000 per word.)

Although there was no hint of it, either in the bill itself or in the 310-page committee report explaining the bill, those particular words had been specially tailored for and specially inserted into the bill on behalf of a single company: Uniroyal, Inc., the nation's sixty-eighth largest corporation and one of the leading tire makers of America.

THE FOLLOWING HYPOTHETICAL ACCOUNT may help view the "Uniroyal amendment" in context:

When George and Linda Nichols sold their suburban lakefront home, they could hardly believe they got $75,000 for the house they had paid just $20,000 for back in 1947. Of course, back then, when they had plunked down their life savings and mortgaged themselves up to their eyebrows for the house and an acre of ground, their friends had thought them crazy to move "into the middle of nowhere"—twenty miles from the center of town. But with freeways and the population explosion, the value of their precious lake frontage had soared. So, with the children gone and George retired, they decided to "cash in" and build a house in *real* country—Michigan's North Woods, up near Canada.

And that's where their luck changed: the first contractor went broke; the second got sick; the third came so late to the job that a ground-freeze stalled the project for the winter. After a freak-ishly late thaw, there were labor troubles and more delays—so that by the time the Nichols' could move into their dream house, eighteen months and one week had passed since they sold their lakefront house near the city.

Presently, they received a letter from Internal Revenue advising them that they would have to pay a tax of $10,000 on the profit they had made on the sale of their old house. The Nichols' were stunned: they were sure the law said there would be no tax if you put those profits into another personal residence. Several exchanges of letters with the IRS produced the fact that, in order to avoid the tax, they would have had to move into their new house within eighteen months of selling their old one. Since they had missed that deadline by one week, they would have to pay.

With the bank pressing for payments on the new mortgage, the Nichols' gathered up all the files and letters they had carefully kept and journeyed to the nearest IRS office to explain that the delays had been due to circumstances over which they had no control. The IRS agent was sympathetic. He agreed the delay had not been their fault. But, he told them, his hands were tied. He showed them what it said, in black and white, on page 104 of the Internal Revenue publication "Your Federal Income Tax":

No extension of time for replacement and occupancy beyond the . . . 18-month period is permitted. . . . Thus, if you did not buy or occupy another residence [within 18 months] (*even though you were pre-vented from doing so because of conditions beyond your control*) no additional time may be granted.

The agent underlined the parenthetical phrase for them, to show them there was nothing he could do, much as he, personally, would like to help. He even went so far as to say that common sense and justice were on their side. "But," he said, "the law's the law."

O N J U N E 3 0 , 1 9 6 9 , the House of Representatives passed a tax bill repealing the investment tax credit* on machinery and equipment bought or contracted for after April 18, 1969. The House bill was cause for concern among the executives of Uniroyal, Inc. (better known, perhaps, under its former name, U.S. Rubber Company), who had been counting on the investment credit to yield a tax saving of about $3 million on equipment for a new plant to be built for Uniroyal by the city of Ardmore, Oklahoma. As of the magic date of April 18, the company had signed an agreement with the city to lease the plant, and had even filed a description of the project with the Securities and Exchange Commission in Washington. (If you are a detective-story reader who likes to solve the mystery for yourself, remember that last fact. It's a clue.) But construction had not begun, nor had the equipment been ordered. The House bill made it uncertain whether the equipment would qualify for the credit, because in order to qualify, under the general rule set forth in the bill, the equipment had to be "specified" in the lease itself. Unhappily, the description of the equipment in the lease was sufficiently unspecific as to raise doubt that the tax credit would apply and that the company would get its $3 million tax saving. In short, as far as Uniroyal was concerned, there was a distinct possibility of what might be called a three-million-dollar misunderstanding if the House bill became the law of the land. And after all, as the IRS agent had observed to George and Linda Nichols, "the law's the law."

Well, the law may be the law for people such as the Nichols', but not, it seems, for a company the size of Uniroyal (1971 sales: nearly $1.7 *billion*). Not if you know someone who knows someone who has the ear of an accommodating United States Senator, especially one who is a member of the Finance Committee. Because if you are someone with "connections," like Uniroyal, you can have a special law written, tailored to your own specifications, just to meet your particular situation.

---

* A provision enacted in 1962 that permitted U.S. industry to enjoy large tax savings on most of its purchases of new machinery and equipment. See pp. 214–219 for more detail.

And that's precisely what Uniroyal arranged. For lo, when the Senate Finance Committee approved and sent to the Senate the huge 585-page tax bill, there, on page 420, tucked away in the middle of a sentence so as to be virtually unnoticeable by even the most eagle-eyed Senator, were thirty-seven words that had not been part of the House bill. But they were sufficient to remove any doubt that Uniroyal would get its $3 million tax saving. For, according to the words added by the thoughtful Finance Committee, where future equipment was to be bought pursuant to a lease, it would qualify for the investment credit if it was "specified" either in the lease itself (as under the House bill) *"or in a related document filed before April 19, 1969, with a Federal regulatory agency. . . ."* (Emphasis added.) How convenient for Uniroyal—since, as you may recall, the company just happened to have "filed a document" describing the plant and equipment "with a Federal regulatory agency"—namely and to wit, the Securities and Exchange Commission.

How did the Senate Finance Committee come to know that fact, so that it could tailor the thirty-seven words to fit Uniroyal's situation so neatly? One possibility is that Uniroyal had taken advantage of the twenty-two days of public hearings the Finance Committee held to afford taxpayers like Uniroyal a chance to tell of any problems they might have with the House-passed bill. That was one possible route, but it was not the avenue that Uniroyal chose, for one can examine the index of the 6,777 pages of Senate hearings without finding any evidence that Uniroyal had spread its plight upon the public record. So how *had* the Finance Committee learned of the company's situation? From whom? When? Was it in a formal meeting of the Committee? Or through a private approach to individual members of the Committee? The public record contains no evidence to contradict the conclusion that the Committee's accommodation of Uniroyal was a Private Agreement, Privately Arrived At.

How many other companies in the United States had unbought and unordered equipment that might be disqualified for the investment credit because of this or that borderline provision of the House-passed bill? Doubtless there were some—only they lacked either the presence of mind or the "connections" to get a special law passed, all their own, so they would not get the blessings of the investment credit. But, thanks to a sympathetic Congress, Uniroyal, Inc., would. For, after all, even if the law is tailor-made just to fit one company, the law's the law.

Isn't it?

THE UNIROYAL AMENDMENT was by no means the only specially tailored provision secreted namelessly within the 585 pages of the tax measure approved by the Senate Committee that October day of 1969. Also embedded in it, with nary a mention—either in the bill or in the Committee's extensive explanation of it—of any particular companies or individuals the Committee had in mind, were:

•   a provision that meant a $14 million tax saving for the Lockheed Corporation and an additional $6.5 million saving for the McDonnell Douglas Corporation. These were the circumstances: both companies were actively at work building new three-engine jumbo jets (Lockheed, the L–1011; McDonnell Douglas, the DC–10). Both companies had still to buy substantial amounts of machinery and equipment to complete the huge planes, but, because the jetliners were of new design, the exact nature of the new machinery was still uncertain. Hence none of it was under binding contract on the crucial date of April 18 and therefore, under the general rule that all other companies would have to abide by, would not qualify for the investment credit.

But general rules need not necessarily apply to the giants of the aerospace industry for, without divulging their request to the general public by appearing publicly before the Ways and Means Committee, the Lockheed Corporation (thirty-first largest in America, with 1971 sales of nearly $3 billion) somehow persuaded the Committee to write into the law a special exception to the general rule that would qualify the as yet unbought and unknown machinery and equipment for the investment credit and thus bring about a $14 million tax saving. However, the Committee thoughtlessly (though inadvertently, no doubt) wrote the provision in such a way as to exclude Lockheed's arch-competitor, McDonnell Douglas, from its benefactions. The Senate Finance Committee considered this a clear injustice,* and with the addition of but four words, and the changing of the figure "60" to "50," it assured McDonnell, too, of the investment credit and of its $6.5

---

* In this case, McDonnell Douglas departed from the norm and presented its plea to the Finance Committee in a public hearing.

million saving. Mathematicians among the readers of these words may already have calculated that if four words could save $6.5 million, that comes out to $1,625,000 per word. There was, in this case, another departure from the usual practice: in announcing to the press its approval of the bill, the Finance Committee specified that it had expanded the Lockheed amendment to include McDonnell Douglas. But if any Senator happened to miss that press announcement, he had no way of knowing that the two companies were the beneficiaries of special provisions in the tax bill, for the Committee's 310-page official explanation of the measure made no mention of either company.

• a provision that meant a saving of $12.6 million for the Mobil Oil Corporation. Mobil had bought the land for a new $180 million refinery it planned to build in Joliet, Illinois, but as of the April 18 cutoff date no construction contract had been signed. Under the generally applicable law, therefore, Mobil was due to lose a $12.6 million investment tax credit on the refinery. But the Senate Finance Committee obligingly concocted a bit of make-believe designed to save the credit for Mobil. Under the seemingly general, apparently innocuous Committee provision, where a company had acquired the land for a new refinery (no other kind of plant would do), but hadn't actually begun construction, the law would, in effect, make believe that construction had begun on the date of the site purchase. Presto! The Mobil refinery would thus qualify for the repealed investment credit and its $12.6 million tax saving would be salvaged. (While this imaginative provision passed the Senate, the hard-hearted members of the House-Senate conference committee named to iron out differences between the House and Senate versions of the bill, alas for Mobil, saw fit to drop the amendment before the measure became law.)

• an amendment that gave the corporate executives of just one company—Litton Industries—four years longer than the officers of any other company to enjoy the liberal rules governing stock options (see page 78) that were coming to an end with the 1969 bill.

• an amendment that facilitated a transaction between a family foundation and Washington super-hostess Gwendolyn Cafritz, celebrated winer-and-diner of many a Senator and Congressman. The transaction involved an exchange of stock in the family-owned real-estate corporation between Mrs. Cafritz and the

Cafritz Foundation. Without the specially tailored provision, that would have subjected the Foundation to a tax and to the difficulty of divesting itself of the stock in a very short period of time. While experts in the foundation field say that the Cafritz Foundation was not alone in benefiting from the Senate's provision, they have little doubt that when the Finance Committee, in its official explanation of the bill, cited the nameless example of "a substantial donor to a foundation [who] leaves a number of business holdings jointly to his widow and his foundation," this was no theoretical example; the widow the Committee had in mind was none other than Mrs. Cafritz.*

All told, the 1969 bill contained at least fifteen such hand-tailored amendments, of which the most intriguingly worded was Section 121(b) (2) (C), providing for an exemption from the tax that the bill was imposing, for the first time, on church-owned businesses. Section 121(b) (2) (C), like all the others, named no names. But Committee insiders chortled over the section, knowing that embedded in it was a coded, Sherlock Holmes-ish clue to the identity of the favored company. For, according to the section, the nex tax was not to apply "in the case of a trade or business . . .

> (A) Which consists of . . .
> (B) Which is carried on by . . .
> (C) Less than 10% of the net income of which. . . ."

The clue lay in the initials of the first words—W, W and L— of provisos (A), (B) and (C). The favored "trade or business" was radio-TV stations WWL, the CBS affiliates in New Orleans, owned by Loyola University. According to the *Wall Street Journal*, "Capitol sources swear there was no coincidence" in the coded clue; and an ex-Senate staff member has written that this was "an example of [Committee Chairman Russell] Long's sense of humor." Why would Chairman Long have had a connection with this particular amendment? Because WWL was one of the most important TV stations in Senator Long's home state of Louisiana.

So far as Congressional tax experts are aware, WWL was the first organization to have a special tax provision that was

---

* As was true of McDonnell Douglas, a representative of the Cafritz Foundation testified publicly before Congress and set forth the problem that beset the Foundation and Mrs. Cafritz.

not only tailored to its particular needs but even carried its own personal monogram! The phenomenon of such individually honed provisions, however, was by no means a "first" in the 1969 bill. They had been tucked away in abundance, over the years, in previous tax measures. Perhaps the most celebrated is Section 1240 of the Internal Revenue Code. As with all the other similar provisions, on the surface there seems nothing unusual about Section 1240—it looks just like any other provision of the tax law. It reads as follows (to aid in deciphering the legal terminology, a layman's translation is provided):

Section 1240	Layman's Translation
Amounts received from the assignment or release by an employee, after more than 20 years' employment, of all his rights to receive, after termination of his employment and for a period of not less than 5 years (or for a period ending with his death), a percentage of future profits or receipts of his employer shall be	*If* you've worked 20 years for one company . . . and *if* you have rights to future profits of the company for at least 5 years after you leave its employ . . . and *if* you sell those rights . . .
considered an amount received from the sale or exchange of a capital asset held for more than 6 months if—	the proceeds are taxed at the special 25 percent capital gains rate . . .
(1) such rights were included in the terms of the employment of such employee for not less that 12 years,	*provided* you've had those rights at least 12 years before you stop work . . .
(2) such rights were included in the terms of the employment of such employee before the date of enactment of this title, and	and *provided* those rights were in your contract before August 16, 1954 . . .
(3) the total of the amounts received for such assignment or release is received in one taxable year and after the termination of such employment.	and *provided* you sell your rights after you leave and all in a single year.

Even your tax lawyer (if you have one) would probably pass over the section as meaningless, on the assumption that no client of his could ever comply with all those "ifs" and "provideds."

But to the late Louis B. Mayer, former head of Metro-Goldwyn-Mayer studios in Hollywood, Section 1240 was far from meaningless. For him, it had a special meaning: it saved him roughly $2 million in taxes. He had no trouble meeting all the "ifs" and "provideds"—and for a very simple reason: Section 1240 was written with him specifically in mind, tailored to fit his own individual situation. It didn't mention him by name, but it might just as well have.

There is nothing unique about Congress's granting legislative relief to designated individuals: hundreds of "private laws" entitled "An Act for the Relief of John Doe" are enacted every year, granting individual exceptions to the immigration quotas, dealing with claims or other grievances against the government, or simply relieving specific hardships. But these measures do not wear the disguise of a supposedly general provision of law. Not only is "John Doe" named, but the amount of relief sought and the reasons for it are fully set forth in Congressional proceedings for all to see and judge.

But there was no such disclosure in the case of the Uniroyal amendment or the Lockheed–McDonnell Douglas provision or the Gwendolyn Cafritz amendment—or the Louis B. Mayer amendment, which is namelessly headed "Taxability to Employes of Termination Payments."

The background of the Mayer amendment has been described by tax attorney Louis Eisenstein with special felicity:

Mr. Mayer was about to retire from his eminent position as a contributor to American culture. He had faithfully served his employer for about 20 years; on retirement he was entitled to share in the future profits of his employer for about five years or until his death; and his contract of employment had so provided for about 12 years. Instead of assuming the risk of future operations, Mr. Mayer desired to depart with one large lump-sum payment. However, if he took the payment, relatively little would remain after taxes. The [Senate] Finance Committee was informed of his acute problem and proved to be a friend in need. It declared that an employee so unfortunately situated was in a peculiarly distressing situation. He was caught between the bleak prospect of an "unduly harsh" tax and the unpleasant alternative of leaving "his retirement income dependent upon the operation of the business."

Mr. Mayer's "plight" was brought to the attention of the Senate Finance Committee in the form of a proposed amendment offered by Mr. Mayer's lawyer, Ellsworth C. Alvord, appearing not in his capacity as a private attorney but as the official spokesman of the United States Chamber of Commerce. Anyone else in Mr. Mayer's position would have paid the regular tax rates that had prevailed (in this case, presumably 91 percent) on a termination settlement of this kind. But the amendment proposed by Mr. Alvord, presented as though enjoying official Chamber of Commerce blessing, sought to spare the movie executive this unpleasantness and permit him, instead, to pay the far more favorable 25 percent capital gains rate that prevailed then.

The Finance Committee adopted Mr. Alvord's proposal, bolstering its action with a phrase frequently invoked to allay the apprehensions of other Senators and ease the passage of special provisions. "The revenue loss from this amendment," said the Committee, "will be negligible." (It is doubtful that Mr. Mayer considered his $2 million tax saving "negligible.") As but one trivial provision tucked away in a major revenue-raising bill, the Mayer provision passed the Senate unnoticed, without opposition or debate, in large part because no Senator (other than Finance Committee members) knew its true significance.

Three years later, in 1954, in the process of completely overhauling the tax code, the House of Representatives unaccommodatingly omitted the Mayer provision, perhaps on the assumption that it had already served its purpose and had no further utility. The alert Mr. Alvord, however, was on hand to point out the omission to the Senate Finance Committee, which reenacted the provision "in such a way as not to affect" the past Mayer, but also in such a way as to bar future Mayers from equal treatment (see clause (2) of the provision, page 41. There will, in short, be no poaching on the "Hollywood Rajah's" private preserve.

The Mayer story has a sequel, for in 1963, twelve years after Ellsworth C. Alvord had arranged a $2 million special amendment for his celebrated client, it was Alvord himself who needed similar special attention from the tax-law writers. Alvord, it seemed, had acquired considerable holdings in a Canadian holding company called Hekor and, under the general rule contained in U.S. tax law, there was no way for either Alvord or his heirs to liquidate Hekor (as Alvord desired to do) and sell its stockholdings without paying a capital gains tax of about $1 million. The Alvord amendment, by making a specific exception for certain companies (the description of which was made-to-order for Alvord's company) would permit Alvord's estate to achieve Hekor's liquidation without paying the million-dollar tax.* And so it came to pass that the tailor-made technique that Alvord had used so effectively for his client was later used to handsomely benefit Alvord himself.

The story of the Mayer amendment also has a postscript, for later the provision was inadvertently adopted by Mayer's home state of California. In 1953, California, in revising its own statutes, bodily lifted and inserted into the state income tax laws great sections of the Federal tax code, including, perhaps unwittingly, Section 1240—a provision that had once greatly blessed one of the state's most renowned citizens, but which, as revised in 1954, can no longer benefit anyone, in or out of the Golden State.

THE ESTATE OF Charles E. Merrill, of Merrill Lynch fame, is the beneficiary of another anonymous provision of the tax code—to wit, Section 512(b)(13). At his death on October 6, 1956, Mr. Merrill willed an interest in his firm to a charitable trust. Under the generally applicable law, the trust's share of the firm's income would be taxable. But, thanks to Section 512(b) (13), the general rule does not apply in the case of a partnership interest willed by "an individual who died after August 16, 1954†

---

* At the time the Alvord amendment was enacted, his legal associates said that the restrictive wording of the amendment, which apparently confined it to Alvord's case alone, was not of their doing or asking but resulted from the Treasury Department's rejection of a more general tax concession that Alvord favored. Moreover, they said, the provision was more a matter of convenience than necessity for Alvord, since his heirs could have achieved the same result by another means. Why, then, go to all the trouble of drafting and persuading the Congress to enact an enormously complex special provision? Because, tax experts said at the time, the alternative maneuver open to Alvord's heirs would have been subject to government challenge as purely tax-motivated. The enactment of the Alvord amendment, on the other hand, left Internal Revenue powerless to make such a challenge, and powerless to collect the million-dollar capital gains tax.

† The date of enactment of the 1954 Revenue Code.

and before January 1, 1957." Any decedent other than Mr. Merrill, in order to obtain similar treatment, would have to have been endowed with special prescience, for Section 512(b)(13) did not become law until April 7, 1958—fifteen months *after* the provision's final cutoff date.

M A N Y   I S   T H E   L A W Y E R   (or client), caught by the frailties of human foresight, who has wished that the past might be reopened and all the advantages of hindsight applied to decisions that went awry. Usually, the law is sternly intolerant of oversight. But on page 1075 of Volume 70 of the General Statutes of the United States lies a statute (Public Law 1011, 84th Congress, 2nd Session) that made that wish a reality. PL 1011 made it possible to erase the effects of some unhappily unforesighted estate planning (or lack of it) and to save $4 million in taxes for the estate of Mary Hill Swope, wife of former General Electric president Gerard Swope.

Mrs. Swope died on October 28, 1955, leaving a sizable estate in trust and giving her husband power to dispose of it at his death, either to their children or to charity. From a tax viewpoint, there were two unfortunate aspects to Mrs. Swope's will. One was that it was written in such a way as to deprive Mrs. Swope of the privilege of leaving half her estate tax-free to her husband* (the will was written in 1947, before that privilege was part of the law and apparently was unrevised in the subsequent eighteen years so as to take advantage of the 1948 provision). The other was that by the time of her death, Mr. Swope had already amply provided for their children and wished her estate to go entirely to charity. Had anyone thought to accommodate Mrs. Swope's will to that fact, she could easily have bequeathed her estate directly to charity and paid no estate tax on it. As it was, though, because of these two unfortunate oversights which neither foresight nor hindsight could now correct, her estate was liable for some $4 million in taxes.

At the behest of a bipartisan pair of New York Congressmen —Democrat Eugene Keogh of Brooklyn and Republican Daniel Reed of Sheridan—Congress reopened the past and expunged the consequences of unprescient decisions. The measure Messrs.

---

* The so-called estate tax "marital deduction." See p. 327.

Keogh and Reed shepherded through* made, of course, no mention of Mr. or Mrs. Swope or the perfectly understandable human
frailties the measure sought to remedy. Instead, it bestowed a
special power on husbands (and wives) who are over eighty at
the time of the spouse's death (Mr. Swope was one month short
of eighty-three when his wife died). If such a surviving spouse
(no one younger than eighty may qualify), within a year of his
wife's death, exercises the power under her will to transmit her
property to charity, the law will treat this as if she had decided to
do this herself. Thus, the charitable gifts may be subtracted from
her taxable estate and not be subjected to tax.

Public Law 1011 remains in the tax code today, as Section
2055(b)(2), but Treasury officials are not aware of any other
eighty-year-old surviving spouses who have come along to take
advantage of it.

THE LEO SANDERS AMENDMENT, fully as anony-
mous as the Mayer, Merrill or Swope provisions, is a testimonial
to the efficacy of the late Senator Robert S. Kerr of Oklahoma.
Barely four months elapsed between the Supreme Court's rejection
of Mr. Sanders' tax case and the enactment of a tailor-made provision, sponsored by the Senator from Oklahoma, reversing the
court verdicts.

Leo Sanders was a general contractor in Oklahoma City, who,
in 1949, received settlement from the government of $955,000 in
connection with a World War II contract. Although the tax law
provides for such settlements to be taxed at the regular income
tax rates, at first Sanders failed to include any of the $955,000 on
his income tax return.† Then, after government prodding, he
claimed the bulk of the settlement as a "capital gain," taxable at
the special 25 percent tax rate. The government filed suit for
$729,446 in tax deficiencies and $226,258 in delinquencies for

---

* With the aid of the special "member's bill" procedure peculiar to the
Ways and Means Committee. Under this procedure, at selected intervals
each year, at closed-door Committee meetings and without any public hearings, each Ways and Means member is permitted to call up a bill of his own
choosing which, by a gentleman's agreement and in a spirit of mutual helpfulness, generally wins unanimous Committee approval. Usually, though not
invariably, a member's bill is addressed to (or at least springs from) the
tax problem of a lone taxpayer.

† He claimed a government attorney had told him there would be no tax
to pay on the settlement, which the lawyer denied.

failing to file proper tax returns (for three years, Sanders had filed blank returns). In 1955, the Tax Court* ruled against Sanders and sharply criticized him for his tax-filing practices which, the court found, were "due to willful neglect." The Supreme Court denied an appeal on February 27, 1956.

Precisely two months and one day later, a bill emerged from the Senate Finance Committee. Ostensibly, it had nothing to do with Mr. Sanders (its main title involved the transfer of patent rights), but tucked away in it was an extraneous section entitled "Certain Claims Against the United States." In order to qualify under the section, these "certain claims" had to meet certain qualifications. They had to (1) arise "under a contract for the construction of installations of facilities for any branch of the Armed Services of the United States" (2) which "remained unpaid for more than 5 years" and (3) which were paid in the year 1949 (six years prior to the enactment of this provision)—no sooner, no later. For the happy taxpayer whose claim could meet all of these specifications, the maximum tax rate was 33 percent, instead of the 90 or 91 percent top rate that would otherwise have applied. In addition, the provision excused Sanders from the massive penalties for his failure to file proper tax returns, despite the Tax Court's findings that "all excuses [for improper filing] have been carefully considered and found inadequate upon analysis."

None of these circumstances was even hinted at in the Congressional report accompanying the measure. The bill slipped easily through the Senate, without explanation or debate. There is, however, a suggestion that those appointed to reconcile the differences between the House and Senate versions of the bill were not entirely comfortable about the Sanders provision, for they took pains to make clear their "understanding" that the provision was "not to be considered a precedent for future legislative action."

But Leo Sanders needed no "future legislative action." His made-to-order provision—you won't find it in the tax code itself, because it lies tucked away in Volume 70 of the General Statutes of the United States—was quite sufficient to save him a large part of the $955,000 the Tax Court had said he owed the government.

LEO SANDERS is not the only fortunate individual who has lost in the courts of law only to win later in the halls of Con-

---

* See Glossary.

gress. On June 12, 1952, the Tax Court ruled against a Mr. L. R. McKee, a wholesale and retail feed and grain dealer from Muscatine, Iowa, for claimed deficiencies totaling more than $190,000 for the years 1946, 1947 and 1948. By the time the case came before the Court of Appeals in October, 1953, the pertinent section of the law had been changed—not just for the future but, under certain conditions, retroactive for seven years, to include "taxable years beginning after December 31, 1945," just far enough back to relieve Mr. McKee of the effect of the Tax Court's adverse ruling.

Section 1342 of the Internal Revenue Code is entitled "Computation of Tax Where Taxpayer Recovers Substantial Amount Held by Another under Claim of Right." Anyone can avail himself of this provision *if* he was involved in a patent infringement suit and *if* he claimed a tax deduction for certain expenses in connection with the suit, and *if* the deduction was later disallowed because the decision in the suit was found to have been "induced by fraud or undue influence," and *if* the disallowed deductions exceeded $3,000. It would be miraculous if this remarkable array of specifications should fit more than a single company. But, then, one shouldn't expect too much—it did, at least, fit the one company for which it had been so carefully tailored: the Universal Oil Products Company, which had been involved in a patent infringement suit in which the decision was later found to have been fraudulent because the judge was bribed, and certain of whose expense deductions in connection with the suit were later disallowed.

MEMBERS OF CONGRESS at times show a tender solicitude toward each other's needs. For example, although as a general rule cousins may not be claimed as dependents, Section 152(a)(10) of the tax law provides that a "descendant of a brother or sister of the father or mother of the taxpayer" (i.e., a cousin) may be claimed as a dependent if he or she first resides with the taxpayer and then receives institutional care. One such cousin belonged to Representative Jere Cooper of Tennessee, formerly Chairman of the tax-writing House Ways and Means Committee.

The section defining "head-of-household" is said to have been carefully written so as not to bar the lower head-of-household tax rates* to North Carolina's venerable Representative Robert L. ("Muley") Doughton, Representative Cooper's predecessor as Ways and Means Chairman. At the time the head-of-household provisions were enacted, Representative Doughton was a widower whose daughter was living with him. Consideration was given to requiring that children and grandchildren living with heads-of-household earn less than $600 per year, but this would not have suited Representative Doughton's fancy, since his daughter, at the time, was on his Congressional office payroll, and earning considerably more than $600 a year.

Private Law 490 of 1955 is namelessly entitled "An Act To Provide Tax Relief to a Charitable Foundation and the Contributors Thereto." A reading of the law itself discloses that the principal "contributors thereto" are Mr. and Mrs. Clarence Cannon of Elsberry, Missouri—the same Representative Clarence Cannon who for eighteen years presided powerfully over the House Appropriations Committee. Mr. Cannon's influence on Capitol Hill was eloquently demonstrated in the dispatch with which the legislators acted on Private Law 490, which decreed that the Cannon Foundation was indeed a tax-free institution, any doubts to the contrary notwithstanding. A bill to this effect was introduced in the House on Saturday, July 30, 1955. On Monday morning it was referred to the House Judiciary Committee and, no more than three minutes later, "approved" by that committee and, simultaneously, passed by the House. The following day it received the Senate's blessing. Hours later, Congress adjourned until the following January—but not without having resolved the doubts that apparently had existed about the tax-exempt status of the Cannon Foundation of Elsberry, Missouri.

EXAMINE ANY WARTIME excess profits tax law and you will soon find a number of provisions so narrowly drawn that they could only apply to one company—or, perhaps, to a select few companies.

For example, Section 518 of the Revenue Act of 1951 provides special relief for any taxpayer "engaged primarily in the newspaper publishing business" which in a certain limited time period "consolidated its mechanical, circulation, advertising and

*See p. 127.

accounting operations" with those of another newspaper "in the same area"—a circumstance that happened to fit two Fort Wayne, Indiana, newspapers, the *Journal-Gazette* and the *Sentinel*. Almost surely, no other newspaper in the country could qualify.

Section 516 of that same law had its own peculiar restrictions. All a company had to do to reap its advantages was: (1) to have been in business prior to 1940; (2) to have assets as of a certain date worth not more than ten million dollars; (3) to have government contracts account for more than 70 percent of its total income in 1942–45 but less than 20 percent in 1950; and (4) to have profits in 1945 and the average of 1948 and 1949 at least three times as great as average profits in 1946 and 1947. The Owens-Corning Fiberglas Corporation was able to wedge itself within the confines of those limitations, but could any other?

The following year, excess profits relief was specifically granted to the Budd Company of Philadelphia (maker of railroad cars), the Sangamo Electric Company of Springfield, Illinois, and the Bridgeport Brass Company—and, possibly, a few other independent brass fabricators.*

THE CUSTOM-MADE PROVISIONS mentioned so far are those for which the beneficiaries have somehow been identified. But there are dozens of other statutes which seem clearly fashioned for a lone taxpayer perhaps known only to himself, his attorney (or lobbyist) and the lawmaker who favored him by sponsoring his made-to-order provision.

If you are interested in sleuthing these provisions yourself, one telltale signal is a retroactive date, for chances are its purpose is to reach back and take care of a single taxpayer's *past* difficulty, perhaps with the courts, perhaps with the Internal Revenue Service. And don't confine your searches to the tax code itself. Many of these custom-tailored provisions are, like the Leo Sanders amendment, tucked away in the General Statutes. If, for example, you chanced to open Volume 70 of the General Statutes, you would find five tax measures in a row (Public Laws 396 through 400) of which four have retroactive provisions.

---

* Some contend (with considerable reason) that specially tailored excess profits provisions of this sort result from the inherent awkwardness of the excess profits tax itself—relying, as it does, on an arbitrary "base period" that cannot accommodate the individual peculiarities of particular companies' growth patterns.

Even in the tax code itself, though, you will find provisions so narrowly circumscribed that they seem clearly to have been written with a single taxpayer in mind. For example, as a general rule, noncitizens of the United States do not qualify as "dependents." But Section 152 (b) (3) (A) of the Internal Revenue Code provides an exception to this rule, applicable to any child of a taxpayer (1) "born to him, or legally adopted by him, in the Philippine Islands"; (2) if the birth or adoption occurred "prior to January 1, 1956"; (3) if the child was a resident of the Philippines; and (4) "if the taxpayer was a member of the Armed Forces of the United States at the time the child was born to him or legally adopted by him." The amendment, enacted on August 9, 1955, reached back eight years, and was effective as of 1947.

Ordinarily, you may not claim a charitable deduction for contributing to organizations engaged in electioneering. But, thanks to Section 29 of the Revenue Act of 1962, anyone was allowed to deduct contributions made *during 1962 only*—not before, not after—to organizations electioneering for or against state or local judicial reform proposals "with respect to which a referendum [occurred] during . . . 1962." Section 29 was specifically tailored to help the fund-raising efforts of the Chicago and Illinois Bar Associations in backing a judicial reform program voted on in November, 1962.

ONE OBJECTION to the specially designed tax provisions is that while they may, in the first instance, be designed to help out one person, they can sometimes become an acorn from which a sizable oak later grows.

The classic illustration is the case of the "Philadelphia nun." In 1924 a provision was enacted for the express benefit of a wealthy member of the Drexel family who wished to bestow all of her substantial riches upon the religious order which she was entering. The generally applicable tax law would have given her a tax deduction on only a limited portion of this generous gift, but the 1924 special provision permitted her a deduction on the entire donation. Later, however, other affluent taxpayers perceived in the "Philadelphia nun" provision (which later came to be known as the "unlimited charitable deduction" provision) a means whereby they could combine generosity with total tax avoidance, and by 1966 some 100 taxpayers, all of whom had incomes in excess of $1 million, were using the provision as a means of paying zero taxes. One fortunate individual was able, one year, to shield from the tax collectors a total income of $20 million, on which he paid not a penny of taxes.

What began as a seemingly unexceptionable provision for a Philadelphia nun ended up as a $25 million yearly drain on the U.S. Treasury. Forty-five years passed before Congress, in 1969, finally cut down the oak that had grown from the tiny acorn.

THE BENEFICIARIES of these special statutes are not always anonymous. In rare instances, they are actually named. Section 25 of the Revenue Act of 1962, for example, is entitled "Pension Plan of Local Union Numbered 435, International Hod Carriers' Building and Common Laborers' Union of America" and grants tax exemption to that pension plan roughly a year earlier than would otherwise have been the case.

In other instances, while the bill itself may name no names, its object is openly acknowledged. When, in 1961, Congress debated a bill entitled "Distributions of Stock Pursuant to Orders Enforcing Antitrust Laws," it was stated that the measure made a specific tax-law exception for the sale of nearly $3 billion worth of General Motors stock by owners of DuPont, following a Federal court antitrust order. A similar bill, before Congress in 1962 and again in 1963, named no names, but its retroactive provisions were known to apply specifically to the court-ordered sale by the Hilton Hotels Corporation of certain of its properties. A minority report by Ways and Means Committee members opposed to the bill pointed out that the bill was broad enough, potentially, to excuse nineteen other companies from the tax consequences of their antimonopoly offenses.

And it was no secret that a provision of the 1962 tax bill entitled "Income Tax Treatment of Certain Losses Sustained in Converting from Street Railway to Bus Operations" applied exclusively to the Twin Cities Rapid Transit Company of Minneapolis–St. aul, Minnesota. Senator Eugene McCarthy explained to the Senate that the company's management had made a too-rapid changeover from streetcars to buses "in order to complete [certain] fraudulent activities quickly, intentionally disregarding the income tax consequences"—incurring losses so large that they could not be fully tax-deducted in the required period of time. As a result, the company, now under new management, was left with over $5 million of losses for which it could get no tax advantages. The proponents of the provision argued that the new management of the transit company should not have to bear the consequences of fraudulent activity by their predecessors in which they took no part.

The Twin Cities provision was not new; it had been passed by Congress in 1961 as a separate bill, and had been vetoed by President Kennedy. Now, by tacking the same provision onto the omnibus 1962 tax bill, which the Kennedy Administration had been struggling to pass for the better part of two years, its sponsors had made the measure veto-proof.

Also enjoying a free ride as part of the 1962 bill was a previously vetoed provision for the specific benefit of Howard F. Knipp of Baltimore, Maryland, but here there is an important difference from the Twin Cities case. As a result of a special partnership arrangement and the death of Mr. Knipp's partner-uncle in 1946, Internal Revenue ruled that nearly two years' income was taxable to Mr. Knipp in the single year 1947, causing him to pay roughly $110,000 in additional taxes. After losing in both the Tax Court and the Appeals Court, Knipp's attorneys sought relief through a "private law," openly entitled "A Bill for the Relief of Howard F. Knipp." Congressional committee reports set forth all the circumstances of the case and, as did not occur in the Leo Sanders case, candidly acknowledged that the measure would reverse court decisions. The Treasury Department opposed the measure as an "undesirable precedent" that would invite others to seek Congressional reversal of adverse decisions, and the private law was vetoed. Thus thwarted, Knipp's protagonists sought relief via the nameless "general law" route and finally succeeded in tacking onto the 1962 Revenue Act the Knipp amendment—retroactive fifteen years to take care of Mr. Knipp's 1947 tax problem.

THE KNIPP CASE, in illustrating the two means by which Congress can accommodate an individual taxpayer's problem (either by a "private law" or by a nameless "general" provision), illuminates the central question posed by these tailor-made measures: if Congress wishes to bestow a tax favor on Louis B. Mayer or Leo Sanders or Charles Merrill or Howard F. Knipp, why not come right out and say so?

If, as with the first Knipp bill, the Mayer, Sanders and Merrill provisions had set forth the reasons for requesting special relief, Congress, the public and the President, with his veto power, would have had a means of judging the measure on its merits, based on all the facts. Why mask these actions behind the thin disguise of a "general" law?

To the practical politician, the answer is self-evident. The Treasury Department and the President rarely perceive as clearly as does Congress why a lone taxpayer should be exempted from the laws and rules applicable to others. Thus most efforts to grant tax relief through the more candid "private law" route have, like the Knipp bill, succumbed to a Presidential veto. Therefore, explains one Ways and Means Committee member, when he is appealed to by a taxpayer with a case he considers meritorious, he has no choice but to disguise his tailored provision as a general law and attach it, if possible, to an unvetoable measure. Besides, the anonymous-bill method avoids the annoyance of having to explain why special relief should be granted to a taxpayer such as Leo Sanders, who has availed himself of all the regular channels of justice and whose case has been found wanting by the courts.

Moreover, members of the tax-writing committees, observing their Congressional colleagues on other committees dispensing subsidies, public works and politically lucrative appropriation items, are understandably reluctant to have tax bills diverted to the respective judiciary committees to which, under Congressional rules, private relief bills of the Knipp variety are referred.

There is another defense of the "general law" method of dispensing single-taxpayer relief. When Taxpayer A, with a meritorious case, seeks relief, how, it is asked, can anyone know that there aren't dozens of others—Taxpayers B, C, D, and so on—in the same predicament? To name Taxpayer A in a bill for his exclusive relief would be to discriminate against B, C, D, and all the others. But this argument collapses when applied to the Sanders provision (six years retroactive) or the Merrill amendment (applicable only to those who died fifteen months *prior* to its enactment). It is, moreover, a transparently thin defense of such absurdly hedged-in provisions as the Mayer amendment.

Ironically, in many cases, the very narrowness of these statutes results from the urgings of the Treasury Department itself, which reasons (e.g., in the case of the provision for Ellsworth Alvord) that if special relief is to be granted at all, better to protect the Federal revenues by confining the relief to the narrowest possible circumstances.

In opposing these made-to-order relief provisions, the Treasury usually finds itself a lonely Horatio at the bridge. The few outside persons, such as, say, law professors or Naderesque public-interest research groups, who might be disposed to speak up against such provisions, have no way of knowing (in time, at any rate) that Amendment A is for the McDonnell Douglas Corporation or that Provision B is for Gwendolyn Cafritz and her foundation, and in most cases the identity of the favored beneficiary does not become publicly known until after the specially designed provisions have been safely enacted into law. One notable and rare exception occurred in 1969, when Senator Edward M. Kennedy had the temerity (and the courage) to stand up on the Senate floor and publicly identify at least fifteen tailor-made provisions (including the McDonnell Douglas, Lockheed, and Mobil Oil amendments and the others cited at the outset of this chapter) that were embedded in the huge tax bill the Senate was then considering. "These special provisions," Kennedy complained, "are generally hidden from public view. As this has been the case historically, it is also the case with the bill before us."

Finance Committee Chairman Russell Long was incensed by the charge of secrecy. "All the Senator has to do is read the newspapers," he said. As his committee had adopted the various special provisions, he insisted, he had announced to the press the identity of the person or company at whose behest it had been enacted. For example, he said, regarding the specially monogrammed WWL amendment, Father Jolley of Loyola University, the station's owner, had openly testified before Senate Finance, and Long himself had explicitly announced the station's identity to the press when the Committee approved the provision.

Kennedy was evidently prepared for this rebuttal for he and his staff had reviewed the newspapers and had found that "a number of different amendments were accepted which were not reported in the newspapers."* Long, in effect, confirmed this, in a

---

* A review of all the Finance Committee's press releases on its 1969 decisions fails to disclose any naming of a special beneficiary other than Lockheed and McDonnell Douglas.

Senatorial barb seemingly intended to embarrass Kennedy: "I regret," he said, "that we did not identify the Western Massachusetts Electric Company," which also had a special provision in the bill in which Kennedy had taken an interest. But Kennedy had been careful to place the Massachusetts company's provision at the top of his list of examples, insisting that "there is nothing in the Massachusetts case that ought to receive special consideration, outside of the merits." His main complaint, he said, was that "nowhere in the [committee] report or the 585-page bill, is there any indication of these special provisions. . . ."; public acknowledgment of these provisions was important to "public confidence in public processes":

It is not a secret that special provisions find their way into the various tax bills passed by the Congress and are signed by the President. But it is usually a secret which groups or individuals benefit from them. And this aura of secrecy generates an impression that the provisions are hidden because their sponsors have something to hide. I do not believe this to be the case. Anything given the force of Federal law should—indeed must—be able to stand the test of public scrutiny if we are to expect the public to have continuing faith in our government processes.

These arguments were evidently not persuasive to Chairman Long, who offered two seemingly contradictory defenses of the Committee's existing procedure. On the one hand, he argued that to name the particular beneficiary of a provision was questionable, in part because the Committee had no way of knowing that the provision would not also apply to other taxpayers (and thus it would be unfair to single out Lockheed, Mobil Oil or Gwendolyn Cafritz) and in part because the identity of the beneficiary should have nothing to do with the merits and the justice of the provision itself. "I voted on *some* of the [special] measures without regard to who was involved. With regard to the Cafritz matter, it made no difference to me who was involved." (Emphasis added.)

Later the Senator waxed eloquent on the subject:

I personally . . . cling to the . . . concept of justice as the lady who stands there blindfolded and holds the scale of justice. She does not know who has an interest on the left side or who has an interest on the right side. She just tries to do what is right on the matter that is involved. That is how we should do these things.

But there were some inconsistencies in Senator Long's pronouncement. For one thing, his Finance Committee certainly didn't operate blindfoldedly when it adopted the special provisions. The names of the individuals and companies seeking special treatment were freely discussed in the Committee's closed-door deliberations. Moreover, if Senator Long's goal was "Justice Blindfolded," why had he named *some* of the beneficiaries in his own announcements to the press? And was his position consistent with his insistence that "if [Kennedy] had inquired . . . I would have been glad to have identified for him any taxpayer who expressed any interest in the bill." If it was appropriate for members of the Senate (and, where Long chose, the press and public) to know the names of the beneficiaries, why was it not also appropriate to name them in the Committee report, together with the *reasons* for exempting Uniroyal or the Litton executives or the Cafritz Foundation from the general rules by which other taxpayers would have to abide?

One of the main difficulties in identifying the special provisions is the conspiracy of silence entered into by those who know who is getting what from which provision. Finance Committee members, for example, generally know who the lucky taxpayers are; yet not even the most reform-minded Senators on the Committee will divulge their identity to the public.*

Equally tight-lipped is the fraternity of Washington tax attorneys, many of whom, in the course of pressing their own clients' interests, learn via the grapevine of many of the special provisions that others are pushing. If they were willing to "blow the whistle," they could be very helpful in blocking these tailor-made raids on the U.S. Treasury, for often even Treasury Department officials have difficulty in detecting the beneficiary of this or that amendment. The mutual protectiveness among legislators, though of doubtful defensibility, is understandable. No Senator can, with

---

* Delaware's Republican Senator John J. Williams, a member of the Committee who asserted, during the Senate debate, that he had opposed some of the special provisions contained in the bill as passed by the House, openly told Kennedy, "I know two or three more special exemptions he missed"—but he would not identify or try to eliminate them from the bill.

equanimity, deny favors to his own constituents while less fastidi-
ous colleagues are pushing through special provisions for theirs.
In defending the Twin Cities amendment, for example, Minnesota's Senator Hubert Humphrey, one of the most vocal opponents
of tax loopholes, acknowledged that his was "special legislation."
But, he said, "it is not unique."

Few Senators are immune from the charge of having pushed
a particular provision on behalf of a favored constituent. When,
for example, Ohio's Senator Lausche protested the Twin Cities
amendment, Senator Kerr turned on him savagely and accused
him of having objected, at the behest of an Ohio constituent, to
one aspect of a "loophole-closing" provision, a charge indignantly
denied by Senator Lausche. In a gentler manner, Senator Eugene
McCarthy reminded Illinois' Paul Douglas, principal objector to
the Twin Cities amendment, that "we passed a bill for the Senator
from Illinois" providing retroactive relief for a union pension
fund.

IF THE PORTRAIT PAINTED thus far in this chap-
ter is that of a tax law riddled with individually tailored provisions
and of a Congress wholly pliant to the pressures of blandishments
of special pleaders, it is an incomplete picture. Provisions of the
Lockheed, Cafritz or Mayer variety make up a small part of the
tax law. And, although the pressures on the tax-writing committees of Congress are great (the greater, perhaps, because they have
shown themselves willing to let down the bars at propitious times),
they do turn down many requests for special favors (e.g., the
Mobil Oil amendment, which died in the House-Senate conference). Even among those that win the sponsorship of a legislator,
few are finally enacted.

One knowledgeable critic of tax preferences, Professor Walter
Blum of the University of Chicago, is restrained in his criticism
of the tailor-made tax provision. Because so few taxpayers are
involved, he says, these measures do not complicate the tax system "to any appreciable extent" or lend themselves to "spawning
new preferential provisions by suggesting analogous situations."

Nevertheless, the average hard-pressed taxpayers—like the
Nichols', whose situation was recounted at the outset of this chapter—are entitled to be outraged that raw political power or close
acquaintanceship with a member of Congress (or a tax lobbyist)

satisfactorily qualifies a citizen for favorable tax treatment not generally available to other taxpayers. It has been observed that "popular imagination holds taxes to be as ruthless in the certainty of their incidence as is death." If that is true, then popular imagination is not familiar with the efficacy of lobbyists or the ways of legislators.

Columbia law professor William L. Cary (later Chairman of the Securities and Exchange Commission) was once prompted to write an entire article on special tax provisions inspired in considerable measure by the "casual remark" of one Washington lawyer, who asked, "What is the point of litigating a tax case when we can have the statute amended for the same outlay of time and money?"

Cary posed this question:

Can relief be scattered sporadically among a few individuals—whose only common characteristic is access to Congress—without making a mockery of the revenue laws? For every person who successfully argues [before Congress] that he is discriminated against, there are thousands of others, inarticulate or ineffective, who are suffering the same fate in silence.

4

The Mightily-Privileged Few

QUESTION: What percent of the taxpayers of the United States make more than $30,000 a year?

What percent make more than $50,000? More than $25,000?

Over a period of years, I have asked these questions of a large number of people. I have encountered almost no one—even among people sophisticated in the facts of economic life—who could come anywhere near answering them correctly.* Many of the answers were off the mark tenfold.

Can you do better?

Before reading further, make your own guesses.

THE ANSWERS ARE:

—If you make more than $25,000 a year, you are in the top three percent of all taxpayers.

—If you make more than $30,000 a year, you are in the top two percent of all taxpayers.

—If your income is more than $50,000 a year, you are in the top *six-tenths of one percent.*

---

* This is not because the figures are particularly hard to find. They are published every year by the Internal Revenue Service, in a statistical portrait of American taxpayers entitled *Statistics of Income.* That portrait is based on "adjusted gross income" of taxpayers, which omits certain items of income such as interest on state and local bonds and half of all capital gains. Thus it differs with figures based on *total* income, developed by Drs. Pechman and Okner and cited elsewhere in this book (see p. 9).

Now, if you're not in that top three percent—if you don't make $25,000 a year—take fair warning. This chapter is not about you. As a matter of fact, chances are this chapter doesn't mention you unless you're in the top six-tenths of one percent. (But don't skip over the chapter; these tax features have a direct bearing on you—they cause you to pay higher taxes to make up for the billions of revenue they cost the Treasury every year.)

Do you own any (or many) tax-exempt bonds? Do you get a salary of more than $200,000? Do you have large oil investments or substantial amounts of "capital gains"? Do you happen to have a "stock option" arrangement with your employer? No? Then none of the tax preferences described in this chapter will do you any good.

If, however, you *are* a beneficiary of these particular tax preferences, you are indeed blessed, for great are the tax savings therefrom.

How great? Well, for example, over two and a half billion dollars annually to the owners of state and local tax-free bonds. Three hundred million dollars a year to corporation stockholders. About fifty million dollars to the fortunate holders of corporate stock options.

Since in each case these bountiful tax favors go to a comparative handful of taxpayers, the savings for each can be mighty.

Take, for example, the case of Mrs. Horace Dodge, Sr. (see next page), who reportedly came to own the astonishing sum of $100 million in state and local bonds, the interest on which is nontaxable. Her annual tax savings: nearly $3,500,000.

Or consider the case of Mr. Thomas J. Watson, head of IBM, who, over the years, has been permitted to buy shares of his company for *$5 million less than the going market price.* If Mr. Watson took advantage of his good luck, sold the stock and realized that $5 million profit, his tax saving would almost surely have been in excess of $2 million.

Great, therefore, are the blessings, but few are the blessed, since the ownership of tax-free bonds and corporation stock and the benefactions of stock option arrangements are heavily concentrated in that top six-tenth of one percent of the population fortunate enough to make more than $50,000 a year.

In the case of no other tax preference is the above so dramatically true as with tax-exempt bonds, so that is where we shall begin our examination of the mightily-privileged few.

Tax-Free Bonds

How would you like to have $5,000,000 of income every year and not even have to bother filing a tax return?

All you have to do is put your entire multi-million-dollar inheritance into state and local bonds (as the late Mrs. Horace Dodge did) so that you end up owning $100 million worth of those bonds, and if the bonds yield an average 5 percent return, you're all set.

Why, even with a staggering $5 million of income, wouldn't you have to file a tax return? Because as far as Internal Revenue is concerned, the interest you receive on state and municipal bonds doesn't even exist: page 5 of the Form 1040 instructions specifically lists it as "income which should not be reported" on your tax return. And since (under the above assumption) all your wealth is in such bonds and the tax-exempt interest from these bonds therefore constitutes your entire income, you have zero "gross income" to report—and you are excused from filing a tax return.

Now, if you were to ask around among your friends whether they own any state or municipal bonds, assuming your friends have fairly average incomes, chances are about a hundred to one the answer would be no. If, however, you happen to travel in a circle of, say, Long Island estate owners, you'd get a far different answer, for among *individual* bond owners (as distinct from corporations, banks and other institutions), people of wealth own virtually all the tax-free bonds, as graphically shown by the following table:

This share of the population . . .	owned . . .	this share of tax-free state and local bonds
The top 1/10 of 1%		69.2%
The top 7/100 of 1%		39.7%
The top 4/1,000 of 1%		8.2%

It is little wonder that even so conservative an individual as former Republican Congressman John Byrnes of Wisconsin (who fought valiantly to curb the benefits of this exemption in 1969) should have seen fit to label this exemption as little more than "a tax saving for the wealthy."

There is a common-sense explanation for this extreme concentration of tax-free bonds among the super-rich. For one thing, a family with, say, $5,000 to $8,000 of income rarely has any spare dollars lying around to invest; even if they do, a 5 percent state or local bond is distinctly unalluring, what with savings accounts paying 5 to 6 percent interest.

By contrast, to a top-bracket Long Island estate owner, with plenty of cash to spare for investments, a 5 percent tax-free bond is intensely appetizing. Ordinarily, he would expect as much as 70 percent of any investment income to go into taxes, so that only 30 percent would actually reach him. But with state and local bonds, the entire return comes to him untouched by Internal Revenue. If he is in the 70 percent tax bracket, it would take a 16.7 percent return on a *taxable* investment to leave him 5 percent after-tax "keeping money." The following table shows how the allure of the tax-free bonds increases as the owner's income rises:

If your taxable income is:	A 5 percent tax-free bond is equivalent to a taxable stock or bond yielding:
$4,000–$8,000	6.2%
$20,000–$24,000	7.4%
$52,000–$64,000	10.6%
$100,000–$120,000	13.2%
Over $200,000	16.7%

From this it is clear that these seemingly magical bonds are not tailored to the needs of the hoi polloi, as one beleaguered taxpayer discovered when he asked the "Daily Investor" column of the Washington *Daily News* about buying such bonds for his children. The answer: "All of us like to minimize our taxes wherever we can, but municipal bonds . . . *don't necessarily fill the bill unless certain other conditions are present—a high tax bracket, for example.*" (Emphasis added.) And an advertisement in the New York *Times* by a bond-selling company in New York pictured three individuals, right hands raised in oath-like fashion, declaring, ON MY HONOR, I RESOLVE TO BUY TAX-EXEMPT BONDS BEFORE ANOTHER APRIL 15TH PASSES. Was any of the three a laborer or a blue-collar worker? Not bloody likely (as Eliza Doolittle might have put it): one was a white-coated, be-stethoscoped doctor; one was a blue-serge-suited executive type; the third was a white-haired and unmistakably well-tailored matron.

Investing in tax-free bonds results in handsome tax savings for the unneedy, with almost insultingly low tax benefits for the more hard-pressed:

Income Group	Average Annual Tax Savings from Tax-Free Bonds
$1,000,000 or more	$36,000
$500,000–$1,000,000	$18,000
$25,000–$50,000	$24
$10,000–$15,000	80 cents
$5,000–$10,000	10 cents

Naturally, with the top-bracket families owning most of the bonds and getting the biggest tax bang for a buck invested, the tax benefits are heavily concentrated in the economic stratosphere:

This percent of all families . . .	gets . . .	this percent of the tax benefits from tax-free bonds
The richest 7.6%		96%
The richest 1.2%		87%
The richest 0.8%		76%

These tax savings certainly can't be justified as an incentive to risk-taking on the part of the purchasers of state and local bonds. The Wall Street underwriters and sellers of such bonds habitually point out, in the enticing brochures, that these bonds are almost as safe as U.S. government bonds, showing that even during the worst depression, no more than 2 percent of these bonds were in default (and even those ultimately met their obligation).

IN ADDITION TO the tax-free bonds owned by individuals, an even greater quantity belongs to commercial banks, corporations and other institutions, which derive handsome tax benefits therefrom. For example, as of December 31, 1971, the Bank of America, the nation's largest, owned nearly three *billion* dollars' worth of these bonds, from which it presumably derived about $150 million of wholly untaxed income,* and a tax saving of nearly $72 million, for 1971 alone.

---

* Assuming an aggregate 5 percent return on the bonds.

The nontaxable bondholdings and the resulting tax savings enjoyed by other large banks are as follows:

Bank	Amount of Tax-Free Bonds Owned*	Approximate Annual Tax Saving
Chase Manhattan	$1,591,107,501	$38,000,000
First National City of New York	$915,163,000	$22,000,000

* As of December 31, 1970.

Banks and insurance companies enjoy a double-edged advantage from their tax-free bonds. They are allowed full tax deductions on their interest payments to depositors and policyholders; yet they may turn around and invest the deposits and premiums in tax-exempt bonds and enjoy wholly untaxed income.*

TAX-FREE BONDS date back to the original income tax law of 1913 when Congress, notwithstanding its new power under the Sixteenth Amendment to tax incomes "from whatever source derived," voluntarily relinquished the taxes on state and local bond interest. Why? Because of assurances given key governors while the Sixteenth Amendment was before the states for ratification and because there existed, then, a doubt as to the constitutionality of taxing the states.

But as the volume of state and local bonds has risen to $143 billion, their small cost in 1913 has grown into a $2.5 billion annual revenue loss to the Treasury. Over the years, many Presidents and Secretaries of the Treasury—including such conservatives as Calvin Coolidge, Carter Glass and Andrew Mellon, not to mention the Investment Bankers Association—recommended repeal of the exemption, but the howls by the states and cities always killed the proposal dead in its tracks. In 1969, those highly vocal protests dissuaded Congress from even the most infinitesimal curtailment of this tax privilege.†

---

* Commercial banks also enjoy another special advantage: they are permitted to deduct all the expenses of administering their tax-exempt investments, whereas personal trusts that own tax-free bonds are disallowed deductions on a proportionate share of their administrative expenses.

† Not only did Congress refuse to subject tax-exempt bond interest to the "minimum tax" (p. 71); it also declined to require that state and local bond interest merely be *reported* on tax returns, even though retaining its tax-free character.

To hard-pressed states, counties and towns, taxation of their bond interest raises the specter of higher borrowing costs, since it is the tax-exempt feature that makes the bonds attractive to wealthy investors. Yet the Federal Treasury *loses* far more revenue (many experts believe twice as much) than the states and localities *save* in lower borrowing costs. Hence, tax reformers argue, the Federal government could well afford to pay a direct subsidy of as much as 50 percent to states and cities to prevent a rise in their borrowing costs, and still break even on revenue (not to mention improving the equity of the Federal tax system).*

That thought has led reformers to propose a solution that would sidetrack the constitutional doubt about Federal authority to tax the states. Under the proposal, states and localities could choose between continuing to issue tax-free bonds at their present low rate or, alternatively, issuing taxable bonds that would bear higher interest rates but would qualify for a Federal subsidy. If the subsidy were as high as 50 percent (as proposed by Senator Gaylord Nelson of Wisconsin), a state or town could issue an 8 percent *taxable* bond, receive a 4 percent subsidy and end up paying only 4 percent—less than most localities and states are now paying on their tax-free bonds. Under those circumstances, the phenomenon of untaxed bond interest for the well-to-do would (in Marxian terms) "wither away," and the Federal tax system would be considerably fairer than it is today.†

---

* The states would gain a side advantage from this: since the mutual nontaxation "truce" between them and the Federal government would be ended, the states could begin taxing the interest on Federal bonds and would pick up an added $180 million of revenue for themselves by so doing.

† Some argue that a Federal subsidy would reduce the independence of the states and localities, but the existing exemption of their bond interest is nothing but an indirect subsidy. It is an irrationally dispensed subsidy at that, since the more a state or city borrows, the greater its subsidy, and since the richer states borrow more (and hence get more of a subsidy) than the poorer and needier states. One study showed that in 1969 (the latest year for which figures are readily available) the average per capita debt in Southern and border states was just $145, compared with nearly $784 in Delaware. Moreover, the neediest communities—those with the poorest credit ratings and the highest interest rates—receive the least assistance under the existing system. A directly appropriated Federal subsidy could, in theory at least, be so structured as to correct some of these incongruities.

The "Minimum Tax"

On January 17, 1969, just three days before the Johnson Administration left office, outgoing Treasury Secretary Joseph Barr attracted nationwide attention when he told Congress that in 1967, 155 Americans with incomes of $200,000 or more had paid not a penny of Federal income taxes. Twenty-three of those fortunate individuals had contrived to enjoy incomes of a million dollars or more, without paying any tax whatever.

As mentioned in Chapter 1, the taxlessness among the very rich of which Barr spoke was a rapidly growing phenomenon. Here, once again, are the figures:

Income* Group	Number in Group Who Paid No Tax in		
	1960	1967	1969
Above $1,000,000	11	23	56
Above $500,000	23	63	117
Above $200,000	70	167	301
Above $100,000	104	399	761

* These figures understate the extent of tax avoidance among the very rich. For one thing, "income," as used here, means "adjusted gross income" (AGI), which is computed *after* a person deducts from his total income his business deductions, including "paper" deductions in the case of real-estate investors (see p. 175). Thus AGI can be vastly less than a person's real income. (One wealthy real-estate investor had total income of $1,433,000—but an "adjusted gross income" of zero!)

For another, the figures in the above table deal only with those wealthy people who achieved *total* taxlessness. They omit the "near misses"—affluent persons who paid a pittance in taxes (e.g., an actual taxpayer cited in a Treasury Department study who had total income of $1,284,000 and paid just $274 in taxes).

In revealing these figures, Barr talked of "the possibility of a taxpayer revolt"—and not without reason. As Barr observed, "millions of middle class families and individuals" were paying taxes "based on the full ordinary [tax] rates." But even more striking, the same tax law that was levying no tax on hundreds of millionaires was, at the same time, extracting *some* taxes from 2,200,000 Americans who were living below the officially designated "poverty" level.

It was all very embarrassing. Clearly, something had to be done to banish from the headlines this awkward phenomenon of tax-free millionaires. The most direct way to achieve this would have been to close up the loopholes through which the wealthy were escaping taxation. But that remedy would surely have produced anguish and even vocal protest from the beneficiaries of the loopholes, and Congress exhibited no enthusiasm for the direct, loophole-closing approach. Instead it elected, in 1969, to enact a "minimum tax" whose object, according to the Senate Finance Committee, was to "make sure that those receiving [tax] preferences . . . pay a share of the tax burden."

Done, done and done.

But wait. Not so fast. Time passed and when the facts about 1970 (the first year of the "minimum tax") came in, it was clear that something was amiss—for a large number of highly prosperous citizens had done it again. Despite the "minimum tax," no fewer than 394—count 'em, 394—families making more than $100,000 a year had once again contrived to pass by April 15 without paying one red cent to Uncle Sam! One hundred and twelve of them took in more than $200,000, and nineteen had incomes of more than a half-million dollars that they were able to keep wholly untouched by Internal Revenue.

Moreover, despite the "minimum tax," total tax avoidance remained a widespread phenomenon among the moderately well-to-do. More than *three thousand* families (3,314, to be precise) made more than thirty thousand dollars in 1970, yet were free of any tax burden. One thousand three hundred and thirty-eight of them made more than fifty thousand dollars that year.

But most spectacular (or most outrageous) were the three families at the very pinnacle *whose 1970 "adjusted gross income"** averaged *more than three and a third million dollars* but who paid no income tax whatever. (Their average income from corporate dividends alone was nearly two and a half million dollars per family—which would imply corporate shareholdings of about seventy-five million dollars per family.)

All of these families were exempt from the Senatorial pronunciamento about "pay[ing] a share of the tax burden." Clearly, even in this new "anti-loophole" law, there were loopholes.

---

* As noted earlier, "adjusted gross income" usually significantly understates total dollar intake, since it does not include half of all capital gains and does not include income offset by certain business deductions (real estate, oil, etc.).

Of course, not every super-rich family slipped cleanly through the new "minimum tax." But the statistics on those who *were* tripped up by it (i.e., those who otherwise would have paid no tax) merely dramatize the feebleness of the new tax. In 1970, for example, 318 families making more than $100,000 would have paid no tax but for the "minimum tax." The following shows the impact of the law on those families, divided into three groups: Group 1 making between $100,000 and $500,000; Group 2 between $500,000 and $1,000,000; and lucky Group 3 making more than $1,000,000.

Group	Number of Families	Average Total Income	Tax Due Without "Minimum Tax"	Average "Minimum Tax" Amount	Average "Minimum Tax" Percent of Total Income
1	279	$471,220	0	$14,122	3%
2	31	$1,397,420	0	$61,742	4.4%
3	8	$1,703,750	0	$67,375	4%

Technically, then, all of those 318 families were living up to the Senatorial criterion of "pay[ing] a share of the tax burden." But was it a *fair** share? Judge for yourself. Let's look at the situation of those families from another perspective—the amount they were able to keep *after* paying the "minimum tax":

	Average "Keeping Money"		
Group	Full Year	Per Week	Percent of Total Income
1	$457,098	$8,790	97%
2	$1,335,678	$25,686	95.6%
3	$1,636,375	$31,469	96%

Those figures take on still another perspective when viewed through the eyes of Ralph Senters, the laborer at the Otis Elevator factory in Cleveland, mentioned in Chapter 1. Mr. Senters' year's work brought him $7,371.72, out of which he paid taxes of $1,131.47—nearly 16 percent of his income. Side by side, the figures look like this:

---

* The Senate Finance Committee conspicuously omitted that word.

	Year's Income	Percent of Income Paid in Taxes
Group 3	$1,703,750	4%
Ralph Senters	$7,372	16%

The "keeping money" enjoyed *each week* by families in Group 3 was five times Ralph Senters' "keeping money" *for the entire year*.

It would seem, from the above figures, that Congress chose just the right word when it called the new 1969 tax a "minimum" tax. It would also appear that in enacting the new provision, the lawmakers exhibited a careful and tender regard for the formerly taxless well-to-do.

How was that tender regard manifested? In a number of ways.

First, in the astounding gentleness of the "minimum tax" itself. Congress, after placing generous amounts of the tax-favored income outside the reach of the "minimum tax" (you'll read more about that in a moment), chose to impose, on the remainder, a tax amounting to just 10 percent.* This seems an act of great generosity, considering that ordinarily, but for the loopholes, wealthy families would be obliged to pay tax rates of 40, 50 or even 70 percent on their tax-sheltered income. Nonetheless, the "minimum tax" was fixed at a mere 10 percent. Even the poorest taxpayers—those with taxable incomes as low as $1,000 a year—are subject to a tax rate nearly half again as high as that (14 percent).

What's more, Congress made it a flat 10 percent tax, no matter how much tax-favored income a family enjoyed. For other taxpayers, tax rates rise as income increases; but not for the "minimum tax" payers: the rate is fixed at 10 percent, no higher, whether their tax-favored income is $100 or $1,000 or $100,000 (and remember that, on the average, families in Group 3 above had tax-favored income of $703,750 in 1970).

Recalling that Congress elected *not to* close up the avenues of tax avoidance but, instead, to impose this "minimum tax," the 10 percent figure might be looked at in another way: namely, it

---

* Had the Senate Finance Committee had its way, the "minimum tax" would have been even more negligible—just 5 percent.

permits the users of various tax loopholes to continue to enjoy 90 percent of the benefits they have always received from them. It was a small price to pay.

But you have yet to hear the worst: as to many kinds of tax-favored income, Congress refused to take away even 10 percent of the traditional benefits.

In the first place, Congress allowed each tax-favored family to keep a generous amount of its formerly untaxed income— $30,000 at a rock-bottom minimum, and possibly much more than that (see pages 72–73)—wholly free of the "minimum tax." Thus it is not surprising that more than three thousand families making more than that $30,000 figure paid no taxes at all in 1970.

Secondly, the legislators decreed that certain highly effective tax-avoiding devices should remain undisturbed by the "minimum tax." For example, there were the wealthy oil investors about whom you will read in Chapter 11, who had consistently managed to pay no taxes, year after year, by virtue of their "intangible drilling" deductions (see page 235). Congress concluded that these gentlemen were so worthy and deserving that they should be allowed to continue that tax-avoiding practice, unmolested. Likewise, the wealthy individuals whose business acumen suddenly deserted them when they engaged in farming ventures (see pages 187–199) are spared the effects of the "minimum tax" when they shield their dividend and other income from taxation by means of their large farm "losses."

In addition, Congress insisted on continuing to treat as wholly fictional and nonexistent the $50,000 that the average million-and-over-income family receives each year in interest on state and local bonds. While that $50,000 must seem real enough to the families who receive and spend it, an ostrich-like Congress treats it as fictional, for, as we have seen, not only does it not have to be reported as income on tax returns, but it is also not treated as income for purposes of the "minimum tax."

Finally, the lawmakers exempted from the "minimum tax" a device by which rich people can derive huge income-sheltering deductions from gifts to charity in a manner not available to propertyless taxpayers.*

---

* The device consists of donating to charity stock or other kinds of property that has undergone a large increase in value since the donor acquired it. Let's say, for example, that a member of the Mellon family

And so, armed with this knowledge about the escape hatches that Congress wrote into the 1969 law, it is not difficult to understand how some families can have stupendous incomes and still pay no tax to Uncle Sam.

Here's how a hypothetical Mr. A, for example, might enjoy a total dollar intake of $1,500,000 and get to keep every penny of it. To begin with, he might receive $500,000 of interest on state and local bonds, which is wholly nontaxable (as well as nonreportable). He might also have $1,000,000 of dividend income, which would be taxable except that fortunate and ingenious Mr. A is able to cancel it out by arranging $300,000 of "intangible drilling expense" deductions on his oil investments; $500,000 of charitable deductions consisting of a gift of stock that had been almost valueless when acquired; $100,000 of deductible interest expenses on that year's borrowings; $70,000 in other personal deductions (state taxes, casualty losses and the like); and $30,000 of percentage depletion deductions,* also from his oil investment. The tax-exempt bond income and all of the other deduction-sheltered income are exempt from the effects of the "minimum tax," with one exception: the $30,000 sheltered by the "excess percentage depletion" deduction. But remember that Congress kindly allows Mr. A a basic $30,000 exemption from the "minimum tax," so that, too, escapes the new law. Net result: zero tax for lucky Mr. A.

I MENTIONED ABOVE that a rock-bottom minimum of $30,000 a year could escape the "minimum tax" and that the exemption might in many cases be much larger than that. Wealthy

---

donates Gulf Oil stock that was worth only $100,000 when acquired many years ago but is now valued at $1,100,000. In general, the average property-less taxpayer can only get a charitable tax deducton by giving cash (e.g., to the church plate on Sunday), for that's about all he has to give. If Mr. or Mrs. Mellon were subject to that same condition (i.e., could only become entitled to a charitable deduction by giving cash), he or she would be obliged to sell the Gulf Oil stock for a million-dollar profit, and pay a $350,000 capital gains tax. But under certain conditions, the tax law permits a Mellon to have his (or her) cake and eat it too: that is, to donate the stock to charity and get the full $1.1 million charitable deduction *as if* the stock had been sold and cash had been donated—but without paying the capital gains tax. That income-shielding device, too, was spared the effects of the "minimum tax."

* Over and above what "cost depletion" would allow (see Glossary).

tax avoiders can thank the U.S. Senate for enlarging the $30,000
by the amount of regular taxes paid in a given year. Suppose, for
example, that Herman Tycoon managed his affairs sloppily
enough to have to pay $100,000 of regular taxes. This would
enable him to enjoy $130,000* of tax-sheltered income that year,
free of the "minimum tax."

That, at any rate, was how the law stood when the "minimum
tax" was first enacted in 1969. But before the new tax could take
effect, in 1970, Congress concluded that even that was not a
sufficiently generous exemption. On December 31, 1970—the last
day of the first year of the "minimum tax"—the lawmakers
enlarged the exemption still further (retroactively, of course, so
that it could be used to soften even that first year's "minimum").
What the Congressmen said, that New Year's Eve, was that the
exemption would be supplemented not only by the regular taxes
paid in the *current* year, but by certain of the taxes that had been
paid *in the seven previous years!*†

This enlarging of the exemption went a long way toward
emasculating the already feeble "minimum tax." For example, as
regards that greatest of all tax-savers-for-the-rich—the special capital gains tax—the expansion of the exemption served to reduce
the "minimum tax" from an already mild 10 percent to a paltry
and almost painless 1.5 percent.‡

IN MARCH, 1972, looking back on the "minimum
tax" that Congress had enacted three years earlier, Wisconsin
Senator Gaylord Nelson concluded that, rather than achieving its
purpose of "end[ing] tax avoidance by the rich," the purported
"minimum" had "turned out to be a gentle 'love tap' to the rich."

---

* The $100,000 of taxes plus the $30,000 exemption available to all
those to whom the "minimum tax" applies.

† Specifically, if in any of those seven years the taxes paid exceeded the
amount of tax-sheltered income, the excess could be carried forward and
used to enlarge this year's "minimum tax" exemption.

‡ To understand how the 1.5 percent rate came about, suppose that
Montague Wellborn, a 70-percent-bracket taxpayer, has $100,000 of capital
gains. The $50,000 that he is allowed to exclude in figuring up his tax is
theoretically subject to the "minimum tax." But on the other $50,000 that
is subject to tax, Wellborn must pay a tax of $35,000 (70 percent of
$50,000)—and Congress has permitted him to use that to reduce the amount
subject to the "minimum" to just $15,000 ($50,000 minus the $35,000 paid
in taxes). The 10 percent tax on this comes to only $1,500, or 1.5 percent of
the total capital gain of $100,000.

It was a "love tap" that resulted in huge savings for the wealthy. Senator Nelson proposed just four changes in the 1969 law—principally lowering the exemption from $30,000 to $12,000, making state and local bond interest subject to the "minimum tax," and substituting for the flat 10 percent rate a graduated tax schedule half as high as the regular one—and estimated that *these changes alone would increase tax collections from the wealthy by $3 billion a year.* That is a measure of the savings to the affluent from Congress's 1969 "love tap."

The "Double-Dip" Tax Advantage

Congress's solicitous attitude toward the taxless wealthy was also exhibited by its refusal, in 1969, to close up another major tax-escape boulevard that involves a "double-dip" tax advantage.

To illustrate this double saving, take the case of two taxpayers, A and B. Each has total income of $100,000. Each makes a charitable donation of $50,000. It would be reasonable to expect, given the sameness of their respective situations, that both would pay the same tax. But they don't. Why? Because A's $100,000 of income consists entirely of corporate dividends, which are fully taxable, while only $50,000 of B's income comes from dividends, the other $50,000 being in the form of interest on state and local bonds which, as you know, is nontaxable. Here is how the two fare, come April 15.

		Taxpayer A	Taxpayer B
Income Sources	*Taxable?*		
Dividend income	Yes	$100,000	$50,000
State/local bond interest	No	—	$50,000
Total income		$100,000	$100,000
Tax Calculation			
Initial taxable income		$100,000	$50,000
Minus charitable deduction		$50,000	$50,000
Final taxable income		$50,000	0
Tax		$17,060	0

Thus B has been able, in effect, to shelter $100,000 of income from taxation with a charitable donation of just $50,000.

To illustrate how the "double-dip" benefit comes about, assume that, for our convenience, B was kind enough to keep the two halves of his income in separate bank accounts, and that he gave the nontaxable $50,000 to his favorite charity. The double advantage arises from the fact that this $50,000 did not create a taxable "plus" on his return; nonetheless, he could use it to create a "minus" that offset the taxable part of his income, thus doubling the amount of tax-free income from $50,000 to $100,000.

Of course, tax-exempt bond interest is not the only kind of income that produces no "plus" on the tax return. Half of all long-term capital gains are also excluded, but they, too, can be used to produce tax-sheltering deductions that, in effect, give the double benefit.

That device was used to exquisite advantage by an actual taxpayer, whom we'll call Mr. C, cited in a Treasury Department study. Mr. C could not be said to be courting the poorhouse: his total income, that year, came to $1,284,000.*

Fortunately for him, practically all of that—$1,210,000 of it, to be precise—consisted of long-term capital gains, half of which (about $600,000) he could, under the generous tax treatment of such gains, wholly exclude from his taxable income. That single step cut in half Mr. C's task of finding other tax deductions to cancel out the remaining $600,000. Evidently, charitable impulses did not course strongly through Mr. C's veins (since, out of a total income of $1,284,000, the total of his tax-deductible charitable gifts came to just $463). Instead, the credit-worthy Mr. C chose another route: he borrowed about $10 million, the wholly deductible interest charges on which came to $587,000†—just about enough to cancel out his remaining taxable income. There was, of course, nothing to prevent the evidently acquisitive Mr. C from channeling the $10 million into additional tax-saving investments, such as real-estate or oil ventures, thus causing further incursions on the Treasury, at the expense of all the rest of the U.S. taxpayers. (If one imagines Mr. C paying those interest charges out of the untaxed half of his immense capital gains, one wincingly perceives, again, the double tax advantage of dollars that added

---

* His dividend income of $76,000 suggested that he owned stocks worth more than $2,250,000.

† Interest deductions of this magnitude would probably not be allowed today, under a provision enacted in 1969 (see p. 367).

no "plus" on the tax return being used to generate a "minus," thus doubling the number of tax-spared dollars.)

The net result of all this was that Mr. C ended up, in that particular year, writing a check to Internal Revenue for just $274 —about two one-hundredths of one percent of his $1,300,000 income. (By contrast, an unmarried person making as little as $1,700 for the year paid, at the then existing tax rates, *seven* percent of his meager income to the U.S. Treasury.)

A Treasury Department analysis showed how intensely meaningful this double advantage has been to top-bracket taxpayers. For about a thousand families in the million-and-over income group, it meant average annual tax savings of $64,400; for thirteen of those families, it was the stepping stone to paying zero tax. In fact, in 1969 this "double-dip" tax advantage paved the way for total taxlessness for no fewer than 124 families with incomes greater than $100,000 a year!

All told, it represents annual tax savings of more than $400 million. Most of that goes to the top six-tenths of one percent of the taxpayers. In other words, the "double-dip" means a nearly half-billion-dollar tax burden shifted onto the shoulders of the other 99.4 percent of the taxpayers.

How avoid this $400 million "double-dip" tax advantage? The Treasury Department offered a simple, common-sense solution: require taxpayers to allocate their nonbusiness tax deductions between their taxable income and their tax-sheltered or untaxed income. Under such a proposal, for example, Mr. C would have been able to take tax deductions on only half of his huge interest payments, since only about half of his income was subject to tax.* Had that been the case, instead of paying just $287 in taxes, he would have paid about $180,000.

The House of Representatives, in 1969, thought this a fair proposal, but the U.S. Senate was evidently more concerned about imposing an added burden on the richest six-tenths of one percent of the taxpayers than about relieving that burden from the other 99.4 percent, for it eliminated the deduction-allocation provision from the 1969 bill, a step to which the House later acceded. Thus the elimination of the "double-dip" advantage remains on the tax-reform agenda.

---

* Remember that in figuring up his taxable income, he could exclude half of his capital gains.

The "Maximum Tax"—for a Few

In the same year that Congress enacted a "minimum tax," it also passed a "maximum tax."

More accurately, Congress further diluted the principle of "ability to pay" by decreeing that dollars received in the form of salary and other kinds of "earned income" are less able to pay taxes than dollars received in the form of dividends and other kinds of "unearned" income. As a result of the 1969 law, "earned income" dollars are subject to a maximum top-bracket rate of 50 percent—twenty percentage points lower than the top rate for "unearned income."*

According to one estimate, that single stroke saved $100 million annually for just 30,000 top-bracket taxpayers—most of them high-salaried corporate executives and some professional men. That is, it shifted a $100 million burden onto the shoulders of the other less affluent taxpayers.

Congress's reasoning for making this change is intriguing: it "was adopted as a means of reducing the pressure for the use of tax loopholes." That is, Congress reasoned, if super-salaried persons weren't subjected to such high tax rates, they wouldn't spend so much "time and effort [in] 'tax planning'" and this, in turn, would "contribute to maintaining the integrity of the system." The lawmakers did not seek to explain how they were "maintain[ing] the integrity of the system" by violating the integrity of the basic principle underlying the system—namely, the principle of "ability to pay." Cleveland laborer Ralph Senters' $1,131 tax on his $7,372 income is reckoned on the "ability to pay" system, but the tax of Harold Geneen, Chairman of the Board of ITT with an annual salary-plus-bonus of $812,494, is not.

As Congress saw it, "one of the most effective ways to prevent the use of tax avoidance devices is to reduce the incentive for engaging in such activities by reducing the high tax rates on earned income." Others might have concluded that an even more "effective" way to achieve that end would have been to close up the loopholes and put an end to the "tax avoidance devices." But Congress felt otherwise.

---

* There is an interconnection between the "minimum tax" and the "maximum tax," in that any tax-sheltered income (in excess of $30,000) that is subject to the "minimum tax" also reduces, dollar for dollar, the amount of a person's salary income that qualifies for the special 50 percent top rate.

The notion of the state whisking away 70 cents of a person's topmost hard-earned dollars is not an appealing one, and Congress's desire to bring relief from that notion may strike a sympathetic chord in the hearts of all save those who would use the tax system as a means of redistributing wealth (a not unrespectable point of view).

Fairness dictates, however, that if top-bracket rates are lowered, (a) they should be lowered for *all* wealthy people, and not just for some; and (b) all taxpayers should share in the abatement— i.e., tax rates should be lowered all down the line. The final chapter of this book suggests that, if all the loopholes were closed, all tax rates could be lowered by at least 40 percent.

But the "maximum tax" for just a few is not the answer.

Stock Options and Other "Fringe Benefits" for Corporation Executives

Probably the most select group among "the mightily-privileged few" are the enjoyers of executive stock options,* for they have been said to be limited to the top executives of roughly 1,500 corporations in the entire country. One study showed that the average of about $540,000 a year).

The following actual case will show how a stock option arrangement works, to the colossal benefit of its recipient. In 1956, the International Business Machines Corporation granted to its president, Thomas J. Watson, Jr., the right, for ten years,† to buy a total of 11,464 shares of company stock at $91.80 per share. The price of IBM stock soared, and five years later, when the stock was selling at $576 a share, Mr. Watson exercised his purchase rights on 3,887 shares. A sale after six months by Mr. Watson at the $576 price would have netted him a $1,882,085.40

---

* Throughout this discussion, we will be considering only one type of executive stock option—in which the option plans meet certain requirements set forth in the tax law, so as to yield the lucky executive the tax advantages about which you are about to read. These are called "qualified" option plans. But there are, in addition, other kinds of stock option plans that do not meet the tax law's requirements and hence do not receive tax-favored treatment.

† A subsequent change in the law limits the purchase right to five years, if the option arrangement is to qualify as a tax-favored plan.

profit—*all taxable at the favorable 25 percent capital gains tax rate then in effect.* Assuming (conservatively) that Mr. Watson was in at least the 75 percent tax bracket, his tax saving from the special 25 percent rate would have been at least half* of his $1,800,000 profit—that is, about $950,000. To the extent he elects to hold on to his stock until he dies, under present law he will never pay any income tax on this handsome profit (see page 99).

A prime feature of a stock option arrangement is that if IBM stock had gone *down* in price, Mr. Watson would have risked and lost nothing, since there was no obligation on his part to buy the stock. That is, heads he won, tails he did not lose.

Happily for Mr. Watson, his good fortune did not end with the highly profitable transaction described above. In the five years 1966 through 1970, stock option plans enabled him to purchase nearly 18,000 shares of IBM stock for just $421,053—even though their market value on the day he bought them was *more than three million dollars,* so that if he had sold the shares immediately† he would have realized a profit of $2,733,189. (This was in addition to the "salary and percentage compensation" paid Mr. Watson which, over those five years, came to $2,704,011 (or an average of about $540,000 a year).

In those same five years (or, more precisely, in the four years before he resigned to become the American ambassador in Paris), Mr. Watson's brother, Arthur, bought some 12,400 shares of IBM for two million dollars less than he would have had to pay in the open market. All told, forty-two officers of IBM were enabled, by the generosity of the other shareholders who approved the stock option plan, to purchase some 130,491 shares of IBM for *twenty-four and a half million dollars* under their going market price!

While IBM executives fared spectacularly well, they were not unique. In 1970, ITT chairman Harold S. Geneen (labeled "Hungry Hal" by one "confidential letter to chief executives") was the nation's highest paid corporate executive, with a salary-plus-bonus of $766,755.‡ But apparently ITT didn't consider that sufficient, for, under stock options granted by the company, Mr. Geneen was able to buy 33,334 shares of ITT for nearly

---

* Seventy-five percent minus 25 percent equals 50 percent.

† Under present law, any optioned stock sold within three years of its purchase does not qualify for the favorable capital gains tax rate.

‡ In 1971, President Nixon's Phase II wage-price controls notwithstanding, Mr. Geneen was awarded an increase to $812,494.

$800,000 less than the going market price. All told, that year officers of ITT bought 141,000 shares of ITT at nearly three million dollars under market price. (Even after doing that, they still had the privilege of buying three and a half times that much—some 520,000 additional shares—under their unexercised options.)

Also in 1970 (the year of that unfortunate auto workers' strike that cut badly into auto company profits), General Motors executives had to do without their usual bonuses, and company president Edward N. Cole received only his regular salary of $225,000.* But chances are Mr. Cole had enough to tide him over that bonus-less year, for between January 1, 1966, and December 31, 1970, he was able to buy 14,226 shares of GM for $575,658 below their going market price. Richard C. Gerstenberg (since elevated to board chairman) bought 11,907 shares for about a quarter-million dollars below market value, and GM officers and directors as a group bought more than 329,000 shares for $2,149,000 below market. Not a bad collective saving.

While these options are supposed to be either rewards or incentives to executives for making their corporations bigger, better and/or more profitable, occasionally they are bestowed even in the face of *losses*. For example, at the 1971 annual meeting of Continental Airlines, shareholders received the bad news of a $2,790,000 loss for the preceding year. At the same time, however, they were asked to approve a plan whereby company president Robert F. Six, who had presided over the prior losing year, could buy 125,000 shares of Continental for just $9.60 a share. This did not sit well with shareholder Gerald Armstrong, who rose to point out that, as of the date of the shareholders' meeting, Continental stock had risen to 17⅝, so that Mr. Six stood to make a profit of about $800,000 if he exercised his option. According to an account of the meeting in the Denver *Post*, Mr. Six "grinned and said he has no such plan." Mr. Six's option was overwhelmingly approved.

T A X - F A V O R E D stock options are neither as spectacularly beneficial nor as alluring as they were in the 1950's, when the stock market was soaring and the tax law governing the options

---

* In 1971, the bonus was restored. The cash amounted to $269,007. Outgoing chairman James M. Roche not only received a salary increase from $250,000 to $275,000, but also got a bonus that brought his total pay to $838,750.

was more liberal. Nonetheless, the law still permits the executives of giant corporations to be paid in a gently taxed manner that is not available to other generously high-salaried persons.

"Qualified" stock options yield three separate advantages to the fortunate executives who receive them.

First, at the very instant the option is issued, the executive receives—entirely tax-free—something of substantial value: the right to "play the market" for the next five years, without laying out, or even risking, a dime of his own. Say, for example, an executive is granted an option to buy 1,000 shares of his company's stock, currently selling for $100 a share. If that stock goes up in price, he can cash in on the rise at a bargain price; but if the stock goes down, he hasn't lost a penny (unlike the ordinary investor, who puts his $100,000 at risk when he buys the stock, and hence suffers if his stock declines in price).

People pay cold hard cash (in the so-called "put-and-call" market) for the right to "play the market" without actually buying stock. In the case of executive stock options, it is estimated that the immediate value of the five-year right to do so is 25 to 40 percent of the market price of the optioned stock. Thus, in the above example (where the optioned stock was worth $100,000 at the time the option was granted), that lucky executive received the equivalent of $25,000 to $40,000—*on which he did not have to pay one penny of tax!*

Advantage Number Two* occurs if that same company's stock rises in value (to, say, $150 a share) and the executive exercises his option and buys the full 1,000 shares at his option price of $100 per share. This means he pays $100,000 for shares that are worth $150,000, so that there is a $50,000 "bargain element" in the purchase. Under other circumstances (e.g., if his company were, in a fit of generosity, to sell him, on the spot, $150,000 worth of stock for $100,000), he would have to pay a tax at "ordinary income" rates on the "bargain element." But when he buys optioned stock, he is excused from paying any such tax.

The third advantage lies in the favorable capital gains treatment that the executive receives when (and if) he actually sells the optioned stock for more than he paid for it (after holding it at least three years). The Supreme Court has held that these option

---

* This is, in a sense, a later manifestation of Advantage Number One. Imposing a tax at regular rates at either time would cure the problem.

profits are really salary supplements—that is, essentially no different from salaries. For most people, salaries are taxed at rates up to 50 percent. But Mr. Watson and other fortunate optioned executives are not "most people." Rather, they are a privileged class of people, a large portion of whose "compensation" is taxed only half as severely as other people's salary income.

Actually, the term "salary supplements" may unfairly belittle option benefits, for in many cases (as with the Watson brothers and General Motors president Cole), they have loomed far larger than the regular salary.

STOCK OPTIONS were almost unknown before 1950, when Congress decided to accord capital gains treatment to option profits, with two apparent purposes in mind: (a) to enable companies to attract and hold executive talent; and (b) to give officials a "proprietary" (i.e., ownership) interest in their companies, as an incentive to better performances.

Critics acknowledge that stock options have succeeded brilliantly in bestowing lavish tax benefits on favored executives. But, they charge, options were not needed and/or were poorly tailored to achieve either purpose (a) or purpose (b). As to attracting and holding executive talent, they say, a great majority of the option rights have been accorded senior executives already established in their companies and therefore the least likely to move. (One firm, for example, allotted over half its optioned stock to nine executives who *averaged* over sixty years of age and thirty-five years of service.) Moreover, option opponents ask, what is gained by bestowing a tax advantage to the Thomas J. Watsons of this world, who already have large holdings of their companies' stock (Watson owned outright or in trust $40 million of IBM stock prior to his option purchases) and who therefore feel the requisite proprietary love for their companies even without stock options?

Some contend that stock options have simply introduced an artificial element into intercompany competition for executive talent, and that repealing this tax feature would still leave all companies on an equal footing in trying to entice executives into their employ.

Critics also maintain that the suitability of stock options for achieving purpose (b) (providing executives with a performance incentive) rests on a demonstrably false assumption: namely, that a company's success or failure on the stock market is an accurate reflection and result of managerial performance. Often, a single company's stock may *rise* in price, even though its profits and earnings per share *decline** (connoting *poor* management). But, massive rises in overall stock prices may occur not because of any managerial genius but simply because investors as a whole are willing to pay higher prices for stocks. Between 1950 and 1962, for example, corporate profits as a whole rose only 15 percent, *but overall stock prices trebled*, because investors were satisfied to pay nineteen times earnings per share, compared with only 7½ times earnings per share a decade earlier. Thus, optioned executives stood to gain handsomely, thanks largely to the expansiveness of the investing public.

One study sought to determine the effectiveness of stock options in a commendably scientific way: by comparing the stock market success of thirty-eight matched pairs of option and non-option companies, with results not overly kind to option plans. While in fourteen cases the option company did appreciably better than its mate, in nineteen cases it fared appreciably worse. (Five cases were a draw.)

Stock options rest on another sharply questioned premise: namely, that the process of making a company official an actual or would-be stockholder, via options, inherently imbues him with a sense of oneness with other shareholders. Ah, say the critics, but while optioned executives share the bliss of other stockholders if the market price *rises*, they do not share their misfortune if the stock happens to *decline*. They have no obligation to buy the proffered stock and, unlike other shareholders, they have risked nothing.

Some detractors contend that options can actually create a conflict (rather than a oneness) of interests between optioned officials and other shareholders. Tennessee's former Senator Albert Gore has said that corporate insiders told him of instances where, in order to "show a good profit and loss statement" and "run up the price of [company] stock" just prior to selling some optioned shares, executives have cut "to the bone" such things as advertising and research expenditures, without due regard for the long-

---

* Examples: between 1950 and 1960, the earnings per share of Bethlehem Steel and of Westinghouse Electric *declined* 17 percent. Nevertheless, the price of their stock rose 225 percent and 188 percent, respectively.

run well-being of their company. Doubtless this is the exception rather than the rule; nevertheless, say seasoned corporate observers, stock options, with their premium on short-run, flashy profit and market showings, create a temptation to sacrifice long-range corporate growth.

A true identity of interests between management and stockholders would be far better achieved, some contend, by encouraging and, perhaps, helping executives to acquire company stock on the open market (rather than through risk-free stock options) so that they would share adversity as well as prosperity on the same basis as other shareholders.

The catalog of objections to stock options does not end there. Other criticisms:

• *The true cost of stock options is not made sufficiently apparent to the stockholders who bear that cost:* For one thing, options involve issuing more shares of stock, which means that each existing share gets a smaller share of the dividends. For another, when new stock that would ordinarily bring $1,000,000 on the open market is sold to an optioned executive for only $600,000, the cost to the company is $400,000. That is, the company receives $400,000 less than it would get if it sold the same stock on the open market. But shareholders will look in vain through the glossy four-color annual report of their company for a listing of any such costs. Some information on executives' options may be contained in the "proxy statements" mailed out in advance of annual meetings, but unless a shareholder (a) saves these from year to year and (b) is an astute mathematician, he is unlikely to glean any useful information as to the outcome and true cost of the options.

• *Stock options are far costlier to corporations than straight salary bonuses:* Option benefits, unlike salaries and bonuses, are *not* tax-deductible to corporations, hence involve more than twice the "out-of-pocket" costs. For example, if the $400,000 option benefit in the example above had been paid as a tax-deductible bonus, Uncle Sam would have borne 48 percent of the cost* and the corporation would have been out of pocket only $208,000 instead of the full $400,000. Of course, a bonus would not bring the executive the tax pleasures of a capital gains stock option. Even so, for many optioned executives (those with taxable income

---

* Under the current corporation tax rate of 48 percent.

below $40,000), a $192 bonus would work out better, after taxes, *for both the corporation* and the executive,* than a $100 option profit.

• *To the extent executives sell their optioned stock—and the law leaves them fairly free to do so—the incentive effects of stock options are negated:* An executive who has sold *all* his optioned stock (and a 1958–1960 survey indicated the proportion of such executives was sharply increasing) may experience a residual gratitude for the low-taxed profit he made on the deal, but now that he is no longer a shareholder the much-touted feeling of *proprietary* devotion may wane. This problem was eased somewhat by a requirement enacted in 1964 that, in order to obtain the capital gains advantage, executives hold their optioned stock for three years before selling. The problem may also be lessened to the extent an executive retains unexercised options or is granted new ones.

• *Stock options may be least useful to the very companies that need them the most:* It is the small, struggling company, rather than the well-established giant, that faces the greatest difficulty in recruiting and holding executive talent. Yet those small companies often do not enjoy the ready market for the sale of their stock that the giants do; accordingly, their stock options may not hold the same appeal as those offered by the colossi.

• *Stock options, unlike other tax-favored pay schemes, are permitted to discriminate against company employees:* In order to qualify for favorable tax treatment, pension and profit-sharing plans must cover a reasonable number of employees in a non-discriminatory manner. Stock option plans, by contrast, may be as discriminatory as the company desires and limited to a select few executives.

STOCK OPTIONS are by no means the only way corporations have devised to lure or hold their executives. For example, they are, increasingly, acting as friendly bankers for favored officers, especially those to whom they have granted large stock options. Suppose an executive has an option on half a million dollars' worth of stock, and the market booms and he just can't

---

* The bonus does have one disadvantage from the company's point of view: unlike the stock option, it necessitates a withdrawal of cash from the company coffers.

afford to pass up the chance to exercise the option. Problem: how does he raise half a million dollars in cash to buy the stock? Answer: the company may lend him the money, usually at a very favorable interest rate—maybe even interest-free.

For example, according to *Dun's* magazine, when Allied Chemical was trying to lure John Connor, then Secretary of Commerce, to its presidency, it lent him the money to purchase 25,000 shares of company stock at about half the going rate*—and the 5¼ percent interest rate charged Mr. Connor was more than covered by the dividends from his newly purchased shares.

The Xerox Corporation seems to win the prize for loans to company executives. In its 1970 proxy statement to its shareholders, it listed outstanding loans of no less than $10 million to sixteen top executives at a modest interest rate of 4 percent. (Shareholders may have wondered where *they* came out in the deal since the company must have been paying far more than 4 percent for any money it was borrowing: moreover, corporations of Xerox's size can usually make in excess of 12 percent if they put their capital to use in other ways. If that's true of Xerox, the $10 million of 4 percent loans to top company executives was costing Xerox $800,000 a year.) These loans represented the full amount these sixteen executives needed to buy "restricted" company stock at half of its going market price. One compensation consultant termed the Xerox loan program "a bit flamboyant."

Some companies (e.g., Ford Motor Company) have actually lent money to their executives without any interest charge. However, according to *Dun's,* company lawyers do not encourage such a move, for it stirs the interest of Internal Revenue and may cause IRS to tax the executive on the "bargain element" of the interest. To avoid IRS inquiry, tax advisers suggest a minimum 4 percent rate, and that, says *Dun's,* is the most popular rate used by corporations-doubling-as-bankers-for-their-favored-executives.

Another form of executive enticement has come into vogue, bearing the name "phantom" stock bonus. This plan tends to be less costly both to the corporation and to the executive, but can be highly beneficial to the latter. Under it, both parties make believe that a certain number of company stock shares have been set aside and put into a special make-believe account for the executive. Say,

---

* So-called "restricted" stock, which Mr. Connor would not be as free to sell as would normally be the case; this is different from a stock option.

for example, on January 1, 1973, Universal Widget Company pretends that 10,000 shares of company stock are placed in the account of company president Robert E. Profitmaker. Assume, too, that each share is worth $50 and pays an annual dividend of $1. Once each year, the make-believe stops for a moment while the company pays Mr. Profitmaker the $10,000 of dividends that would come to him if he really owned the stock. (If the dividend rose to $1.50, he would get $15,000.) Then, at the end of an agreed-upon period, there would again be a pause in the make-believe while both sides reckoned up what had happened to the price of Universal Widget since the pretend game began. If it had risen from its original $50 per share to, say, $60 per share, the company would pay Mr. Profitmaker $100,000 ($10 per share rise times 10,000 shares). But that is taxable the same as salary.

In addition to salaries, bonuses and options, *Dun's* observes that companies "have a cornucopia of lesser perquisites at their disposal" which, "beyond their obvious value as status symbols," add up to a neat dollar-value package, which one consulting firm prices as follows:

Company car and gasoline	$2,700
Country club membership	750
Luncheon club	385
Financial counseling	1,000
Physical examination	50
Total	$4,885

To the extent that the executive uses any part of these emoluments (e.g., the car or the country club) for personal rather than business reasons, a portion of these perquisites *technically* represents taxable income to the executive. But persons close to the field believe that in actual practice IRS does not police this closely.

HOW SHOULD stock options be taxed so as to place optioned executives on a par with others who receive only salaries?

First, if capital gains were taxed at the same rates as ordinary income, as suggested in this book,* that would resolve the existing

---

* With, of course, an averaging scheme for spreading out the gain and avoiding the "bunched income" problem. (See pp. 112–113 and Glossary.)

unfairness of allowing special low rates on option benefits which the Supreme Court has held to be essentially the same as salary income. But that step would not put optioned executives on an equal footing with others, for they would still be receiving, tax-free, the highly valuable right to "play the market" for a period of years, without having to buy any stock or take any risks. Hence, equal treatment would require placing a value on that right* and taxing that as part of the executive's salary at the time the option is granted.

But, at the very least, the option benefits† should be taxed at the same rates as other salary payments. Stock option advocates really shouldn't have any objection to this—*if*, that is, their true objective is to provide *ownership incentives*‡ and not simply windfall tax advantages to favored executives. After all, even if the benefits were taxed at the regular income tax rates, corporations who believe in the ownership-incentive principle could go right on granting stock options just as they do now.

But Congress did not see it that way, and in 1964, while tidying up some fringe abuses,§ it rejected the Kennedy Administration's proposal to end the capital gains treatment of stock option benefits.

A combination of changes in the tax laws has reduced both the allure and the voguishness of stock options. Principal among these is the lowering of the top tax rate on salaries from 70 to 50 percent and the raising of the top capital gains rate to 35 percent,

---

* While the valuation can present some difficulty, it is a common problem that is solved in other areas of taxation. For example, if the executive were to die before exercising his stock option, a value would be placed on it for estate-tax purposes.

† I.e., the "bargain element" or difference between the option price and the market price at the time the executive exercises his option and buys the stock.

‡ And, for small companies, to avoid the cash drain of high salaries.

§ The right to purchase is now confined to five instead of ten years; the option may not be issued at less than the going price for the stock at the time of issue; options may no longer be canceled and reissued at a lower price if the company's stock fares badly in the market; to get capital gains treatment, executives exercising their purchase rights must hold the stock three years before selling it; and options may no longer be issued to executives who own more than 5 or 10 percent of the company's stock (depending on the company's size), so that they cannot be used, as they once were, to benefit important shareholders of small, closely held companies; and option plans must be approved by all shareholders within twelve months of adoption by company officials (but this is *pro forma*, given the almost automatic acquiescence or inactivity of most shareholders).

which markedly reduces the advantages of, in effect, being paid in a capital-gains-rather-than-salary format.* Moreover, according to executive compensation specialists, there may be as many as ten separate steps involved in getting a new option plan approved by various company, legal and governmental authorities, which makes such plans far less attractive to many corporations. Nonetheless, 110 out of 120 corporations surveyed by *Dun's* magazine responded "yes" on the question of whether or not they have stock option plans, and in most cases, even when no new plan will be instituted, executives still have significant option privileges they haven't yet exercised. Thus many corporate executives will continue to enjoy tax-favored treatment of much of their compensation.

The Dividend Exclusion

Few sounds or sights are as poignant as the Congressional rhetorician in full flight, bemoaning the plight of the "little stockholders"—the widow, the orphan, the retired, and the aged—who, you are led to believe, make up the bulk of the investing and stockholding public in America.

Few affirmations are as thoroughly decimated by the cold statistics, which show the following: (figures, the most recent available, apply to 1962)

This group ...	owns ...	this percent of all individually held* corporate stock
Richest 1%		62%
Richest 5%		86%
Richest 20%		97%
Middle 60%		3%
Poorest 20%		less than 1%

* As distinct from stock owned by corporations, banks and other institutions.

Hence it should come as no surprise that the bulk of the $700 or so million tax benefaction that Congress accords to corporate shareholders goes to the top 1 or 2 percent of the taxpayers with whom this chapter is concerned.

---

* In addition, to the extent the "bargain element" exceeds $30,000, the excess (a) is subject to the 10 percent "minimum tax" and (b) reduces the amount of the executive's salary income eligible for the new 50 percent top rate.

That tax bounty stems from the fact that for married owners of corporate stock, the first $200 of their dividend income is wholly tax-free.

The $200 of tax-free income is available in full only to couples wealthy enough to own something in excess of $6,000 worth of stock.* It is a favor that Congress has failed to bestow upon Mr. and Mrs. Middle America who, lacking the spare cash to buy stock, instead are more likely to put their meager savings into the local savings and loan association. Every penny of the interest they draw is taxable. No tax-free $200 for *them*.

As usual, this untaxed income accords far more benefit to top-bracket shareholders than to those with more modest incomes:

Couple's Taxable Income	Couple's Top Tax Bracket	$200 of Tax-Free Dividends	
		Means This Much Tax Saving	Is Equivalent to This Much Taxable Income
Over $200,000	70%	$140	$667
$12,000–$16,000	25%	$50	$267

That fact compounds the heavy concentration of stock ownership among the well-to-do and produces an even greater concentration of the tax benefits from the dividend exclusion:

This percent of all families ...	gets ...	this percent of the $700 million of tax benefits from the dividend exclusion
The richest 14.7%		63%
The richest 7.6%		48%
The richest 1.2%		16%

Between 1954 and 1964, the tax benefits to the fortunate owners of corporate stock were vastly more generous than they are today, for during those years, in addition to what was then a $50 dividend exclusion, they were allowed to *reduce their taxes owed* to Uncle Sam by 4 percent of their dividend income (via the so-called "dividend credit"). To General Motors' largest single stockholder, Charles Stewart Mott, who at one time was said to own

---

* Anything less than that would be unlikely to return the full $200 of dividend income.

more than 2,600,000 shares of GM, this meant, at the time, roughly $315,000 of extra spending money per year.

In 1964, however, Congress concluded that the 4 percent "dividend credit"* was unwise, and they repealed it. To soften the blow to shareholders, though, they doubled (from $100 to $200) the amount of tax-free dividends that each couple could enjoy.

The ostensible reason that Congress gives for bestowing tax favors upon the owners of corporation stock is that it eases, to some degree, the extent of "double taxation" that supposedly arises because each dollar of dividends is taxed once when received by the corporation, as part of profits, and a second time when it is received by the individual shareholder in the form of a dividend.

But is "double taxation" per se an intolerable inequity, as the defenders of this three-quarter-billion-dollar tax preference contend? If so, Congress must lose no time in performing major surgery on the entire tax system to relieve the oppressed. Dwight D. Eisenhower's celebrated 1952 campaign complaint about the hundred different ways eggs are taxed was a graphic (if slightly exaggerated) reminder that our tax system is shot thrconstruct not just with "double taxation" but with "multiple taxation." As but one illustration, do you remember the last time you bought automobile tires? You paid an excise tax, using the already taxed dollars of your "take-home pay," and thus were the victim of "double taxation." But that is not the whole story, for the price of the tires also included allowances for taxes paid by the retailer, and the wholesaler before him and the manufacturer before him and the materials supplier before him.

Hence, you may be prompted to wonder why a single class of taxpayers—the corporation shareholders—should be singled out for relief from mere *double* taxation, while you remain prey to *multiple* taxation on your tires and, if General Eisenhower was correct, a full hundred taxes on your morning egg.†

Furthermore, it is far from clear just how much "double taxation" of corporate dividends really exists. Many—including, sig-

---

* At the time, this feature was costing the U.S. Treasury (i.e., the non-shareholders in America) nearly half a billion dollars every year.

† Some tax economists say the "double taxation" argument is spurious in that our tax system has always levied different taxes for different purposes against different persons at different points in the economic process. For example, just as the income and the estate tax are two different *kinds* of taxes, so are the personal and the corporate income tax.

nificantly enough, some of the most ardent defenders of the dividend tax preferences—believe that corporations do not bear the burden of the corporate tax, but pass it along either to consumers (in higher prices) or to workers (in lower wages). The very sponsor of the dividend credit, the late Representative Daniel Reed, blamed "inordinately high" consumer prices in part on the fact that "all products are increased in price in the exact proportion of taxation." And the redoubtable former Speaker of the House, Representative Martin of Massachusetts, has affirmed that "any graduate economist can tell us that corporations compute profits after taxes, and not before, and their price scales are adjusted accordingly."

Most economists are not so dogmatic. The more modest will acknowledge that in any given instance no one knows just how much a corporation bears—and how much it shifts—its tax burden, but most believe there is always some shifting, and to that extent the "double taxation" problem is lessened.

It is also eased by the fact that stock market investors take account of the corporate tax in calculating the price they are willing to pay for their share of stock (i.e., they pay less for stocks than they would if there were no corporate tax and if 100 percent of company earnings were available for dividends). Therefore, it is argued, to the extent they have already allowed for the corporate tax in the lower purchase price of their stock, shareholders are unaffected by "double taxation."

BECAUSE OF THE WIDESPREAD ownership of corporation stock—seventeen million owners, according to the New York Stock Exchange—some may wonder why the dividend tax provisions were included in this book under the heading of "The Mightily-Privileged Few" instead of "The Slightly-Privileged Many" (see Chapter 18). The following facts will explain why:

HOW MANY ACTUALLY RECEIVED DIVIDENDS IN 1970

Income Group	How Many in This Group Reported Any Dividends	How Much of This Group's Income Came from Dividends
Under $5,000	1 in 18	1.8%
$5,000–$10,000	1 in 13	1.0%
$20,000–$50,000	1 in 5	4.1%
$100,000–$200,000	87 out of 100	19.8%
$1,000,000 and over	97 out of 100	40.0%

5

The Great Capital
Gains Trial*

[*The scene is a packed U.S. courtroom. The occasion: the trial of* People v. The Capital Gains Tax. *The twelve jurors have been chosen, and the opposing lawyers are scheduled to make their opening statements. The noise in the courtroom subsides as the Judge enters.*]

CLERK: Oyez, oyez, oyez! All persons having business before this honorable court are admonished to draw near and give their attention, for the court is now sitting. God save the United States and this honorable court.

JUDGE: Be seated, please. The jury having been duly selected, we may now proceed with the case of *People v. The Capital Gains Tax.*

This case is, of course, most unusual. The Defendant, the Capital Gains Tax, stands accused of two contradictory offenses. On the one hand, the People contend that because the tax is so *low*, it is guilty of injecting unfairness and complexity into the American tax system. On the other, the Investors, in a separate brief, main-

---

* The capital gains tax has here been placed on hypothetical trial as a means of simplifying and dramatizing the arguments, pro and con. Readers who happen to be trial attorneys are asked to indulge the obvious deviations from regular courtroom procedure, especially the freedom accorded the jury to question counsel and to debate issues in open court. At the conclusion of the trial the author appears, thinly disguised as the Foreman of the Jury.

93

tain that because the tax is so *high*, it is hampering the free flow of American capital. Apparently, the Defendant can do no right.

Counsel for the People, you may proceed with your opening statement.

PEOPLE'S COUNSEL: Thank you, Your Honor.

Ladies and gentlemen of the jury, you should understand at the outset just what is on trial here. Capital gains are the profits a person makes on the sale of stocks, bonds, land, buildings and other kinds of property. That is, if you buy a share of stock for $10 and sell it for $100, you have a "capital gain" of $90.

Now such gains, when realized during your lifetime, are taxed at no more than *half* the rates to which other kinds of income are subject. And those value increases that have accrued on property you own at the time of your death are not taxed at all.

With that as background, let me say that His Honor, with his usual succinctness, has ably stated the People's case. Our charge is twofold: first, that the Defendant, the Capital Gains Tax, is perhaps the greatest source of unfairness in the American tax system; and second, that it is the most significant single cause of tax complexity.

On the question of inequity, more eloquent than any words I could invoke are the plain facts about the top-heavy manner in which the tax benefits from the capital gains preference—in other words, the capital gains "tax welfare" handouts—are dispensed. Those facts about the average per-family "tax welfare" payments are displayed in tabular form on this easel I've placed before you.

Family's Yearly Income	Average Yearly "Tax Welfare" per Family from Capital Gains
Over $1,000,000	$641,000
$500,000–$1,000,000	$165,000
$100,000–$500,000	$23,000
$20,000–$25,000	$120
$15,000–$20,000	$55
$5,000–$10,000	$8
$3,000–$5,000	$1

LABOR-LEADER JURYMAN: That's fantastic! You mean to tell me that the government gives $641,000 a year to those multimillionaires, while the workingman gets only eight lousy bucks?

PEOPLE'S COUNSEL: That's what it amounts to. To put it in more common language, the multimillionaire is getting about $12,300 in added "take-home pay" every *week*.

LAWYER JURYMAN*: I must say that makes me mighty envious. I'm struck, Counsel, not only by the tiny benefits that go to the workingman, but even more by the sharp drop-off below the $500,000 income level. Can you tell us why the tax breaks from capital gains are so lopsided for the wealthy?

PEOPLE'S COUNSEL: It's really quite unmysterious when you consider the nature of capital gains. They are, after all, the profits flowing from the ownership of *property* that has risen in value. So to enjoy capital gains, you have to own property, and the only people who can acquire property—stocks and bonds and real estate and the like—are the people who have some spare cash left over after paying their grocery bills and their medical bills, payments on their house, their car and the like.

So right away that freezes out of the capital gains picture every American family that's struggling to keep its nose above the financial waters.

It's not really surprising, then, that only one taxpayer in ten reports *any* capital gains.

LABOR-LEADER JURYMAN: One in ten! Do you mean to say that nine out of ten people are completely denied what you call these "tax welfare" handouts?

PEOPLE'S COUNSEL: That's precisely what the government statistics show. Not only that: even among the one in ten, the capital gains are concentrated among a very few at the pinnacle of the economic pyramid. I've prepared a chart to show you the latest statistics on this, taken from 1969 tax returns:

Those with incomes of:	Comprise only this percent of all taxpayers:	But get this percent of all capital gains:
$200,000 and over	2/100 of 10%	27.8%
$100,000 and over	1/10 of 1%	37.7%
$50,000 and over	6/10 of 1%	49.9%
$25,000 and over	2.9%	64.5%
$10,000 and over	31.9%	87.1%

* The presence of a lawyer on the jury is a literary license, since ordinarily atttorneys may not serve as jurors.

ENGINEER JURYMAN: But that still doesn't explain why the benefits to that million-and-over income group are so colossal. I mean, $641,000 a year—that's unbelievable.

PEOPLE'S COUNSEL: Not when you realize what a colossal proportion of those multimillionaires' income is in the form of these low-taxed capital gains.

Let me give you an example: some recent figures on the stratospherically rich families of America* showed that on the average their total annual dollar intake, including capital gains, was about $9 million—and two-thirds of that, or about $6 million, was in the more gently taxed capital gains. Now if that six million were taxed at the top-bracket rate of 70 percent,† the tax on it would be over $4,000,000. But under the special rates accorded capital gains, which reach no higher than 35 percent, they would pay only half that much—so that for those super-hyper-extra-affluent families, the tax savings from this one feature of the tax law would amount to more than $2,000,000 a year. Or, put more simply, it would mean more than $40,000 added "take-home pay" —or more cash spending money—every week.

Compared with that, the $641,000 saving by the *average* million-and-over-income family seems almost paltry.

Which brings me to another aspect of the capital gains loophole that strikes me as grossly unfair: namely, that the higher a family's total income, the greater the portion of that income that's made up of lightly taxed capital gains. Here are the figures:

Income Group	Percent of People in This Income Group Having Any Capital Gains	Percent of Their Incomes That Comes from Capital Gains
Under $5,000	4.5%	1.9%
$10,000–$25,000	14.0%	2.4%
$50,000–$100,000	55.3%	15.6%
$1,000,000 and over	90.9%	82.1%

HOUSEWIFE JURYWOMAN: Wait a minute. You said that these capital gains are taxed at just half the rates that apply to income that's earned by the sweat of the brow. My husband,

---

* Those whose total incomes, including capital gains, exceeded five million dollars a year.

† *Un*earned income, such as dividends and interest, is still subject to the top tax rate of 70 percent. The 50 percent maximum rate applies only to salary and other *earned* income.

who works hard all day, is out driving a cab every damned night just so we can keep up the payments on the house. Are you telling me that somebody who made the same money on some stock market deal that my husband makes working eighteen hours a day pays just *half* what we have to pay?

PEOPLE'S COUNSEL: On the income (or profits) that somebody gets from the stock market deal, that's exactly what I'm telling you.

But the situation is even more unfair than that, and at the risk of raising your blood pressure still further, I shall explain how.

You're familiar, I'm sure, with the principle of "ability to pay" under which the higher your income, the stiffer your tax rates.

So when your husband took on his moonlighting job, my guess is the extra income put you both in a higher top tax bracket.

HOUSEWIFE JURYWOMAN: You can say that again!

PEOPLE'S COUNSEL: And, Mr. Lawyer Juryman, if you win a big case, and get an unusually large fee for it, that boosts your top tax bracket, too, doesn't it? I don't mean to pry, but would I be guessing wrong to say that such a fee would put you up to the 50 percent top bracket?

LAWYER JURYMAN: I'm afraid you're only too correct, Counsel.

PEOPLE'S COUNSEL: Well, I wonder how it makes you feel to know that the receivers of capital gains are exempt from the "ability to pay" rule.

Let me give you a hypothetical example, using a real name, if Your Honor will permit. Nelson Rockefeller almost surely has an income that runs into the millions. But suppose that, on top of his already huge income, he hits a stock market bonanza worth several million more. He still pays no more than a 35 percent tax* on the extra millions—less, Mr. Lawyer Juryman, than the 50 percent you would have to pay on your hard-earned extra fee.

ENGINEER JURYMAN: Wait, let me get this straight. Say that Nelson Rockefeller invests some money in a company like, maybe, Xerox. Then he sits back while the people at Xerox do all the work, and because of *their* work and *their* success Xerox stock goes sky-high. Are you telling me that Nelson Rockefeller, who didn't lift a finger, gets to rake in the profits and yet pays less tax than my lawyer friend here? Is that the way it goes?

---

* If Mr. Rockefeller's gains were subject to the "minimum tax" as well as to the capital gains tax, the overall rate would be 36½ percent. (For an explanation, see p. 73.)

PEOPLE'S COUNSEL: You have stated the People's case admirably. The fact is that under our tax system, the Work of Money is rewarded far more handsomely than the Work of Men.

PROFESSOR JURYMAN: I had always been brought up to believe in the virtues of Hard Work and Personal Initiative and all that. But from what you're telling us, the tax system makes Horatio Alger look like a sucker instead of a hero.

PEOPLE'S COUNSEL: As a matter of fact, very wealthy people get even more advantage than we've talked about so far from the way in which capital gains are taxed.

I've said that capital gains are taxed at no more than half the rate that applies to regular income, but the *way* that comes about brings an important advantage to the prosperous. What happens is that half of all capital gains can be totally discarded, totally ignored, in computing your taxable income, and the other half that is included is taxed at the regular rates.*

ENGINEER JURYMAN: I don't see that it makes any difference whether you tax the whole thing at half the rates, or tax half the gain at the regular rates. Doesn't it come out the same either way?

PEOPLE'S COUNSEL: No, in some cases the difference can be enormous. Let me give you an example of an actual taxpayer whom we'll call Mr. C, cited in a Treasury tax study,† who exploited that difference so as to practically wipe out his tax.

Mr. C enjoyed a total income of $1,284,000, nearly all of which —$1,210,000—was in the form of capital gains. Half of those gains—about $605,000—was automatically tossed aside, placed wholly outside the reach of the tax collector, and ignored in computing his taxable income.

Now that's where the advantage to Mr. C comes in, because *that step reduced by half the amount of income that Mr. C had to offset with other deductions.* And he managed that simply by borrowing about $10 million, on which he paid interest—entirely tax-deductible, of course—of $587,000.‡ That plus a few other deductions very nearly canceled out his otherwise-taxable income.

---

* On the first $50,000 of a person's capital gains each year, the top rate on the included half is 50 percent, so that the maximum rate on the entire gain is 25 percent (50 percent of the included 50 percent).

† This case was also cited on pp. 75–76.

‡ As noted, interest deductions as large as this might not be allowed today (see p. 367).

What was the result? On his total intake of over a million and a quarter dollars, he ended up paying a total tax of just $274— three one-hundredths of one percent of his income.

LABOR-LEADER JURYMAN: Two seventy-four! Hell, just about everybody I know pays more taxes than that.

PEOPLE'S COUNSEL: That's right. The Treasury Department study that described the machinations of Mr. C noted, at the time, that the average single person living at the official "poverty line" was paying nearly 7 percent of his income in taxes—twenty times as much, proportionately, as multimillionaire Mr. C. Incidentally, Mr. C may well have used the proceeds of that $10 million loan to invest in other "tax shelters," so as to magnify even further his "raid" on the U.S. Treasury.

ENGINEER JURYMAN: Counsel, you mentioned at the outset that profits that have accrued at the time of a person's death are not taxed at all. Can you explain that to us?

PEOPLE'S COUNSEL: Gladly. Again, let me use a specific example—that of Mr. Charles Stewart Mott. Mr. Mott sold his company to General Motors way back in 1913, got a lot of GM stock in those early days, and is now said to be worth between $300 and $500 million. A lot of his wealth, I'm sure, is in GM stock that cost just a tiny fraction of what it's worth today. Let's say that $105 million of that GM stock only cost him $5 million when he got it. If he were to sell that stock during his lifetime, there would be a capital gain of $100 million, on which he would have to pay a tax of $35 million.

But if he leaves that stock to his wife in his will, she can sell it for the full $105 million *but pay no capital gains tax at all!*

LABOR-LEADER JURYMAN: And save $35 million? How come? The stock only cost him $5 million. Why isn't the gain taxed?

PEOPLE'S COUNSEL: Because, in this area, the law gets into a game of make-believe. Let me explain. Ordinarily, you'd say that the capital gain in a given situation is the price you sell it for minus your "cost"—that is, the price of the stock when you bought it or were given it. In other words, if the stock's "cost" was $5 and you sell it for $105, there's a capital gain of $100.

But when you die, the law makes believe that the "cost" of the stock was *not* its price when you got it, *but its price on the date of your death.*

If we go back to the situation of Mr. and Mrs. Mott, the law pretends that the "cost" of all that GM stock he leaves his wife is not $5 million, but the $105 million it's worth when he dies. So if she should turn around and sell it the next day, also for $105 million, there is no capital gain and therefore no tax.

HOUSEWIFE JURYWOMAN: What you're saying, if I understand it, is that there's a zero tax on all the gains that pass at death.

PEOPLE'S COUNSEL: That's a good way to put it.

LAWYER JURYMAN: That's not quite fair, though, Counsel. The $100 million doesn't really pass tax-free since there's an estate, or death tax to pay on it.

PEOPLE'S COUNSEL: Not necessarily. Mr. Mott could leave $50 million of it tax-free to his wife and could leave the other $50 million, also tax-free, to charity.* So there need not be any death tax at all. But even if there were, there's still an enormous advantage to leaving capital gain property over leaving cash. Suppose in your case, Mr. Attorney, that all you can leave your wife is the cash you've managed to build up from your law practice. You've already paid an income tax on it—*and you pay a death tax besides.* But in the case of Mr. Mott, who leaves the General Motors stock, there is no income or capital gains tax involved, but only a death tax. So *his* heirs end up way ahead of yours.

LAWYER JURYMAN: But, Counsel, is it really as important as you make it out to be? After all, I would imagine most of the gains are left by just a few rich people, so the number of dollars that escape tax at death must be pretty small.

PEOPLE'S COUNSEL: Sir, I think you are in for a major surprise. Not one person I have ever asked about this has come anywhere near guessing the right answer. The fact is, though, that *more than $10 billion escapes tax at death every year.* This one feature of the tax law costs the U.S. taxpayers nearly $4½ billion dollars each year—which is to say that $4½ billion of "tax welfare" is handed out every year in this manner. Of course, most of that "tax welfare" goes to the very rich, who have very large estates. Just think of the "tax welfare" that must have been involved in the case of Mrs. Ailsa Mellon Bruce, who died in 1969 leaving an estate of *over half a billion dollars.* Almost surely a large

---
* See Chapter 16.

part of that estate was in Gulf Oil and Alcoa stock that came into the Mellon family many decades ago. So in her case the untaxed gains must have been in the hundreds of millions.

ENGINEER JURYMAN: And how much is it costing the taxpayers to give that special half-rate to capital gains that people get during their lifetime?

PEOPLE'S COUNSEL: Nearly nine and a half billion dollars a year—so that when you combine the two, the total capital gains "tax welfare" comes to nearly $14 billion a year.

LABOR-LEADER JURYMAN: Fourteen billion! I remember that Nixon vetoed an education bill that cost less than a third that much because he said it was "inflationary." I don't remember hearing him complaining about *this* $14 billion as "inflationary."

PEOPLE'S COUNSEL: One tax expert estimates that if you were to tax capital gains the same as ordinary income, it would be possible to lower the top tax rate on unearned as well as earned income from 70 to 50 percent and make a significant cut in all other tax rates and still raise the same amount of revenue for the U.S. government. Taking the top rate down to 50 percent ought to please all the people in the 60 and 70 percent bracket who moan about Uncle Sam being their "majority partner."

LABOR-LEADER JURYMAN: Yeah, but what a sop to the rich, bringing the top rate down to 50 percent.

PEOPLE'S COUNSEL: That's the way it looks at first glance. But did you know that not very long ago, when the top-bracket rate was 91 percent—much higher than it is now—families with yearly incomes of *more than five million dollars*, the super-super-rich, were paying taxes, on the average, of only 25 percent?

LABOR-LEADER JURYMAN: That's impossible—having an income of five million and paying that little tax.

PEOPLE'S COUNSEL: But remember what I said earlier: two-thirds of those people's income was in capital gains, which then was taxed at no more than 25 percent. That is, two-thirds of their incomes escaped the regular tax rates. So you see, lowering the top rate to 50 percent, coupled with ending the special rate on capital gains, wouldn't necessarily be a "sop to the rich."

LAWYER JURYMAN: But didn't you tell us that the top capital gains rate is now 35 percent? So aren't those super-rich people paying more?

PEOPLE'S COUNSEL: Yes, but even with that increase, families with annual incomes of more than a million dollars a year are still paying just 32 percent of it in taxes. That's just half what you'd expect, looking at the tax rates that are published in your tax return every year. And by far the biggest single factor that accounts for the difference is the half-rate taxation of capital gains. That's why I said, in the beginning, that I think this is *the* single greatest cause of unfairness in our entire tax system.

JUDGE: Counsel, you told the jury, at the outset, that there was a second count to your indictment against the Capital Gains Tax. You charge, as I recall, that it's the greatest cause of complexity as well as unfairness in our tax system. What about the matter of complexity?

PEOPLE'S COUNSEL: To understand that second charge, Your Honor and members of the jury, picture, if you will, a dam in a river—high water behind it, low water in front. As you know, the high water exerts steady pressure against the dam as it seeks the level of the lower water.

Our tax system is not unlike that. On the high side of the tax dam lies what the tax laws call "ordinary income"—the wages and salaries all of us earn, as well as any interest or dividends we might receive. Most of this "ordinary income" is subject to the regular income tax rates that run as high as 70 percent on unearned income.

On the low side of the dam are so-called "capital gains" which, as we've noted, are taxed no more than half as severely as "ordinary income."

The pressure on the dam results from the difference between the rates. Everybody in the upper brackets would naturally like to pay less taxes—and they're constantly badgering Congress and the courts to have this or that kind of income classified—and taxed—as a "capital gain." After years of pressure, the dam has deteriorated quite a bit so that today the distinction between so-called "ordinary income" and "capital gains" sometimes doesn't make much sense.

In order to ilustrate this point to you ladies and gentlemen of the jury, I have prepared signs describing certain ordinary income and capital gains situations, which I have placed side by side on easels in front of you, for easy comparison. As you consider these various situations, bear in mind that the tax is only 25 percent on the first $50,000 of a person's capital gain:

Ordinary Income Situation No. 1	*Capital Gains Situation No. 1*
You are a novelist.	You are an inventor.
You have written a widely acclaimed, best-selling novel.	You have invented a new pretzel bender.
You have just sold your novel to the movies for $300,000.	You have just sold your invention to a pretzel company for $300,000.
You pay a tax of $180,980.	You pay a tax of $100,000.
You get to keep $119,020.	You get to keep $200,000.

FOREMAN OF THE JURY: You mean to say, Counsel, that the inventor gets to keep nearly twice what the novelist keeps?

PEOPLE'S COUNSEL: That's right.

FOREMAN OF THE JURY: But why? What's the difference between them? They've both used their brains to create something of value. Why should one pay nearly twice as much tax as the other?

PEOPLE'S COUNSEL: Because Congress says so.

FOREMAN OF THE JURY: What do you mean?

PEOPLE'S COUNSEL: In 1950 Congress simply decreed, in effect, that the proceeds of an invention can be classified as capital gains, whereas the proceeds from a "literary, musical or artistic composition" must be classified as ordinary income.

ENGINEER JURYMAN: It's a kind of "legislative alchemy," isn't it? You take a dollar that comes from selling an invention: one day it's "ordinary income" and then, presto! Congress transforms it into a "capital gain." It's the same dollar, from the same source, earned in the same manner—but it's suddenly taxed differently.

FOREMAN OF THE JURY: It doesn't make sense. Did Congress give any reason for all this?

PEOPLE'S COUNSEL: They just said it was desirable to "foster" the work of inventors. Let's look at the second pair of signs.

Ordinary Income Situation No. 2	*Capital Gains Situation No. 2*
You are an apple farmer, with a top rate of 50%.	You are a Christmas-tree farmer, with a top tax rate of 50%.
You make a $4,000 profit on the apples you have grown.	You make a $4,000 profit on the Christmas trees you've raised.
You pay a tax of $2,000.	You pay a tax of $1,000.
You get to keep $2,000.	You get to keep $3,000.

LABOR-LEADER JURYMAN: Christmas trees! You mean there's something special in the tax law for Christmas trees?

PEOPLE'S COUNSEL: I quote, sir, from Section 631(a) of the Internal Revenue Code which states that the capital gains treatment for timber specifically extends to "evergreen trees which are more than 6 years old at the time severed from the roots and are sold for ornamental purposes." In plain English, this means Christmas trees.

LABOR-LEADER JURYMAN: But why? Why Christmas trees?

PEOPLE'S COUNSEL: Well, when Congress gave capital gains treatment to certain tree sales—another case of legislative alchemy, by the way—Internal Revenue ruled that Christmas trees were ineligible. Of course, the Christmas-tree growers complained of discrimination, so Congress changed the law.

The next pair of signs illustrates a far more important point:

Ordinary Income Situation No. 3	*Capital Gains Situation No. 3*
You are a lawyer.	You are a corporation vice-president.
Your top tax bracket on your earned income is 50%.	Your top tax bracket on your earned income is 50%.
By working extra-long hours on a big case, you earn an extra $25,000.	For your extra-hours work and superlative job performance, your company has given you the right to buy company stock at a favored price. You buy the stock and later sell it for a $25,000 profit.
On your added $25,000 you pay a tax of $12,500.	On your added $25,000 you pay a tax of $6,250.
You get to keep $12,500.	You get to keep $18,750.

LAWYER JURYMAN: Counsel, that one really hits home with me. No matter how hard I work, or how big a practice I build up, everything I earn from my practice is ordinary income, and even with the new top-bracket rate of 50 percent on earned income, Uncle Sam ends up with a big chunk of what I make.

LABOR-LEADER JURYMAN: What's wrong with that? Your fees are no different from my weekly pay check. It's all ordinary income, isn't it?

LAWYER JURYMAN: That's right, and if the rule applied to everybody, I wouldn't kick. But these stock options* are nothing

---
* Discussed more fully on pp. 78–89.

but salary bonuses, and what gets me is seeing some of my own clients getting twice the income I do, but paying a lot less in taxes —just because they happen to work for a corporation. I read about one lawyer who quit Wall Street and went to work as general counsel of Ford, and it wasn't long before he had nearly half a million dollars' worth of these stock options. He certainly couldn't have done that as a Wall Street lawyer.

ENGINEER JURYMAN: Nearly everybody on this jury is in the same boat. All we have to sell is our services—and the more successful we are, the rougher our taxes are.

PEOPLE'S COUNSEL: You gentlemen have made my point for me. Why should people be taxed differently on their earnings just because of their profession?

The next pair of signs illustrates a point that we've already discussed, but it's so important that it's worth reemphasizing:

Ordinary Income Situation No. 4	*Capital Gains Situation No. 4*
You are a junior executive, single, with a taxable income of $32,000.	You are a junior tycoon, single, with a taxable income of $200,000.
Your hard work has earned you a $1,000 raise in your yearly salary.	Your broker has sold one of your stocks for a $1,000 profit.
Your top income tax bracket is 50%; your extra $1,000 of salary is taxed at 50%.	Your top income tax bracket is 70% but your $1,000 stock profit is taxed at 25%.
On your added $1,000 you pay a tax of $500.	On your added $1,000 you pay a tax of $250.
You get to keep $500.	You get to keep $750.

As you can see, the junior tycoon has more than six times the income of the junior executive, but, even though he hasn't done a lick of work for his stock market profit, his tax is just half what the young executive's is.

LAWYER JURYMAN: Isn't this the same point you were making earlier, Counsel, that this capital gains loophole just makes a mockery out of the principle of "ability to pay"?

PEOPLE'S COUNSEL: That's absolutely correct: the capital gains tax and the principle of "ability to pay" have nothing to do with each other. In fact, the junior tycoon might have had *fifty or a hundred* times the income of the junior executive and still paid less taxes on the extra thousand.

JUDGE: Counsel, would you proceed with your next illustration?

Ordinary Income Situation No. 5	*Capital Gains Situation No. 5*
You are a single lady, supporting your aged aunt.	You are a single lady, supporting your aged aunt.
Your taxable income is $14,000.	Your taxable income is $200,000.
On May 1, you buy a share of Allegheny Stovepipe, for $40.	On May 1, you buy a share of Allegheny Stovepipe, for $40.
Five months and 29 days later—October 30—you sell the stock for $60 in order to meet an insurance premium payment.	Six months and one day later—November 2—you sell your stock for $60.
Your profit on the sale of the stock is taxed at your regular income tax rate of 31%.	Your profit on the sale of the stock is taxed at the special capital gains rate of 25%.

HOUSEWIFE JURYWOMAN: Why, that's perfectly outrageous! Why should that poor lady with the $14,000 income pay a higher tax than the other lady with more than thirty times as much income?

PEOPLE'S COUNSEL: Because, madam, the $14,000 lady is a "speculator" while the $200,000 lady is an "investor."

HOUSEWIFE JURYWOMAN: What do you mean—"speculator"?

PEOPLE'S COUNSEL: She sold her stock in less than six months—and that makes her a speculator, at least as far as the tax law is concerned.

HOUSEWIFE JURYWOMAN: How ridiculous! She sold that stock to keep her insurance from lapsing. She's no speculator.

PEOPLE'S COUNSEL: This, strangely enough, is one point on which the People and the Investors agree. We both feel it's ridiculous to distinguish speculators from investors by an artificial time cutoff. But the law has always required a person to hold on to property a certain length of time in order to get the capital gains rate. At first it was two years, but now it's been shortened to six months.*

ENGINEER JURYMAN: Counsel, all these examples are either perplexing or outraging or both, but I don't think you've

---

* In 1963, President Kennedy proposed lengthening the holding period to one year, but Congress would have none of it.

persuaded me as to why and how the capital gains tax is the greatest cause of complexity in the tax law.

PEOPLE'S COUNSEL: The explanation lies in the image of the dam I cited earlier, with the high water pressing against it, seeking the lower level of the water below. Taxpayers on the high side of our two-level tax system exert a similar pressure as they seek the lower-level capital gains tax below the dam. They press upon the Treasury, Internal Revenue, the Congress and the courts in a never-ending battle to create new and more ingenious ways by which ordinary income can be alchemized into capital gains. They devise schemes with intriguing names like "collapsible corporations" and "corporation spin-offs."

Where does the complexity come in? Well, as an example, Congress's effort to prevent tax avoidance through the "collapsibles" ended up adding 3,000 words to the tax law itself, and the Treasury added 5,600 words to its own tax regulations. "Spin-offs"* were slightly easier to control—it only took 1,000 words in the law and 4,000 words of added regulations to curb them.

Those, of course, are only two of the capital gains contrivances in the law. There are a host of others—stock options, real-estate and cattle-raising "tax shelters," timber, lump-sum pension settlements,† and many others. Government officials estimate that roughly half of all tax cases in the courts involve the capital gains field. It would be difficult to measure or describe to you the effort, talent and ingenuity devoted to "working the capital gains angle." What a shame this talent isn't being channeled into minimizing costs and prices and maximizing profits.

I submit, members of the jury, that we should put an end to the preferred status that capital gains enjoy in our tax laws. Our tax laws should recognize the unassailable fact that a dollar of capital gains income and a dollar of ordinary income each endow the person who receives it with 100 cents of "ability to pay" for necessities, luxuries—or taxes. We should tax all income at uniform rates, whether the income be from wages or the sale of stock, from novels or inventions. And we should end the zero tax on capital gains passing at death. We should, of course, recognize the problem of unfairly taxing in a single year capital gains that have accrued

---

* See Glossary.

† Described in more detail on pp. 78–89, 165–187, 187–193, 287–294 and 301, respectively.

over a period of years—the so-called "bunched income" problem that I'm sure Defense Counsel will explain to you in a moment. To take care of that problem, the taxing of capital gains should include a system of income averaging* such as we already have in the tax law to take care of other "bunched income" situations.

If we took these steps, we could—and many feel we should— reduce the top tax rates, down to a 50 percent maximum.

I ask you, members of the jury, to envisage the dramatic benefits that would flow from such a reform.

It would make our tax system fairer: everyone would be taxed according to the same rate schedule, and according to his ability to pay.

It would restore sensible values to our society; no longer would the work of *money* be vastly favored over the work of *people*.

It would put an end to much of the pressure for special tax treatment, and would liberate much of the energy and talent now devoted to tax avoidance.

It would mean nearly $14 billion of added Federal revenue, which could be devoted either to solving urgent national needs— such as feeding hungry Americans or rebuilding the ghettos and providing decent housing—or to reducing tax rates for the non-capital gains recipients, or a combination of both.

I submit, Your Honor and members of the jury, that the abolition of the special capital gains tax rate preference is one of the greatest tax reforms this nation could undertake.

JUDGE: Counsel for the Defense, you may proceed with your opening statement.

DEFENSE COUNSEL: Your Honor, I am aghast at the radical proposal made by People's Counsel, which would, of course, shake the very foundations of our enterprise system. This country has had a separate capital gains rate ever since 1921, and so far as I know, Congress has never, in all those years, seriously questioned the principle of a separate rate.

JUDGE: Would you tell the jury what prompted Congress to enact the separate rate in 1921?

DEFENSE COUNSEL: Two considerations, Your Honor, which remain the principal reasons behind the special capital gains rate today.

The first is the manifest unfairness of taxing, *in a single year,*

---

* See Glossary.

all the gains that may have accrued over a number of years, in, say, a share of stock or a piece of land. Clearly, to do so would push a taxpayer into an artificially high tax bracket. For instance, take a man in, say, the 36 percent tax bracket, who buys a piece of land, holds it for twenty years and sells it for a $100,000 profit. Now if that were to be taxed as if the gain had occurred evenly over the twenty years he held the property, it would mean just $5,000 of added income a year, which would put him in only the 39 percent bracket. But if the entire $100,000 were taxed in the year he sells the land, he would suddenly be catapulted into the 64 percent or 70 percent bracket (depending on whether he's married or single), and the government would take most of his profit. This is the so-called "bunched income" problem to which People's Counsel referred a moment ago. As long as the tax rates get stiffer as a person's income goes up, this so-called "bunching" effect is going to be unfair.

JUDGE: What was the second main reason for the capital gains tax, Counsel?

DEFENSE COUNSEL: Congress felt that having to pay a tax on the sale of stocks and other properties tended to make people hold on to them instead of selling them, and that capital was becoming too "frozen."

There is, members of the jury, a crucial difference between capital gains and ordinary income. Most of the income you receive —salaries, wages, interest, dividends and the like—involves no *choice* on your part. The income is paid to you, you're taxed on it, and that's that.

But with capital gains, you do have a choice. Either you can sell a particular stock or bond or piece of land, and pay a capital gains tax, or you can hold on to the property and pay no tax. It's this element of *choice* that creates a tax barrier to selling property —and it's this that justifies special tax treatment of capital gains. It's important to lower that barrier and make capital more mobile.

JUDGE: Perhaps, Counsel, a numerical example would illustrate what you mean by a "barrier."

DEFENSE COUNSEL: Well, suppose you have a share of stock you bought for $20. It's now selling for $100 and paying you a $3 dividend. Your broker suggests you sell. If you do, of course, you'll pay a $20 capital gains tax and have only $80 left to reinvest in a new security.

Now, that may make you pretty reluctant to sell. Say, for instance, you're mainly interested in maintaining the $3 dividend you've been getting. If that's the case, you ought to turn down your broker's suggestion unless he can find you a stock with a 3.75 percent return—considerably higher than the 3 percent return your old stock paid. Remember, after paying the $20 tax, you'll only have $80 to put into a new stock and it takes a 3.75 percent return for an $80 stock to pay a $3 dividend.

On the other hand, if you're more interested in preserving your $100 of *capital*, it won't pay you to sell unless you can find a stock you're pretty sure will go up from $80 to $100 in the reasonably near future. At best, you'll be trading the *chance* that your new stock will go up for the *certainty* of having to pay the $20 tax and having only $80 to reinvest.

So, you see, the capital gains tax gives you every incentive to stay "locked in" to your existing investments, instead of switching to new ones. Of course, raising the tax, as People's Counsel proposes, would only intensify the locked-in effect.

So if People's Counsel, with his tender regard for the Treasury, is trying to increase revenues by raising the capital gains rate, he's going about it the wrong way, because raising the rate will simply make people hold on to their stocks instead of selling and paying the tax, and the Treasury will raise less, not more, through the capital gains tax.

ENGINEER JURYMAN: Let me make sure of one point. You don't contend, do you, that the tax deters *new* capital from coming into the market? After all, a person pays no tax when he makes a new investment.

DEFENSE COUNSEL: That's correct.

ENGINEER JURYMAN: So your point is not that the tax "starves" industry from getting the volume of capital it needs, but merely that it deters people from switching the money they've already put into the market from one particular investment to another.

DEFENSE COUNSEL: Right again.

ENGINEER JURYMAN: Well, I don't understand what's so "bad" about people holding on to the stocks they have and what's so "good" about their switching from one stock to another.

DEFENSE COUNSEL: Well, "switching," as you call it, is the way capital finds its way out of the staid old conservative blue-chip stocks and into the pioneering, venturesome new companies. It's an essential ingredient to a dynamic and forward-moving economy.

Your Honor, that is the essence of the two main arguments the Defense will offer.

JUDGE: People's Counsel, do you wish to rebut the points made by the Defense?

PEOPLE'S COUNSEL: Thank you, Your Honor. I shall try to take them up point by point.

First, Defense argues that we should not change the preferential capital gains rate because it has been in the law since 1921. But must we accept the notion that just because a provision has been in the tax laws for years, it is *ipso facto* virtuous, just and immutable? If so, we might as well end this trial and give up all thought of tax reform.

Besides, the special capital gains rate does not enjoy the historical sanctity with which my adversary seeks to endow it. On the contrary, my supposedly "radical" proposal is, in reality, the soul of conservatism. It simply calls for reverting to what the Founding Fathers of our tax system wrote into the original 1913 income tax law. In fact, this "radical" plan of mine prevailed for a full nine years for individual taxpayers, and for nearly thirty years for corporations. Yet the country survived quite nicely.

DEFENSE COUNSEL: Ah, yes, but the 1913 law had a top tax rate of 7 percent. You can't compare that with the 70 percent rate we have today.

PEOPLE'S COUNSEL: True, but during the first nine years, the tax rates went as high as 77 percent—even higher than we have today.

DEFENSE COUNSEL: And soon after that, Congress saw the error of its original decision, and established a 12½ percent rate for individual taxpayers' capital gains.

PEOPLE'S COUNSEL: But for the most specious reasons. Take, first, the so-called "bunched income" reason—as exquisite an exercise in illogic as the mind of man could invent. Now, I readily admit there *is* a "bunched income" *problem* with capital gains. But as a *solution*, a flat preferential tax rate is the acme of absurdity.

First of all, the six months' holding period makes a mockery of Defense's "bunched income" argument. Suppose a man sells a stock for a profit after holding it just six months and a day. His gain all took place in one year and he is taxed in the same year. He has no "bunched income" problem—yet if the stock profit is $50,000 or less, he gets the same rate as the man who held his stock for twenty years.

ENGINEER JURYMAN: And what about corporations? I don't see why the "bunched income" argument applies to them, since no matter how "bunched" their income is, its always taxed at their flat 48 percent rate. Why do *they* need a special rate?*

PEOPLE'S COUNSEL: As to that, sir, I am as baffled as you. Now, if the capital gains rate were *really* what it is supposed to be—a device for averaging out the "ordinary income" rates—you'd expect it to go up and down as the regular income tax rates rise and fall. But it hasn't. For instance, in 1950, the income tax rates went up some 10 to 25 percent, to finance the Korean war, but the increase in the capital gains rate only amounted to about 4 percent. Conversely, the top capital gains rate was increased in 1969 without an accompanying increase in the "ordinary income" rates. So, clearly, Congress does not seriously regard the capital gains rate as an averaging device.

ENGINEER JURYMAN: I would seem to me, Counsel, that to the extent there is a hardship from "bunched income," it would be different in every case, depending on a person's income and tax bracket, the length of time he's held the property, the amount of the gain, and so on. How can a single flat rate, such as we have now, be an accurate and fair answer to the "bunched income" problem in every case?

PEOPLE'S COUNSEL: It can't—and as a matter of fact, the present capital gains tax rate is so low that it more than offsets any "bunched income" hardship and really gives most taxpayers a big windfall tax break. For example, take a person with a $40,000 taxable income who suddenly realizes a $25,000 capital gain on a stock he's held for twenty years. Taxing the entire $25,000 to him in the year he sells the stock makes him pay a little over 51 percent of it in taxes. If, however, you tax him as if he'd received the $25,000 evenly over the twenty years he owned the stock, he'd only have to pay 48 percent of it in taxes—but that would remove the "bunched income" problem. That would be the fair way to handle the case, and of course there's no difficulty about writing a provision into the law for averaging or "smoothing out" capital gains income. The law already has such a provision for

---

* The capital gains rate for corporations is 30 percent.

smoothing out other kinds of income that may vary greatly from year to year. But the existing capital gains tax goes far beyond that. Instead of paying 48 percent (which would be fair), he only has to pay 25 percent. In other words, he gets nearly *twice* the concession that equity requires. And, of course, the wealthier he is, the greater his windfall tax break, as the table in front of you clearly shows.

THE "BUNCHED INCOME" PROBLEM AND TWO SOLUTIONS
(Comparison of tax that has to be paid)

Income Level	Problem	Two Solutions	
	Income "Bunched"*	Income "Unbunched"†	Capital Gains Rate‡
On a Gain of $50,000			
$5,000	37.7%	19.0%	14.1%
$25,000	48.9%	36.0%	25.0%
$100,000	63.6%	62.0%	25.0%
$500,000	70.0%	70.0%	25.0%
On a Gain of $100,000			
$5,000	47.5%	20.2%	18.8%
$25,000	54.8%	37.2%	24.5%
$100,000	65.8%	62.0%	31.8%
$500,000	70.0%	70.0%	35.0%

* Entire gain taxed all in one year.

† Gain spread evenly over twenty years (on the assumption the property has been held for that period)—i.e., tax is computed as if one-twentieth of the gain had been taxed in each of twenty years.

‡ On a married couple's capital gains under $50,000 ($25,000 for a single person) the rate is never higher than 25 percent. But it can be lower than 25 percent, since a taxpayer is entitled to choose between having his gain taxed at 25 percent (the maximum), or at *half* his regular top-bracket rate. If this latter is less than 50 percent, it pays to choose the second method. In the above table, it is assumed that the $50,000 gain applicable to the first group of figures qualifies for these rules.

PEOPLE'S COUNSEL: Turning now to Defense Counsel's second argument—the so-called "locked in" argument—my adversary has the right charge, but the wrong culprit. The existing system does have a locked-in effect, but the preferred capital gains tax rate is not to blame—in fact, it produces an opposite or anti-locked-in effect. No, the real culprit is the failure to tax capital gains at death.

FOREMAN OF THE JURY: Counsel, you covered too

much ground in one breath. Could you explain *why* the failure to tax gains at death creates a locked-in effect?

PEOPLE'S COUNSEL: Because, as Defense Counsel has explained, the deterrent to selling comes from a person asking himself, "Shall I sell and pay a tax or hold on and pay no tax?" But he's able to pose the question in this way only because if he holds on long enough—namely, until he dies—he will indeed "pay no tax." So of course there's an incentive to hold on rather than sell.

But if the rules were changed, and gains were taxed at death, then a person would pose the question differently: "Shall I sell and pay the tax now or hold on *and pay the tax later*?" Either way, the tax would have to be paid; it would really be a matter of timing, and while there would still be some incentive to hold on, it would be much less.

FOREMAN OF THE JURY: And why do you say that the existing capital gains tax encourages "switching"—an "anti-locked-in" effect, I think you called it?

PEOPLE'S COUNSEL: Well, put yourself in the shoes of a person in the 70 percent tax bracket. You have two choices: you can leave your money in AT&T stock, which fluctuates very little in price but pays a nice, steady dividend, on which you keep only 30 cents out of every dollar. Or you can sell your AT&T and put your money in a stock that stands a good chance of doubling in price in the next three years, *with you keeping up to 65 to 75 cents out of every dollar of profit, instead of 30 cents*. Which would you do? Wouldn't you be tempted to sell the AT&T and go for the stock profit?

ENGINEER JURYMAN: Your argument sounds logical in theory. But does it work out in actual practice?

PEOPLE'S COUNSEL: Three professors of the Harvard Business School made a nationwide survey of the habits and behavior of actual investors, and show that "quite contrary to the indictment . . . it is precisely in drawing funds into new ventures and unseasoned securities that the capital gains tax at present rates exerts its strongest influences."

Actually, as far as overall stock sales and purchases are concerned, *non*-tax reasons seem to be much more powerful than tax considerations. Take the years 1922 through 1933, for example. During that time, both the income tax and the capital gains tax rates were consistently at fairly low levels so that the supposed tax impediments my adversary has conjured up were at a minimum. Yet those years included both the fattest and the leanest in history in the volume of capital gains. The point is that economic conditions and market judgments are far more important than the level of taxes.

A perfect illustration is what happened in the wake of the 1969 increase in the top capital gains rate, from 25 to 35 percent. Let me quote from what Dr. Joseph Pechman, the top tax expert at the Brookings Institution, said in 1972, when asked whether raising the capital gains rate discourages people from selling their stocks:

Many financial analysts think so. But they also felt the same way when the maximum rate of capital gains was 25 percent. Yet the 1969 law increased it to 36½ percent* and the roof didn't cave in. In fact, we've had one of the sharpest and most sustained stock market recoveries in history since the 1969 law was passed. Realized capital gains [as a result of people selling their stocks for a profit] probably set a record in 1971....

Also, a large proportion of stock buying and selling is done by colleges, pension funds, foundations and insurance companies that are wholly or partially tax-exempt. For them, of course, taxes *couldn't* be a factor.

DOCTOR JURYMAN: Counsel, I am quite persuaded by what you say about the *present* tax system, but frankly I am concerned about what would happen to the economy if we were to tax capital gains the same as ordinary income—at rates as high as 50 or 70 percent.

For instance, you yourself have admitted that the present special capital gains rate has powerfully attracted investment into so-called venture or pioneering companies, where the risk is high and dividends may be years away. Where are those companies going to get capital under your proposal?

PEOPLE'S COUNSEL: You've raised an important point that causes many people concern. But I think there are convincing answers to it.

---

* Dr. Pechman was referring to the maximum tax rate that can apply if a person is subject to both the capital gains tax and the "minimum tax" enacted in 1969 (see p. 73).

The first is that corporations get only a tiny fraction of their needed capital from new stock issues. Over the decade of the Sixties, for example, *American corporations derived only 1.5 percent of their capital from stocks!* That is, they met more than 98 percent of their needs from other sources—plowed-back earnings and borrowing and the like. That fact is crucial to bear in mind. For even if a higher tax rate did discourage stock market investors (and as I've just said, the post-1969 experience suggests that the effect of the tax rate is much less than most suppose), they play a marginal rather than central role in meeting corporations' capital needs. Even if stock market investment were to shrink by half— which to me is almost inconceivable—that would affect less than one percent of all the capital that corporations need.

What's more, to counter any inhibiting effect on investment there might be in taxing capital gains the same as other kinds of income, under my plan, investment *losses* that offset investment profits in any year would be deductible at the regular rates (which they aren't under existing law). That ought to be a considerable added inducement to risk investment by top-bracket taxpayers— because if a risky venture went sour, the government would, in effect, pay a far greater share of their losses than is now the case.

Secondly, does anyone on this jury really believe that as long as people think they can make money in the stock market, they are going to pass up that chance just because they'll have to pay a hunk of it in taxes? Ask yourself: if you were convinced that a given stock was going to double in value, or even that its price was going to rise by half, assuming you had some money to invest, would you pass up the chance entirely because of the tax? Even if the tax were high, you'd be able to keep some of your profit. Of course, you'd be looking around to see how much you could make by doing other things with your money. But don't forget, if capital gains were taxed the same as other kinds of income, as I'm proposing, any place you'd put your money, the tax would be the same.

Ladies and gentlemen of the jury, Defense Counsel has sought to characterize the People's proposal as radical. Actually, it is based on the old-fashioned, laissez-faire, free-enterprise principle that a free market is the best regulator, sifter and adjuster of economic forces.

The People believe that investors, given a free choice and

free competition among companies for capital, will make sound decisions. Worthwhile ventures will get all the money they need. Since when did we need to subsidize risk-taking in America? After all, men invest—or even gamble—their personal energies and talents, even though they are taxed at the regular income tax rates. Is money so much more precious than a man's own talent that its risks must be coddled?

JUDGE : I'm afraid we may be turning this trial into a seminar on economics. If neither side has anything further to submit to the jury at this time, this trial will stand adjourned for the day.

JUDGE: Mr. Foreman, has the jury concluded its deliberations?

FOREMAN OF THE JURY: Yes, Your Honor, and we are prepared to render our conclusions.

We start from a simple proposition: a dollar is a dollar, no matter how it was earned or where it came from. It will buy just as much in groceries, or shoes, mink coats or Cadillacs, whether it was made from a sale of stock or from the sweat of a man's brow or the fruits of his brain. It will pay taxes just as well, too. The voice of Equity, therefore, calls clearly and eloquently for taxing *uniformly* "all income, *from whatever source derived"*—to use the words of the tax law itself.

The voice of Simplicity speaks, too, telling us that the closing off of a major avenue of tax avoidance would enormously lessen the incessant pressure for special tax treatment. It would permit doing away with the very complex sections of the tax law that are there solely to stop or minimize abuse of the capital gains preference. Energies now devoted to minimizing taxes could be more constructively dedicated to minimizing costs and prices and maximizing profits, as People's Counsel put it.

We note the apprehension felt by many that the equal taxation of capital gains and ordinary income will dry up the wellsprings of capital and greatly reduce American risk-taking. But this viewpoint supposes the American economy to be so frail as to require a subsidy for risk-taking. We do not share such a view, although we recognize that taxing capital gains equally with ordinary income might well dissuade *some* people from investing. But I remind you again of the very small share of their capital—less than two percent in the decade of the Sixties—that corporations de-

rive from stock market investors. I remind you, too, of the historic
evidence, most recently in the post-1969 period, that raising the
tax rate on capital gains has little discernible effect on investment.

Your Honor, the People have faith in the American economy.
We do not believe that risk-taking need be subsidized. In any
event, if a subsidy *is* needed, it should certainly be through a device
less clumsy and ill-directed than a blanket tax preference to *all*
investment, safe as well as risky.

We have faith in the free enterprise system. We believe the
free play of the market is the best regulator of economic forces—
that investors, operating freely amid a free and open competition
for capital, will produce the soundest economic and investment
decisions. Institutions and investors will adjust themselves. Values
will find a new—and sounder—level. As long as there are reasonable opportunities in America to invest and make a profit, there
will be investors and capital to take advantage of them, with or
without a tax subsidy. But if no such opportunities exist, no
amount of tax preference will lure investors into the market.

We are well aware, Your Honor, that what we propose would
be a sharp departure from the past. But we are persuaded by
People's Counsel when he says that this would be "one of the
greatest tax reforms this nation could undertake." And as Justice
Brandeis once said, "If we would guide by the light of reason, we
must let our minds be bold."

The light of reason tells us that we can have a far simpler and
far fairer tax system. The question is whether our minds are bold
enough to make this a reality.

6

Your Wife
May Be Worth
a Million

JUST THIS ONE MORNING, make an exception. Lower your breakfast-time newspaper and take a look at your wife. How much do you think she's worth? Oh, *of course* she's the priceless gem without which your life would be an utter void. But try, for a moment, to be wholly unsentimental, and to make a coldly practical dollars-and-cents calculation of just what she is worth to you in hard cash. The results may surprise you.

If you are a young executive with a $25,000-a-year salary, the little woman is an asset worth precisely $31,562.50. If you are a junior vice-president with a salary of $50,000 per year, the image of your wife is likely to be more dazzling, for she is the equivalent of $100,777.77. If you have reached the $125,000 level, you should experience a certain humility, for you are in the presence of a half-million-dollar asset. To be precise, her worth has ascended to $536,666.66.

If you are a corporation president drawing a salary of $200,000, you may feel an impulse to go out and buy your spouse an expensive present upon discovering that her cash value to you is $771,666.66. If you are able to so arrange your life as to have an annual income of $245,731.77, your joy and wonder attain peak levels, your helpmate having attained the lustrous value of $807,333.32.

Time was when the cash value of a spouse kept on skyrocket-

119

ing until her husband's taxable income reached $445,777.78. From then on her value began to plummet, and in those days husbands were encouraged to be at pains to prevent their incomes from exceeding $1,399,555.55 for, at that point in the income scale, their wives became worthless (in a monetary sense, at least).*

The experience of having a worthless wife was not, however, reserved to those in the over-$1,399,555.55 group. On the contrary, it was shared, in those days, by every married man with an annual income of less than $2,889. Today, it is an experience common to married men earning less than $2,800. But that is hardly the most "exclusive" of clubs since, according to the latest available government statistics, some three million men belong.

Moreover, to the nearly four million married men with incomes of around $4,000, filing a joint return with the lady of the house represents added spending money of only 37 cents a week—which a husband of surly disposition might say makes her worthless.

ALL OF THIS comes to pass by virtue of a fiction written into the tax laws in 1948. In most American homes, if there is only one breadwinner, it is the husband. The weekly pay check is made out in his name. Nevertheless, the tax laws permit the husband, in making out his tax return, to make believe that half of the pay check has been earned by his spouse. This fiction comes to pass because of special tax rates that may be used by couples filing a joint return.

This is an enormously expensive fiction: even most experts are astonished at its prodigious cost, but according to the Brookings Institution computer analysis, this one feature of the tax law costs the U.S. Treasury *about twenty-one and a half billion dollars every year*! Its bounties, moreover, are dispensed with singular unevenness. When it was enacted, 97 percent of its benefits went to the top 5 percent of the taxpayers. On the other hand, nearly four-fifths of the married couples of the nation were entirely denied its benefactions. While subsequent changes in the

---

* This phenomenon resulted from a provision of the tax law, repealed in 1964, that stipulated that a person's tax could in no event exceed 87 percent of his taxable income. This ceiling began to take effect, and began to reduce the tax savings from marriage, when a person's income reached $445,777.78. At an income level of $1,399,555.55, the ceiling was fully effective and the matrimonial tax savings were zero.

tax rates have lessened the lopsidedness, even today Married Couple A, with twenty times the income of Married Couple B, can enjoy ninety-seven times as much tax benefit.

A hypothetical illustration will demonstrate how the application of this fiction makes marriage financially as well as spiritually rewarding.* Picture a promising young executive, Jeremy Hornblower, who at this point in his budding career earns $25,000 and has taxable income of $20,000.

It is his wedding day: at noon he is to become conjugally joined with a delectable Southern maiden, Sue Alice Beauregard. But until noon he remains a bachelor, obligated to Uncle Sam for an annual $5,230—$2,090 on the first $10,000 of his income and $3,140 on the second $10,000 (since the tax rates rise as income increases).

At 12:17 the minister ties the knot, and at that instant Jeremy's annual tax bill drops to $4,380.† Why? Because, as of 12:18 P.M., the government suddenly permits him to make believe that half of the $20,000 is earned by the former Miss Beauregard. As far as the government is concerned, his $20,000 income is now divided into two separate but equal parcels, labeled "His" and "Hers." The taxes on "His" half are $2,190, the taxes on "Hers" also $2,190, for a total tax of $4,380—$850 less than his tax as a bachelor.

Clearly, then, his new bride is not only an ornamental but a monetarily valuable asset. How valuable? Well, at his salary level, 36 cents out of every *added* dollar of income goes to the government. Hence, in order to enjoy an additional $850 of after-tax "keeping money," he would have to earn $1,328.13 more. He would get precisely that amount of added income if suddenly a rich aunt were to deposit in his savings account $26,562.50 drawing 5 percent interest.

Thus, days later, basking on the beach at Waikiki, our honeymooning bridegroom can take a satisfied glance at that $26,562.50

---

* Simplicity and clarity compel disregarding the extra $750 exemption that comes with the bridal "package."

† Again in the interest of simplicity and clarity, this illustration is based on pre-1969 tax rates, when the principle of income-splitting that Congress enacted in 1948 was still in effect. In 1969, in order to lessen the disparity between the taxes paid by married couples and single taxpayers, Congress modified that principle and altered the relationship between the two. Accordingly, while this illustration would be more up-to-date if it were based on current tax rates, it would also be less illuminating.

asset lying by his side (for that is her equivalent cash value). If he closes his eyes and indulges in Walter Mitty dreams of ascending the corporate promotion ladder, she becomes monetarily even more alluring. When his taxable income reaches $50,-000, he calculates, Sue Alice will mean added "keeping money" of $3,130 each year. At the 62 percent bracket* into which he will have ascended, this will require $8,236.84 of before-tax income—the equivalent of an annual 5 percent return on a $164,736.80 deposit in his savings account.

His calculations assume that she does not earn a penny of her own, and, since the advantages of income-splitting are greatest when the wife's income is zero, if she wishes to keep her cash value at a maximum she must at all costs avoid remunerative activity.

The following table will give male readers an opportunity to gain a true appreciation of the value of the wife they so often take for granted.

Annual Income* of Husband	Cash Value of Wife†
$5,000	$1,197.53
$7,500	$2,506.33
$10,000	$5,197.31
$25,000	$25,937.50
$100,000	$354,062.50
$200,000	$771,666.66
$245,731.77 and over	$807,333.32

* "Adjusted gross income." Assumes personal deductions of 18 percent on incomes of $25,000 and over.

† This is the amount of cash which, drawing 5 percent interest, would net a husband the same increase in *after-tax* dollars he receives, thanks to marital income-splitting, again leaving aside the extra exemption attached to the blushing bride. Figures in this table assume that upper-income taxpayers have enough *un*earned income to place them in higher than a 50 percent bracket (which is now the ceiling on *earned* income).

This information should be used with the utmost discretion and selectivity. Clearly, it should at all costs be concealed from

---

* Remember that this illustration is based on pre-1969 tax rates—that is, before the 50 percent ceiling on salary and other earned income was put into the law. The same is true of the figures in the tables that follow the written illustration. While in the middle- and upper-middle-income brackets, this may result in an overstatement of the wife's value, the same is not likely to be true in the top income brackets, where taxpayers generally have enough unearned income to place them in higher than a 50 percent top tax bracket.

one's wife who, upon learning her true cash value, will forthwith enlist in Women's Lib and begin making demands on the family budget that theretofore would have been considered outrageous.

The above table can, however, be usefully referred to by the husband whose pique at his wife's proverbial tardiness (or, more likely, his infatuation with another woman) leads him to consider severing the conjugal tie. A quick glance at the statistics would readily convince him that he cannot afford *not* to be married.

Ludwig S. Hellborn, a research economist with the General Motors Corporation who originated many of the concepts described above, terms the income-splitting feature of the U.S. tax laws "Uncle Sam's Dowry"—quite different from the private dowry customary in many parts of Europe.* There, the size of the dowry varies with the wealth of the bride's father rather than that of the bridegroom. To the romanticists of Europe, therefore, the most satisfying event is the marriage of the worthy pauper to the millionaire's daughter, whereas in America the dowry reaches its maximum when Cinderella marries a Rockefeller. In Europe, moreover, the dowry is a one-time gift. But kindly, magnanimous Uncle Sam renews the dowry annually, in even more generous amounts as the husband's affluence grows.

These lighter aspects of income-splitting are not likely to be appreciated by struggling young marrieds at the lowest end of the economic scale, who are virtually or wholly excluded from the joys and benefits of this tax feature. Nor is there likely to be great amusement among the single people who are obliged to support, say, aged and ailing relatives, but for whom the tax laws show only part of the mercy proffered to *all* middle- and upper-income married couples, no matter how small their obligations.

THE FICTION of income-splitting became part of the U.S. tax laws in 1948, largely because of a distinction between the property laws of the various states. Eight so-called "community property" states,† taking their laws from Spain or France rather than from England, treated half the income and property of the husband as if it legally belonged to the wife. Hence, before 1948, the married citizens of those eight states enjoyed all the Federal tax

---

* West Germany and France also provide a governmental dowry since their tax laws provide for income-splitting.

† Louisiana, Texas, Idaho, Washington, Arizona, Colorado, Nevada and New Mexico.

advantages accruing to the hypothetical Jeremy Hornblower when he took his bride—a pleasure denied the citizens of the other forty states. For low-income taxpayers, the difference was small ($26 a year for those with $4,000 incomes), but for the well-to-do (those with $500,000 incomes) living in one of the favored eight states meant $25,180 a year more spending money. Or, to use a more widely used term, it meant $484.23 in added *weekly* "take-home pay."

To close the gap, various state legislatures began enacting "community property" laws of their own—Oklahoma in 1945 (to prevent an exodus of wealthy oilmen to the "community property" comfort of neighboring Texas); Oregon, Michigan, Nebraska and Pennsylvania in 1947. Other states were impatient to pass similar laws. The pressure was on Congress to act.

Politics was a factor, too. The Republican Eightieth Congress was pledged to a tax cut, but President Truman had successfully vetoed two G.O.P. tax bills. Income-splitting seemed a hopeful way of breaking the impasse: it enjoyed the support of some in the Truman Administration, and it offered those primarily interested in bestowing tax relief on the middle- and upper-income groups a way of doing so under the respectable guise of "reform."

And so Congress proceeded to act, but with great illogic. It ended one discrimination but created another. The very distinction that had been considered so unfair to the married citizens of forty states was picked up bodily and imposed upon the *single* people of *all* the states. The results are shown in the following table:

To those with taxable incomes of:	Joint-return filing* brings this tax bliss:	
	Amount	Percent
$3,000	$4.00	2.9%
$4,000	$19.00	6.3%
$5,000	$48.50	9.9%
$7,500	$99.00	10.0%
$10,000	$197.50	12.9%
$25,000	$830.00	16.1%
$50,000	$2,267.50	15.6%
$100,000	$5,665.00	14.3%
$150,000	$9,135.00	13.4%
$200,000 and over	$12,110.00	9.8%

* Leaving aside the extra exemption that the new bride brings.

The following figures may further aid your judgment as to whether the advantages of joint-return filing are fairly or unfairly distributed:

Families with total incomes of:	*Comprise this percent of all families*:*	*But get this percent of the benefits of joint-return filing:*
Less than $5,000	18.1%	2/100 of 1%
Less than $10,000	45.5%	2.5%
Less than $15,000	70.2%	14.3%
Less than $20,000	85.3%	32.2%
More than $25,000	7.6%	52.1%
More than $50,000	1.2%	21.3%
More than $100,000	0.3%	7.7%

* These figures differ from those on p. 60 because these are based on *total* income, whereas those on p. 60 are based on "adjusted gross income," which leaves out various income items of which the two most significant are the half of all capital gains that now is excluded from taxation, and government-benefit income. For more detail see Notes and Sources.

There is a tinge of political irony to the events of 1948. Clearly, income-splitting, which by-passes the poor and bestows lavish favors on the wealthy, does violence to the principle of "ability to pay"* historically embraced by the Democratic party. Yet the Congressional Democrats of the day, far from denying this offspring, proudly claimed paternity, boasting they had impelled the Republicans "toward consideration of equity and the elimination of discrimination in the tax system."

Apparently the lawmakers of 1948 considered the equity of income-splitting self-evident, for committee reports at the time omitted the customary justification of the new provision. Some have since sought to rationalize it on two principal grounds. First, they contend, it is both unfair and socially undesirable that two people should pay more taxes when married than they would pay on the same total income if they were earning it as single persons. Imagine, for example, Sophie and Ray, each leading separate and desolate lives, each with $7,500 of taxable income, each paying $1,470 of taxes (or $2,940 between them). Were it not for income-splitting, love and matrimony would increase their

---
* See Glossary.

combined tax bill on their newly combined $15,000 income to $3,520. Surely (say the defenders of income-splitting), we do not wish thus to discourage marriage. (Strangely enough, Congress itself undermined this last argument in 1969 by enacting a provision that *does* provide a financial incentive to certain happily married couples to obtain a divorce and continue their joint ménage in illicit cohabitation. Details may be found on page 342.)

But, counter the critics of income-splitting, if husband and wife pool their incomes (as most compatible couples do) and share as one, why should they not be taxed as one? Besides, they say, if the institution of marriage is so frail as to depend on the slender reed of a tax incentive, how does one explain the popularity of matrimony among those with incomes of less than $2,050 —who do not share in the blessings of income-splitting?

The second main defense of income-splitting, invoking economic reasons, holds that, contrary to the maxim, two *cannot* live as cheaply as one, and hence deserve to be taxed more gently than one. But logic deals this argument a fatal blow. For, if the purpose of this tax concession is to help married couples make financial ends meet, *why are those with the lowest incomes either wholly or virtually excluded from its benefits—while, at the same time, couples with $200,000 of income (hardly on the brink of starvation) are blessed with $12,110 of added spending money?* (Even for childless couples with incomes of less than $7,500, income-splitting means a tax saving of only $99 a year, or about $1.90 a week.)

The "economic" defense founders on another shoal. The most expensive part of marriage is the rearing of children; yet income-splitting bestows the same advantages to childless couples as to those with ten children. To be sure, each new offspring brings the tax saving of an added $750 exemption, but consider how this compares with the benefit to the American male (taxable income, $50,000) when he quits the state of bachelorhood.

	His tax bill is:	So that next step saved him:
As a blissful bachelor	$20,190	—
As an even more blissful bridegroom	$17,060	$3,130
As the proud father of one	$16,685	$375
As the even prouder father of two	$16,310	$375

If the gentleman in question is fortunate enough to have a taxable income of $150,000, the statistics are even more striking:

	Tax	Saving
Bachelor	$88,090	—
Bridegroom	$76,980	$11,110
Father of one	$76,485	$495
Father of two	$75,490	$495

Moreover, is it *always* true, as income-splitting assumes, that single people are better able to pay taxes than married persons? What if they must take care of aged (and perhaps ailing) parents? What if they suddenly find themselves responsible for the care of children, in the wake of a bereavement or divorce? Their burden may well be far heavier than, say, that of a couple without children; yet the original 1948 income-splitting provision denied them the tender treatment accorded married couples.

In 1951, Congress acknowledged this logical defect of the 1948 provision and granted *one-half* the benefits of income-splitting to so-called "heads-of-household": unmarried persons obliged to support children, grandchildren or other dependent relatives actually living with them, or dependent parents, wherever they might live. But this modification suffers the same basic defect as the 1948 provision: those with the lowest incomes, on whom the burdens of dependency press the hardest, are excluded from its benefits. In 1970 there were over three and a half million heads-of-household, *nearly one-fifth of whom gained nothing from semi-income-splitting*. Moreover, although the responsibilities of heads-of-household can easily be greater than those of a married couple, they still receive only *half* the tax concession accorded the married.

In 1954, an effort by the House of Representatives to place heads-of-household on a par with married couples and to ease the living-in requirement for dependents was defeated by the Senate. As if to show they were not wholly devoid of compassion, however, Senators did grant to widows and widowers a two-year extension of their income-splitting privileges after the demise of their spouses.

Those actions, humanitarian as they were, served to further isolate, discriminate against and enrage the unmarried citizens of the nation, and their protests led Congress in 1969 to lower their rates so as to cut roughly in half the "penalty" for being single (i.e., instead of paying 30 to 40 percent more than married couples with like taxable incomes, single people now pay 15 to 20 percent more). Nevertheless, the discrimination remains, and so does the resentment of the unmarried, now mobilized and expressed by a new lobbying group with the intriguing acronym CO$T, signifying Committee of $ingle Taxpayers, whose efforts to end the tax disadvantage of single people (at an annual revenue cost of $1.6 billion) are described more fully on page 302.

THERE IS A GENERAL BELIEF, even among those who feel that income-splitting is illogic and injustice personified, that nothing can be done to undo the deed without reverting to the chaos of the pre-1948 situation, with the "community property" states once again enjoying a favored tax position over the other states.

Such is not the case, and the solution is remarkably simple: permit income-splitting, but abolish its benefits.

This could be accomplished by providing a special schedule of tax rates for married persons who filed separate returns (those who wanted to split their incomes). In this special schedule, the "brackets" (i.e., the range of income to which a given rate applies) would be half as wide as in the schedule that other tax-payers would use. It would look like this (for selected income groups, assuming 1973 tax rates):

SCHEDULE A
(For single persons and married couples filing just one return)

If taxable income is:	Then tax would be:
$0–$500	14%
$500–$1,000	$70 plus 15% of excess over $500
$1,000–$1,500	$145 plus 16% of excess over $1,000
$1,500–$2,000	$225 plus 17% of excess over $1,500
$2,000–$4,000	$310 plus 19% of excess over $2,000
$8,000–$10,000	$1,630 plus 28% of excess over $8,000
$14,000–$16,000	$3,550 plus 39% of excess over $14,000
$20,000–$22,000	$6,070 plus 48% of excess over $20,000
$38,000–$44,000	$15,510 plus 58% of excess over $38,000
$70,000–$80,000	$35,190 plus 66% of excess over $70,000
Over $100,000	$55,490 plus 70% of excess over $100,000

SCHEDULE B
(For married couples filing separate returns)

If taxable income is:	Then tax would be:		
$0–$250		14%	
$250–$500	$35	plus 15% of excess over	$250
$500–$750	$72.50	plus 16% of excess over	$500
$750–$1,000	$112.50	plus 17% of excess over	$750
$1,000–$2,000	$155	plus 19% of excess over	$1,000
$4,000–$5,000	$815	plus 28% of excess over	$4,000
$7,000–$8,000	$1,775	plus 39% of excess over	$7,000
$10,000–$11,000	$3,035	plus 48% of excess over	$10,000
$19,000–$22,000	$7,755	plus 58% of excess over	$19,000
$35,000–$40,000	$17,595	plus 66% of excess over	$35,000
Over $50,000	$27,745	plus 70% of excess over	$50,000

Under Schedule A above, single people with taxable incomes of $8,000 would pay a tax of $1,630. So would married couples with the same taxable income ($8,000) filing just one tax return.

But if a couple in California,* also with $8,000 of taxable income, asserted the claim that under California's "community property" law $4,000 belonged to the husband and $4,000 to the wife, then they would have to use Schedule B. Under that schedule, the tax on $4,000 is $815, and when each had paid that tax, the couple would have paid $1,630—exactly the same as the other taxpayers who didn't "split their incomes."

This would not only achieve tax equality for all family units (married or single) with the same taxable income; it would also reduce the number of special rate schedules from the present four to just two.†

Setting up the tax rate schedules as proposed above would, in a single stroke, raise the prodigious total of $21.5 billion‡ in

---

* Or any other "community property" state.

† The existence of two rate schedules, one with half the "bracket width" of the other, is not novel. Congress enacted just that in 1969, when it created two rate schedules for married couples—one for joint-return filers and the other for couples filing separate returns, the latter having half the "bracket width" of the former.

‡ This assumes that Congress would bring the tax rates for single persons and heads-of-household into line with the rate schedule now provided for married persons filing separate returns.

added revenues—a sum that can be expected to grow as national income rises.*

To date, when the idea of tampering with the joint-return tax advantages has been put to politicians, they have responded about as enthusiastically as if one were suggesting they shake hands with a leper. Yet the $21.5 billion that would be raised through such a reform could make it very seductive to taxpayers if properly presented. It is, for example, considerably larger than the enticement the Nixon Administration was reportedly considering in 1972, whereby some $13 billion to $16 billion would be raised through a "value added tax" (which is generally regarded as a disguised national sales tax [see Glossary]), and the proceeds would be used to lighten the burden of the property tax as a school-financing source. What if Congress were to promise to devote the much larger proceeds of income-splitting (joint-return) reform to some such universally popular cause?

And would not the now leprous idea become even more politically appealing if political leaders were to emphasize the facts about who-now-gets-what-tax-advantages-from-income-splitting (joint-return filing)—facts such as that:

- nearly half of all families—those earning less than $10,000 a year—are getting less than 3 percent of those advantages;
- more than two-thirds of all families—those making less than $15,000 a year—are getting only one-seventh of all the benefits;
- more than eleven billion dollars of income-splitting "tax welfare" is going to the richest 8 percent of American families—those making $25,000 or more;
- more than four and a half billion dollars of that "tax welfare" is going to the richest one percent of American families—those making more than $50,000;
- more than a billion and a half dollars of that "tax welfare" is going to the richest three-tenths of one percent of American families—those making more than $100,000 a year.

Can facts such as those fail to have popular impact?

---

* It would also be possible to achieve tax parity by *lowering* the taxes of the single people to the level of married couples. This would be accomplished by having "tax brackets" for married people filing separate returns twice as large as those for single persons (rather than half as large, as in the above table). But this would result in a $1.6 billion *loss* in revenue, rather than a $21.5 billion *gain*.

IF ALL THE HAPPY consequences described above can spring from a mere *two*-way splitting of income—between husband and wife—think of the added joy that can flow from a three-, four- or five-way division. One hundred thousand dollars of taxable income in the hands of Father alone, for example, would mean a tax of $53,090. The filing of a joint return with Mother brings the tax down to $45,180. If Junior can somehow be brought into the picture, in a three-way split, the tax becomes $32,870. Include Sister in a four-way split and the tax is reduced to $28,760—only a little over half of a single man's tax.

But can this be done? Few things are too difficult for the mind whose ingenuity is stimulated by the possibility of a 40 percent tax saving—for self or for client.

One solution, popular some years ago but somewhat more difficult to employ effectively today, is the family partnership, an intimate arrangement in which infants are sometimes born into the world as full business partners in a thriving enterprise.

Take the actual case, for example, of Paysoff Tinkoff, a New York accountant who operated his firm as a partnership. For a time the enterprise consisted of himself and his wife, with the partnership income divided equally between them, thus giving them the benefits of marital income-splitting. On November 11, 1929, an infant son, Paysoff Tinkoff, Jr., was born to them, and on that very day, the partnership agreement was amended to include the diapered infant. Thereafter, the partnership income was divided *three* ways equally, among father, mother and son. Yet, as a court later found, neither mother nor son "ever contributed any capital or services to the business. . . ." (The judges were unkind enough to point out that Mrs. Tinkoff was not "a lawyer, accountant, bookkeeper or stenographer" and had "never worked in an office.")

Vintage readers will recall Stanback Headache Powders ("Snap Back with Stanback"). These powders, together with the less celebrated Stanback Liver Fixers, were the product of a company owned by two Stanback brothers, Thomas and Fred. Each brother had a wife and two minor children who were duly made full partners in the business, though the brothers retained full control and management.

Although the courts were unkind to both these arrangements, and ruled them invalid for tax purposes, apparently other family partnerships were faring better, for between 1939 and 1948 the number of partnership tax returns more than trebled, and in 1947 nearly a third of them indicated that the partnership included the wife or child of one of the partners.

The court cases that resulted from this proliferation of family partnerships were sometimes illuminating. In one case, the eager and forward-looking parents caused all the necessary partnership legal documents to be drawn up during the wife's pregnancy, leaving only the name and sex of the prospective new partner to be filled in. Thus, once the infant was safely in the world, the papers could be promptly filed and not an hour would be lost in the quest for greater splitting of the family income.

During another court case, involving a partnership made up of a husband, wife and four children, aged seven, five, two and three months, the partner-wife was asked:

Q. Now, do you participate in the management of the business of the La Salle Livestock Company?
A. Well, I have been producing partners.
Q. Beg pardon?
A. I have been too busy producing partners so far.

Up until 1951, the law, as interpreted by the courts, permitted family partnerships to be invalidated, for tax purposes, unless "the parties, in good faith *and acting with a business purpose* [emphasis added]," intended to join together in the present conduct of the enterprise. But in 1951 the "business purpose" test was dispensed with in cases where a bona fide and outright gift of a partnership interest had been made—even if the gift was to an infant child who had no intention or capacity to engage in "the present conduct of the enterprise." If a father were to give his son stocks or bonds, it was argued, the income from them would certainly be taxed to the son and not to the father. Why not apply the same principles of ownership to a part interest in the family business? Senatorial defenders of the 1951 provision were careful to point to its supposed safeguards* designed to prevent a father from artificially shifting partnership income away from himself and his own high tax brackets and into the hands of less heavily taxed family members. These Senators failed, however, to ex-

---

*Described in Notes and Sources.

plain why the 1951 provision should be made retroactive all the way back to 1939, the effect of which was peremptorily to decide a great many pending government challenges of family partnership arrangements against the government and in the taxpayers' favor.

Tax experts who have probed the details of many a family partnership insist that the supposed safeguards in the 1951 law were not the effective bulwark against tax avoidance that their protagonists claimed they were. In an ordinary arm's-length business partnership, the incentives are all against the artificial shifting of partnership income, since each partner will insist on his proper share. Not so in a family partnership, where the dividing up of the business income is not done by arm's-length negotiation (especially where one of the partners is an infant) and where the father has every incentive to allocate as much income as he can to his lightly taxed offspring.

This is not mere theory, as actual court cases show. Take the case of the Uneeda Doll Company, a highly profitable venture (profits $327,350.97 one year) in which a paltry $15,000 capital contribution (made on his behalf by his father) won a 15 percent interest for a minor son. This $15,000 contribution netted the son a 300 percent return which the government termed "inordinate," arguing that it was really the firm's trade name, good will and know-how that accounted for the profits. The court agreed in principle but said it had no power to reallocate the profits, and the arrangement was permitted to stand.

Another case involved a highly reputable West Coast construction company engaged in building highly complex multi-million-dollar bridges, office buildings and stadiums. A family partnership was formed and a 6 percent share given, in trust, to the son of one of the partners, in return for a mere $20,000 given by his father. By contrast, the adult partners received *no* share of the profits for the $80,000 of capital *they* put up. The government argued that the firm's success rested on its reputation, business contacts, bank credit and know-how—all built up by the adult partners—and that a $20,000 capital input could play only the most minuscule role. Yet the court held that since a bona fide gift had been made, the arrangement could not be challenged.

Those most familiar with such court cases feel this way: family partnerships are, after all, supposedly business arrangements. Why shouldn't they be subjected to a "business purpose" test?

Would the Uneeda Doll Company, with over $300,000 in annual profits, sell a 15 percent interest to an outsider for only $15,000? Would the partners in a major construction firm ordinarily accept no profit share for their $80,000 capital contribution, and then give up a 6 percent share for $20,000? If not, why shouldn't such arrangements be subject to challenge as mere tax-avoidance devices?

BUT THE FAMILY partnership device is only the tail on the income-splitting dog. The body of the problem lies in the prodigious advantages that income-splitting now accords wealthy married people. Very few are aware of the nature—or even the existence—of this enormous upside-down "tax welfare" handout, and reform in this area is about as politically unthinkable as capital gains reform was ten or fifteen years ago. Yet, as regards capital gains reform, the situation has changed; there has begun to be a public awareness of the "tax welfare" entailed in the favorable taxation of capital gains (about which you read in the previous chapter), and in 1972, for the first time, a Presidential candidate proposed ending the capital gains tax advantages. Hopefully, in time, the public will be made aware of the facts about income-splitting and the lopsidedness of the benefits it bestows, and one day a Presidential candidate will propose reform in this area, too.

7

The "Treasury Papers" Episode
or
A Dollar Lost
Is a Dollar Spent

Dear Government:

I have just passed my 65th birthday, which I understand makes me eligible for a special government welfare payment. I really need every penny I can get: I am crippled up with arthritis, and the medicine costs so very much. I'm all alone. I can't work, and have to live on just my late husband's pension. Won't you help me?

Despairingly yours,
Grace G. Elderly*

Dear Mrs. Elderly:

You are correct. Being 65, you are eligible for a special government benefit. In your case, unfortunately, it won't be very much. All we can pay you is $105 a year, and we enclose a check in that amount.

Regretfully yours,
United S. Government

Dear Government:

This may seem a strange question, coming from someone as rich as I am—those gossip-column reports about me being worth a quarter of a billion dollars are not too far off—but I'm curious about some-

---

* Mrs. Elderly and the other writers of the letters contained in this chapter have obviously read the writings of Professor Stanley Surrey of the Harvard Law School, and the author of this book cannot allow them to borrow Mr. Surrey's brainchildren without proper acknowledgment.

thing. I am 67 years old and a friend told me that being over 65 entitles me to a special government subsidy. I can't honestly say that I need it; but still, I'd like to know if, despite my great wealth, I'm entitled to this subsidy, and if so, how much it amounts to.

Curiously yours,
John D. Rockemellon

Dear Mr. Rockemellon:

Your government would like to assure you that it does not discriminate against a person either on grounds of race, religion, creed— or just because he happens to be filthy rich, like you.

On the contrary, we are inclined, in certain instances, to bend over backwards to avoid even the slightest hint of any such discrimination. For instance, we recently received a request identical to yours from a Mrs. Grace G. Elderly and we advised her the most we could send her was $105. But, just to show you our hearts are in the right place when it comes to lending a helping hand to the rich, we are hereby enclosing a check for five times that amount.

While none of us here has been able to imagine what a person with your income will possibly find to spend it on, we all hope you spend it in good health.

Warm-heartedly yours,
"Gov"

THESE WERE THE FIRST of what were to become known as, not "The Pentagon Papers," but "The Treasury Papers,"* first published in the New York *Times.* Official Washington was, of course, intensely annoyed by the unauthorized disclosure of the closely held letters, and was threatening to subpoena every known editor and reporter of the *Times* when a second installment appeared in the "Washington Merry-Go-Round" column of Jack Anderson:

Dear Government:

I am not very rich—too poor, in fact, to pay any income tax. But the Salvation Army helped me in time of need, and I am sending it $5.

---

* All of which are fictional, as are the references to Jack Anderson and the letters' publication by the New York *Times* and the Washington *Post.*

I wondered if maybe, with all the money you have, you could send the Salvation Army a little something, to match what I'm giving.

> Pennilessly yours,
> Horace T. Pauper

Dear Mr. Pauper:

We have received your letter, and are deeply touched by your generosity and your sacrifice. But in this situation, we cannot make the contribution you request.

> Callously yours,
> United S. Government

It seemed a strange response, especially when compared with the government's reply to one Herman Greenbacks, a millionaire who wrote as follows:

Dear Government:

Inasmuch as my income this prosperous year is fast approaching $500,000, I find I have some spare cash, and I have decided to donate $30,000 to my favorite charity: the Society for the Preservation of Hog Calling in Arkansas. I am writing to inquire whether you might also make a donation to this indisputably worthy cause.

> Inquiringly yours,
> Herman Greenbacks

Dear Mr. Greenbacks:

We are in receipt of your letter and will be delighted to be of assistance. In fact, so eager are we to help the cause of Hog Calling in Arkansas that we are prepared to match your own $30,000 contribution more than two to one. Accordingly, we are forthwith sending a government check for $70,000 to the Hog Calling Society, confident that this will help this priceless American institution.

> Eagerly yours,
> U. States Government

But perhaps the strangest exchange of all was with Roger Croesus, heir to the huge Croesus fortune:

Dear Government:

I need to raise some cash—my present yacht is now three years old and just frightfully obsolete—and thus I plan to dispose of about

$2 million worth of stock I inherited from my grandfather to buy a new yacht and to take care of one or two other odds and ends.

I am also writing to express my strong endorsement of the Antique Car Society of America and, while I have decided not to make a contribution to the Society myself at this time, I thought perhaps you might have an interest in supporting this fine charity.

Avariciously yours,
Roger Croesus

Dear Mr. Croesus:

We will be delighted to send a $2 million contribution to the Antique Car Society and will be glad to say that the contribution is in your name. Moreover, in appreciation of your thoughtfulness in suggesting this fine idea to us—and confident your new yacht will need outfitting—we are sending you a check for $100,000—tax-free, of course.

Generously yours,
U.S. Government

With this second disclosure, official embarrassment and anger intensified, but just as the FBI was zeroing in on the suspected source of the leak to the *Times* and to Anderson, the Washington *Post* published still a third exchange of letters between the government and citizens seeking Federal assistance. The first appeal came from Mr. and Mrs. Van der Meer Opulent, of New York, Newport and Palm Beach, whose annual income, according to the *Post,* was "in excess of $500,000." As the *Post* reported it, the Opulents wrote as follows:

Dear Government:

As we're sure you know from all the newspaper accounts, we have been accustomed to wintering in Palm Beach and summering at Newport. However, in recent summers, the mid-August temperatures at Newport have become absolutely insufferable, even with the air conditioning, and now we plan to purchase an additional summer residence at Southwest Harbor, Maine. We hereby request your assistance in paying the mortgage interest, which we understand amounts to 7 percent.

Mr. and Mrs. Van der Meer Opulent

Dear Mr. and Mrs. Opulent:

We have received your heartrending request for assistance and hasten to reply that we will be only too delighted to pay 5 percent of your mortgage interest, so that you can effect the purchase of your much-needed Southwest Harbor residence paying an interest rate of just 2 percent.

Sympathetically yours,
U.S.

The second letter came from Mr. and Mrs. Wallace Comfortable, of East Suburbia, Michigan. The Washington *Post* reported that the Comfortables enjoyed an income of "about $50,000 a year."

Dear Government:

While we are comfortably housed in East Suburbia, we are anxious to purchase a summer cottage on Lake Michigan and would like your help in paying the 7 percent mortgage interest.

Expectantly yours,
Mr. and Mrs. Wallace Comfortable

Dear Mr. and Mrs. Comfortable:

Thank you for letting us know about your new summer cottage, which we will be glad to help you purchase. We will furnish half of the mortgage interest, leaving you to pay only 3.5 percent on the cottage's purchase.

Understandingly yours,
United S. Government

The third letter was from Mr. and Mrs. George Lowly, of Recession Center, West Virginia. The Lowlys' annual income, according to the *Post*, amounted to "in the neighborhood of $7,000." The exchange was as follows:

Dear Government:

We have always dreamed of owning a home of our own and now a little house that just seems to suit us has come on the market. But we're not sure we can swing it with the 7 percent mortgage interest. We figured it down to the penny, and 4½ percent is the most we can carry. We're dying to get out of this crummy place we're renting

(please don't tell our landlord we said so), and to have a place we
can really call our own. Please—it's not much to ask.

Pleadingly yours,
Mr. and Mrs. George Lowly

Dear Mr. and Mrs. Lowly:

Receipt is acknowledged of your request for assistance. Note has
been taken of the fact that this will be the first house you have ever
owned and assurance is hereby given of the government's sympathetic interest. However, under the restrictions imposed by law,
the most your government can do is to pay 1 percent interest for you
which, under the circumstances, will make it necessary for you to
pay the balance of 6 percent mortgage interest.

Bureaucratically yours,
The Government of
the United States of America

This last series of letters, dealing as it did with housing assistance, sent newsmen scurrying to the Department of Housing and
Urban Development (HUD) for an explanation of this seemingly
upside-down subsidy program. But HUD officials said the program
did not come within their jurisdiction and, in fact, denied knowledge of its existence.

Reporters who went to the Department of Health, Education
and Welfare (HEW) seeking clarification of the Rockemellon–
Elderly correspondence on the over-sixty-five welfare payment
got a similar response: HEW officials disclaimed both responsi-
bility for and knowledge of the program.

Finally, not knowing where to turn, reporters approached the
Treasury Department (even though Treasury had no known subsidy programs). There, officials sheepishly admitted that the various citizen requests for aid had been routed to Treasury and that
the responses had indeed originated there.

Meanwhile, revelation of "The Treasury Papers" and the
seemingly hard-hearted government policies suggested in them
had stirred unexpectedly heated reactions around the country.
There were calls for Congressional investigations. By the time
reporters tracked down the source of the "Papers" to the Treasury Department, the furor had reached such proportions that the

White House instructed all cabinet members to participate with Treasury officials in an extraordinary press conference, the transcript of which follows:

Q. (*To Treasury official, who tremblingly insisted he not be identified*) Can you tell us, sir, why these various requests were routed to Treasury and not to the various other departments? For instance, why did the Opulent–Comfortable–Lowly requests for housing assistance go to you, rather than to HUD?

A. Because the subsidy involved was not a direct subsidy. It was a tax subsidy. Or you might call it a "tax expenditure."

Q. What do you mean—"tax subsidy" and "tax expenditure"?

A. I mean that, rather than being appropriated by Congress and spent directly out of the Treasury, this subsidy springs from the tax law—in this case, the provision that makes mortgage interest tax-deductible.

As you know, any tax deduction reduces a person's taxable income and therefore lowers his tax. But as far as the U.S. Treasury is concerned, it's exactly the same as if we'd written out a check and paid it to each of those families.

Q. How do you figure that?

A. Because on April 15, when, say, Mr. Opulent sends the Treasury a smaller check than he would have if there were no such tax deduction, Mr. Opulent is that much richer, and the U.S. Treasury is that much poorer than if the tax deduction weren't in the law. Exactly the same would be true if the Treasury wrote out a check for the same amount: the person receiving the check would be that much richer, the Treasury would be that much worse off.

Q. But how come the Opulents got so much more than the Lowlys?

A. Because the Opulents, with their enormous income, are in the 70 percent tax bracket, so every dollar of tax deductions saves them 70 cents. That is to say, the U.S. Treasury (or, more precisely, all the rest of the U.S. taxpayers) end up footing 70 percent of the Opulents' mortgage interest payments.

But the unfortunate Lowlys are only in the 15 percent tax bracket, so 85 cents of every dollar of mortgage interest comes out of *their* pockets. They only get 15 cents' worth of help from the Treasury.

Q. I imagine that explains why the government responded so

generously to Mr. Greenbacks, and sent $70,000 to the Hog Call-
ing Society.

A. Precisely. Since Mr. Greenbacks is in the 70 percent bracket,
a $100,000 tax-deductible charitable gift by him to the Hog Call-
ing Society lowered his tax by $70,000. So he ended up contribut-
ing just $30,000 out of his own pocket, with the U.S. Treasury
(that is, all the rest of the American taxpayers) providing the
remaining $70,000.

Q. You mean regardless of whether or not I give a damn
about preserving hog calling, part of *my* tax dollars were used to
help that crazy outfit?

A. That's exactly right.

Q. But why did the government turn down poor Horace
Pauper cold, and refuse to contribute a cent to the Salvation
Army? That seems rather hard-hearted.

A. I know it must seem that way, but we had no choice in the
matter. That's the way the law is written.

Q. What do you mean?

A. Well, you'll remember that Mr. Pauper said he was so poor
that he didn't have to pay any income tax. That being the case,
he had no taxable income from which to deduct his contribution.
Therefore, the donation didn't save him anything, and he had to
foot the entire bill out of his own pocket. The contribution by the
U.S. Treasury was zero.

Q. What about the incredible response to Roger Croesus'
request? How does that come about?

A. The explanation for that is a bit technical, and if you're
really interested in pursuing it, I wish you would see my technical assistant, here, after the press conference.*

Q. And does the difference in tax brackets explain why Mrs.

---

* A Treasury aide later explained to newsmen that the response to Mr.
Croesus was occasioned by Mr. Croesus' 70 percent top tax bracket and his
decision to make a tax-deductible gift to the Antique Car Society of $2 mil-
lion in stock that was virtually valueless when he inherited it from his
grandfather. In that circumstance, his tax saving (i.e., the U.S. Treasury's
contribution referred to in the government's response) was $1,400,000 of
income tax, resulting from the $2 million deduction, plus the avoidance of
$700,000 in capital gains tax—for a total saving of $2,100,000, or $100,000
more than his $2 million gift. In that sense, not a penny of his $2 million
charitable gift came out of Mr. Croesus' pocket—which is what he meant
when he said in his "letter" to the government that he did not intend to
make a contribution of his own to the Antique Car Society. Not only that:

Elderly got only $105 but John D. Rockemellon got five times that much as his old-age tax subsidy?

A. Exactly. Each of them became entitled to an extra $750 exemption when they turned sixty-five. But for Mr. Rockemellon, who's in the 70 percent bracket, that saved him $525, while poor arthritic Mrs. Elderly was saved only $105.

Q. But that seems crazy. Why give the least help to the people who need it the most?

A. Because, sir, that's the way these tax subsidies work. It springs from the very nature of the tax system. So I suggest you put that question to the people who write the tax laws—not to us.

Q. You mean we should ask Congress about this?

A. *You* said that, sir, not I. I want the record to show that.

But there's something more you should know about the housing tax subsidies. Not only do the Opulents get a bigger bang for *each* tax-deductible buck; *they also spend vastly more tax-deductible bucks* (because obviously their new summer mansion costs much more than the bungalow the Lowlys wanted to buy). So the advantage to the rich over the poor is multiplied even further.

I call your attention, ladies and gentlemen, to a study by the Brookings Institution that showed that the tax benefits of all the tax subsidies to home owners (over home renters) comes to just 66 cents per year for the lowest-bracket families—but amounts to 10,000 times that much (over *six thousand dollars* a year) for the richest families.

Q. That's fantastic! That must cost the Treasury a pretty penny.

A. Well, from our point of view, it's not very "pretty," because so many people take advantage of this subsidy, it costs the Treasury nearly ten *billion* dollars a year.

Q. Ten billion! (*Leafing through budget of Department of Housing and Urban Development*) I don't find anything in HUD's budget about spending $10 billion for assistance to home owners.

A. (*From Secretary of HUD*) No, because it isn't *in* the HUD budget.

Q. Shouldn't it be?

A. Of course it should. After all, it's by far the largest major

---

even after the government (i.e., the rest of the taxpayers) had paid for the entire charitable contribution, Mr. Croesus enjoyed a $100,000 after-tax profit—also provided by the other taxpayers.

outlay of taxpayers' money in the housing field. In fact, it's two and a half times the budget of my entire department and *six times* what the Federal government spends in direct housing assistance.

Q. Mr. Secretary, if you started from scratch to devise a subsidy program to encourage home ownership, would it be anything like the tax subsidy we've just heard described?

A. Are you kidding? Not a chance—because any direct subsidy program I would cook up I'd have to justify to Congress every year—otherwise I wouldn't get the money. Can't you just picture me trying to explain to Congress every year why I'm giving just 66 cents to the poorest families and $6,000 to the richest? Why, I'd be laughed out of Washington—or ridden out of town on a rail.

Q. (*To Treasury Department spokesman*) Don't you Treasury people have to go before Congress every year and justify these tax subsidies?

A. Certainly not.

Q. You mean Congress permits $10 billion to be "spent" that way year in and year out, without asking any questions about it?

A. That's exactly the case, incredible as it may seem.

Q. How does that come about?

A. Because all these tax subsidies are embedded in the tax laws and stay in effect year after year, as long as Congress doesn't vote to change them.

Q. Isn't that just the opposite of a direct subsidy—I mean one that's spent directly out of the Treasury?

A. (*From the Secretary of Agriculture*) It certainly is—I can testify to that from painful personal experience. The farm subsidy, for instance, is a directly appropriated subsidy, and every damn year I have to go before Congress and justify every penny of what I'm spending. And if Congress doesn't approve of what I'm doing, and doesn't vote the money, the farm subsidy could come to a dead halt.

But just the opposite is true of the tax subsidies that go to what I call the "tax farmers"—the rich city folk who invest in cattle and pistachio groves and the like, solely or mostly for the tax savings. Most of them never go near their "farms" and they're really hurting the true honest-to-God farmers by artificially bidding up the price of farm land. Yet *their* tax subsidy goes on and on, forever, unless Congress takes some action to change the law and stop the subsidy.

Q. (*To the Secretary of the Interior*) Mr. Secretary, what about the oil depletion allowance in the tax laws? Unless I'm mistaken, that represents a tax subsidy or a "tax expenditure" of more than a billion and a half dollars every year—supposedly to encourage oil discoveries. Now since your department is in charge of natural resource development, and since oil is one of our most important resources, wouldn't it be logical for that billion and a half to be part of your Interior Department budget?

A. Of course. By rights it should be, unless we're going to kid the taxpayers about how much of their money we're spending on resource development every year. As it is now, the billion and a half is, in effect, hidden from the taxpayers' view. No one thinks of it as an annual outlay.

Q. Would it make much of a difference if that billion and a half were a direct expenditure, rather than a "tax expenditure"?

A. All the difference in the world. If it were a direct expenditure, it would be subject to sharp questioning every year, not just by Congress, but by me, and by the President's Budget Director, who's sitting next to me here and who fixes his beady eye on every one of my projects and programs before he'll include it in the President's budget. You see, I have to fight for every penny that goes into my budget, so that if this oil-exploration incentive were a direct subsidy instead of a tax subsidy, it would have to compete with, and measure up against, every other program in my budget.

As it is, though, the depletion allowance, being part of the permanent tax law, hasn't been subject to that yearly scrutiny, which partly explains why it remained absolutely unchanged for forty-three years—from 1926 to 1969—even though the supply of oil and the techniques for finding it changed drastically during that time.

Q. Wasn't there a study recently that showed there was something like a 90 percent waste factor in the depletion subsidy?

A. Yes, a study commissioned by the government in 1968 indicated that although the American taxpayers shell out a billion and a half dollars every year—through tax subsidies—supposedly to promote new oil discoveries, all they get for their money is a measly $150 million in added outlays for oil exploration. That's just a 10 percent return, which means, as you say, that there's a 90 percent waste factor. I doubt that any direct-subsidy program would survive very long with that much "waste."

Q. (*To Treasury official*) Do these tax subsisides—or "tax expenditures" as you call them—add up to very much money, in total?

A. If you call seventy-seven billion dollars "very much money," they certainly do.

Q. Seventy-seven billion dollars! That's about *one-third* the size of the entire Federal budget?

A. That's right.

Q. And you say that every dollar of "tax expenditures" is just as much of a drain on the Federal Treasury—and contributes just as much to government deficits—as a dollar of direct spending?

A. Precisely.

Q. Then the government of the United States is, in effect, understating the extent of its spending by about *a third*.

A. I guess you could say that.

Q. I'm surprised that the Democrats haven't made a big issue of that, considering how President Nixon berated them for being big spenders.

A. I suspect the reason the Democrats didn't press the point is that they never included the "tax expenditures" in their budgets when they were in office, either (although in fairness it has to be said that the concept of "tax expenditures" did originate with Assistant Treasury Secretary Stanley Surrey in a Democratic administration).

Q. (*To the Secretary of Commerce*) Mr. Secretary, you were a highly successful company president before you came into the Cabinet. Would you, as a businessman, have dared to present to your board of directors, or to your stockholders, a financial statement that totally omitted 30 percent of what you were spending?

A. No, of course not. For one thing, I wouldn't have wanted to do any such thing, because I would only have been kidding myself, my board and my shareholders. For another, my accountants would never have let me get away with such a gross distortion of the facts. So from the point of view of a person who likes to see things done in a businesslike manner, I would very much applaud having the "tax expenditures" included as part of the President's budget every year.

Q. (*To the President's Budget Director*) Didn't Congress consider requiring just that?

A. Yes, there was such a provision in the 1971 tax bill at one point, but Congress knocked it out before the bill finally passed.

Q. Why did they do that?

A. Partly because the Nixon Administration threw its weight against the provision. Say, can we go off the record for a moment? (*Off the record*) My guess is that neither the Administration nor the Congress wanted the public to know how much they hand out every year in "hidden spending." That's especially true of the Congress. After all, they do have to preserve their carefully built reputation as the guardians of the taxpayers' dollars, and the watchdogs over the Treasury. The truth is, though, that every year they are "spending" tens of billions of dollars that leak out of the Treasury through the tax loopholes, and they "spend" those billions without asking any questions as to whether the money is doing what it's supposed to or reaching the people who need the help.

Q. Can you give us examples of tax subsidies that don't reach the people who really need them?

A. Sure. There are lots of examples. The tax subsidy connected with tax-free state and local bonds* is an ideal case. Most people think of it as a subsidy to the states and localities, by enabling them to borrow money at lower interest rates. But studies have shown that this subsidy costs the Federal government twice as much as the states and counties and towns save in interest costs. That means that only half the subsidy goes to the intended beneficiaries. The people who really benefit are the super-rich individuals and the banks that buy and own those bonds and get the income from them entirely tax-free.

Q. What about that extra exemption for the elderly—that sounded like it was giving most of the help to the rich who don't need it.

A. Yes, that's another good example. It *sounds* like a humanitarian act on Congress's part—until you find out not only that a John D. Rockemellon gets five times as much benefit from it as poor Mrs. Elderly, but also that old people who are too poor to pay any tax anyway—the people who need help the most—get *zero* benefit from the extra exemption.

Another crazily designed tax subsidy results from the tax credits and deductions for political contributions, passed, as you know, in 1971. This is supposed to be a country of "one man/one

---

* See pp. 62–66.

vote." But if you use the political-contribution *deduction,* the richer you are, the greater the Federal government's share of the gift. But even worse than that, people who are too poor to have to pay taxes—and that's fully one-fourth of the electorate—all those people are barred from having the government make *any* contribution to their candidates. What could be more undemocratic? Yet that's inherent in using the tax system, to achieve even the worthiest of objectives.

Look at the basic $750 exemption that applies to every taxpayer and his dependents. The purpose of that is to spare poor families from being taxed on what they need to meet "some minimum essential living costs." And yet that seemingly unarguable feature of the tax law confers *four billion dollars* of "tax welfare" on families making more than $15,000 a year.

And the home owners' tax deductions for mortgage interest and taxes—they represent a "tax expenditure" of nearly *six billion dollars* a year. Maybe if Congress held hearings on that every year, as they do with the direct expenditures, they'd find out only 30 cents out of every dollar of that goes to families making less than $10,000 a year. Maybe then Congress would stop and ask, Is that the most efficient—the most humanitarian—way to spend $6 billion helping home owners? But no one seems to raise that question, and so the $6 billion goes on being "spent," year after year.

Then there are tax subsidies that are so poorly targeted that lots of the money doesn't even accomplish the supposed objective. When that happens, of course, huge amounts of the taxpayers' dollars are wasted.

Q. For instance?

A. For instance, the oil depletion allowance, one of the main justifications for which is to encourage risk-taking in the exploration for new oil. From that point of view, giving the depletion benefits to the passive landowner who takes no risk whatever in allowing someone else to drill on his land is an utter waste of the taxpayers' money.

Or take the investment tax credit* and the so-called "DISC,"† which were, respectively, supposed to bring about *increases* in machinery investment and *increases* in exports. Now, to grant

---

* See pp. 214–219.
† See pp. 271–274.

those multi-billion-dollar tax subsidies, as Congress did, to companies that simply invest as usual, or export as usual—that is, companies that do nothing they wouldn't have done anyway—is once again a total waste of the taxpayers' money.

A. (*By Secretary of Commerce*) Let me illustrate that, if I may. As a businessman, when I wanted to give my salesmen an incentive to do better, I gave them a bonus based on their *increases* in sales over last year. I wouldn't have dreamed of giving them a bonus just for doing the same as last year's performance. I would have been throwing my money away.

Yet that's just what Congress did when it enacted those billions of "tax spending" for business, in the investment tax credit and the DISC. It gave the "tax bonuses" to companies for doing no more in the way of plant investment or exports than they had done before and would have done anyway. I call that throwing away taxpayers' money. Congress should have limited the tax benefits to *increases* in plant investment and *increases* in exports.

Q. (*To Secretary of Commerce*) Mr. Secretary, this is another question directed to you as a businessman: don't these tax subsidies or "tax expenditures" represent government intervention—or government "meddling"—in the free enterprise system? Doesn't it violate the "laissez-faire" philosophy that most businessmen favor?

A. You have a good point there. When you come to look on the tax preferences as tax subsidies or "tax expenditures," they don't square with the Free Enterprise philosophy—or at any rate with the Free Enterprise *rhetoric*.

For instance, I remember what John Connally told Congress in 1971 when he was Secretary of the Treasury and was explaining President Nixon's "New Economic Policy." He said it involved a "fiscal policy which places maximum reliance on our free enterprise economy, and less reliance on expanding the already-large government sector." At the same time, though, Mr. Connally and President Nixon were urging the Congress to enact literally billions in new government subsidies to business. Not *direct* subsidies, mind you. That would have been "expanding the already-large government sector" in an obvious way. No, these were hidden subsidies—tax subsidies: the investment tax credit and the so-called "ADR."* Of course, those tax provisions were using the

_____
* See pp. 219–227.

taxpayers' dollars just as much as a direct subsidy, but the public doesn't understand that. So the tax subsidies are a lot easier to sell.

Let me read you a newspaper editorial that seriously questions using the tax system for creating "incentives." "It soon gets the entire tax structure out of kilter, creating loopholes for some taxpayers, and transferring to others the burden that has been lifted from the fortunate. The result is a sense of unfairness and ill will among taxpayers, which is the first step toward wide-scale tax evasion."

Q. Where does that come from—some left-wing newspaper?

A. I hardly think the *Wall Street Journal* qualifies as a "leftwing" publication. Let me read you what else the *Journal* said: "There is a serious flaw in the idea that subsidizing industry somehow makes it more competitive. A subsidy supplies the means to become less, not more competitive. . . ."

Q. Doesn't a subsidy sometimes entice people into ventures that make no economic sense? For instance, for a while there were terrific tax incentives to build office buildings, and I've read articles about office space going begging in New York as the result of overbuilding.

A. There's no doubt that the tax incentives played some part in bringing about the oversupply of office space—although when you bring up that argument with the real-estate people, they downplay the importance of the tax factor. They insist it's "just one of a large number of considerations" that determine whether or not a building is built.

A. (*By the President's Budget Director*) Yes, I know they say that, but then if you say to them, "Well, if the tax incentives are so unimportant, surely it won't make much difference if we close the loophole and do away with the tax advantage," all of a sudden the tune changes and you get a parade of industry people wailing to Congress that if you take away the tax favors, their entire industry will collapse in a heap, building will come to a sudden halt, there will be massive unemployment, and so forth and so on.

Another trouble with tax subsidies is that once Congress has created one, it's almost impossible to put a fence around it and limit its use to the purpose for which it was intended.

Q. What's an example of that?

A. For instance the DISC tax provision we've been talking about. As I just said, the supposed purpose of that was to increase

U.S. exports—but I heard of a clever New York tax lawyer who was talking about a scheme whereby the head of a family-owned business could use the DISC provision to avoid estate and gift taxes. I'm sure Congress never intended the DISC to be used that way, but now that the provision is in the law, there is no way to prevent that kind of "spillover"—again, at the taxpayers' expense.

You see, with tax subsidies, the people who benefit from them essentially write their own ticket, and sometimes that results in a crazy distortion of priorities in the "spending" of the taxpayers' money. For instance, in 1968, the Treasury estimated that three-quarters of a billion dollars a year was being "spent" in tax favors for real-estate construction of various kinds. And where were all those hundreds of millions being spent? Two-thirds—that's a half-billion dollars a year—was going into motels, office buildings, shopping centers and other commercial projects. And only one-tenth that much—just $50 million a year—was going into low-rent housing. One hundred million was spent for luxury apartments. Only half that much was being spent for low-income housing. That's just a crazy way to spend the taxpayers' money. Anyone who has been through the slums and ghettos of the big city knows that the top priority need isn't for more motels and more shopping centers. And commercial projects like that certainly don't need government subsidies, while low-rent housing can't be built without them.

Now, I realize that since the Treasury study was made, the tax law has been changed so as to place comparatively more emphasis on low-rent housing. But think of the years of huge spending on motels and luxury apartments before the law was changed. And don't forget—the luxury high rises are *still* being built with hidden "tax help" from the taxpayers.*

Q. You mentioned the new emphasis in the tax law supporting low-rent housing. Isn't it true that these new provisions have resulted in more low- and middle-income houses being built?

A. Yes, there has been an increase. I'm not arguing that the tax subsidy had no effect whatever. But *where* were most of those homes built? The answer is that only about one-fourth of them were built in the inner city, where the most crucial need is. Nearly two-thirds of them were built in the fringe areas, where the risks

---

* See the description of the Ocean Towers apartments (pp. 179–182) complete with "swimming pool, gymnasium and sauna and steam rooms."

to the investors are less and the land is cheaper. But that isn't where the poor people are, and it usually isn't near where the factories and the jobs are. As one housing expert put it, "The guy who makes the most money is the guy who builds the projects where they don't need them anyhow."

Which leads back to a question we were talking about earlier: namely, who benefits from the taxpayers' dollars? Is it the poor people who need the housing? Evidently not, for most of the housing is being built in the wrong location for them. So who does benefit? The top-bracket investors, who can get after-tax returns of as high as 35 percent on their money.* And the builder-developers, who sometimes make as much as 400 percent profit—with as little as 10 percent cash outlay and with the government guaranteeing the other 90 percent.

Q. What kind of subsidy would be better as far as reaching the people who really need it?

A. I'd much rather take the same number of dollars that are now going into that tax subsidy and put them into rent supplements for poor and middle-income families—that is, into money that could be used to supplement what they can afford to pay, so that they could rent good housing, and, with the supplement, the building's owners would receive a decent return on their investment. That way, both the owner and the tenants would benefit.

Incidentally, there does exist a rent-supplement program, but because that's a direct-spending program, Congress has been consistently niggardly about voting the money. In 1968, for instance, just before he left office, President Johnson recommended $100 million for rent subsidies. President Nixon, when he came in, cut that back to $50 million; and Congress cut it again, to just $23 million. At the same time, though, for years, Congress had silently been approving more than thirty times that much—about three-fourths of a billion dollars—in tax subsidies for motels and office buildings and luxury apartments—with most of the benefits, of course, going to rich "tax shelter" seekers.

Which brings me to the next point: no one really knows exactly how much that subsidy to the "shelter" seekers is costing, because it's not the government or the Congress who decides or controls how much is being "spent," or *how* it's spent. That's decided by the "tax shelter" seekers. The only limit is how much

* See p. 167.

money they have and are willing to put into "tax shelters." Congress in effect says, "Come one, come all. Collect your 'welfare' tax right here. No limit of one to a customer. Dip in. Write your own ticket."

Q. (*To Treasury official*) I understand there's been a lot of shoddy building in the subsidized projects. There was an Associated Press series on them that said, "The Government's booming billion-dollar apartment building programs are on their way to producing new slums in the inner city." Since the Treasury Department is in effect subsidizing a lot of that housing, what is your department doing to make sure the housing is of decent quality?

A. (*By Treasury official*) That's one of the dilemmas we face with these tax subsidies. We at the Treasury Department are not housing experts, yet we do, as you say, help subsidize housing. We're not antipollution experts, yet Congress has put us in the business of granting subsidies in that area, too, to the tune of $120 million a year.* Really, to be properly supervised, the housing subsidies belong in the Department of Housing and Urban Development, and the antipollution subsidies should be under the Environmental Protection Agency or some other agency that has the experts.

Q. (*To the President's Budget Director*) Is it your position, sir, that *none* of these tax subsidies does any good—that the entire $77 billion of so-called "tax expenditures" is a waste of the taxpayers' money?

A. (*By the Budget Director*) No, that's not what I'm trying to say. Let me put it this way.

I'm trying to make two essential points. The first is that to the extent government assistance or government subsidies are needed, those ought to come through *direct* payments, recommended each year by the President and directly appropriated each year by the Congress. In my view we ought *not* use the tax system for subsidies and incentives. Why? For all the reasons you've heard here this morning:

—because tax subsidies aren't reviewed by Congress every year, as direct subsidies are;

—because they continue in existence as long as Congress fails

---

* The 1969 Tax Act provided rapid tax write-offs for antipollution facilities.

to act, whereas direct subsidies die if Congress fails, each year, to appropriate the money;

—because they are often inefficient, poorly aimed at their supposed target, and therefore waste the taxpayers' money;

—because they provide upside-down subsidies—large "tax welfare" payments for the rich and pittances for the poor—which means they often provide generous help to people who don't need it, while failing to give *any* help to people who are really in need;

—because not only are they "hidden" spending programs that neither the public nor the Congress watches over, but they are also open-ended spending programs over which Congress has very little control.

The second point is that until the day we *do* eliminate the loopholes, all the tax subsidies or "tax expenditures" ought to be included, just like the direct spending programs, in the annual budget of the Government of the United States—so that the public will have an honest picture of how their tax dollars are being spent. To show you what a "tax expenditure" budget looks like, I've prepared one, and it's available for any of you who want to look at it.*

That's the nub of what we've been talking about here this morning: that these "tax expenditures" are no different from direct spending. The trouble is that in all the talk about "high government spending" and "big deficits," the public's eye has been directed toward just part of the target. When an "economy wave" hits, it's the spending bills, not the tax bills, that suffer Presidential vetoes (like President Nixon's vetoing bills for day-care centers and hospitals and medical schools and the like because they cost too much and were too inflationary). It's the food-stamp and rent-supplement programs that fall victim to the Congressional budget-cutting knives, not the billions of "tax welfare" dollars that silently leak out of the Treasury to the wealthy "shelter" seekers and the large corporations. As Professor Stanley Surrey has said, these tax-spending programs come to have a life of their own, largely because the price tags are tucked inside the merchandise, where they can't readily be seen. But it's time the public realized that tax spending is just as costly, just as much of a subsidy, just as much government "meddling" and intervention in the free enterprise system as the direct-spending programs. If the public came

---

* The illustrative budget appears on pp. 155–158.

to realize this fully and insisted that Congress look upon tax spending with the same pinchpenny eye that the direct-spending programs now receive, the taxpayers' dollars would be far better spent, and the country would be far better off.

THE PRESS: Thank you, gentlemen.

(And thus ended the longest press conference in Washington history.)

Illustrative Tax Expenditure Budget
(For Year Ending June 30, 1971)

	Millions
National defense:	
Exclusion of benefits and allowances to Armed Forces personnel	$500
International affairs and finance:	
Exemption for certain income earned abroad by U.S. citizens	40
Western Hemisphere trade corporations	50
Exclusion of gross-up on dividends of less-developed country corporations	55
Exclusion of controlled foreign subsidiaries	165
Exclusion of income earned in U.S. possessions	90
Partial exemption of export income (DISC)	ª 170
Total	570
Agriculture and rural development:	
Farming: Expensing and capital gains treatment	820
Timber: Capital gains treatment for certain income	130
Total	950
Natural resources:	
Expensing of exploration and development costs	325
Excess of percentage over cost depletion	980
Capital gains treatment of royalties on coal and iron ore	5
5-year amortization of pollution control facilities in pre-1969 plants	ª 120
5-year amortization of coal mine safety equipment	ª 1
Total	1,431

Millions

Commerce and transportation:
Investment credit	ª 3,600
Excess depreciation on buildings (other than rental housing)	500
Dividend exclusion	280
Capital gains: Corporation (other than agriculture and natural resources)	425
Excess bad debt reserves of financial institutions	380
Exemption of credit unions	40
Deductibility of interest on consumer credit	1,700
Expensing of research and development expenditures	540
$25,000 surtax exemption	2,000
Deferral of tax on shipping companies	10
5-year amortization of railroad rolling stock	105
Class lives for depreciation—20 percent reduction	ª 2,400
Total	11,980

Community development and housing:
Deductibility of interest on mortgages on owner-occupied homes	2,800
Deductibility of property taxes on owner occupied homes	2,000
Excess depreciation on rental housing	255
5-year amortization of housing rehabilitation expenditures	ª 330
Deferral of capital gain on sale to occupants of certain low-income housing	(¹)
Total	6,285

Income security:
Disability insurance benefits	130
Provisions relating to aged, blind, and disabled:	
Combined cost for additional exemption for aged, retirement income credit, and exclusions of social security payments	2,950
Additional exemption for blind	10
"Sick pay" exclusion	105
Exclusion of unemployment insurance benefits	400
Exclusion of workmen's compensation benefits	210
Exclusion of public assistance benefits	50
Treatment of pension plans:	
Plans for employees	3,075
Plans for self-employed persons	175

Millions

Income security—Continued
    Exclusion of other employee benefits:

Premiums on group term life insurance	440
Deductibility of accident and death benefits	25
Privately financed supplementary unemployment benefits	20
Meals and lodging	170
Exclusion of interest on life insurance savings	1,050
Deductibility of charitable contributions (other than education)	3,550
Deductibility of child and dependent care and household expenses	ª 145
Deductibility of casualty losses	80
Standard deduction	3,000
Total	15,585

Health:

Deductibility of medical expenses	1,700
Exclusion of medical insurance premiums and medical care	1,450
Total	3,150

Education and manpower:

Additional personal exemption for students	500
Deductibility of contributions to educational institutions	200
Exclusion of scholarships and fellowships	60
5-year amortization of employer child care and on-the-job training facilities	(¹)
Credit for employment of public assistance recipients under WIN (Work Incentive) Program	ª 25
Total	785

Veterans benefits and services:

Exclusion of certain benefits	650

Aid to State and local governments:

Exemption of interest on State and local debt	2,300
Deductibility of nonbusiness State and local taxes (other than on owner-occupied homes)	5,600
Total	7,900

Millions

Election process:
Credit and deduction for political contributions   [a] 90

The 1968 Treasury tables* contained the following:
Capital gains—Individual income tax: Special provisions
(increase in basis at death: exclusion of one-half of long-
term gains: maximum tax rates of 25 percent on long-
term gains)   5,500–8,500

[1] Not available.
([a]) The estimates marked with ([a]) are for fiscal years other than 1971.
* This refers to the first "tax expenditure" budget developed by the Treasury Department and included in the 1968 Annual Report of the Secretary of the Treasury.

8

A Dollar Delayed
Can Be
Many Dollars Saved

IF YOU FEEL LIKE pampering yourself, indulge the following Walter Mitty fantasy:

There's a knock on the door. You open it, to find a neatly suited, crew-cut gentleman proffering for your examination a leathered-encased, clearly official identification:

INTERNAL REVENUE SERVICE

You are frightened. What have you done? How much is it going to cost you? But, remembering you are Walter Mitty, you decide to play it cool.

A good decision. For this man's mission is quite extraordinary. Not at all what you expected.

"Good morning, sir. Name is Tedley. Internal Revenue. I've come to tell you about the availability of one of our lesser-known services: our interest-free loan offer.

"It's really quite unique, we think. You determine the size of the loan you'd like to take out. No need to consult us—just decide what you need, and it's yours. You decide when you want it—and it's immediately available, no questions asked. And, as I say, there's no interest charge at all.

Even in your Walter Mitty role, you can't help showing surprise. Internal Revenue offering *you* something—and for nothing?

159

What's the gag? (But your speculations are interrupted as Tedley continues.)

If, at any time, you'd like to increase *the amount of your loan, why that's perfectly all right with us, too.*

"But the best feature of all—I'm sure you'll agree—is that it's up to you when *you pay back the loan*—or even whether *you pay it back. Many of our clients have kept their loans outstanding for years, without paying back a penny of them. We're really very tolerant about it.*

"In fact, under certain circumstances, we are perfectly willing to transform your load into an outright gift—at no extra cost to you, of course.

"Now, Mr. Mitty, how much of an interest-free loan would appeal to you—shall we start with $100,000? Or would you like to make it a million? Remember, you can write your own ticket."

At this point, your earlier doubts are magnified. You fix Tedley with your most Mittyish gimlet-eyed stare. What's his game? He *seems* on the level. Yet he doesn't *talk* like a Revenue agent. You ask to see his identification again. It's OK; he really *is* from Internal Revenue. But still—what's he up to, offering interest-free loans for any amount, any length of time? There must be *something* fishy about the deal. . . .

CHANCES ARE you've never had such a visit from an Internal Revenue agent; chances are, too, that you never will.

Nonetheless, the service that the imaginary Mr. Tedley was offering *is* available to you and every other taxpayer, and *is* used regularly, and in large amounts, by certain kinds of taxpayers. *Rich* taxpayers. And corporations.

Only it isn't called an "interest-free loan." It's called "tax deferral." All you have to do to avail yourself of the service is contrive to *postpone* a tax you owe Uncle Sam.* It's as simple as that.

To illustrate: suppose General Motors is able, one way or another, to defer for a year a million dollars in taxes that would otherwise be due right away. The result is that during the year's

---

* I am not talking about postponement by means of late payment or a dispute with IRS about the amount of tax due. Delays of that kind are not interest-free; they cost you 6 percent interest.

delay, GM, not Uncle Sam, has the use of that million dollars. And since large corporations like GM expect a return of at least 10 to 12 percent on leftover cash of that sort,* the mere one-year *delay* of paying that million-dollar tax is worth $100,000 to $120,000, cash in hand, to America's largest corporation. If GM can manage to postpone the million-dollar tax payment for *five* years, the delay (assuming a 10 percent rate of return) is worth $611,000. A *ten*-year deferral carries a total value of $1,594,000. (At a 12 percent return, which is more likely, the deferrals are considerably more valuable: $762,000 for the five-year delay, and $2,106,000 for the ten-year postponement.)

So Agent Tedley's offer could hardly be considered niggardly.

HOW CAN SUCH LUCRATIVE tax deferrals be arranged?

Sometimes it requires artificial contrivances, such as the one that bears the intriguing name "Mexican vegetable roll-over." Although that sounds like a combination platter in a Latin-style restaurant, it is in fact a device (described more fully on page 196) for investing in a Mexican vegetable farm venture in such a way as to get large and immediate tax deductions that shields this year's income from taxation and postpones payment of the tax on that income until at least next year.†

At times, Congress explicitly and intentionally legislates a tax deferral—as in the case of the domestic international sales corporations (the DISC's described on pages 270–274). That law enables exporting corporations that set up DISC's to defer the tax on half of their export profits.

But the explicit, publicly avowed tax deferral is more the exception than the rule. More often, IRS's special interest-free loan offer is an unacknowledged, built-in feature of the law, widely available to rich "shelter"-seeking taxpayers without the special convolutions of a "Mexican vegetable roll-over." It is, for example, not only available to, but abundantly used by, every investor in an

---

* Some corporations are said to be dissatisfied if they fail to get as much as an 18 or 20 percent return.

† Such a device is well-suited to a high-salaried individual who finds himself, toward year's end, with more income or less "tax shelter" than he had expected, and who needs to buy some time until next year, when his income might be lower or when, given some time, he might be able to generate a North-of-the-border "tax shelter."

apartment house venture where the law still permits "accelerated depreciation" deductions* (see pages 172–175). For a 70 percent taxpayer owning a $3 million apartment building, the tax saving (i.e., the interest-free government loan) arising solely from the "acceleration" comes to $52,500 in the first year alone. If the lucky owner is permitted to keep that loan for ten years—which he could easily expect to do—that would represent a free gift from Uncle Sam (i.e., from all the other taxpayers) valued at $61,000.

THERE ARE A FEW ASPECTS of Agent Tedley's magnanimous offer to Walter Mitty that deserve further explanation.

For example, Tedley generously said that Internal Revenue would go along with whatever *amount* Mitty might decide he wanted to borrow, interest-free. How come?

Well, when any American corporation takes the legally approved "accelerated depreciation" deductions in excess of the true wearing-out pattern of its plant and equipment, it gets the same kind of interest-free loan the apartment house investor gets. And of course it is General Motors or ITT or IBM, and not Internal Revenue, that determines the level of its outlays (and deductions) for plant and equipment. Hence each company, not IRS, determines the size of its interest-free loan. If, say, GM spends $1 billion rather than $500 million on a new plant, that represents a unilateral decision on GM's part to take out twice as large an IRS loan; and IRS has no choice but to go along.

What's more, GM or ITT can, without enormous difficulty, arrange it so that its interest-free loan *never* has to be repaid. All the company has to do is to maintain a constant level of plant-and-equipment investment. If it does that, just at the time the faster-than-average deductions on Equipment Batch A turn into slower-than-average deductions (i.e., just at the time when the "loan" begins to come due), the company buys Equipment Batch B and puts *it* into service with the tax-saving faster-than-average deductions that go with its early years. It's very much like a revolving credit account: as soon as one loan is repaid, the company takes out a new loan, and the bank never gets its original money back.

---

* Most experts believe that these "accelerated" deductions are far in excess of the *real* wearing out that takes place, especially in the early years of a building's life, and it is the excess that results, in effect, in a deferral of tax.

And any time the company elects to *increase* the level of its plant and equipment outlays, it automatically increases the amount of its interest-free loans outstanding, again with IRS's helpless assent.

General Motors' ability to defer indefinitely the repayment of its accelerated-depreciation loan, simply by maintaining a constant rate of equipment replacement, explains Agent Tedley's big-hearted offer to transform IRS's loans into outright gifts; obviously, the longer the loan repayment can be postponed, the greater the value of enjoying the money interest-free. If General Motors can delay the payment of a million-dollar tax for a little over seven years, assuming a conservative 10 percent return, the value to GM of the deferral itself is a million dollars, and what started out as a million-dollar loan has, in effect, been transformed into a million-dollar outright gift.

T H E   M O R A L of this story is simple: *when* you pay can be as important as *how much* you pay.

This is a scantly understood fact. For example, when you read Chapter 9, it may, at first blush, seem a mere technicality that the high-salaried city slickers who invest in cattle herds and pistachio groves are permitted to horn in on farmers' cash-accounting methods rather than having to abide by the "accrual-accounting" system demanded for their other business ventures. But this "technicality" lies at the heart of the huge tax savings—mainly from tax *deferrals*—enjoyed by those "gentlemen farmers" (see pages 187–199).

Typical of the pooh-poohing of tax deferrals is the Nixon Administration's efforts to shrug off the criticism that its DISC proposal (pages 270–274) would mean heavy revenue losses to the U.S. Treasury. Nonsense, said the Treasury Department; in the long run, the DISC won't save anybody any taxes. It's just a tax deferral, not a tax forgiveness.*

You now know enough, from the above discussion, to label that kind of argument as pure baloney. The Treasury was being far more honest when one of its officials, in talking to a group of lawyers and accountants, said, "I need not tell this group that tax deferral is the name of the game."

And a lucrative game it is.

---

* Actually, for any corporation with a constant volume of export business, the DISC means a *permanent* deferral of tax.

Running
for Shelter

> shel·ter \'sheltə(r)\ *n* . . . something that covers or affords protection . . . something that provides refuge or defense (as from . . . danger, or annoyance). . . .
>
> —Webster's Third New
> International Dictionary (unabridged)

For a highly select group of Americans—those with huge incomes—the word "shelter" is frequently preceded by another word: "tax."

These "tax shelters" do precisely what the dictionary says: they afford "protection . . . refuge or defense" from the "danger, or annoyance" of having to pay tax (the full tax, at any rate) on the substantial incomes enjoyed by the "shelter"-seeking wealthy.

Often the "shelter" comes in a quite expectable form: an office building or apartment house. But other "shelters" are not so conventional. One can, for example, imagine a high-bracket taxpayer sheltered, somewhat after the manner of Romulus and Remus, under the udder of a cow or even beneath a bull. Quite literally—cows and bulls. Or race horses. Or they might seek refuge in the shade of a pistachio grove.

If those unorthodox modes of "shelter" sound bizarre, don't get the idea they are jokes. They are deadly serious, high-dollar affairs that can be enormously effective tax savers for the rich and super-rich. In general, the "shelters" achieve this happy result by providing the wealthy with enormous tax deductions that serve to reduce the "taxable income" figure they enter on their Form 1040. And, of course, the smaller the taxable income, the smaller the tax. If the deductions are sufficiently large and fall into the proper category, they can shrink "taxable income" to zero, which also reduces the tax to zero.*

That was precisely the result achieved by Mr. J, an actual taxpayer (or non-taxpayer) cited in a Treasury Department study. Mr. J, one year, enjoyed no less than $1,433,000 of income and yet reported to Internal Revenue, that year, that he *lost* $3,000.†

How did he manage such an apparently nonsensical result? Primarily with the aid of tax deductions of $864,000 from real-estate investments (plus the exclusion from taxation of half of his $1.2 million in capital gains, in the manner described on pages 98–99).

Another actual case cited in the same Treasury study concerned a Mr. K, whose total income was a mere $738,203. But he, too, contrived to pay none of it to Internal Revenue, principally because of what would appear to be a horrendous business judgment: he invested in a farm that lost $450,000 (according to what he told Internal Revenue). That colossal red-ink figure, wholly tax-deductible, shielded most of his income from taxation. (He, too, was able to exclude a large amount of capital gains—about a quarter of a million dollars—from his taxable income.) His tax saving: at least $300.000.‡

If you are baffled as to just how Messrs. J and K pulled off these tax-saving capers, be patient. The details will be revealed to you presently.

"Tax Shelters" in Real Estate

For those sufficiently endowed with financial wealth and resourceful tax advisers, the rewards that come from "tax-sheltered" investments are indeed enviable. If, for example, you are becoming restive about the modest 5 percent return on your little savings account, perhaps you would like to invest your money and get,

---

* The "minimum tax" enacted in 1969 (see pp. 67–73) made it more difficult than it had been to achieve zero taxable income via "tax shelters," but, as you have read, it can still be done, especially with oil "shelters."

† Of course, that meant he paid not a penny of tax on his nearly million and a half of income, and saved roughly half a million in taxes.

‡ Both of these tax-avoiding feats were accomplished before the enactment of the Tax Reform Act of 1969, which cut back somewhat on the "tax sheltering" capabilities of real-estate and farm investments. But, as you will see, there are still manifold "shelter" possibilities in both fields.

say, a 35 percent return. Sound alluring? It's no pipe dream. That's the actual rate of return offered on a real-life apartment house venture near Washington, D.C. But there's one hitch: that super-duper rate of return *includes* the tax savings you get from the venture; and to get a 35 percent rate of return, you have to be in the 60 percent tax bracket (i.e., have taxable unearned income* of at least $88,000 a year). If you are merely in the 50 percent bracket, your rate of return drops to a paltry 24 percent (still far from disgraceful). Ironically, if you are a more typical person in, say, the 19 percent bracket (taxable income, $4,000–$8,000), this particular investment would not be profitable, since your tax saving, at that low bracket, would just equal the cash you had to put into the venture. But don't fret excessively: that deal wouldn't be for you—you can't get in for less than $58,500, cold hard cash.

To whet your appetite (and perhaps your envy) just a bit more, you should know that some of the "shelter" deals allow a top-bracket investor to play the profit game entirely with *other people's* dollars (*your* dollars, in fact). That is, the tax savings (the amount the rest of the taxpayers—including you—put into the deal) are so large and so immediate that the investor, in effect, risks no dollars of his own in the venture. No, it's even more amazing than that: he actually realizes an after-tax *profit,* wholly at your expense, without risking a dime of his own. The details of just such a miraculous venture are spelled out on pages 167–169, but, once again, don't get your hopes up about participating in such Midas-like deals: you don't get to play in that particular poker game unless you can put up a whale of a lot of cash "front money"—$114,000 in one particular "shelter" deal. (I call it "front money" because the investor recoups his cash outlay within a year, in the form of tax savings† that equal or exceed the initial cash outlay.)

In the above-mentioned "shelter" venture involving an apartment development in a suburb of Washington, D.C., the prospectus (a document that describes the venture for would-be investors)

---

* Unearned income (such as from corporate dividends) is not subject to the top 50 percent rate that applies to earned (i.e., salary) income.

† These tax savings are dependent on the investor's having income at least equal to the depreciation deductions, i.e., income that can be offset, or "sheltered," by the deductions. Throughout this discussion, it is assumed that the investors do have that much income so that they can take full advantage of their deductions.

invites a 70 percent taxpayer to invest $114,000, but advises that his cash return over fifteen years will amount to only $78,750. That would indicate a cash *loss* of $35,250—and yet the prospectus promises him an after-tax *profit* of $120,875.

A 60 percent taxpayer who invests in another apartment project in western Massachusetts puts $58,500 into the venture and extracts cash of only $48,516, yet nonetheless is able to realize an after-tax profit of $160,456—*an annual return on his money of nearly 35 percent.*

All of this may sound odd, since in the realm of real estate, with which we will begin our scrutiny of "tax shelters," profits are somehow losses and losses highly profitable. Yet, illogical as they may sound, the ventures just mentioned are real-life examples.

How? Why?

A hypothetical flight of fancy into the future will suggest the How.

AT 7:07 A.M. of April 2, 1974, ground was broken and construction began on the new Providential Apartments. A year and a half later the building was finished and ready for occupancy, most of its apartments already rented.

The Providential Apartments were aptly named, for in the ensuing years they were to bring sparkling financial rewards for a succession of owner-investors.

The first was Allan Welloff, a polo-playing heir of the Welloff fortune, whose prodigious income from corporate dividends threw him into the 70 percent tax bracket.

For a person in that lofty bracket, Providential was an ideal investment, from many points of view. Even though it would not bring any cash return for the first five years of its existence, it would yield something equally precious: immediate and extremely rewarding tax deductions—mainly for depreciation (the supposed wearing out of the buildings). Come tax time, the fortunate Welloff could use these deductions to cancel out large portions of his dividend income, with the result that he could, in effect, enjoy that income tax-free.

In fact, so large were those deductions and the tax savings therefrom that, from the very first year of the project to the last, his tax savings always exceeded his cash investment in the Providential Apartments. As a result, he never, at any time, had a dollar of his own at risk in the structure.* In that sense, all of his profits sprang, in effect, from an investment of funds magnanimously provided him by all of the other taxpayers of the United States. Here's the way the first four years of the Providential project worked out for lucky Allan Welloff (called "W" for short):†

Year	W puts in:	W saves in taxes (i.e., all other tax-payers put in):	W's net input	W's "tax profit" This year	Total
1	$150,000	$182,582	0	$32,582	$32,582
2	$335,000	$476,640	0	$141,640	$174,222
3	$110,000	$943,880	0	$833,880	$1,008,100
4	$85,000	$1,003,840	0	$918,840	$1,926,940

Even though that profit of nearly $2 million was short-lived (as you'll see in a moment), no matter how you slice it that's a pretty fair return, even if temporary, on a zero net investment.

In the fifth year, the venture called upon Mr. Welloff to put in a very large bundle of money—$1,600,000 to be exact—although, when that amount was reduced by his fifth-year tax savings, his net input for the year was $1,285,780. But remember, at the end of the fourth year he was ahead of the game by nearly $2 million, so that even after his very large fifth-year input, he enjoyed an after-tax profit of $640,940‡—still not a bad return considering that he had not jeopardized a penny of his own and that all the net investment was provided by the rest of the U.S. taxpayers.

Earning a profit like that was an especially neat trick considering the fact that during each of those first four years, the Providential Apartments project didn't pay a penny of cash profit to Mr. Welloff. It all gets to seem like Alice in Wonderland when you look at it this way:

---

* Except during the comparatively brief interval between his cash outlays to the venture and the filing of his next tax return, at which time he realized a tax saving of more than his cash outlay and thus, in effect, has more than recouped his investment.

† The figures in this table are actual, taken from the prospectus for the apartment project in the suburbs of Washington, D.C., discussed on pp. 166–167.

‡ That is, the accumulated "profit" of $1,926,940 he had built up after the fourth year minus his fifth-year net input of $1,285,780.

Year	Cash Input by W	Cash Outflow to W	Apparent Result	Actual After-Tax Result
1	$150,000	0	$150,000 loss	$32,582 *profit*
2	$335,000	0	$335,000 loss	$141,640 *profit*

Et cetera, et cetera, ad nauseam—clearly not Mr. Welloff's nauseam, but that of you and the rest of the U.S. taxpayers who put up all the money yet then suffer only losses, reaping no profits from the venture. (A foreign visitor, unaware that you and the rest are not consulted about putting your dollars into such ventures, might conclude that you are not very prudent with your money. You, on the other hand, might reach the simpler conclusion that you and your fellow taxpayers are being played for suckers.)

The Saga of the Providential Apartments continues. The year is now 1989. Although the Providential project has just celebrated its fourteenth birthday, Allan Welloff has yet to risk the first dollar of his own money in the project. But for Welloff the Providential Apartments have lost their tax allure: the lucrative tax deductions that once went with the project have long since expired, and, rather than *saving* him taxes, the project has actually been causing Mr. Welloff to *pay* some taxes. Clearly that will never do; it is time to dispose of this annoyance.

Fortunately, at this very moment, he receives an important caller: an agent representing Consolidated Tax Shelters, Inc., a syndicate of top-bracket taxpayers who share Mr. Welloff's antipathy to paying taxes and are on the lookout for some deductions. By this time, despite the large wear-and-tear deductions that Allan Welloff has taken—which have substantially reduced the "book value" (i.e., the "worth" of the building, as shown on his accounting books)—the agent, miraculously enough, is offering to pay Welloff precisely what the building cost in the first instance.

Welloff quickly accepts the offer. Not only will the cash enable him to go out and buy a new building on which he can begin the depreciation-deduction cycle anew; he will also come out with a handsome tax profit on the sale. The tax deductions he had taken on the Providential Apartments had saved him 70 cents of every deducted dollar; but the capital gains tax he'll have to pay on his "book profit" (the excess of the purchase price over "book value") will be only 25 or 35 cents on the dollar.* With a 70 cent saving and only a 25 or 35 cent pay-back, the transaction just had to be a winner.

Allan Welloff is pleased. So are the new buyers, Consolidated Tax Shelters, Inc., whose top-bracket investors will be able to grasp the depreciation wheel and give it another spin—not based on the "book value" (original cost minus all the Welloff wear-and-tear deductions) but on the new purchase price of the building. And since Consolidated paid just what the building cost initially, it's as if the building hadn't undergone any wear and tear at all.† It's enough to make a person question whether all those wear-and-tear deductions that Allan Welloff took were really justified.

Everyone has profited—except the silent partners in these various transactions: you and the other taxpayers who were footing most of the bill. But all of you were not present to protest, and thus were destined to continue being not only silent but involuntary partners in real estate.

IT IS TIME, now, to inquire how the Allen Welloffs of this world come by these immense tax deductions and the savings that flow therefrom. These resulted primarily from the tax deductions the law permits for the wearing out, or "depreciation," of buildings like the Providential Apartments.‡

These depreciation deductions are easily understandable when applied, say, to factory machinery. If, for example, a widget-making machine will last only ten years before it is worn out or

---

* The tax on the first $50,000 of capital gains each year is only 25 percent, rather than 35 percent. So if, in any venture, the sale price can be divided up among several partners, or stretched out over a period of years, so as to keep each person's (or each year's capital gains profit below the $50,000 mark, the 25 percent rate will apply.

† In this respect, buildings receive far more favorable tax treatment than machinery and equipment. When A sells a machine to B for more than its depreciated or "book" value, that is regarded as an automatic sign that A took more depreciation deductions than were warranted, and, at the time of sale, A is required, in effect, to pay back the tax advantages gained from the unwarranted deductions. When a *building* is sold, such a requirement is, at most, only partially imposed, and under certain circumstances (e.g., when all the depreciation on a building has been of the "straight-line," or even-rate variety) the requirement is waived entirely.

‡ In addition, there were substantial deductions for interest on both the temporary construction loan and the permanent mortgage.

obsolete and has to be replaced, then part of the cost of making each year's widgets is one-tenth the cost of the machine. And since, in our system, all true business costs are tax-deductible, such deductions are generally considered appropriate.

But buildings are, in some respects, different from factory equipment. For them, depreciation deductions are not always as manifestly plausible. For one thing, the hypothetical Amalgamated Widget Company has no choice but to buy a new widget-making machine when the old one wears out. Hence, the company both needs and uses its depreciation tax savings for that purpose. But in real estate, many, if not most investors do not contemplate paying out the money to replace the buildings they put up. More often, they do what Allan Welloff did: sell them to other buyers. Hence, in many or most cases, their tax savings are neither needed nor used in the same way as the machine owners'.

More important, however, is the question of whether the depreciation deductions are a *true* measure of the wear and tear on a building (and of its consequent loss of value). Presumably, if they were, no one would want to pay more than its "book value." Yet buildings are constantly being bought and sold for considerably more than their depreciated worth. This leads critics to conclude that the deductions do not, in fact, correspond with the building's *actual* loss in value. To the extent this is so, the deductions confer an unwarranted tax advantage on the building's owner.

Defenders of the depreciation deductions argue that the phenomenon of buildings selling for more than their depreciated worth doesn't mean that wear and tear wasn't taking place but, rather, reflects a rise in the value of the *land* on which the building rests (which, after years of population growth, may have become more scarce and sought-after). At least one student of the problem, Professor Charles Davenport of the University of California at Davis, says there is little evidence to support that view. He even argues that a properly built and maintained building may undergo little if any depreciation (*viz.*, the "buildings in Europe that have been used for a millennium"), although changes of circumstances or neighborhood may render them obsolete. But even if the realtors' argument regarding land-value rises is correct, it merely points up one of the weak spots in the whole real-estate depreciation system. Under the law, the new purchasers of a building

compute *their* depreciation deductions on the entire portion of the
purchase price that is allocated to the building, even though in
many, if not most real-estate transactions, a considerable part of
this in reality represents the value of land, which is *not* depreciable
under the tax laws.

In the case of new buildings, the potential discrepancy between
depreciation deductions and actual wear and tear is heightened
by the so-called "accelerated" or faster-than-average depreciation
permitted during the early years of a building's life. The simplest
method of depreciation is the so-called "straight-line" formula,
whereby a uniform deduction is taken during each year of the
building's "useful life." (For example, the deductions each year
for a $100,000 building with a twenty-five-year life would come
to $4,000.) But on *new* apartment buildings (like the Providential
Apartments), twice this amount is permitted in the first year (so
that the deduction would be $8,000 instead of $4,000). These
deductions decline each year until, *theoretically,* in the latter
years of a building's life, the lower-than-average deductions offset
the larger-than-average deductions of the earlier years, and everybody comes out even.

That's the *theory*. But, here again, if the owner is as shrewd
as Allan Welloff, and sells the building at the proper time, he
avoids the unpleasantness of those lower-than-average deduction
years. Not only does he end up ahead of the game, but the new
owner starts at the beginning again, with his own tax-saving
deductions. If he, in turn, sells at the proper time, he too will
escape some or all of the lower-than-average years, and the
Treasury (i.e., you and the rest of the taxpayers) never catches up.
And on each sale, provided the timing is right, the depreciation-
capital gain advantage (deduction savings up to 70 cents on the
dollar, pay-backs of only 25 cents or 35 cents) may come into
play.

Before 1969, the rules of the real-estate "shelter" game were
freer than they are today. In 1969, though, Congress put a few
crimps in the real-estate tax laws (but not enough to prevent the
Providential Apartments caper described above). For one thing,
the possibilities of magically alchemizing high-taxed regular income
into low-taxed capital gains, by means of fast depreciation and the
rapid owner-to-owner sale of buildings, have been curbed somewhat. Unless the owner of an apartment building holds on to it a

certain amount of time before selling,* he'll find that an uncomfortable portion of his profit above "book value" that stems from faster-than-average depreciation deductions will be taxed, not at the favorable capital gains rates, but at his regular income tax rates. (And if the proceeds of the sale flood in on him all in one year, that could push him into a lofty tax bracket.) On nonresidential property, profits from faster-than-average deductions are all denied the capital gains advantage, no matter how long the building is held. But two things are worth noting: first, even in those cases where *no* capital gains advantage is available, the depreciation deductions permit the happy investor to *postpone* large amounts of tax until such time as the building is sold—and, as described in Chapter 8, that is equivalent to bestowing an interest-free loan upon him, often in large amounts and often for several years. As Chapter 8 recounts, the value of that, especially for a high-bracket taxpayer, is hardly to be sneezed at. Secondly, the capital gains "alchemy" is still totally available on buildings that are held the requisite amount of time; that is, it is available to the investor with a lot of capital and a bit of patience.

Because of another 1969 cutback in the real-estate tax advantages, the fast-depreciation deductions are no longer as widely available as they once were. Buyers of *used* buildings (such as Consolidated Tax Shelters, Inc., in the above Saga) can no longer avail themselves of the zippy rapid write-off deductions they used to expect and receive.† The really lucrative double-rate write-offs are now denied office buildings and other nonresidential property (whose owners must content themselves with one and a half times the "straight-line," or even-rate deductions). But the double deductions are still available on new residential rental properties, and as of this writing, that is where the real-estate "tax shelter" "action" is.‡

---

* On government-assisted apartment buildings, most realtors regard the minimum profitable holding time as about seven years; on other residential rental properties, about twelve years is considered the practical minimum ownership span. For an explanation of why this is so, see Notes and Sources.

† Used apartment buildings having twenty years' remaining "useful life" may still be depreciated at one and one-fourth the "straight-line" rate, but that offers less than spectacular advantages.

‡ Especially is this true in government-assisted apartment projects, where, even though there is a legal ceiling on the investor's before-tax return, two significant tax advantages await the savvy investor who puts his money into such a project and later has a chance to sell his interest at a profit. For

In the past, Treasury Department experts have argued that any fast-depreciation formula—but especially the double-rate one—is the exact *opposite* of what is happening to the building. They contend that in reality, the value drops off more slowly in early years and faster later*—a pattern that conforms precisely with the assumption underlying the repayment patterns that mortgage bankers permit on real-estate loans (slow repayment in early years, faster in later years).

To emphasize the discrepancy between these repayment practices and depreciation deductions, the Treasury Department has cited this example, taken from the magazine *Architectural Forum*:†

Five-Year Depreciation Deductions	Five-Year Mortgage Repayment
(Loss of value in the eyes of the tax laws)	(Loss of value in the eyes of the bank)
$203,600	$70,900

One leading real-estate expert supported the Treasury contention when he told Congress that "it seems to be accepted in the real estate industry that depreciation is measured by mortgage amortization [loan repayment]—*the amount that you have to pay off on the mortgage, by and large, is considered about equivalent to current wastage* [wearing out] *of the asset.*" (Emphasis added.)

Real-estate spokesmen say this evidence should not be given undue weight, for the repayment patterns in the lending industry

one thing, the capital gains advantages are more readily obtainable here than in any other kind of real-estate investment. For another, even the capital gains tax can be postponed if the investor elects to plow his profits back into another government-aided project (which, once again, represents an interest-free loan, courtesy of Uncle Sam). Such government-aided projects generally expect investors to put up a minimum of $50,000 to $100,000. Thus, such ventures, and the special postponement advantage associated with them, are out of bounds to the small investor who may have enough spare dollars to buy a few shares of this or that stock, but who can't postpone the capital gains tax if he decides to cash in and reinvest in another kind of stock.

* To the extent that is really the case, even so-called "straight-line," or constant-rate depreciation yields early-year deductions that are faster than the reality warrants, and confers upon the real-estate investor an interest-free loan in the form of early-year taxes postponed until a later year.

† Involving a $900,000 building on a $100,000 site, with a forty-year life, depreciated on a double-rate basis.

are based on purely practical considerations, principally the popularity and success of the even-monthly-payment formula, which inherently involves low debt repayments in the early years. Nevertheless, Treasury experts have said, since sound lending institutions would not tolerate a discrepancy in values as large as that reflected in the *Architectural Forum* example, that example supports the point that fast depreciation is not an accurate measure of wear and tear and value loss in buildings.

THE TAX DEDUCTIONS involved in real estate carry a special advantage over the kind of deductions that most taxpayers use. When a paterfamilias of modest means puts some money into the church platter on Sunday or writes a check for his state income taxes, he becomes entitled to a deduction that lowers his taxable income and, hence, his tax.

But that mode of securing a tax deduction requires an outlay of hard cash (to church or to state in the above examples). This is an inconvenience which affluent real-estate investors are spared, for their depreciation deductions are mere "paper" deductions, calculated by an accountant to the limit the law allows and entered on the investor's tax return *with no outlay of his own cash*.* Thus, unlike the church contributor, who must part with the cash in order to get the deduction, the real-estate investor gets the deduction (and the tax saving)—and gets to keep the cash. For him, the cake and the eating of it go hand in hand.

IF YOU WILL LOOK BACK at the Saga of the Providential Apartments, you will note that Allan Welloff sank $2,280,000 into the project—and though each of his cash inputs was quickly offset by a tax savings, still $2,280,000 is a pretty piece of change to raise and tie up, even temporarily.

In fact, however, he need not have tied up anything like that amount, for the law permits him to borrow most of the necessary

---

* In theory, the "paper" deduction is supposed to make provision for the day the investors will have to lay out real cash to replace the building when it has given up the ghost. But they get the benefit of the "paper" deduction *whether or not they ever pay for the building's replacement*, and, as we have seen, for most real-estate investors, who sell their interest in the building long before its "useful life" is ended, that day of reckoning remains a theoretical one. As time goes on, however, the advantage of these "paper" deductions is reduced to the extent the investor repays the mortgage loan.

capital, risk only a tiny fraction out of his own pocket, *and still get the full depreciation deductions as if every penny of it had come from him personally.* That generous treatment is accorded him even if the bank merely looks to the apartment building as security on the loan—that is, *even if neither Mr. Welloff's cash nor his personal wealth and credit are "on the line."*

In fact, under certain circumstances (if the real-estate venture is owned by a legal partnership) the tax advantages may actually depend on Welloff and his partners' having *no* personal liability for the borrowed money.

Sometimes the cash input can be minuscule indeed. In one instance, a Mr. Manuel D. Mayerson contrived to purchase a $332,500 office building at the corner of 8th and Walnut streets, Cincinnati, with a cash down payment of just $10,000 with ninety-nine years to pay the balance of $322,500. When, despite his astoundingly low cash investment of just 3 percent of the total price, Mr. Mayerson and his conjugal joint-return filer, Rhoda, claimed depreciation deductions on the full $200,000 worth of the building,* Internal Revenue balked, claiming that this unusual transaction really amounted to a lease, not a purchase. But the Tax Court disagreed, ruling that the 3 percent tail could wag the 97 percent of the dog so as to produce 100 percent deductions.

While the 3 percent down payment arranged by Mr. Mayerson was unusually small, it is by no means unheard-of. You will run into it again soon in The Case of the Ocean Towers Apartments (page 179), a super-deluxe apartment project also financed with a 97 percent loan. In most real-estate deals today, investors in private real-estate ventures are easily able to borrow 75 percent of the total capital needed; where a government guarantee is involved, up to 90 to 95 percent borrowing is available.† Yet the investor's 5 to 25 percent cash input nets him the full 100 percent of deductions, even if the loan is guaranteed by the government.

---

* The remaining $132,500 was the value assigned to the land beneath the building, on which depreciation deductions may not be taken.

† Usually these government guarantees cover 90-plus percent of "cost," which includes the promoter's profit. In such a case, the promoter's profit accounts for more than the remaining 10 percent, and it is frequently possible to get a loan covering 100 percent of the cash outlay. In that case, the investor's risk is confined to what is called "sweat equity"—the very considerable time, trouble and worry that go into putting a major real-estate deal together.

But that is not the end of the story. For, in addition to the depreciation deductions on the building, the investors' huge borrowings generate still another tax deduction: their interest payments on the mortgage loan.

IN MANY a carefully chosen and well-run real-estate venture, where the location becomes increasingly valuable as time goes by, the value of the project or building soars—and that opens the way for the investors to rake in the profits, reaping most of the advantages of actually selling the building but without paying any of the taxes that would be imposed upon a sale at a profit

How is this done? Simply by going to a bank and refinancing the project—that is, getting a new loan, bigger than before, secured not on the personal credit of the investors but solely on the enhanced value of the real estate. Assume, for example, that a building originally costing $2 million has come to be valued by most appraisal experts at $3 million. If initially there was a $1.5 million loan on the building, the investors would probably have no trouble in obtaining a new loan of $2,250,000. The joyous investors could then receive the added three-quarters of a million entirely tax-free (since the proceeds of a loan are not taxable) and use it to buy caviar or yachts or whatever might strike their fancy—just as if they had *sold* the building at a profit. But the refinancing arrangement is better, for if they had *sold* the building they would have to pay some tax on the profit. As it is, not only do they postpone that tax, but their increased loan means increased interest payments which means increased tax deductions. Of course, a tax may be due if the time ever comes when the owners sell the building for a profit. Even so, they have enjoyed (a) the tax-free use of the loan proceeds; (b) the postponement of the tax for several years (i.e., an interest-free loan for that period); and (c) by stretching out their period of ownership, an increase in the capital gains tax advantage allowed under the law. There is very little reason for any of them to complain.

ON FEBRUARY 9, 1972, the temperature in Washington, D.C., was a frigid twenty degrees—not the ideal time to entice the residents of that city into thinking about buying vacation homes at Bethany Beach, on the Delaware oceanfront. Nonetheless, on that chilly day, the Washington *Post* carried a significant ad for

BEACH PLACES

FOR PROFESSIONAL MEN—TAX SHELTER—INFLATION HEDGE
FROM $20,950 plus lot

The advertiser, Resort Homes, Inc., apparently did not think that just anybody would be interested in buying a place "2 minutes from Bethany's incomparable surf"—for the ad was carefully placed on the *Post*'s business page, aimed (as the ad said) at "professional men" (read *"high-bracket taxpayers"*) who might be in the market for a "tax shelter" and a personal vacation home, all rolled into one.

Whence the "tax shelter?" Well, suppose Joseph Professional, a 50-percent-bracket young executive, were to buy one of these homes and use it for himself and his family for, say, just one month out of the year, offering the place for rent during the rest of the year. Twelve months in a year minus one month for family use leaves eleven months of "availability for rent." Under the tax laws, that means that eleven-twelfths of the expenses for maintenance and the like are tax-deductible. A far more important dividend, though, comes from the depreciation deductions. Mr. Professional can take no such write-offs on his Washington, D.C., residence, which he does not offer up for rent. But he is free to claim eleven-twelfths of the usual depreciation deductions on his Bethany home. (And if he buys it new, those deductions are of the delightful faster-than-average variety.) Note that even if Mr. Professional succeeds in finding tenants for only two out of the twelve months, the eleven-twelfths deductions remain his, for, technically speaking, the house is "available for rent" for the eleven months that the Professionals don't use it themselves.*

Result: the family has itself a brand-new vacation home—paid for, in considerable part, by the rest of the U.S. taxpayers.

NOW THAT YOU HAVE BECOME a minor expert in the ways in which high-bracket taxpayers invest *your* tax dollars

---

* Under the law and regulations, these vacation home advantages may be subject to challenge on the ground that the vacation home was not a venture entered into for profit. But promoters believe such ventures can be structured so as to fend off such challenges.

in real-estate ventures, you are in a position to examine with an informed and critical eye still another of the ventures you are unwittingly and involuntarily helping to finance: the Ocean Towers apartments, a "high-rise luxury apartment project . . . overlooking the Pacific Ocean" in Santa Monica, California. From the point of view of gracious living, the project will no doubt meet your approval: the investment prospectus describes it as "situated on a bluff over the beach, enjoy[ing] an unobstructured view of the ocean and coast." To exploit this view, its 317 apartments are located in two lofty sixteen-story towers. Each apartment has its own balcony, not to mention "carpeting, draperies, range with oven, dishwasher and refrigerator—all furnished courtesy of the management," plus, of course, full air conditioning.

In addition to those basic necessities, however, you are also helping to finance what are called "amenities available to tenants: a swimming pool, gymnasium and sauna and steam rooms," twenty-four-hour message and security service and valet parking— all available to tenants "at no additional charge, or at a small additional charge based on use."

Perhaps you are beginning to fantasy the pleasures of finding *yourself* ensconced in this paradise you are helping to finance. But before you become excessively enthralled with that thought, be advised that one-bedroom units begin at $470 a month, and for a three-bedroom pad the monthly tariff comes to a cool $880.

The Congress of the United States has called on you to be an involuntary partner in this enterprise because it felt that surely you, as a patriotic citizen of a country suffering certain acute housing shortages, would want to help alleviate those well-publicized problems.* Yet, if you live in one of America's urban ghettos, you are likely to take the view that if your dollars are going to be drafted in the war against substandard shelter, your first priority would *not* be to provide the gymnasia, saunas and steam baths and valet parking for the well-to-do who can afford to pay $880 a month for rent. Never mind: you are given no choice in the matter. When Congress offered this tax incentive to *all* residential rental buildings, it laid compulsory claim on your dollars to help finance "tax shelter" projects for the rich as well as the poor.

---

* That is why, when Congress cut back on the double-rate depreciation deductions in 1969, it made an exception for "residential rental properties"— of which Ocean Towers is one.

Your discomfiture might be increased by the knowledge that not only the occupants but also the nominal investors in this luxury project (i.e., the "tax shelter" beneficiaries) will be confined to the well-heeled. The investment prospectus says just that in so many words, set in boldface type for emphasis. This venture, it says, "Should Be Considered Only by Investors in the Higher Income Tax Brackets."

Then it goes on to say something that might give you a queasy feeling about your investment: the venture, says the prospectus, is "Speculative in Nature. . . . Particularly in View of the Substantial Investment Required, Potential Investors Should Consider Carefully the Risks of an Investment Herein and Should Consult Their Own Financial and Tax Advisers. See 'Risk Factors,' Page 4."

Congress, of course, was not thoughtful enough to give you the opportunity to consult *your* "Financial and Tax Adviser" (assuming you have such); you're a partner in this venture whether you like it or not. But anyway, you might want to turn to Page 4 and know what some of those "Risk Factors" are (or were, as of November 8, 1971, when investors were being solicited):

Item: The apartment project "has not been completed and has no history of operations."

Item: "The Corporate General Partner* has only recently been organized, has had no significant operations to date, has no employees other than its six officers, and has never served as a general partner in a limited partnership."

Item: "The Partnership will be totally dependent on the success of a single project [the Ocean Towers apartments]. Moreover, it is intended that apartments will be offered at rentals substantially higher than those generally charged in the area. The number of potential tenants will, therefore, be significantly limited."

Item: "The Partnership cannot predict its cost of operations. . . . There is no assurance that . . . reserves [for repairs, replacements and continuing operations] can be established or that, if established, they will be adequate to cover the expenses and costs of the Partnership."

---

* The corporation whose officers will be spending full time overseeing and managing the project, and on whose management skills the success of the venture depends.

Swell. With all those risks, one might be tempted to wonder how such a venture could possibly succeed. Unhappily, a question of that sort is not yours to ask. Congress expects you to put your money in without protest.

SEVERAL ELEMENTS combine to bestow handsome largesse upon the "high-bracket investors" who made this ocean-side fairyland possible. We've already mentioned the key factor: double-rate depreciation deductions, which were available to this project (a) because it was being newly constructed and (b) because it is residential rental property.

The advantages of these deductions to the investors in Ocean Towers, Ltd., were hugely magnified because the project's promoters arranged the massive $17 million project to be built with a cash input by the investors amounting to just 3 percent of the total. The other 97 percent was borrowed "on a long-term basis" through a loan "secured solely by Ocean Towers Property"—that is, without a penny of liability on the loan or risk to the investors should the project go sour. Despite this, they were allowed to compute their depreciation deductions on the basis of the full $17 million, just as if they had personally put up (or, at the least, been liable for) the total amount. Nice work, if you can get it.

An important added fillip was provided by the fact that while most of the costs of constructing the building can only be deducted bit by bit, over the building's "useful life," certain sizable construction-period expenses may be deducted immediately, all in a lump. These include interest on the special short-term construction loan; certain taxes; and fees paid to make the construction loan possible. Many feel that these expenses are an integral part of the cost of construction and contribute to the capital value of the building in precisely the same way as the brick-and-mortar and labor costs. Therefore, they argue, these expenses should receive the same tax treatment as the brick-and-mortar and labor costs— i.e., should be deductible over a several-year period, rather than immediately-and-in-a-lump—a method that is supported, say its proponents, by most texts on accounting.* Nonetheless, the tax laws provide otherwise, and the immediate deductibility of these

---

* The counterargument to this is that since the law allows immediate deductibility for other kinds of interest and tax expenses, why should the rule be different just because the expenses occurred during the building's construction?

expenses can provide vital assistance to a project's promoter, for the tax savings therefrom often equal his preconstruction promotional outlays. With those expenses recovered (via his tax savings), the promoter has a zero-risk investment in the project virtually from the outset.

In most real-estate "tax shelter" ventures, there are two classes of participants: the organizer-promoters who put together and often manage the project, usually on a full-time basis, and the wealthy investors whose primary, if not sole interest is the "shelter." Congress, in its consistent solicitude for this latter group, has sanctioned some internal manipulations within these ventures that permit the "shelter" seekers to get more than their proper share of the tax advantages. For example, the full-time participants are allowed to forgo their share of the construction-period deductions and bequeath them to the rich "shelter" seekers; likewise, although a new investor who puts up his money in, say, November, is only entitled to two months' deductions that year, the law permits fudging the truth and allocating a full year's deductions to him.

A significant advantage springs from a single sentence that appears in most real-estate "shelter" prospectuses, stating that the venture expects to be "treated for Federal income tax purposes as a partnership and not as an association taxable as a corporation." That may sound technical, but to the investors that sentence spells "advantage," whether the venture shows profits or losses. If there are profits, the investors get twice as much as they would if the venture were taxed as a corporation.* But if it is to be successful as a "tax shelter," a real-estate venture will show, not profits, but large "tax *losses*," in which case the advantage of the partnership form of doing business is that each partner-investor may claim his share of those "tax losses" in a manner not permitted in the case of corporations. Some feel that it is unduly generous to permit these ventures to profit from being taxed as partnerships, since IRS regulations permit them, at the same time, to enjoy many of the advantageous characteristics of corporations.

---

* If taxed as a corporation, the venture would have to pay a 48 percent corporate tax *before* distributing the profits to the investor-shareholders. But if it is treated as a partnership, none of the profits need be shared with Uncle Sam. They are 100 percent available for divvying up among the partners.

The tax advantages for *profitable* real-estate partnerships also flow to investors in so-called "real estate investment trusts," as graphically described by a 1963 pamphlet, "Federal Tax Angles in Real Estate," published by Prentice-Hall:

Before 1962, if a Real Estate Investment Trust (REIT) earned $984,734* before providing for income taxes, here's how the melon was cut up:

To the Government, for income taxes	$478,500
To the shareholders, as dividends	506,234
	$984,734

Assuming the earnings remain constant, here's how the melons will be cut up now:

To the Government, for income taxes	$ Zero
To the shareholders as dividends	984,734
	$984,734†

As the pamphlet aptly points out, "That's a whale of a different set-up—$478,500 more for the shareholders to divide among themselves."

What makes it different? A law was passed in 1960 which in effect excuses so-called "real estate investment trusts" from paying corporation income taxes (by permitting them to deduct their dividend payments to their shareholders in computing their taxable income).

In order to qualify for this, however, they must distribute at least 90 percent of their income to their shareholders, and the justification for excusing them from the corporation tax is that they act, in effect, merely as conduits for rental income, and not as ordinary corporations which actively reinvest their earnings in the business. On the other hand, as the law explicitly acknowledges, they are in every other respect exactly like other corporations. Thus, these groups are able to get all the *advantages* of doing business as a corporation, but unlike others who enjoy these

---

* As the Real Estate Investment Trust of America actually did one year.
† Since that pamphlet appeared, the corporate tax rate has been slightly changed, but the principles involved remain the same.

advantages—even others who may *by choice* pay out 90 percent of their profits as dividends—they pay no corporate income tax.

IF YOU ADMIRE SHEER INGENUITY in skirting the law without breaking it, you'll enjoy the following often-used caper, in which borrower, lender—and even the Internal Revenue Service—join as conspirators.

The law to be skirted is the widespread prohibition, in many state laws, against banks' lending more than 75 percent of the amount needed to finance a real-estate venture. But sometimes, when a bank sees a really juicy piece of real estate, it would like to make a 90 or even a 100 percent loan—which of course would suit the project's owners to a T, since that reduces, or even eliminates, the amount of their own cash they must put up.

What's the solution? Easy. The bank simply buys the building and promptly turns around and leases it back to the sellers—on terms that make it clear that the arrangement is tantamount to a loan (only with a better-than-average return to the bank, for its trouble). So clear, in fact, that the sellers often apply to IRS for —and obtain—a ruling permitting the transaction to be treated as precisely that. This way, they get to take advantage of the depreciation deductions, just as if they had never sold the building to the bank. They even get credit for what would be reasonable interest deductions if it were a loan!

Part of the deal is that the sellers have the right to buy the building back from the bank after a period of years. That leaves them a number of pleasant options: if the building (plus land) goes up in value over time, the original owners can take out a conventional loan of 75 percent of the now increased value, which is likely to be enough to pay off the bank. Or they can simply leave the building in the bank's hands.

It's a nice arrangement.

WHAT SHOULD BE DONE to curb the special tax advantages accorded real estate?

First, rule out "accelerated depreciation" on all real estate, confining the deduction to, at most, "straight-line," or constant-rate depreciation.* Even the prime architect of "accelerated de-

---

* There are some who believe that even this does not reflect the true rate of wear and tear on buildings, and that the deductions should be more akin to mortgage-repayment patterns instituted by bank and other lending institu-

preciation" for machinery and equipment (Dan Throop Smith, the top tax adviser to the Eisenhower Administration) has acknowledged that the fast write-offs are "not needed for real estate."

Second, provide that *all* profits on the sale of buildings over their depreciated or "book" worth be taxed at regular income tax rates at the time of sale. This would put the depreciation rules for buildings on a par with those for machinery and equipment and would put an end to the duplicate depreciation deductions now enjoyed by successive owners of buildings. For example, say that Owner A of a $3 million building takes $2 million of "straight-line" depreciation, leaving a depreciated or "book" value of $1 million. Then suppose he sells the building (exclusive of land) for $2 million. Under existing law, Owner B is allowed to begin a new round of depreciation deductions based on the $2 million price, even though $1 million of those deductions had already been taken on the same building by Owner A. (The duplication is lessened but not eliminated by the capital gains tax that A must pay at the time of sale.) Under the rule suggested here, if A sold the building for more than its depreciated worth, this would be regarded as an automatic sign that he had taken more depreciation deductions than were justified, and he would have to make up for this by paying regular income tax on the "book profit" at the time of sale—the same rule that now applies to machinery and equipment.* One realtor observed that if such a rule were instituted, it would put a virtual end to the sale of buildings, but it is difficult to see who would suffer from that other than the buyers and sellers of buildings and their brokers. The tenants are usually oblivious of, if not unaffected by, the identity of the building's owner.

Third, confine an investor's depreciation deductions to the extent of his personal cash input or to the extent of his personal liability for any loans associated with a given real-estate venture, plus any pay-down of the mortgage. This is not easy to achieve, technically, but the goal is worth pursuing.

---

tions—that is, with smaller-than-average deductions in the early years, increasing as time goes on.

  * Realtors argue that if buildings are put on a par with machinery in the respect suggested here, they ought to be put on a par in other respects, too— which would mean extending to buildings two tax advantages now accorded machinery and equipment: the investment tax credit (see pp. 214–219) plus an extra 20 percent depreciation allowance permitted in a machine's first year.

To the extent Congress concludes that any segment of the real-estate industry (e.g., low- and middle-income housing) requires a subsidy, this can and should be effected by a directly appropriated subsidy—rather than an indirect and hidden tax subsidy—for reasons fully set forth in Chapter 7. In the low- and middle-income housing field, for example, a direct subsidy might take the form of a rent subsidy that would provide a decent return for low- and moderate-cost housing developments while keeping out-of-pocket rent payments at a level that poor and middle-income families could afford.

WHAT WOULD BE THE EFFECT of such changes in the tax law? One leading New York real-estate attorney who has read and commented on this chapter takes the view that if the above suggestions were adopted, the effect would be "disastrous," for it would mean the "disappear[ance]" of the capital the industry now obtains by "team[ing] up with high tax bracket individuals who are prepared to take the risks associated with the projects in exchange for the tax incentives afforded by current law." If those tax incentives were removed, he predicts, "housing activity in the United States would decline drastically and a strong movement for more publicly-owned housing would emerge," with all the drawbacks that public housing has thus far demonstrated. He says that the discussion in this chapter fails to take proper account of "the risky nature of the real estate industry," in which "every piece of real estate is unique" and where "an apartment complex built two blocks away from a highly successful apartment housing project may turn out to be a disaster."

While this chapter admittedly concentrates on the tax joys that flow from real-estate successes, no one should conclude that the industry is nothing but an unbroken succession of bonanzas. Real estate, like any other industry, has its disastrous flops as well as its spectacular successes, and any real-estate investor must face the possibility of foreclosure if the project goes sour. In that case the investor can suffer serious financial consequences from which no amount of tax incentive can protect him. But is the real-estate industry more risky than others? And, even if it were possible to measure and compare its riskiness, is it the proper function of the tax system to compensate for it? If so, in order to be fair, the tax laws would have to take account of the varying risks, not just for each industry but for each occupation and even each person.

Moreover, how valid is the claim that the American housing industry will "decline drastically" unless we perpetuate tax incentives for "high tax bracket individuals"? While the rich do provide a portion of the equity capital, far more is furnished by banks and lending institutions that do not benefit from the "tax angle" but are more influenced by the inherent worth of a real-estate project. In the last analysis, both investors and lenders are looking for a return on their money. Are tax incentives to rich individuals the only way—or, indeed, the best way—of providing that return? No one can seriously doubt the need of low- and middle-income families for better housing. If direct rent subsidies to such families were used to supplement what they can afford to pay, wouldn't the augmented rents make many a housing development financially attractive to *private* builders, without resorting to government ownership?

In a recent seven-year period, the tax laws enabled one real-estate operator to enjoy a total income of $7,500,000 while paying only 11 percent of that to the U.S. government—about the same proportion as was paid by a family of four with an income of just $10,000. Another real-estate investor in Washington, D.C., with a considerably more modest yet highly comfortable income, was confronted with (and complied with) a request from his household maid, one April 15, for a loan of $500 so she could pay her taxes, in a year when he was not only paying no taxes but anticipating a substantial *refund* from the U.S. Treasury. Are results like these the *only* way of encouraging the housing industry in the United States of America?

"Tax Shelters" in Farming

> "I'm a rich cowhand, of the Wall Street brand;
> And I save on tax, to beat the band.
> Oh, I take big deductions the law allows
> And I never even have to see my cows.
> Yippie-yi-yo-ki-yay."

That parody on "The Old Cowhand from the Rio Grande," apparently the creation of an imaginative *Wall Street Journal* writer, is an apt introduction to the next (and more unconventional) forms of "tax shelter," used by those wealthy souls who seek protection from Internal Revenue under pistachio trees, 'mid kiwi groves, and 'neath cows and bulls (or, if they are the sporting kind, 'neath race horses).

These "shelter" seekers are often called "gentlemen farmers," for they are almost all high-salaried city dwellers—doctors, lawyers, stockbrokers, corporate executives and the like, many or most of whom would not dream of getting rural dirt under their fingernails; who indeed rarely even *see* their cattle or their pistachio trees.* What they really are is "tax farmers," and the only harvest that genuinely interests most of them is a harvest of dollars—dollars of tax savings.

Indeed, they are a strange breed, for, judging from their tax returns, they love losing money. The richer they are, the more they seem to like to lose.

Looking at it another way, something curious apparently happens to the well-to-do when they invest in farming ventures, for their usual moneymaking acumen seems to desert them in the most remarkable way. Take, for example, that select group of Americans making between $100,000 and a million dollars a year. When they put their money into *non*-farm ventures, their profits outweigh their losses five to one. But put them into farming enterprises and what happens? Judging from what they tell Uncle Sam on their tax returns, they manage to lose three times as much as they make! (But before you generate excessive pity for their plight, you should bear in mind that these "losses" are serving to shelter from taxation their usually substantial non-farm income (from stockbrokering or doctoring or whatever), with startlingly profitable after-tax results. We have already noted the feat of Taxpayer K (page 165), whose seemingly egregious farm "loss" of $450,000 was sufficient to keep the tax collector from laying a finger on his $738,203 of income.† In this manner, some 2,400 affluent "tax farmers," with non-farm incomes of $100,000 or more, contrived to extract some $90 million of "tax welfare"

---

* Unless they happen to plan a vacation trip in that direction (e.g., to their Florida fruit groves in January or February when the winds blow cold in New York), in which case a side excursion to inspect their investment would make much of the trip tax-deductible. This is an aspect of farm ventures that many a promoter seizes upon as an added lure to the deduction-hungry (see the discussion of "Rent-A-Cow," p. 192).

† As usual, the privilege of excluding from taxation one-half of his large capital gains (a quarter of a million dollars, in his case) greatly facilitated his tax-avoidance exploit.

payments from the Treasury, for an average tax saving to each of about $37,500.

According to one recent estimate, the total of "tax welfare" going to city-dwelling "farmers" is $860 million a year.

TO GET AN IDEA of how these "tax farmers" go about harvesting their tax benefits, let's begin with a problem that ought to be easily solvable by anyone who has completed fourth-grade arithmetic:

Clark Movie Star, a top-bracket screen success, invests $30,000 in a cattle-raising venture from which his expected cash return, over five years, will be $9,500. Will he make money, or lose money, and how much?

What's the answer, class? You say he'll lose $20,500? Terribly sorry, but you're wrong. He'll make $11,000.

Evidently, you went astray because you were using the wrong arithmetic book. *Cowboy Arithmetic* explains the whole thing. *"The raising of livestock,"* it says on page 95, *"gets an income tax treatment in which even the basic principles differ from that afforded most other forms of American business. . . . The over-whelming majority of the differences are most favorable."**

Clark Movie Star's exploitation of *Cowboy Arithmetic* is no theoretical one. It reflects the enticing figures listed in an actual investment prospectus for a cattle venture near Louisville, Kentucky. Here is how things work out for a top-bracket investor, like our own Clark Movie Star, in the first three years after he has plunked down his $30,000 investment:

Year	Clark Movie Star's Share of Cattle Venture's Tax Loss for Year	Clark Movie Star's Tax Saving (70% of tax loss)	
		That Year	*Total*
1	$24,823	$17,376	$17,376
2	$24,855	$17,399	$34,775
3	$11,484	$8,039	$42,814

* This volume, published by the Interstate Printers and Publishers, Inc., of Danville, Illinois, takes pains, however, to disabuse readers that these tax provisions represent a "tax loophole" or "tax gimmick." This is "definitely not the case," says the book. "The special provisions were purposefully put into the law, after long study . . . to encourage private individuals to take over a program that would otherwise have to be handled directly by the government."

Thus, thanks to the generosity of the tax laws, even before the end of the second year our screen star's "tax welfare" payments from Uncle Sam have more than recovered his $30,000 outlay and not a dime of his own remains in the venture. At the end of the third year, he has realized a "tax profit" of nearly $13,000—even while reporting substantial "losses" to Internal Revenue.

In the subsequent years, the cattle herd is sold, and the venture's tax returns actually begin to show a profit. But that is of minor concern to Clark Movie Star, for those early-year losses saved him 70 cents on the dollar, while these later-year profits from the sale of the herd may well be taxed at the special capital gains rate—at only 25 or 35 cents on the dollar. (Remember that the 25 percent rate applies to the first $50,000 of a person's capital gains each year.) Thus, as with the real-estate "tax shelters," Mr. Movie Star has succeeded in transforming high-taxed regular income into low-taxed capital gains.*

As if these tax benefits weren't enough, Congress, in 1971, sweetened the kitty by making cattle eligible for the investment tax credit† (described on pages 214–219) which added $1,000 to Clark Movie Star's tax bounty. Supposedly, this additional tax saving is limited to one per herd, but one ingenious cattle syndicate, undaunted by that restriction, reportedly made plans to sell its herd to another syndicate, simultaneously buying the other syndicate's herd. Result: both syndicates would get a second shot at the investment tax credit.

With tax savings like that in the offing, it is little wonder that cattle investments have attracted top-bracket notables in the entertainment world, such as Alfred Hitchcock, Jack Benny, Richard Rodgers and Groucho Marx—as well as other wealthy people outside of show business, like Winthrop Rockefeller and E. Roland Harriman. One musician-conductor with an annual income of nearly $300,000 reported tax deductions on his cattle invest-

---

* In 1969, Congress supposedly curbed this alchemizing process, but was careful to include generous exemptions that still permit most "gentlemen farmers" to enjoy the advantages on most of their farm ventures. (See pp. 197–198.)

† Since the investment tax credit is more generous for "new" than for "used" property, the application of the ITC to cattle raises a nice question: when is a cow "new" and when it is "used"? One taxpayer has suggested an intriguing definition: if a cow has been inseminated, but has not yet dropped her calf, she is still "new"; only when she becomes a mother does she become "used." That line of reasoning may strike a responsive chord in the hearts of many a diaper-enslaved new mother.

ment of nearly $130,000 in 1959 and 1960, saving him over $100,000 in taxes. And one manufacturer of chain link fence, whose income in 1958, 1959 and 1960 totaled nearly $9,300,000, was saved nearly $500,000 in taxes as a result of his cattle investments.

True, these top-bracket investors had some out-of-pocket outlays to make in these ventures; but, as with real estate, a large part of the tax-saving deductions were "paper" deductions (because the law permits rapid depreciation of a bull or cow)—that is, deductions that involved no cash outlays, and therefore could not be used to shield non-farm income from Internal Revenue.

THE TAX JOYS of being a "gentleman cowboy" were breathlessly depicted in a pamphlet headed, in ersatz Western lingo, "How to Round Up a Tax-Sheltered Second Fortune by Investing in Cattle." The "secret to success," confides the pamphlet, lies in "the population explosion" which is "giving cattlemen a built-in market advantage—*Americans love steak smothered in onions*. And, cattle owners get *preferential tax treatment*." (Emphasis in original.)

TV and movie stars—and corporate executives—are quickly assured that they do not have to be tall in the saddle or quick on the draw, or even know anything about cattle, in order to be "gentlemen cowboys." Everything will be taken care of: heifers will be bought, grazing leases arranged, even bulls supplied for a fee—which itself is tax-deductible. Then, says the pamphlet, the investor can just "sit back and let nature take its course." Lest this allusion be cloudy, the pamphlet embroiders it: "Bulls + Cows = Calves."

Some cattle investors have found, however, that sometimes these details are not as neatly taken care of as they might have wished. In 1970, one of the larger "tax shelter" cattle syndicates, Black Watch Farms, ran out of cash and went into receivership. Court records showed that its 36,000 head of cattle were scattered over sixty-three locations in twenty states—but *whose* cows were *where*? "I got 10 head," said a vice-president of a New York stockbrokerage firm, but "the records are so mangled that I don't know where the animals are." Among the notables who got stuck in the venture: singer Connie Francis and Peter Revson, son of a founder of Revlon cosmetics.

IN THE LATE SIXTIES, Treasury officials were intrigued by a prospectus that heralded a cattle investment program called "Rent-A-Cow," which sought to entice wealthy New Yorkers in the following terms:

Before "Rent-A-Cow," the dream of being a rancher while living in a Fifth Avenue apartment was economically unattainable. . . . Cattle ownership will add a new and exciting dimension to your life. Just imagine having your own herd of fine quality registered cattle and a big cowboy hat! All of your friends will be envious of your new "Rancher" status. You'll be the most popular family in town with . . . visiting privileges* on one of the southwest's most famous ranches . . . . And—you can charge it all off your income tax as a business "inspection trip." Just hop on a jet at New York—we'll meet you in Tulsa with a twin-engined private plane and within 4 short hours from your busy city life, you will be in our luxuriant guest lodge, gazing at your own tax-sheltered registered cow herd. Fishing, hunting, horseback riding, hiking—it's all yours when you become a "Rent-A-Cow" rancher.

How could any self-respecting Fifth Avenue apartment dweller resist the temptation to become the most popular family in town? It could all come true with an outlay of just $450 (fully tax-deductible) for a year's rental of a quality Hereford cow ("the Cattlacs of the industry"), in return for which you would be guaranteed the production of one (1) weaned calf which would be yours, all yours. At that point, you'd have your choice: you could, if you wished, take your calf to your Fifth Avenue apartment; sell it; or, for $150 a year (also tax-deductible), leave it with the Rent-A-Cow company. The long-run prospects (with your calves growing up and producing their own offspring) were rosily portrayed. The promoter's brochure pictured a winsome girl of about five, fondling an adorable calf, with the caption "In 13 years, this calf and its offspring will put this little girl thru college."

And, as the brochure pointedly observed, if you are in the 50 percent tax bracket, "in effect the government will be paying one-half of your herd building expenses." (They didn't say so,

---

* According to the brochure, those privileges were limited to investors who rented twenty or more cows.

but by "government" they really meant all the other taxpayers of the United States.) With installment payments available, and a free cowboy hat thrown in, no wonder, in 1972, there were rumors of a program called "Lease-A-Sow"!

CATTLE are by no means the only "tax shelter" available to those who wish to be "gentlemen farmers." Increasingly, such persons are finding the requisite "shelter" in the shade of fruit trees and grapevines. In 1969, for example, a publication called "Citrus Tax Angles" boasted to a prospective investor that, after just two years, the tax savings would "more than recapture" his initial outlay, and "he still has title to appreciating real estate [the citrus grove]. Think of it," the pamphlet went on, "tax dollars were used to purchase the property, *and are the only dollars invested.*" (Emphasis added.)

Since that time, Congress has put a crimp on the tax savings from citrus and almond groves, which has diverted "shelter"-seeking investors to more exotic kinds of crops. Pistachio nuts have come into vogue; and a California company by the name of Calchico is peddling the virtues of a little-known fruit called a kiwi (sometimes known as a Chinese gooseberry and said to resemble a "fuzzy potato"). The Calchico Kiwi Company extols the *Actinidia chinensis* (its botanical name) as "a new crop . . . that can (1) produce outstanding income; (2) provide lower per acre input than average vegetable crops; and (3) *provide excellent tax shelter possibilities.*" (Emphasis added.) Just incidentally, it's also supposed to taste good ("a combination flavor of strawberries, rhubarb and pineapple guava," according to one gustatory authority).

WHENCE COME the tax savings to "gentlemen farmers"? Basically, in three ways.

The first is that certain major tax deductions which in other forms of business would have to be delayed and spread out over a period of years may, in farming ventures, be taken immediately and in full. To illustrate, take the case of the Empire State Building, which cost $42 million and took one and a half years to build. During the eighteen-month construction period, the owners of the building were laying out about $25 million of construction expenses, but of course no income from those expenses would begin until the building was completed and tenants began to move in and pay rent. Thereafter, barring an earthquake or other catastrophe, the building would go on generating rental income over a long period of time—at least forty years. Therefore, in order to match up the expenses as closely as possible with the income and profits that would result from them, the owners of the Empire State Building were not permitted tax deductions on *any* of the basic construction costs* until the building was completed, and even then they had to spread out their tax deductions over the forty-five-year "useful life" of the building—taking annual deductions of about a million dollars a year (actually one forty-fifth of $41 million, using "straight-line" depreciation methods).

If the law were otherwise—that is, if the building's owners had been permitted to deduct the construction costs immediately —they would have enjoyed huge immediate tax savings, but it would have been years before they had to pay tax on the resulting income. As we learned in Chapter 8, that would have meant an enormous interest-free loan, courtesy of all the other taxpayers in the United States. Clearly, such a rule would be cause for complaint by those other taxpayers.

Yet that is precisely the rule that results in large interest-free loans to "gentlemen farmers" who invest in plants or animals or trees requiring some years of nurturing before they will begin to bring in any income. Plant seedling pistachio trees, for example, and you will have to wait about eight or nine years before they will reach nearly full production, during which time you will have shelled out considerable money in the care and feeding of your trees.

If the rules governing the Empire State Building (and all other business ventures) were to apply, you would not be allowed any deductions at all on the expenses of your pistachio grove until it was at the point of bringing in income; and then you'd have to spread out your development-expense deductions over the income-producing life of the grove. But farming ventures of the sort that attract "shelter"-seeking city folk are exempt from that common-sense rule. The expenses of cultivating, feeding, pruning, etc.—

---

* This description is slightly oversimplified, for illustrative purposes. As already noted, the tax laws do permit immediate deduction, during construction, of interest on construction loans, property taxes and ground rent, which can amount to 5 to 10 percent of total cost.

i.e., of bringing the grove to profitability—are immediately deductible, when incurred.*

In 1969 and 1970 Congress recognized the questionability of that rule by requiring deductions for the expenses of developing citrus and almond groves to be spread out and treated *à la* Empire State Building. But the legislators' wisdom stopped there. They failed to apply to pistachio, kiwi and other fruit trees the principles they found valid for citrus and almond groves.

WE COME NOW to Advantage Number Two to "gentlemen farmers." All of the development expenses are fully deductible against the investor's regular income which, let's say, is subject to a 70 percent top-bracket rate. That is, each dollar of deductible loss has saved him 70 cents. But if, at a later date, he decides to sell his pistachio grove, the profit may be taxed at the special capital gains rate of only 25 or 35 cents.† As already noted, anyone who saves 70 cents on the dollar and has to pay back only 25 or 35 cents is bound to end up ahead. Congress, in 1969, placed a ceiling on that tax-saving practice, but, as we shall see in a minute, it was a generous ceiling—tall enough for most "gentlemen farmers" to fit under without even removing their hats.

Advantage Number Three is that "gentlemen farmers" are allowed to muscle in on a special simplified tax accounting rule that has historically been available to farmers but not to other businessmen: the privilege of treating their expenses (and computing their taxes) on a *cash* basis—i.e., on the basis of when cash was paid out and when it was taken in, regardless of whether the income and outgo were properly "matched."

Other forms of business are not allowed to do that. If, for simplicity's sake, the Amalgamated Widget Company incurs $100,000 of expenses in making 100,000 widgets this year but, at year's end, has 20,000 widgets on hand as unsold inventory, it can claim only $80,000 as a business expense this year, rather than

---

* That is one reason why Clark Movie Star's cattle venture was able to bestow upon him such large and helpful early-year tax "losses." Those resulted from the immediately deductible expenses of feeding his cattle at a time when they weren't bringing in any income. In addition, as noted, there are generous depreciation deductions that involve no cash outlays.

† As mentioned, the 25 percent rate applies to the first $50,000 of a person's capital gains each year.

the full $100,000 it paid out. Why? Because $80,000 was all the expense incurred in making widgets that brought in income *this year*. For the remaining $20,000, the company must wait until the unsold inventory has been disposed of. Similarly, if, in order to get a volume discount, the company buys a huge supply of widget parts, half of which won't be used until next year, it can only deduct half its purchase outlays.

But the syndicated farming "shelters" are exempt from that rule, and are free to manipulate their income and expenses, to great advantage to their investors. For example, cattle ventures can (and do) buy next year's feed grain this year, giving rise to a large tax deduction for an investor who may need it now more than later—netting him, at the least, a one-year interest-free loan on his postponed tax. That same principle lies behind the "Mexican vegetable roll-over" (see page 161): next year's expenses of some Mexican vegetable farms are paid this year. This is of considerable aid and comfort to a hypothetical Charles C. Stockbroker, who, after a few bonanza years, anticipates a slump in his income—and in his top tax bracket—next year.

The special permission for farmers to use cash-accounting methods dates back to the time when most farm operations were small and most farmers had neither the time nor the facilities for sophisticated bookkeeping. Some believe it ought to be abandoned by all but the smallest farmers, for, they submit, large farm operations can and do exploit their tax "losses" on, say, cattle breeding to provide "tax shelter" for their farming income from, perhaps, soybeans. In any event, there is serious question whether cash accounting is either appropriate or necessary to such a highly sophisticated "tax shelter" as the picturesquely named "Fat City," a cattle feeding operation in Monterey, California. Fat City boasts to prospective investors, in its fancy four-color brochure, that "All progress reports are coordinated and reported to the Limited Partners [investors] using modern business systems"—this under a full-color photograph of comely young ladies taking computer print-out reports from the most modern, automated accounting machines.

AN ADDITIONAL adverse effect of "tax shelters" for "tax farmers" is that they encourage city dwellers to go into competition on an artificial and unfair basis with real farmers (who usually aren't in the lofty tax brackets necessary to make the "shelters" profitable). According to one study, fully a third of all farm acquisitions in the late Sixties were by non-farmers, and the U.S. Department of Agriculture predicted that in the next decade at least 100,000 high-bracket city folk would become "tax farmers." The "shelter" seekers bid up the price of farmland, and, since they are not in farming to make a profit, they compete unfairly with the marginal and poorly financed farmer.

HOW DOES ONE set about rectifying this situation? Montana's Senator Lee Metcalf has proposed meeting the problem directly. A bill he has introduced would bar a city-dwelling "tax farmer" (defined as a person who has a non-farm income of more than $15,000) from using his farm "losses" to shelter his non-farm income unless he has computed his farm "losses" in accordance with regular business-accounting methods, spreading out his development cost deductions so as to match them up with the farm "income" they produced. Thus, Senator Metcalf would remove the basic abuses that result in artificial tax losses to non-farmers.*

Congress, however, chose a gentler, more oblique and immensely more complex approach. It left wholly intact two of the three advantages enjoyed by "gentlemen farmers"—the privilege of immediate deductions for expenses that in other businesses would have to be spread out over a period of years, and the privilege of using cash-accounting methods. And the limit Congress imposed on the third advantage (the transforming of ordinary income into low-taxed capital gains) was highly generous. For example, that advantage remains 100 percent intact for any "tax farmer" who has less than $50,000 of non-farm income.†

---

* Some tax experts feel the Metcalf bill did not go far enough, arguing that those same abuses ought to be denied to large, sophisticated and diversified farm operators who are shielding much of their farm income via phony tax losses.

† Actually, the law is more liberal than that would imply, for it permits a "tax farmer" to have $50,000 of non-farm "adjusted gross income," as defined on tax returns, without running afoul of the new restrictions. But "adjusted gross income" does not include income that is offset by such deductions as real-estate depreciation or "intangible drilling" deductions. (For example, Taxpayer J, described on p. 165, above, had total income of $1,433,000 but, after his enormous real-estate deductions, an "adjusted gross income" of zero.) For that reason, rich tax avoiders who diversify their "tax shelters" can enjoy huge amounts of non-farm income without being affected by the new farm "shelter" restrictions.

And even if he has salary or dividend income far in excess of
$50,000, he is still allowed to enjoy $25,000 of farm "losses"
wholly untouched by the so-called "reform." So what do we have
left? *If* your non-farm income is greater than $50,000 and *to the
extent* that your farm "losses" are greater than $25,000 in any one
year, *to that extent only* your profits, upon sale of your cattle herd
or pistachio grove, are taxed, not at the lower capital gains rate
but at your regular income tax rates. Big deal. Little wonder that
one pamphlet on "tax shelters" observed that the 1969 changes
were "not as severe as many anticipated" and that "certain farm
investments still offer favorable tax shelter opportunities. . . ."

Professor Charles Davenport, a student of the farm tax law,
has commented that the 1969 reform "is the most modest [reform]
approach that has been suggested." Davis says the 1969 law "is
so complex as to be almost incomprehensible"; that this complexity "arises from the application of a poor idea . . . to a simple
problem" (premature deduction of costs); that it imposes a
penalty only on persons who sell their herds or groves, and thus
discriminates in favor of those who hold on to their farm property.
And, finally, he is concerned that this Band-Aid "may be accepted
as [genuine] reform, thereby lessening the demand for some
effective change" in the future.

IF YOU WERE GOING OUT to buy a horse, chances
are you wouldn't wear an evening dress and sport all your finest
jewels. On the other hand, you aren't Liz Whitney Tippett, of the
super-rich Whitney family, who appeared at a horse sale in
formerly fashionable Saratoga, a few years ago, together with "an
entourage of her very social friends . . . wearing evening gowns
and sparkling jewels." *Newsweek* magazine described the scene:

Charles Engelhard, the beefy precious-metals magnate, pulled on his
long cigar, gazed at the handsome colt in the Saratoga auction ring,
and nodded his head slowly—to raise his bid to $200,000. Across the
ring, svelte Anne McDonnell Ford held a gold-rimmed lorgnette to
her eyes to glance at her sales catalogue, leaned over to consult an
adviser and finally flicked one slim finger—increasing her own bid on
the colt to $210,000.

As *Newsweek* observed, "Many horse owners would never
think of betting thousands of dollars on a race in which there is

one chance in five to win." Certainly few average taxpayers would do so, even if they had the money to burn—for they would be playing entirely with their own money, rather than the government's (i.e., the other taxpayers'). Yet the Engelhards and the Whitneys and the Fords can and do, with the flick of a finger, spend a fifth of a million on a yearling which, statistically, has no more than a thirty-five-to-one chance of winning back his purchase price. One-fourth of all yearlings never even race. And, reports *Newsweek,* "paying record prices doesn't necessarily increase an owner's chances. Ever hear of Bold Legend? Royal Match? One Bold Bid? All brought record amounts at auctions; not one even raced."

Why are top-bracket taxpayers so willing to risk huge sums at thirty-five-to-one odds? Partly, of course, because they have it to risk; but in large part, it's because they're playing, to a great degree, with other taxpayers' dollars. That is, for a top-bracket taxpayer, 70 percent of what they lay out for buying, feeding and training a race horse* would go to the government anyway (if it were spent for a nondeductible item such as, say, jewelry). So why not put the money into long-shot race horses and have the government (i.e., the other taxpayers) in effect pay 70 percent of the bill? Of course, you do have to be careful about losing money on your race-horse operations over too long a period, for fear the government will challenge your business motives in going into the field. But there are obvious tax joys in race horses; otherwise the thirty-five-to-one odds would be just too much to warrant risking $210,000 at one clip.

OIL MAY SEEM a messy and slippery substance from which to construct a "tax shelter," but the rewards for so doing are not in the least slippery; they are tangible in the extreme.

Oil "shelters" have enjoyed an almost explosive growth in recent years. In 1964, the Securities and Exchange Commission received investment prospectuses for only thirty-four "drilling funds" seeking to raise a mere $85 million. Just four years later, however, the number of such funds had trebled and the amount of money they were seeking to entice into oil-drilling ventures had increased nearly eightfold—to $650 million.

---

* The purchase price is deductible only over a period of years; the training and feeding expenses are immediately deductible.

The publication *Oil Daily* has described these drilling funds as "one way for small oil-gas development investors . . . to spread their risks"—by joining with numerous other small investors in a massive drilling program large enough so that among all the wells drilled, a respectable percentage will turn out to be producers. Indeed, unlike the real-estate syndications that call for minimum investments upward of $50,000, many of the oil-drilling funds will allow a person to "play" for a mere $5,000. If 599 other people join in the "game," each will end up with a fractional interest in $3,000,000 worth of drilling—just like a big oil company!

In such drilling funds, the tax advantages flow from the basic preferences enjoyed by the oil industry, about which you will learn in more detail in Chapter 11. Briefly, if dollars are sunk into a "dry hole," they are 100 percent tax-deductible; if other dollars result in an oil strike, about 70 percent of them are immediately deductible (as "intangible drilling expenses"). Then, when (and as long as) the oil flows, the investors get the benefit of the 22 percent depletion allowance (i.e., 22 percent of the resulting income is tax-free).

The more "sophisticated" drilling funds—where the minimum investments start at $50,000—offer tax-saving wrinkles not available where the admission price is a paltry $5,000 and are not offered to just anyone, as the $5,000-minimum funds are. Instead, they are described in "Confidential Memoranda," which warn, in capital letters, that participation is not recommended unless the investor is in at least the 50 percent tax bracket—which means, for married taxpayers, a taxable income of at least $44,000.

What are the special wrinkles proffered in these "Confidential Memoranda"?

First of all, unlike the smaller investors, the larger-stake players in the oil game need not be limited to a mere one dollar of deductions for each dollar invested. No, they can get two dollars of deductions, sometimes three, for each dollar they put up.

How do they manage that? Simple: an oil company, delighted to have other people put up drilling capital, willingly agrees to lend money to the drilling fund—sometimes as much as 71 percent of the total needed—without any requirement that the individual investors pay back the loan. All the company asks is that it receive an option to buy the oil wells that may result from all the drilling.

To the "shelter"-seeking investor this happy arrangement means deductions based on the total amount sunk into oil-well drilling, not just his own dollars but the borrowed dollars as well, even though he bears not one penny of liability to pay back those borrowed dollars!

Thus, in a fund where a kindly oil company agrees to lend 71 percent of the needed funds, for every $10,000 an investor puts in, the oil company lends about $24,483, so that a total of $34,483 is available to sink into the ground. Assuming that the entire amount becomes tax-deductible, the lucky top-bracket investor who put up a mere ten grand of his own gets tax deductions of nearly three and a half times that amount, and realizes a tax saving of $24,438. So, right away, not only does he have every penny of his own investment back; he has a $14,438 "tax profit"* to show. And every one of those 14,438 dollars was furnished him courtesy the taxpayers of the United States.†

But there can be an even more pleasant consequence for the fortunate investor: namely, that the oil company that lent the money decides to exercise its option and buy the oil wells that sprang from the drilling operations. This the company often achieves simply by "forgiving" the loan—which is the same as giving the investors the money with which to repay the debt. Once again, we see that happy one-way street: the loan gave rise to tax deductions that meant savings of 70 cents on the dollar; but dollars the investors receive to pay back the loan are taxed at the capital gains rate of no more than 25 or 35 cents on the dollar— for a net tax profit of 35 or 45 cents on the dollar. Neat.

Yet that by no means ends the "wrinkles" that have been built into these "sophisticated" drilling funds. In the smaller funds, when the investors' dollars result in a "strike," only 70 percent of those dollars are immediately deductible as "intangible drilling expenses"; the remaining 30 percent can only be deducted over a period of years. Not so in the "sophisticated" funds: there, arrangements are made for someone other than the "shelter"-hungry investors to absorb the nondeductible 30 percent, so that every dollar of the "intangibles" is allocated the "shelter" seekers. That way, what for most people would be mere 70 percent

---

* The $24,438 of tax saving minus the $10,000 he originally put into the venture.

† Internal Revenue has begun to place restrictions on some such arrangements.

deductions becomes 100 percent deductions. Not a dollar is wasted.

The fourth added wrinkle (about which there is considerable legal controversy) is especially tailored for the man who, say, as Christmas approaches, receives a huge bonus or fee that he doesn't expect to be repeated next year, and just *has* to have some offsetting deductions right away, before New Year's Eve and the beginning of a new tax year. January 1 won't do: midnight December 31 is the deadline. Like the Lone Ranger, Geo Dynamics Oil and Gas, Inc., comes riding to the rescue. Its representatives just *happen* to have handy a drilling fund in which the *legal commitments* to drill are all drawn up and ready to sign— and they also just happen to have on hand a legal opinion saying that under these circumstances—even though the drilling itself, and the expenses relative thereto, won't occur until well after New Year's Eve—the deductions can be taken this year, just as if the well was drilled and finished on December 31.

S U P P O S E your transcontinental jet journey, complete with two choices of movie and three choices of entrée (yet *no* choice but to suffer the raucousness emanating from the piano lounge in the rear) were interrupted by a bass (but initially hesitant) voice on the public-address system:

"Uhhhhhhhhhhhh, this is your captain speaking. Uhhhhhhhhh, is there a uhhhhhhhhhh a doctor aboard the airplane?"

Your first reaction, doubtless, would be that there must be a medical emergency on board. But, quite conceivably, the captain might merely be trying to determine if one of the jetliner's *owners* is aboard, perhaps to reassure him that his aircraft is in fine repair and working order, and that the doctor-owner has nothing to worry about.

For, one of the "tax shelters" that, in times past at least, was enormously attractive to doctors, stockbrokers and other high-bracket individuals was part ownership of a Boeing 707 or other high-flying jetliner. Of course, a multi-million-dollar jet is far too expensive for any one individual to buy, and thus the promoters and syndicators would put together "packages," whereby Psychiatrist Spielvogel could join with Lawyer Taney, Stockbroker Gould, Surgeon Schweitzer and several other high-bracket taxpayers and, with the help of a substantial bank loan, purchase the aircraft and lease it to the airline.

The promoters could offer a threefold combination of advantages almost too good to pass up. First of all, there were depreciation deductions of almost unparalleled proportions.* Second, there were the interest deductions on the bank loan. But the crowning glory came from the investment tax credit, which, in 1969, would net the investors in, say, a Boeing 707, a tax saving of about $600,000. Really, the investment credit was the icing that made the cake delectable; without it (i.e., with depreciation deductions the principal advantage), the cake was far less tasty, for if the investors sold the plane, as many do, the depreciation advantages could be greatly diminished by having to pay a large tax at the time of the sale.†

The whole thing was a marvelous deal, not only for the high-bracket purchasers of the huge aircraft, but for the airlines that leased them, for it enabled them to fill out their fleets with other people's money rather than their own. What's more, the tax savings flowing to those "other people" permitted them to lease the plane on terms highly favorable to the airlines. Indeed, as some critics saw it, this was a way by which the airlines could, in effect, "sell" to high-bracket "shelter" seekers tax advantages that they couldn't use themselves (because their own profits were not sufficiently large to take advantage of all the depreciation deductions or even the investment credit).

A hint of the kind of arrangement involved was contained in a single sentence in a New York *Times* report of the dramatic hijacking of a Pan American 747 by Arab guerrillas in the summer of 1970. "The jet, which is owned by the First National City Bank and another bank, not identified, is leased to Pan Am with the Bankers Trust Company as Trustee." That sentence sufficiently intrigued the editors of *The New Yorker* that they arranged a "Talk of the Town" interview with a "financially astute" friend, Martin G. Cashflow. According to Mr. Cashflow, the banks didn't really own the airplanes themselves, but "probably represent a bunch of trust-account customers who have grouped together to buy a 747." They would want to do so, he explained, so that they could

---

* Arising from the double-rate depreciation allowed on new aircraft, coupled with the unusually short "useful life" that the tax law accords jetliners. Together, the two permit 40 percent of the cost of the plane to be deducted in the first investment year.

† Because all of the sale profits above the depreciated worth of the plane would be taxed at each investor's regular income tax rates.

totally depreciate it in five or six years and then sell it again. *The New Yorker* wanted to know who would possibly want to buy a totally depreciated airplane since "if it's totally depreciated, it doesn't exist." Cashflow, suppressing a condescending smile, said patiently, "Of course it exists. It's only for tax purposes that it's totally depreciated. It would still fly and show movies and all that. Also, it would be very valuable for the next owner, because he could totally depreciate it all over again."

Alas for high-bracket doctors, lawyers, stockbrokers and movie actors, the law has since been tightened so that only corporations, and not individuals, are privileged to get the investment tax credit when they purchase items such as aircraft and railroad cars and lease them to other companies. Still and all, corporations are able to attain some pretty fancy returns on such deals—especially with railroad cars, on which Congress, in 1969, bestowed the privilege of an unusually short five-year write-off. According to one actual prospectus, the handsome depreciation deductions, coupled with the investment tax credit, promised a corporate investor an *after-tax* yield on his investment of 33.19 percent.* A 50 percent *individual* taxpayer, who would have to do without the investment credit, would have to content himself with a mere 24 percent return, according to a "tax shelter" pamphlet prepared by the major accounting firm of Arthur Andersen & Co.

THOSE, THEN, are some—but by no means all—of the "tax shelters" available to rich tax avoiders. What average taxpayer wouldn't *love* to shelter part of his hard-earned income and reduce his taxes? But the "shelter" deals, with their sky-high minimum investments, freeze him out. Most of them seem to scream, "FOR THE RICH ONLY." Some even say, explicitly, that they aren't interested in the average man's money, even if he saved up the price of admission. "For high-bracket taxpayers only," they say. So the average person is obliged to pay his taxes, grin and bear it. No—even worse: he is obliged to pay part of

---

* In this case, the entire profit seems to have been at Uncle Sam's expense, for one tax expert, scrutinizing the projected profit contained in this prospectus, protested that, but for the tax advantages, the deal seemed to make no economic sense whatever.

the taxes of the rich people who do have the cash to put into the "shelter" deals.

In theory, at least, such deals ought to arouse the wrath of the National Association of Manufacturers and the Chamber of Commerce and others who express admiration for Adam Smith free-enterprise economics, for the "shelters" encourage people to invest in ventures that on their own merit, leaving the tax advantages aside, may make little or no economic sense. Tax lawyers report that many of their "shelter"-hungry clients tend to throw usual investment caution to the winds when they hear the phrase "It's deductible."

The game of "tax shelter" has become a nationwide pastime that engages the brains and energy of gifted people. It has created an entire industry. Tax advisers to the wealthy say they are deluged with "shelter" literature and besieged by visits from "packagers" of "shelter" deals—who get an 8 percent commission for every deal they sell. (The commission is, of course, fully deductible to the investor.) Whole books devoted to "shelters" are multiplying. Two-day seminars on the latest wrinkles in "shelters" are commonplace—and, naturally, the expense of attending is tax-deductible. Moreover, in a day when, reportedly, six out of seven new brokerage houses go bust, houses specializing in "tax-sheltered" investments—such as the burgeoning Donatelli, Rudolph and Schoen in Washington—are springing up in abundance, having a field day and often outstripping their more staid and well-established competitors.

The universal lure of the "tax shelter" was dramatized to me when I attended my twenty-fifth college reunion and fell into conversation with a classmate who, in his school days, had been the campus radical. Now, a quarter of a century later, about all he was interested in telling me was about the killings he had made playing the tax angle. Even his twenty-fifth class gift to his alma mater had to be a "tax shelter" deal. *Sic transit. . . .*

"Tax Welfare" for the Corporate Giants

December 11, 1971

Mr. Richard C. Gerstenberg
Chairman of the Board
The General Motors Corporation
Detroit, Michigan

Dear Mr. Gerstenberg:

We, the members of the Congress of the United States, take pleasure in advising you that we have, this day, caused to be dispatched to your company a gift that will amount, over the next ten years, to about $550 million. Yes; you read that correctly: *over half a billion dollars*! Of this, about $300,000,000 is a renewal of a gift we sent you earlier (from 1962 to 1969). The other $250,000,000 is a new gift that we and President Nixon think you should have.

In all fairness, you should know that GM is not the only corporation receiving these gifts. On the contrary, we are sending them to every American corporation (although strictly between us, most of the money is going to the giants like you).

It would be nice if you would use the $300 million to buy more machinery and equipment than you otherwise would have. But we want to make it clear that the money is yours, even if you just do "business as usual" and don't spend a nickel more than you would have even without our gift.

Also, we've told the public that "job development" is one of the main reasons for this gift, so it would make us look a lot better if you could somehow hire more people than you otherwise would have. We're not entirely clear on how you're going to do that, if you put this gift money into new, more efficient labor-saving machinery—which would probably mean *fewer* jobs, and not more. But we want to repeat and emphasize, the gift is yours to keep, whether you hire more people or less people or just keep your payrolls the same. As you know, we never asked you for an accounting when we gave you a $300 million gift in the Sixties (so we don't really know what you did with the money and what effect it had on jobs or modernization). We see no reason to change our practices now.

Some people might call this a slipshod way of handing out money, especially since when you add up all the gifts of this sort that we plan to send to corporations over the next ten years, they add up to something like *ninety billion dollars*. But, as you know, we Congressmen are an optimistic and trusting bunch, especially when it comes to dispensing gifts to big corporations.

Besides, it's not our money.

> Yours for trickle-down prosperity,
> The United States Congress

Of course, the Congress wrote no such letter to Mr. Gerstenberg. But it might have, for the letter describes quite accurately the multi-billion-dollar blessings the Congress (at the urging of the Nixon Administration) bestowed upon American corporations —mostly the huge ones—in a tax law enacted in 1971. According to Senator Gaylord Nelson, the 1971 law reduced corporation taxes by about 15 percent—one of the greatest corporate tax reductions in history.

Even the pro-business investment banking firm Goldman Sachs & Co. acknowledged, in a 1972 analysis, that the 1971 law had lightened the tax load of corporations considerably more than that of individual taxpayers. In the short space of a year, the report said, the share of corporate profits being paid in taxes had taken a 10 percent drop—and, as of mid-1972, it was still declining. The tax relief voted to individuals since 1969 "hasn't been nearly as sharp."

The 1971 law was the culmination of a series of tax provisions that began in 1954 and that have produced a miraculous result (miraculous, that is, from the point of view of the corporations). For, while keeping the corporation tax *rates* substantially unchanged, the Congress has managed to lighten the tax *burden* of the corporations by about one-fourth. That is, before Congress began dispensing these multi-billion-dollar tax breaks to American business, corporations as a whole were paying a little more than 38 percent taxes. By 1969, with the corporation tax rate slightly *higher* than it had been in the early Fifties,* corporations as a whole were paying only about 29 percent in taxes. The savings: about $15 billion a year.

As a result of Congress's generosity, corporations furnish only about a seventh of total Federal tax collections today—whereas, in 1960, they accounted for nearly one-fourth of all taxes. In 1960, they were the second largest source of revenues; now they are third—far behind the skyrocketing payroll taxes, borne almost entirely by the nation's hard-pressed wage earners.

Apparently, the corporate giants have been able to take better advantage of Congress's generosity than the smaller corporations, for, according to one analysis, the 100 largest corporations paid just 27 percent taxes in 1969, while the smaller corporations paid 44 percent. Since the giants clearly make higher dollar profits than the smaller companies, that would seem to be a reversal of the "ability to pay" principle on which the individual income tax is theoretically based.

The tax-escape achievements of individual corporations are even more impressive (or infuriating) than the record of corporations taken as a whole. A group of experts examining reports submitted to the Securities and Exchange Commission by various large corporations concluded that at least eight of America's largest companies had managed to pay not a penny of Federal income taxes in either 1970 or 1971—despite amassing a total of $788 million in profits before taxes, and despite paying $568 million —more than half a *billion* dollars—to their shareholders in cash dividends. One might have thought that companies prosperous enough to be paying such handsome dividends ought to be "able

---

* In 1969, corporations were paying 48 percent plus a 4.8 percent surcharge, or a total of 52.8 percent, compared with a 52 percent rate that prevailed in the early Fifties.

to pay" some taxes; but, as noted (page 17), the tax laws enacted by Congress imposed no such burden on the following major corporations: *

Corporation	Net Profits Before Taxes	Dividends Paid to Shareholders	Federal Income Taxes Paid	Income Tax Refund
	(In thousands)	(In thousands)		(In thousands)
1971				
Alcoa Aluminum	$50,199	$41,300	0	$17,036
Continental Oil	$109,030	$76,329	0	$24,472
Gulf & Western	$51,381	$15,939	0	$29,350
McDonnell Douglas	$144,613	$38,904	0	$8,087
1970				
Bethlehem Steel	$122,071	$78,917	0	$13,000
Consolidated Edison	$110,027	$108,021	0	$17,500
National Steel	$73,449	$41,009	0	$19,825
Republic Steel	$18,264	$40,440	0	$9,916
U.S. Steel*	$109,491	$127,691	0	$66,100

* TV viewers are doubtless familiar with this company's slogan: "At U.S. Steel, we're involved." Judging from the above, however, the paying of income taxes is one American institution in which U.S. Steel is, on occasion, definitely *not* involved.

How many of the tens of thousands of people who work for those corporate giants contrived to pay no taxes in 1970 or 1971?

According to *Business Week,* for the company through whom you send all your telegrams (Western Union) 1971 "marked the eighth year in a row that it paid no Federal income tax, even though it turned a profit in each of those years." The basic reason: the company uses certain accounting methods for the tax collector, but different accounting methods in figuring up the profits it wants to report to its shareholders.

AT TIMES, corporate chieftains have exhibited an acute tenderness to the charge that their companies pay less than their share of taxes. One such, whose response was astounding, if only for its gall, was Stewart S. Cort, Board Chairman of the Bethlehem Steel Corporation. In September, 1972, Mr. Cort felt moved to have his company take out a full-page advertisement (tax-deductible, of

* In fact, these corporations reported that credits or refunds totaling nearly $78 million were due them.

course) in *Forbes* magazine. It featured a personal message from Chairman Cort which sought, in part, to rebut the contention, made in the 1972 Presidential campaign, that his company and other corporations "aren't . . . paying our 'fair share'" of taxes. How can that be, Mr. Cort wondered, when "our total tax expense was . . . $155 million in 1970"? An odd phrase, "total tax expense." What did it mean? Close scrutiny of company reports discloses that this "tax expense" is made up of Social Security taxes, property taxes, and state and foreign taxes. The phrase omits any mention of Federal *income* tax—perhaps because Bethlehem Steel paid none in either 1969 or 1970 (when it received *refunds* from Uncle Sam of $53 million and $14 million, respectively, *despite before-tax profits of nearly $300 million in those two years*). Yet Mr. Cort's tax-deductible message asks the reader to "think twice before swallowing all this baloney about large corporations not carrying their fair share of the tax burden." All of this might have been less objectionable had it not been part of an ad headlined I SAY LET'S KEEP THE CAMPAIGN HONEST and urging the reader to beware of candidates' statements that may be "faulty, ill-founded, or misleading."

INTERNAL REVENUE STATISTICS show that of the 1.7 million American corporations, about 726,000—or 43 percent*—paid no Federal income tax in 1970. In about 620,000 cases, this was either because they suffered business losses or because they had no income that was subject to tax (due to various allowances, deductions and the like). One hundred and six thousand corporations told the government they had some taxable income, but this was canceled out by various tax deductions (about which you will read more below).

Some corporate colossi, while not achieving *total* taxlessness, come remarkably close to it. For example, ITT (of Dita Beard and shredding-machine fame) seems to have paid only 5 percent tax on $413,000,000 of profits in 1971. Texaco, on the other hand, put ITT to shame: it paid the U.S. government just 2.3 percent tax on nearly a *billion* dollars of net profits. How many readers of

---

* The 43 percent figure omits additional corporations that pay no tax because of the investment tax credit and foreign tax credits (the latter described in Chapter 12). In 1968, the last year for which complete data are available, 48 percent of all corporations paid no tax.

this book paid as little as 3 percent of their income in taxes in 1971?

If you or I or any other non-corporate taxpayer should make more money this year than last, we would take it for granted (even if we didn't like it) that we would have to pay more taxes. That's in the very nature of "ability to pay" taxation. In the case of the individual income tax, that principle finds expression in the rising tax-rate schedule that calls upon the rich to pay a higher propor- tion of their incomes in taxes than the poor. But corporations are exempt from the principle of "ability to pay." Their tax rate on all profits over $25,000 is a flat 48 percent, whether they are General Motors or the panty-hose factory in the neighboring town.*

The absence of "ability to pay" in corporate taxation sometimes shows up dramatically in actual practice. Take, for example, the remarkable case of the American Electric Power Company. In 1969 its profits were about $138 million, and it paid taxes of about 23 percent. Two years later, its profits had risen to $149 million—yet, rather than paying more taxes, as you or I would have had to, American Electric's tax dropped to just 4.5 percent.

IF YOU ARE MYSTIFIED by much of this, you have reason to be. When you enter the realm of corporate and business taxation, you are entering a new and baffling world, filled with "loss carry-backs" and "deferred tax accounts" and other perplex- ing terms. Even more confusing, you will find a marked discrep- ancy between what a corporation tells its shareholders (or even the Securities and Exchange Commission) on the one hand, and what it tells the tax collector on the other.

For example, to make its shareholders happy (and to encour- age them to buy even more of the company stock), a company's annual report portrays the earnings and profits in the rosiest

---

* Even the strongest "ability to pay" adherents are not convinced there should be a graduated tax rate for corporations. They ask, for example, does American Motors, which is struggling to stay alive in competition with GM, Ford and Chrysler, have the same "ability to pay" as a company of comparable size and profitability that dominates its industry, and hence is financially secure? They believe that in the field of corporate taxation the principle of "ability to pay" would be better served by, say, a tax on *un*distributed corporate profits. That would give companies a great incentive to distribute their profits to shareholders who *do* (in theory at least) pay taxes according to an "ability to pay" graduated tax schedule.

possible terms. But if it reported the same high profits to Internal Revenue, the government would expect it to pay very high taxes, which of course would be most unpleasant; so the picture the company paints on its tax return is the most woebegone it can lawfully convey.

Case in point: the 1970 and 1971 tax returns of Consolidated Edison, the big New York utility, conveyed to Internal Revenue that it had *lost* money (for purposes of reckoning its taxes) in years when the company had enough profits to pay its shareholders $108 million in dividends in 1970 and more than $119 million in 1971. Congressman Charles Vanik of Cleveland, who has been strenuously trying to unravel the corporate tax mysteries, has likened the corporations to the medieval peasants of Europe: for their stockholders they wear their wedding clothes; for the tax man, they wear rags.*

To illustrate this: the tax laws permit corporations to compute the wear-and-tear tax deductions on machinery and equipment (a) as if they were wearing out faster in earlier years than in later years—resulting in larger early-year tax deductions, and (b) as if the machinery had a very short "useful life"—and the shorter the "useful life," the larger the annual wear-and-tear duction.† So, in reporting the wear-and-tear factor to Internal Revenue, most corporations take the largest legally allowable deductions—using fast early-year write-offs and the shortest possible "useful life." But if the companies reported such a large wear-and-tear factor to their *shareholders,* that would considerably dim the profit picture. The solution: tell the tax collector one thing and the shareholders another.

The difference is colossal. In 1966, for example, the oil indus-

---

* Also, to its stockholders, a company often speaks a strange and unintelligible language, for its annual reports frequently seem more bent on confusing than enlightening. Thus, the truth about the taxes a company really pays often lies buried in a combination of figuresalllumpedtogethersoyoucan'ttellwhichiswhich, plus an endless chain of footnotes—the words of which, when looked at separately, *appear* to be in English but, when strung into sentences, form a clearly alien tongue. For that reason, many of the figures presented above represent the best efforts of Congressman Vanik and his staff, aided by some accountants, to portray each company's taxes based on its published reports. The companies' tax returns are, of course, confidential.

† For example, if a $100,000 machine is assumed to last twenty years, the annual deductions are only $5,000; if, on the other hand, it is assumed to wear out in just ten years, the annual deductions are $10,000, or twice as large.

try showed profits of more than $3 billion on its own books of account, yet reported profits of only half that amount—about a billion and a half dollars—to Internal Revenue. Similarly, the profits of banks and trust companies according to their own books of account amounted to $2.5 billion—well over twice the $1.1 billion of profits they reported to the IRS. One Congressional tax-reform proposal would require corporations to choose one method of reporting the wear-and-tear factor, and stick to it in making out its tax returns *and* in reporting to shareholders.* It was estimated that if all corporations limited their wear-and-tear *tax* deductions to what they have been telling shareholders, they would have to pay several billion dollars more in taxes. Ironically, the principal author of the original write-off provision, Dan Throop Smith, later came to regret that the law did not impose such a requirement on corporations when the provision was first enacted in 1954.

WHILE THE FIELD of business taxation *is* complex, you will be relieved to know (a) that some of the tax favors that Congress has granted corporations are not difficult to understand, and (b) that this chapter will attempt to describe only those simpler ones.

As mentioned in Congress's "letter" to Mr. Gerstenberg of General Motors, the gift Congress bestowed on corporate America in the 1971 tax law will amount to some *ninety billion* dollars over the next ten years. Basically, that gift came in three packages, whose labels might be mysterious to the general public, but whose cost to the public is both unmysterious and immense.

Label 1: ITC (investment tax credit). Ten-year price tag: $52 billion.

Label 2: ADR (asset depreciation range). Ten-year gift to corporations: $30.4 billion.

Label 3: DISC (domestic international sales corporation). Ten-year boon to corporate America: a mere $3.6 billion. (Since the DISC portion of the gift relates to the taxation of corporations' *foreign* operations, you'll find the discussion of DISC in Chapter 12.)

With price tags of that magnitude, each of those acts of Congressional generosity is worth understanding.

---

* This sensible suggestion has precedent in the tax law: certain inventory practices may be used for tax purposes, only if they are also used in reports to shareholders.

ITC (Investment Tax Credit)

This feature of the tax law, defended as an incentive to corporations to invest more in modernizing their plant and equipment, has had two incarnations. During its first appearance in the law (from 1962 to 1969), it brought tax gifts from the American people to the General Motors Corporation of nearly a third of a billion dollars ($297 million to be precise). To the nation's largest steel company, United States Steel, it brought benefactions of nearly $207 million, netting that company a 35 percent tax saving in 1969 and a 31 percent saving in 1967. To American corporations as a whole, it meant benefits, over the seven years, totaling nearly *thirteen and a half billion dollars.*

In 1969, however, Congress found the ITC guilty of feeding the fires of inflation and, for its sins, repealed it. In less than two years' time, however, those selfsame Congressmen, never sticklers for consistency, concluded that the ITC would be "of material assistance in *combating* inflation" (emphasis added) and, under the politically appealing label "job development credit" (who could be against job development?) gave it a new lease on life— on even more generous terms than before.

How does the ITC save General Motors an average of $40 million a year? Very simple; it reduces General Motors' taxes by a certain percent of what the company spends on new machinery and equipment. If, for example, GM buys a new $100,000 machine that it expects to use for seven years or more, that act reduces the company's tax by $7,000.* That is, we taxpayers have, in effect, paid $7,000 of the cost of the machine, and the price, net, to GM is only $93,000.† Since it is estimated that General Motors spends, each year, more than six hundred million dollars on machinery that qualifies for that special tax treatment,

---

* Seven percent of $100,000—since the law provides a 7 percent investment tax credit on machinery expected to last seven years or more; for shorter-lived equipment the credit is smaller.

† Since GM ends up paying only $93,000 for the machine ($100,000 minus the $7,000 tax saving), it was originally thought reasonable that GM's depreciation deductions ought to be based on the $93,000 net out-of-pocket cost rather than the full $100,000, and the original investment credit law of 1962 was written that way. But two years later Congress concluded it had been too niggardly and decreed that the depreciation deductions should be based on the full $100,000, even though GM hadn't paid that much (after taxes) for the machine.

the ITC is the equivalent of handing the General Motors Corporation, the largest corporation in the world (net profits: $1.7 billion annually), a Federal check for $40 million (for that was the approximate annual saving in the 1962–1969 period of the first ITC).

All told, the ITC means handing Federal checks of $3.3 billion each year to American corporations; and if the history of the 1962–1969 ITC (when 57 percent of the benefits went to just 260 corporations) repeats itself, the giants will again get the lion's share of this brand of "tax welfare."

Does the public get its money's worth for those "tax welfare" checks? Both the Kennedy and Nixon administrations, in appealing for the ITC, argued that American industry needed to be spurred to replace and modernize their machinery and equipment faster than they otherwise would have, so as to keep pace with their foreign competitors. Does the ITC really do that? Many believe it's open to serious question.

First and most important, as noted in Congress's "letter" to GM Chairman Gerstenberg, General Motors gets a tax break from the ITC even when it buys machinery and equipment that it needed *and would have bought anyway,* even without a tax handout from Uncle Sam. To the extent that's true, the public gets zero benefit from the "incentive," and GM ends up with a windfall profit.*

Second, there is serious question about the job-creating effectiveness of the investment credit—which, you will recall, is now labeled "job development credit." Congressman Vanik, for example, says that the top 100 U.S. corporations—the ones that get the great bulk of the ITC benefits since they do the bulk of machinery-buying—are actually providing *fewer* jobs as their sales increase. According to Mr. Vanik, between 1969 and 1971, while the sales of those 100 companies rose by 12.5 percent, their

---

* As the "Secretary of Commerce" put it in the imaginary press conference in Chapter 7, that makes as little sense as giving a salesman an incentive bonus even if he sells no more than he did in prior years. (See p. 149.) From that point of view, the ITC originally proposed by the Kennedy Administration in 1962 was far better devised than the version that was finally enacted. The initial Kennedy proposal would have provided a smaller credit for "normal" investments and a larger one for investment *increases* over prior years. But Congress rejected that in favor of a uniform credit for all investments.

employment *declined* by 5.2 percent, or approximately 500,000 jobs.*

There is also the question as to whether tax stimulants to corporate investment are the most efficient means of creating jobs. To illustrate, in 1971 the Nixon Administration proposed $5.8 billion of such stimulants (through renewing the ITC and allowing greater wear-and-tear deductions through ADR, which will be discussed next) and estimated that this would create between 500,000 and a million new jobs. One Congressman calculated that this would represent a cost of between $6,000 and $12,000 per job created. Yet of course the six to twelve thousand dollars would go not to the workers involved but as tax savings—sometimes windfall savings—to the corporations, whether or not they increased their employment.

Common sense also obliges one to question whether modernization of equipment is likely to be job-*creating*, since in many cases the more modern equipment is more fully automated and requires less rather than more manpower.

The ITC has also been justified on the ground that it is needed to spur American companies to modernize so as to be on a par with their overseas competitors. But the tax favors of ITC are not confined to those industries, such as steel, where foreign companies are considerably more modern than America's. As two Senatorial ITC critics pointed out when the credit was originally passed, it can and does apply to "a new ski lift in Sun Valley, klieg lights in a burlesque house and martini-mixing machines in a bar."† In its 1971 version, the ITC even applies to the costs of producing a motion picture—a field where the crucial competitive factors (artistic talent and imaginativeness rather than modern machinery) are hardly likely to be fostered by a mere tax incentive.

Moreover, like so many tax subsidies, the investment credit thwarts all logic and common sense. Any logical modernization

---

* By contrast, the last 100 corporations in the *Fortune* magazine top-500 list experienced a 16 percent increase in sales, but also increased their employment by 1.4 percent. Yet those corporations do not get nearly the benefits from the ITC that the giant ones do.

† Just where these two Senators might have seen a martini-mixing machine is not clear. Perhaps there is secreted, in the Senate cloakroom, a fully mechanized bar where martinis are not favored with the bartender's personal ministrations.

incentive ought to give top priority to a company such as the Penn Central Railroad, whose financial difficulties spring largely from its very failure to keep its machinery and equipment sparkling and modern. Far lower priority would sensibly be assigned a huge and prospering company such as General Motors. But the investment credit, being a *tax* subsidy, works just the opposite; as noted, it confers handsome benefits upon General Motors but is worthless to the Penn Central, which is in the red, hence has no taxable income, hence owes no tax to the government, hence has nothing from which to subtract its tax credit.

But while Penn Central derives no benefit from the ITC, wealthy doctors and other high-bracket taxpayers have in past years been able to take advantage of the ITC in most lucrative fashion. For example, as discussed on pages 202–204, that shiny airliner that whisks you through the air at several hundred miles an hour may have the United or American or Pan Am insignia affixed to its aluminum skin, but its owners may well be a group of brain surgeons or psychiatrists or some other mixture of high-bracket taxpayers who have banded together in a business partnership and, borrowing heavily to do so, have bought themselves a $9 million Boeing 707 which they lease to United or American or Pan Am. It worked out just fine for everyone: the doctors enjoyed a bevy of tax benefits* (if tax benefits come in bevies), which in turn enabled them to lease the airplane at a favorable rate to the airline. For everyone concerned, Uncle Sam made the going great.

Such arrangements proved too lucrative even for the generous Congressmen who made the ITC possible, and so in 1971 they barred high-bracket individuals from such handsome leasing arrangements, which are now confined to corporations. But the enticements even to corporations are alluring indeed. As noted on page 204, one, being circulated in early 1972 on a railroad car leasing deal, offered the prospect of a 33 percent return on the investment—after taxes, of course. On its merits, leaving aside the tax lure, the investment made little or no economic sense.

---

* Even though the high-bracket owners put up cash of only, say, one-tenth the price of the airliner, they are able to get both the investment tax credit *and* fast tax write-offs computed *as if they had paid the entire purchase price of the airplane in cash.* And, as if that weren't enough, the nine-tenths they borrow to buy the plane nets them additional deductions for the interest payments.

ITC critics also question Congress's decision to extend ITC benefits to the equipment purchases of public utilities—gas and electric companies and the like: an act of extreme (and, some think, needless) generosity (a) since utilities are required, under the law, to make whatever investments are necessary to furnish needed services to the public and (b) since the law also provides that utility rates should be high enough to give the companies a fair return on whatever investments they make. So why do they need a tax incentive to do what the law requires and assures them they'll be paid to do?

The Kennedy Administration, which initially proposed the ITC, concluded there was no such need, and suggested that the utilities be excluded from the benefactions of the ITC. The utilities protested hotly. Congress listened—and heeded; and although the utilities' credit was less generous than for other companies (3 percent—increased to 4 percent in 1971—compared with the 7 percent accorded other firms), Congress nonetheless bestowed tax joy on those companies amounting to more than a third of a billion dollars in 1967 and estimated at half a billion in 1972.

Of course, the tax savings from the investment credit meant that the utilities were spending less, net, for their new machinery and equipment. Since, under the law, the rates that these companies charge the public are supposed to be set so as to yield them no more than a "fair return" on their investment, some regulatory agencies began to wonder whether the lower investment costs should be passed on to the public in the form of rate reductions. Again the utilities protested, saying that such a pass-through would deprive them of the tax favor that Congress intended that they, the companies, should receive. Again Congress heeded, and decreed that the investment credit must not be given to companies that pass the benefits on to its customers in the form of lower rates.

Perish the thought that the consumers should benefit.

IT WOULD BE WRONG to suggest that the investment tax credit has produced no results: any program that dispenses more than $13 billion (which the 1962–1969 ITC tax favors added up to), whether in tax incentives or in direct expenditures, is bound to have some effect, and economists generally acknowledge that the ITC brought about some added machinery-and-equipment investment that would not otherwise have taken place. How much—and how many jobs it created—is a matter of dispute, if not conjecture.*

Some have questioned whether the ITC was needed in the first place. Senators Douglas of Illinois and Gore of Tennessee, protesting the initial enactment of the ITC in 1962, pointed out that corporations at the time had some five *billion* dollars of liquid *un*invested assets that could have been put into new machinery and equipment—*if* corporate managers had felt the need for it; so, asked Gore and Douglas, why "spend" the taxpayers' money to create an even larger pool of investable funds?

Many businessmen themselves discount tax incentives as the determining factor in their investment decisions. In 1961, the secretary-treasurer of the Hewlett-Packard Company in California said, "We're not going to build a plant simply because there's a Federal tax attraction." A decade later, James M. Roche, then chairman of General Motors, echoed that statement: "It should be understood," said Roche, "that most companies of any size determine their purchases of equipment by the needs of the business and not by any short-term tax advantages." But apparently Congress wasn't listening to Mr. Roche, for, in the year he made that statement, they went ahead and reenacted the investment tax credit which, during the decade of the Seventies, is expected to cost the American taxpayers about *fifty-two billion dollars.*

ADR (Asset Depreciation Range)

It's not likely that many Americans know what "asset depreciation range" means. You can bet, though, that Thomas J. Watson, Chairman of IBM, knows what it means (even though he may not understand all its technicalities). *It means that IBM will pay nearly $500 million less taxes during the decade of the Seventies.*

And, although the words "asset depreciation range" have a mysterious ring to them, their meaning to every American is also very simple: over the next ten years, ADR is expected to confer more than $30 *billion* of tax bounty on American corporations,

---

* That is one of the major drawbacks of tax subsidies: the difficulty of measuring what results emanated from using the taxpayers' dollars.

with a highly questionable return to the rest of the American tax-payers who, as usual, will have to foot the bill, one way or the other.

Also as usual, the bulk of the $30 billion of benefits will go to the corporate giants. Senator Alan Bible of Nevada has stated that 55 percent of the benefits will go to the 103 largest corporations, and 80 percent will go to the largest 2,500 companies—who comprise just one-twentieth of one percent of all U.S. businesses. "This seems to leave the remaining 20 percent to the other $99\frac{19}{20}$ percent of the Nation's business," Senator Bible comments.

How will ADR reduce IBM's tax by $500 million over the next decade?

Well, every year, IBM spends the colossal total of about a billion dollars on new plant, equipment and machinery, all of which wear out a little each year and ultimately have to be replaced. The tax law makes allowance for this annual wearing-out of plant and equipment as part of the cost of doing business, by allowing, each year, a "depreciation deduction"—a subtraction from the amount of IBM's income that is subject to tax.

The question is, How large a deduction is proper? How fast is the plant or equipment really wearing out and/or losing value? That is a question of enormous complexity, since IBM's inventory of machinery and equipment ranges from machine tools in factories to typewriters to computers, each category of which lasts a different amount of time before having to be replaced. What's more, IBM may replace its machines or its typewriters faster or slower than, say, Xerox or General Motors or ITT. Or, with the fast pace of computer progress, a new invention may come along that suddenly prompts IBM to retire certain equipment much sooner than originally expected. It's all very complicated, even for the most sophisticated accountant; and there is no precise answer as to what's correct.

Two things *are* clear, however. One is that the more depreciation IBM can manage to subtract from its income, the lower its taxable profits, and the lower its taxes. This, naturally, creates a battleground between IBM and the Internal Revenue: IBM wants to maximize the depreciation deduction and minimize its taxes; Internal Revenue has the opposite interest.

Another thing is simple: the faster IBM can "depreciate" a piece of machinery, the greater its depreciation deductions and the smaller its taxes during the period of the write-off. Suppose IBM has a $10,000 card-punching machine. If IRS says that such a machine must be depreciated over a ten-year period, the annual deductions are $1,000 a year (assuming an even rate of depreciation* and that the machine has no salvage value). But if IRS were to decree that this same machine could be depreciated in just *eight* years, the annual deductions would be $1,250; if a five-year write-off were allowed, the yearly deductions would come to a handsome $2,000.

One tax advisory service, Commerce Clearing House (CCH), gave its readers a specific example of the tax-deferral benefits that went with the advent of ADR on a $10,000 machine that, in pre-ADR days, had to be written off over a ten-year period but under ADR could be written off in only eight years:

| | Depreciation Deductions | | |
Year	Pre-ADR	ADR	Cumulative Tax Deferral
1	$500	$625	$60
2	$1,000	$1,250	$180
3	$1,000	$1,250	$300
4	$1,000	$1,250	$420
5	$1,000	$1,250	$540
6	$1,000	$1,250	$660
7	$1,000	$1,250	$780
8	$1,000	$1,250	$900
9	$1,000	$625	$720
10	$1,000	—	$240
11	$500	—	—

After giving these numerical examples, CCH let the real cat out of the bag. While noting that "the deferral is used up in the later years of the period" (where the "cumulative tax deferral"

---

* The tax laws permit companies to depart from this even rate of depreciation, taking larger-than-average deductions in the early years and smaller-than-average deductions in the later years a given piece of equipment is in use. This "accelerated depreciation," enacted in 1954, is one of the major reasons corporations are now paying far lower taxes today than they were in the early Fifties, even though the corporate tax rates have remained about the same.

in the right-hand column goes down to zero in the eleventh year),
CCH goes on to emphasize that if the company "regularly buys
equipment every year, however, *the deferral would generally be
permanent, like an interest-free loan."* (Emphasis added.) CCH
calculated that for a company that put a new $10,000 machine into
service every year, ADR would confer "a continuing income tax
deferral"—i.e., an interest-free loan—"of $4,800 after a 10-year
period."

Armed with that easy concept, you are now about to become
an expert on the meaning of ADR, for it simply amounts to a
government decree that all plant and equipment can be written
off 20 percent faster than before ADR. Simple as that.

For IBM, with roughly $600 million of plant and equipment
subject to the ADR formula, the ADR speed-up means added
annual deductions of about $63 million and annual tax savings
of about $30 million.

Now, if that 20 percent speed-up corresponds to the actual
corporate practices (that is, if it could be proved that corporations
are *actually* replacing all of their plant and equipment at this
accelerated ADR rate), then the new and larger deductions would
be perfectly appropriate, for they would reflect the true cost of
doing business. Nobody would be getting away with a thing. But
is that really the case?

There is really only one way of telling: namely, by determining how rapidly a company *actually* retires its equipment, and
comparing that with the rate at which a corporation writes off
its equipment, for tax purposes.

In 1962, the Treasury Department devised a way of applying
that actual-experience assessment. It bore a somewhat mysterious
and not very revealing name, the Reserve Ratio Test. The formula
was complex, and, while many businessmen argued that it was
unworkably complex, that view was contradicted by a member of
the large and prestigious accounting firm Price, Waterhouse & Co.,
who testified that "the Reserve Ratio Test, to a professional
accountant, is relatively easy to compute."* According to the

---

* There is reason to question some of the public protestations by businessmen about the unworkability of the Reserve Ratio Test, for one attorney
who is conversant with the internal practices of corporations says that
many companies make the Reserve Ratio Test calculations for their own
purposes, even though they may not use them in making out their tax
returns.

Treasury Department, the test provided an accurate way of determining whether or not a corporation was *in fact* replacing its equipment as fast as its depreciation deductions assumed. If IBM was using a five-year tax write-off on a class of machinery that it was actually keeping in service for ten years, that fact would show up in the Reserve Ratio Test, and IBM would be obliged to slow down its write-off rate so as to bring it into line with its actual practices. The test was, however, designed as more than a way of keeping corporations "honest"; it was a way of minimizing the historic battles between corporations and Internal Revenue agents and, indeed, of tailoring each company's tax deductions to its own equipment-replacement practices in a far more flexible way than an overall Federal fiat or IRS surveillance could achieve. This very view was espoused by the Treasury Department in July 1970 (during the Nixon Administration) when it warned that, in view of the enormous diversity of company write-off practices, replacement of the Reserve Ratio Test with what it called "a system of arbitrary capital allowances" would result in "inequalities" and would thrust "Congress and the Treasury Department . . . into the role of arbiter of industrial asset replacement policy."

Yet when the Nixon Administration, just a few months later, sought to accelerate corporate write-offs by 20 percent, the Reserve Ratio Test stood in the way. For if the 20 percent speed-up turned out to differ from actual corporate practices, the Reserve Ratio Test would give off telltale signs and reveal that embarrassing fact. More serious, it would compel the offending deductor to mend his errant ways and correct his fast write-off practices. Result: the benefactions of ADR would soon (to borrow from Marx) wither away. So the Treasury Department swallowed its earlier espousal of the Reserve Ratio Test and, instead, proposed its demise, which was ratified by Congress's 1971 enactment of ADR.

So today, there remains the crucial question of whether the 20 percent depreciation speed-up is justified. Does it reflect actual experience? Or is it really just a speeded-up version of reality, much like an old Mack Sennett comedy? Here are some facts on which to judge that question.

Fact No. 1: There had already been just recently (in 1962) a 15 to 20 percent speed-up in allowable write-offs.

Fact No. 2: That 1962 acceleration was based on a nationwide Treasury Department survey of corporate equipment write-off practices, comprising individual data from more than a thousand of the country's largest corporations as well as special investigations and conferences with many industry spokesmen.

Fact No. 3: The new and faster "guidelines" that emanated from that study did not merely reflect *average* corporate practices. Instead, they were conservatively (some might say generously) fixed at a level where 70 percent of corporations were replacing their equipment at a *slower* rate than the "guidelines" assumed, and only 30 percent were doing so at a faster rate.

Fact No. 4: At the time of the 1971 speed-up, most industries had not had time to go through a full replacement cycle on their machinery, so there was no real basis (other than the Reserve Ratio Test) for determining whether the 1962 "guidelines" were inaccurate, as the ADR allowances assumed.

Fact No. 5: Despite the Administration's acknowledgment that equipment replacement practices vary greatly among various industries, and even among the companies within an industry, President Nixon's ADR recommendation assumed that *every* company in *every* industry was entitled to a 20 percent speed-up in its depreciation tax write-offs. For at least some companies, therefore, the recommendation had to mean a windfall tax break.

Fact No. 6: Unlike the 1962 acceleration, the 1971 speed-up was *not* based on any systematic government survey of industry practices. So what reason, what evidence, was there for allowing corporations 20 percent faster depreciation deductions? Whence came the idea for this new speed-up? That leads to ·

Fact No. 7: The idea originated with the Presidential Task Force on Business Taxation, named in September 1969 by President Nixon. Its membership (which was not made public until nine days after the Task Force not only had been formed but had held its first meeting) consisted of the following:

> 4 lawyers from firms with substantial corporate practices (including as Chairman of the Task Force a former law partner of President Nixon's and a law partner of John Connally's, later to become Mr. Nixon's Treasury Secretary;
>
> 2 investment bankers from large New York investment banking houses;
>
> 3 representatives of large accounting firms that have giant corporations as clients;

2 top officials of large industrial corporations;

3 industry-oriented economists.

Conspicuous by their absence from this cozily homogeneous group were any spokesmen for the nonbusiness taxpayers of the country who would have to foot the bill for, and hence would have an incentive to question critically, any tax favors the Task Force might recommend for American business.

Opponents of ADR raised other questions about the advisability of this multi-billion-dollar tax dispensation—questions (that also apply to the ITC "tax welfare" provision) such as:

• Since, at the time ADR was proposed, about 25 percent of the nation's plant capacity was already unused, why was it necessary to enact an "incentive" to build still more?

• If there was to be any government subsidy for job creation, wasn't it more important to subsidize the development of *human* capital (with aid for job training), the business-profit returns on which are far more uncertain and difficult to measure?

• Since there had already been a seven-year boom in *private* plant and equipment (stimulated by seven years and $13 billion of tax stimulus from the investment credit), wouldn't more jobs be created more quickly, and more urgent needs be met, by putting the ADR "tax expenditures" into *public* "plant and equipment" (rebuilding ghettos, antiquated schools and hospitals, etc.)?

• Was it sensible to lay out these billions in ADR "tax expenditures" when Administration officials were so vague about how much additional investment these billions would bring about? (Assistant Treasury Secretary Cohen: "We think this will have a substantial impact on investment in plant and equipment, but I wouldn't make an effort to quantify it.")

Administration officials argued that even with the enactment of ADR and the investment credit combined, American companies would still be at a disadvantage compared with their foreign competitors, in view of the more generous plant write-off provisions of foreign tax laws. ADR opponents countered with several arguments:

• The devaluation of the dollar (which would lower the price of American goods abroad) would (and did) have vastly more effect on American export power than would these tax aids.

• In each of the twenty-five years since World War II, America has succeeded in exporting substantially more than she imported, indicating that American industry was doing all right in world competition.

• These tax aids would, at bèst, give a competitive boost to only some American companies (those whose products require heavy investments in plant and equipment) while giving little or no aid to companies and industries where plant and equipment play a smaller role.

Ironically, one of the most eloquent arguments against the ADR was a declaration of faith in the free enterprise system. Why, said Northwestern Economics Professor Robert Eisner, was there a need for the government to interfere, via this tax subsidy, with the corporate decision-making process? Sounding more like the U.S. Chamber of Commerce than like an academic longhair, Professor Eisner said, "I am a firm believer . . . that government should be restrained in its intervention [in the economy]. . . . There is no need for a handout to American industry to persuade them to do what should be in their own interest, [which] is to have the optimal capital and investment policies for their own efficiency and profits."

Indeed, there is a certain irony, if not an inconsistency, in the vigorous espousal of these multi-billion-dollar tax subsidies to business by an Administration that professed, through its Treasury Secretary, John Connally, that it wanted to place "maximum reliance in our free enterprise economy, and less reliance on expanding the already-large government sector." Apparently, dispensing billions in hidden government "tax dollars" to American corporations does not come under the heading of "expanding the already large government sector."

BEFORE LEAVING these major items of tax largesse bestowed upon the corporate world, a few words are in order on behalf of "small business," whose share of the profit and sales "pie" has been declining steadily as the giants' share has grown. The portion of all profits going to small manufacturing firms (those with assets of less than $1 million) declined nearly 45 percent between 1969 and 1970 and fell an additional 4 percent between 1970 and 1971. The share going to the 260 largest corporations (those with assets of more than $1 *billion*), by contrast, rose from 28 percent in 1959 to nearly 55 percent in 1971. The share of *sales* by manufacturing corporations with assets over $100 million rose from 46.4 percent in 1954 to nearly 68 percent in 1971.

All of those facts should be borne in mind when considering the multi-billion-dollar tax favors bestowed on business via the ITC and the ADR—for, as mentioned earlier, 57 percent of the benefactions of the investment tax credit (when it was in effect from 1962 to 1969) went to just 260 corporations—the 260 largest ones, naturally. Similarly, it is estimated that 55 percent of the benefits of ADR will go to the 103 largest corporations, and 80 percent will go to the top one-twentieth of 1 percent of all corporations.

Thus, with corporations, as with individuals, the "tax welfare" makes the rich richer, the large larger, and the small weaker.*

---

* There are many who believe that the tax system also encourages the growth of conglomerates by presenting the aging owner of a family-owned business with a highly tempting proposition: he can exchange the stock of his own business (which he would have difficulty selling to an outsider if he needed money in a hurry) for the stock of a business-gobbling conglomerate that wants to buy him out—and even though he is benefiting from the exchange of a hard-to-sell stock for a readily salable stock of the conglomerate, the tax laws permit him to enjoy that benefit tax-free. While no systematic study has been made of the effect of the tax laws on business takeovers, common sense would indicate that this tax-free exchange provision does nothing to discourage such takeovers.

II

Ah, To Be an Oilman

HAROLDSON LAFAYETTE HUNT, of Dallas, Texas, starting with a borrowed $50 for a broken-down oil-drilling rig, managed, with the help of Lady Luck (and a not insignificant assist from the U.S. tax laws) to build himself up from a barber/ranch hand/lumberjack to an oil tycoon worth between $2 and $3 billion, *with an income estimated (in 1957) at roughly a million dollars a week.*

Despite his prodigious wealth, however, Hunt seems almost a pauper when compared with fellow oilman Jean Paul Getty, who once estimated the worth of his holdings at several billion dollars, yet added, "But remember, a billion dollars isn't worth what it used to be." Getty's income has been estimated at *$300,000 a day.*

With incomes, respectively, of roughly $50 million and $100 million a year, Messrs. Hunt and Getty might have been expected to pay to the U.S. Treasury, under the tax laws prevailing in the early Sixties, taxes of $45 million for Hunt and about $88 million for Getty.*

Yet, according to what President John F. Kennedy privately told two United States Senators, *Messrs. Getty and Hunt each paid income taxes amounting to only a few thousand dollars a year!*

---

* Note that this is what the two might have been expected to pay in the early Sixties, when tax rates were higher than they are today (the top rate was 91 percent compared with 70 percent now). At today's rates, they might be expected to pay roughly $35 million and $70 million, respectively.

228

WHILE H. L. HUNT and Jean Paul Getty could hardly be called your typical oil tycoons, they are far from unique. Consider the cases of

• a Mr. D (cited in a Treasury Department study which by law was obliged to cloak his name), who, in 1960, had an income ("total reported economic income," in Treasury's words) of *over $26 million**—and who not only wholly escaped all Federal taxation, but even managed to file a Federal tax return showing a *loss* of $846,330, much of which could be helpfully used to shield future-year income from taxation;

• a Mr. B, who had total income in the four years 1958–1962 of $9,419,000, *but paid no income taxes in any of those four years*;

• one oil and gas operator, of whom government officials speak privately, who over a twelve-year period sold at least $50 million worth of oil, at times enjoyed an annual income of more than $5,500,000—yet *paid not a penny of income tax for the entire twelve years.*

THE TAX LAW is also strikingly gentle toward the major oil companies, for whom a tax as high as 10 percent would be extraordinary. In 1971, when American corporations as a whole were paying about two-fifths their net income in taxes, this is what the tax law permitted the largest oil companies to pay—and what that cost the U.S. Treasury (i.e., all the rest of the taxpayers):

Company	Before-Tax Profit	Percent Paid in U.S. Taxes	Approximate Loss to U.S. Treasury*
Gulf	$1.324 billion	2.3%	$500 million
Texaco	$1.319 billion	2.3%	$495 million
Mobil	$1.153 billion	7.4%	$375 million
Standard (Cal.)	$.856 billion	1.6%	$330 million
Standard (N.J.)	$2.737 billion	7.7%	$885 million
Total	$7.389 billion	5.0%	$2,585 million

* Difference between what U.S. Treasury did collect from these companies and what it would have collected had these oil companies paid 40 percent of their profits to the U.S. Treasury, as was true of U.S. corporations as a whole.

---

* The Treasury study discloses one interesting detail about Mr. D. As with the other super-rich non-taxpayers cited in Chapter 1, Mr. D earned very little in the way of salary (just $18,150, out of his total income of more than $26 million).

Again, for most of those companies this was no one-year freak result. Here are the same figures for those same companies for the ten years, 1962 through 1971:

Company	Before-Tax Profit	Percent Paid in U.S. Taxes	Approximate Loss to U.S. Treasury*
Gulf	$7.856 billion	4.7%	$2.8 billion
Texaco	$8.702 billion	2.6%	$3.3 billion
Mobil	$6.388 billion	6.1%	$2.2 billion
Standard (Cal.)	$5.186 billion	2.7%	$1.9 billion
Standard (N.J.)	$19.653 billion	7.3%	$6.4 billion
Total	$47.785 billion	5.3%	$16.6 billion

* See footnote to preceding table.

In one respect, Congress is fortunate that its members are immune from investigation by its own Un-American Activities Committee, for the same Congressionally approved tax laws that permitted these companies virtually to escape paying taxes to the U.S. government (at the expense of the American Treasury) simultaneously encouraged those companies to pay enormous amounts to foreign governments (in a manner that will be explained more fully below). Here are the facts:

	Taxes Paid		Percent of Profits Paid	
Company	To U.S. Government	To Foreign Governments*	To U.S. Government	To Foreign Governments
	(In millions)			
Gulf	$365	$2,875	4.7%	36.6%
Texaco	$223	$1,410	2.6%	16.2%
Mobil	$388	$2,114	6.1%	33.1%
Standard (Cal.)	$140	$1,290	2.7%	24.9%
Standard (N.J.)	$1,442	$6,450	7.3%	32.8%

* These figures are approximate, in that they reflect what the companies report they paid in "foreign and state taxes," with no breakdown of how much of that is paid to foreign governments and how much to the various states. But those knowledgeable about the oil industry say that very little of it goes to the states; most of it goes to foreign governments.

It is clear, from all the foregoing, that the Congress of the United States has looked upon the oil industry and its investors with a kindly beneficence by writing into the tax law a number of special features that will be explained momentarily. For the rest of the U.S. taxpayers, it has been an expensive beneficence: according to one estimate, it has cost the grand total of $140 *billion* since Congress first inserted these special features into the law. Even today, they are costing the U.S. Treasury (i.e., the taxpayers) about $1.6 billion every year. That $1.6 billion of tax subsidies —most of which goes to the huge oil companies and to very rich oil investors—amounts to

- nearly four times the amount devoted to the Head Start program for preschool children;
- twenty-one times the funds for the Neighborhood Youth Corps;
- eight times as much as is spent for on-the-job training of veterans;
- eighteen times the Federal support for the arts and humanities.

There are two basic provisions of the law that account for these billions of "tax welfare" to the oil industry. One is called "percentage depletion"; the other involves something intriguingly labeled "intangible drilling expenses." (The expenses may be "intangible," but, as you will see, the tax benefits are tangible in the extreme.)

For those who enjoy its benefits, percentage depletion is a very pleasant experience. To appreciate just how pleasant, imagine how you would feel if the government were to say to you, the earner of $10,000 annually, "We think you are such a nice fellow that we will just forget about $2,200 of your income, for tax purposes. That is, when you make out your tax return, just act as if the $2,200 didn't exist." Chances are you'd feel pretty pleased. Chances are, too, that you would feel absolutely overjoyed if you were told that this would be no one-year temporary phenomenon— that it would last just as long as you went on earning your annual $10,000.

That's pretty much the way percentage depletion works. To all those who receive income from oil and gas ventures, Congress has said, in effect, that in making out their tax returns they may just forget about 22 percent of all their oil and gas income. Congress has, in short, placed that 22 percent of everyone's oil and gas income out of the reach of the tax collector. It is tax-free income. And that tax-free privilege goes on, without limit, *as long as the well keeps on producing oil or gas* (and, of course, dollars).

There is one limitation: in any year, the depletion deduction can't be more than half the net profit from a person's (or company's) oil and gas properties. But that limit has not prevented a dramatic rise in the amount of tax-free income from the "depletion allowance." According to the latest available figures, depletion deductions by corporations (which take the lion's share of such deductions) had climbed from just over $3.2 billion in 1960 to $5.5 billion in 1968.

In addition to this depletion allowance, oil companies and investors are allowed large and immediate tax deductions of their so-called "intangible drilling expenses" in a manner not permitted other taxpayers. For *individual* oil investors (as distinct from the major oil companies), this can be a far more important tax favor than the depletion allowance. It is especially handy for those with an apparent aversion to paying *any* Federal income taxes—ever. As noted in Chapter 1, one oilman has given standing instructions to his tax attorney to "drill up" any potentially taxable income that may loom on his financial horizon. Others are said to guide their drilling decisions with the aid of computers, which make monthly calculations as to income needing "shelter" from IRS.*

In a sense, this "intangible drilling expense" deduction adds insult to injury to the Treasury, since it enables oil investors to use their tax savings (i.e., use what would otherwise be Uncle Sam's money) to help them buy more oil holdings, generate even more tax-favored income and thus make an even larger dent in the U.S. Treasury.

Percentage depletion applies not just to oil and gas but to more than 110 other minerals (ranging from sulfur, coal and iron ore to flowerpot clay, ornamental stone and oyster and clam shells!). But since about 80 percent of the depletion deductions emanate from oil and gas, that is what this chapter will concentrate on.

---

* As described in Chapter 4, when Congress enacted the so-called "minimum tax" in 1969, with the supposed object of putting an end to total tax avoidance of this sort, the legislators took pity on the oilmen who were using "intangible" deductions as a means of paying zero tax. They did so by exempting "intangibles" (although not the depletion deductions) from the effect of the new tax. As a result, the computer-users and "drill-it-up" tax avoiders can still manipulate the system so as to pay no tax. (Use of the "intangible" deductions could, however, increase somewhat the percentage depletions that *are* subject to the "minimum tax.")

Percentage depletion alone costs the Treasury an estimated $1.3 billion per year. In addition, the special "intangible drilling expense" deductions cost about a third of a billion dollars each year, so the total cost of the tax preferences enjoyed by the mineral industries exceeds $1.6 billion.

This prodigious drain on the Federal Treasury is frequently defended as an indispensable incentive to the costly and high-risk exploration for oil and gas. Some find this argument less than convincing. Their doubts are caused by facts such as these:

• The "incentive" offered to comparatively low-risk drilling (in the midst of already-proven wells) is just as generous as that available to high-risk "discovery drilling."

• That same "risk incentive" is even offered to those who take no risk whatever (namely, the passive landowners who simply permit the risk-taking driller to drill on their land).

• The more costly of the two tax "incentives," percentage depletion, taken by itself (i.e., leaving aside the "intangible drilling" feature of the law), does not reward the person who drills and finds no oil but only rewards those who *have found* the oil and who extract the already-found oil from the ground.

TAKE BOOMING INDUSTRIES such as oil and gas; add some lucrative tax advantages; shake well. The result: some spectacularly rich Americans, of whom Jean Paul Getty and H. L. Hunt are but two examples.

The late Hugh Roy Cullen, for instance, who had once worked in a San Antonio candy shop, later became wealthy enough to express both his generosity and his exuberance in grandiose fashion. The object of his generosity was the University of Texas, on which he bestowed the handsome gift of *one hundred million dollars.* Originally, that was all he intended to give; but then, in a moment of elation following the University's upset football victory against Baylor, the overjoyed Mr. Cullen added a "bonus" check of $2,225,000.

In 1958, two fabled oil multimillionaires—Clint Murchison and Sid Richardson—teamed up to contribute $20 million to help Robert R. Young gain control of the New York Central Railroad. Later, it developed that there had been a misunderstanding on Richardson's part. He had thought the deal was for $5 million each instead of $10 million. He called up his partner, not to berate him for the $5 million misunderstanding but simply to inquire, "Say, Clint, what was the name of that railroad?"

In New Orleans, Dr. Martin Miller conducted a quiet practice of surgery and a side practice of investing in oil—so shrewdly that his income was once estimated at between $7 and $8 million a year, according to *Fortune.*

In oil, there is plenty of money to go around. The chauffeur of oilman Michael Late Benedum originally had but one ambition in life: to be guaranteed $50 a week in his old age; but due to the generosity of his employer in cutting him in on oil deals, he was worth $17 million when he died.

The very wealthy consider oil investments almost a "must." One industrialist, worth $85 million, confided to the *Wall Street Journal,* "When a fellow is in my income bracket, he automatically goes into the oil business. This is a legal way to escape confiscation of earnings."

BEFORE READERS rush out to invest their last hard-earned pennies in oil ventures, they should recognize that oil has made paupers as well as millionaires out of the venturesome. But whether luck is with you or against you, the tax laws are on your side. This was neatly summed up by a Houston oil expert who was describing the tax joys of oil ventures to some would-be investors in Cleveland (in the days when the top tax bracket was about 90 percent and the depletion allowance for oil and gas was 27½ percent):

In [oil] exploration, the government permits you to deduct all gambling losses. An individual in the 90 percent tax bracket can consider Uncle Sam as his partner in up to 90 percent of all *losses.* [But] because of the 27½ percent depletion allowance, Uncle Sam takes a relatively modest share of the income of successful ventures. *If you are in the 90 percent tax bracket, you are risking only 10 cents out of a dollar spent on unsuccessful ventures.* As to *successful* ventures, [the average tax rate] to a 90-percent-bracket couple is about 65 percent. [Emphasis added.]

Since the time that advice was given, the tax rates have come down (the top tax bracket is 70 percent and the depletion allowance has been reduced to 22 percent). But while the numbers have changed, the principles remain the same: a person in the 70 percent bracket risks only 30 cents on every dollar he invests in a "dry hole," with Uncle Sam (i.e., the rest of the U.S. taxpayers) a 70 percent partner in the deal.

It may be unpleasant to think of yourself being "taken" in a business deal, but the above description allows no other conclusion. After all, in a normal business arrangement, a person who puts up most of the money and takes most of the risk expects to get back his full share of the profits. But not us non-oil-investing taxpayers. Following the course Congress has set for us, we put up as much as 70 percent of the "risk" money for drilling. If a "dry hole" results, we, as taxpayers, are left holding up to 70 percent of a very empty bag. If the result is a gusher, we must content ourselves, as the Houston oil expert so gracefully put it, with a "relatively modest" share of the proceeds.

IN ALL, investors in oil and gas enjoy three separate, distinct and unique tax advantages. They may be summarized as follows:

	Oil Men	*Others*
Advantage 1	*Immediate* write-off of most capital costs	*Gradual* write-off of most capital costs
Advantage 2	*Double* deduction of initial investment	*Single* deduction of initial investment
Advantage 3	*Continuing* deductions for *no* investment	*No* deductions beyond initial investment

Follow through the simple steps of an oil investment and each of these advantages will be made clear. Suppose you invest $100,000 in drilling an oil well. Roughly $25,000 of this pays for the derrick, the pipe in the ground and other immovable material and equipment. The other $75,000, called "intangible drilling expense," goes for wages and salaries, fuel, and machine and tool rental. Now this $100,000 is, in essence, the cost of developing an income-producing property (namely, the oil well) and is therefore a "capital" cost. In any other industry, the entire $100,000 would be deducted gradually, over the "useful life" of the property. That is, if the well were deemed to have a "useful life"* of twenty

---

* Treasury regulations offer guidelines on the "useful life" of various kinds of machinery, equipment, buildings, etc. For simplicity's sake, the illustrations here assume even, or "straight-line" depreciation (see Glossary).

years, the deductions would come to $5,000 a year; with a ten-year life, they would be $10,000 a year.

But if you are an oilman, such paltry deductions are not considered sufficient. At least three-quarters of your capital costs—the so-called "intangible drilling expenses"—may be deducted *immediately*, in the year you make the outlays, rather than being spread out evenly over the entire "life" of the well. Thus, instead of a first-year deduction of $5,000 or $10,000, *you get a first-year deduction of $75,000 or more.* (The other $25,000, of course, is permitted to be written off gradually, like the capital costs in other industries.)

True, this huge first-year deduction will mean forgoing later deductions. But this does not diminish your enthusiasm, for, as a sensible businessman (or as one who read Chapter 8 of this book and received The Message contained therein), you know that a dollar in hand is worth far more than the expectation of a dollar at some future date. Assuming you have $75,000 of non-oil income that can helpfully be offset by your $75,000 deductions* (and thus escape taxation), you have a splendid opportunity to use Uncle Sam's money to parlay your first well into still others. Thus, if you're smart, you'll follow in the footsteps of many an oil operator before you, and you'll take your tax-free $75,000 and "drill it up" —i.e., put it to work drilling more wells and generating still more depletion-sheltered income.

One student of the oil industry has said that the privilege of the immediate deduction of "intangible expenses" is a more powerful incentive to oil exploration than the depletion allowance. It is certainly generously used: for example, in 1960 (the latest date for which such an analysis was made), corporations taking depletion deductions of $3.2 billion also took $1.1 billion in "intangible" deductions.

Let's move on. Year One has ended, and you have your first well. As Year Two begins, it starts pouring forth liquid gold, and thereafter, with pleasurable monotony, it produces a steady

---

* Of course, if you're the kind of independent, hand-to-mouth "wildcatter" for whom all these incentives were supposedly designed, chances are you don't have the $75,000 of income to offset and the "intangible" deduction won't do you any good. On the other hand, if you're Standard of New Jersey, or a top-bracket taxpayer who uses computers to beat the tax game, you will never want for income to offset so as to take full advantage of these deductions.

$100,000 worth a year.* With even more pleasurable monotony, you are entitled to keep $22,000 of this income—or half your net profit from the well, whichever is smaller—wholly unsullied by the hands of the tax collector. Herein lie Advantages Two and Three.

Remember that your original $100,000 investment has already been taken care of *once*, through the $75,000 of "intangible" deductions you've already taken, plus the deductions scheduled for future years for the remaining $25,000. Now, for most investors this is deemed sufficient; in the case of oil and gas investors, however, Congress apparently wants to make *doubly* sure they get their initial investment back tax-free, for they provide the 22 percent depletion allowance *over and above* the regular deductions to cover their original dollar input.

But apparently, as Congress sees it, even the double deduction does not offer the proper compensation to oil and gas investors. The depletion allowance does not stop even after they have recovered their investment a second time. It goes on and on and on, just as long as the oil or gas well continues to produce. This can get to be extraordinarily generous: in the case of oil, for the year 1966 (the latest year for which an analysis was published), the depletion allowance permitted deductions amounting to *nineteen times* what other industries may deduct. But sulfur puts oil to shame: in the period 1946–1949, the depletion deductions for sulfur came to *two hundred times*† the deductions permitted other industries.

AS MENTIONED ABOVE, the U.S. government (i.e., the U.S. taxpayers) has been making an annual "tax expenditure" of more than one and a half billion dollars per year, via the depletion allowance plus the "intangible drilling" deductions, supposedly to encourage more exploration for oil and gas.

Have the taxpayers been getting their money's worth?

A lengthy and highly technical study commissioned and made public by the U.S. Treasury Department in 1969 suggests that this

---

* The figure of $100,000 is used for simple illustrative purposes, although production controls in many states might at times limit wells to less than this.

† This is because the cost of finding sulfur (usually a by-product of looking for oil) is extraordinarily low in relation to the later sulfur *income* on which the depletion deductions are based.

may be one of the most wasteful expenditures tolerated by the American public. The study concluded that the $1.6 billion annual "tax expenditure" had been resulting in added outlays for oil exploration of just $150 million—only one-tenth the annual revenue loss from depletion and "intangibles."*

THE PERCENTAGE DEPLETION privilege does not stop at the water's edge. American companies enjoy the full benefits of percentage depletion on their foreign oil operations. The domestic depletion allowance is often justified by the high-risk, high-cost character of American oil exploration. Yet, even where fabulous oil pools are found comparatively near the surface and dry holes are rare (as in the Middle East), Congress nonetheless bestows the same 22 percent depletion allowance as for higher-risk, higher-cost domestic production.

This is of substantial comfort to American companies overseas. In 1955 and 1956, the Arabian-American Oil Company (Aramco) (which is owned by the major American oil firms) had depletion deductions amounting to $148 million and $152 million, respectively. This alone benefited the company by (and cost the U.S. Treasury) some $124 million for the two years. So great are the after-tax profits of Aramco that two of its corporate owners— Standard Oil of New Jersey and Mobil—were able to recover their entire original investment in Aramco in a single year.

The Middle East, incidentally, has been a virtual fountain of profits for American oil which, according to one study, made profits totaling $5.8 *billion* on their Mid-East operations from 1963 to 1968.

A second pleasure enjoyed by American oil companies springs from the fact that much of the oil-rich land in the Middle East is owned not by private companies or individuals but by the various national governments. If the land were privately owned, payments by the American oil companies to the landowners for the privilege of extracting the oil would clearly be considered *royalty* payments. But since the land is owned by governments, and payments to governments are usually called "taxes," the payments they receive from the oil companies can be labeled either "royalties" *or* "taxes."

---

* The study also concluded that if the oil and gas tax favors were totally eliminated, the industry would reduce outlays for oil and gas exploration by only a paltry 2.3 percent.

The difference, to the oil companies and the U.S. Treasury—and, indirectly, to the foreign governments—is far more than semantic. The difference is this: suppose Aramco makes a $100 million payment to the government of Saudi Arabia. If that is considered a royalty payment, it is merely treated as a deduction from Aramco's *income* in computing its U.S. taxes. At the current 48 percent corporation tax rate, Aramco is out-of-pocket $52 million, the remaining $48 million in effect being diverted from the U.S. Treasury to the government of Saudi Arabia. If, on the other hand, the $100 million is labeled a *tax* payment, *the law allows Aramco to reduce its U.S. tax payments by the full $100 million* (see Glossary, under "tax credit"). Uncle Sam ends up bearing the entire load.

As indicated, there is, to Saudi Arabia, an indirect advantage in using the "taxes" rather than the "royalties" label, since it and other foreign governments can exact a higher total tribute at no expense to—and hence with little or no complaint from—the American oil companies. Apparently this truth was revealed in all its glory to the various Middle East governments in the early Fifties,* for, beginning about that time, oil company tax payments to the U.S. government underwent a dramatic decline, and their tax payments to foreign governments a correspondingly dramatic increase—a result that some members of Congress might be tempted to label un-American.

For example, from World War II through 1953 the nation's largest oil company, Standard of New Jersey, was paying roughly the same percentage of its profits in foreign and in U.S. taxes (19 and 16 percent, respectively). But suddenly, in 1954, Jersey's U.S. tax dropped to 11 percent, and by 1958 it paid only *1 percent* of its gargantuan profit to the U.S. Treasury, *but more than 40 percent to foreign governments and potentates*!

In the case of the Gulf Oil Company, the transformation occurred a year earlier. Prior to 1952, Gulf was paying roughly 25 percent taxes to the U.S. government. But from 1953 through 1967, the percentage dropped to about 5 percent (for three consecutive years it was less than 1 percent!), with foreign governments getting the 25 percent that had been going into the Federal Treasury.

The loss to the United States was prodigious. If in the ten years, 1962 through 1971, Standard of New Jersey and Gulf had gone on paying American taxes at the rate they did in the late

---

* For details of how this came about, see pp. 281–283.

Forties and early Fifties before "royalties" began to be called "taxes," *the American Treasury would have been more than four and a half billion dollars richer.* (And that is for just *two* of the major oil companies!) Instead, that $4½ billion was siphoned off to foreign governments and had to be made up by the non-oil-owning American taxpayers.

Even one strong supporter of the *domestic* depletion allowances, former Senator Mike Monroney of the oil-rich state of Oklahoma, once expressed strong reservations about the tax privileges enjoyed by overseas companies. The disguising of royalties as "taxes," he said, amounts to giving international oil companies a depletion allowance twice as great as that enjoyed by domestic companies.

THOSE ARE THE BASIC tax advantages which the oil and gas industries find so congenial. But, as with most tax favors, there are one or two other subtle escape routes available to the well-counseled.

There is, for example, the capital gains route, with which you have become familiar in reading of the various "tax shelters" in Chapter 9. When a top-bracket oil operator avails himself of the generous "intangible expense" deduction—and the wealthy oil operator labeled "Mr. B" in the Treasury Department study mentioned on page 229 did so to the tune of $6,600,000 in a four-year period—he is *saving* 70 cents on every deducted dollar. But if he turns around and sells a well, or an interest in it, he pays no more than the special 35 percent capital gains tax rate on his profit.* Clearly, for every dollar on which he has *saved 70 cents* but *pays back no more than 35 cents,* he is ahead of the game *on taxes alone* by 35 cents. On this basis, Mr. B stood to make a "tax profit" of $2,310,000 (35 percent of his $6,600,000 deductions). In 1963 President Kennedy estimated that this pleasant one-way-street arrangement was yielding tax profits totaling $50 million a year, and asked that this one-sided arrangement be made a two-way street.† Congress rejected his proposal outright.

---

* A special maximum tax of 33 percent of the selling price is available under some circumstances on oil and gas properties.

† By providing that profits on a mineral sale that had previously enjoyed a full-rate deduction be taxed at that same full rate instead of at the favorable capital gains rate—as is the case regarding exploration expenses for "hard" minerals.

Another more obscure 1954 provision has been a boon to successful oilmen, and remains quietly in the law today. Ordinarily, when business expenses or deductions result in a taxpayer's showing a net *loss* on his tax return, he is entitled to carry that loss forward and use it to offset income or profits in future years. Prior to 1954, an oil operator was prohibited from carrying his tax losses forward to the extent the losses were due to his percentage depletion deductions. But a little-noticed provision crept into the mammoth 1954 overall code revision, repealing this prohibition and allowing oil-deduction losses to be freely carried forward. At the time, one revenue agent in an oil state predicted that henceforth many large oil operators would cease paying taxes entirely, year after year. He proved right. Look at the record of the Treasury study's Mr. B. Not only did he manage to pay no taxes on $9,419,000 of income during the four-year period from 1958 to 1962; *at the end of that four years, he still had excess deductions (i.e., tax losses) of nearly $2,700,000 that he could carry forward to protect future years' income from taxation.* Thus, the total of his tax-free income, mainly due to his oil deductions, came to $12,100,000.

HOW DID ALL of these preferences come to be written into the tax laws?

Although the term "depletion" was contained in the original 1913 income tax law,* depletion deductions were limited to the *original cost* of the property (the formula that still applies today to nonmineral industries) or its value as of March 1, 1913.† Because this latter qualification was thought to discriminate against new versus pre-1913 discoveries, the law was changed in 1918 to permit an oil investor to base deductions either on original cost or on the "fair market value" of the well at the time of its discovery —a system known as "discovery depletion." But the calculation of this "fair value" proved uncertain and cumbersome, for it led to disputes between oil owners and the government as to the amount and value of the unseen oil that lay deep in the earth. And so, in 1926, percentage depletion—for oil and gas only—was

---

* Technically, there were two prior U.S. income tax laws: the first, enacted in 1861, was repealed in 1872. The second, enacted in 1894, was declared unconstitutional by the Supreme Court in 1895. The 1913 statute was, therefore, the first permanent income tax law.

† This proviso was inserted in order to avoid taxing values that had accrued prior to the adoption of the Sixteenth Amendment.

ushered into the tax law wearing the unarguable garb of "simplicity." The Treasury Department had the unkindness to suggest
that if simplicity was really Congress's object, what could be
simpler than to return to the "original cost" concept of the 1913
law? Apparently that argument did not appeal to Congress.

As you will note elsewhere in this chapter, the percentage
depletion formula that Congress enacted in 1926 has several
apparent defects: (1) while it is justified as compensating for
unusually high *risk,* it is extended equally to low-risk-takers
(drillers in "proven" oil fields) as well as to zero-risk-takers (passive landowners); and (2) the bulk of the benefits go to the
financially well-heeled giant companies rather than to the small
"wildcatter" who really *needs* the incentive. Congress had reason
to be aware of those drawbacks when it enacted percentage depletion, for coincidentally, in that very year, a Senate study revealed
that "discovery depletion" (percentage depletion's predecessor)
had suffered those identical defects. For example, the 1926 study
showed that two-thirds of the "discovery depletion" deductions
were being taken in *proven* oil fields, where the risks were relatively small; that 60 percent of the deductions were benefiting
"large operators" whose extensive drilling operations diminished
their risks; and that deductions were also being taken by landowners who simply leased their lands for oil drillings and "[sat]
idly by and [risked] nothing . . . not risked by every investor in
real estate." Despite these revelations, Congress passed up the
opportunity to cure the defects and, instead, perpetuated them in
the new and more generous percentage depletion provision.

The 1926 law set the depletion allowance for oil and gas at
27½ percent. Why the odd figure? During the forty-three years
that figure remained in the law, the more zealous defenders of the
oil depletion allowance sometimes made it sound as though that
27½ percent was decreed from Heaven, and that to reduce it to,
say, 27¼, or (perish the thought) 27 percent, would cause the
earth to tremble. The fact is, the 27½ percent figure was nothing
but a negotiated compromise—between the 25 percent desired by
the House members and the 30 percent in the Senate version of
the 1926 measure. (An effort to write a 35 percent depletion allowance into the Senate bill lost by a one-vote margin.) Supporters of
the percentage depletion provision acknowledged at the time that
the figure was an "arbitrary" one.

For more than four decades, oil and gas were the undisputed

monarchs of the percentage depletion realm, for they alone were favored with the 27½ percent allowance. But, in 1969, Congress toppled them from their throne and reduced them to the level of the dukes and duchesses among minerals—those that enjoy a 22 percent allowance. The rates for others are, variously, 15, 14, 10, 7½ and 5 percent, always subject to the 50-percent-of-net-income ceiling.

The use of the depletion allowance is increasingly in vogue. Total depletion deductions by corporations quadrupled in the decade 1946–1956—from just under $800 million to over $3.2 billion —and then nearly doubled again, to just under $5.5 billion, by 1967.

The privilege of an immediate write-off for "intangible drilling costs" was first permitted in 1916—not by a law enacted by Congress, but by Internal Revenue regulations. Over the years, there has been considerable legal controversy over whether Internal Revenue had the power to grant this privilege. In 1945, one court held it did not, since these expenditures were in fact "capital outlays" (deductible only over a period of years) and no Internal Revenue regulation could magically transform them into "expenses" (which are immediately deductible). This decision sent a tremor through the oil industry (the shock was the greater since the heresy came from none other than the Fifth Circuit Court of Appeals, whose jurisdiction includes the oil-soaked state of Texas). The tremor was quickly communicated to Congress, which promptly adopted a resolution affirming Internal Revenue's power to grant the more favorable treatment to the "intangible expenses." In 1954, to end all doubt, Congress *directed* Internal Revenue, by statute, to issue such a ruling.

Over the years, under the principle of tax "equity" described in Chapter 14, percentage depletion has been extended to more than 100 specifically enumerated minerals, from A (Anorthosite) to Z (Zinc). So all-encompassing is the list of minerals, in fact, that Congress felt it necessary to specify that it did *not* mean to grant the depletion privilege to "soil, sod, dirt, turf, water or mosses" or to "minerals from sea water, the air or similar inexhaustible sources." Even this has not deterred some imaginative taxpayers from claiming percentage depletion on certain underground water and steam.

WHAT ARE THE REASONS for and against the depletion allowance? To become acquainted with them, one might eavesdrop on a hypothetical discussion between an Oilman and a querulous Taxpayer who experiences some difficulty in understanding why he and others like him should be paying higher taxes in order to make up for the multi-billion-dollar tax preferences for oil, gas and other minerals.

OILMAN: When will everybody learn that oil is different from anything else? Every time you lift a barrel of oil out of the ground, there's one less barrel left, and there's not a thing you can do about it.

Suppose I own just one well, and I'm pumping it at a rate that will dry it up in ten years. Every year, my property gets smaller by ten percent. At the end of the ten years, it's disappeared, vanished, it doesn't exist—and I'm out of business.

You've heard oil called a "wasting asset"? Well, that's why.

TAXPAYER: But isn't *everything* a wasting asset? I mean, a machine doesn't last forever. And once it's worn out, it's just as useless as a worn-out oil well, and there's "not a thing you can do" (to use your words) to get it back. As far as its usefulness is concerned, it might just as well have "disappeared—vanished."

OILMAN: Sure, but you know perfectly well that the tax laws let the machine owner "write off" or depreciate that machine, so that when it's worn out he'll have the money to go out and buy a new one. That's basically what depletion is for the oil industry. It's supposed to give me the money to go out and find a new well to replace my worn-out well.

TAXPAYER: Now, just a minute. First you told me that when a well was used up, there wasn't a thing you could do about it. Now you're saying you need the depletion allowance to go out and look for a new well. What's the difference between that and going out and buying a new machine?

Besides, if we're going to start giving special tax treatment for "irreplaceable" assets, why leave out Raquel Welch and Willie Mays? You can go out and find yourself a new oil well. But what about them, when they grow old? All the money in the world won't buy them back their youth or their beauty. Why not give them a depletion allowance?

OILMAN: Oh, come on now. You can't be serious.

TAXPAYER: Sir, when it comes to potential discriminations against the beauteous Raquel Welch, I am indeed serious. But let's go back for a minute to the oil well–versus–machine example we were talking about. Let's say a toolmaking company buys a new lathe. Under *depreciation*, the toolmaker can never deduct more than the *original cost* of that lathe. But your *depletion* deductions go on as long as your well keeps producing—even though you may deduct one hundred or two hundred times your original cost. How come?

OILMAN: Well, for one thing, the toolmaker can count on his lathe lasting a certain number of years. But I never know for sure how long my oil well is going to produce. It may give out next year. And then where am I?

Besides, I have no way of knowing how much it's going to cost to find new oil. I may hit five or ten or twenty dry holes before I strike a new well—and I might never hit a producing well.

TAXPAYER: But on both scores the toolmaker is in essentially the same boat. For one thing, a new kind of automated lathe might suddenly come along and make his present machine as obsolete and useless as your suddenly worn-out well. For another, he can't tell how much it's going to cost him to replace his lathe— and even if it turns out to cost him twice as much, *he only gets to deduct his original cost.* I still don't see why you oilmen should be special and get deductions for more dollars than you put in.

OILMAN: Obviously, you're not aware that our depletion deductions are less than our outlays. Why, in the late Fifties, for instance, we were laying out $1.18 a barrel looking for new oil— but getting only 80 cents a barrel in depletion deductions.

TAXPAYER: But you're no worse off than any other industry. Nobody gets deductions equal to their *replacement* costs, which is what you keep talking about. Besides, you're leaving out half the picture. You get back your money *once* through your "intangible drilling" and development expense deductions, and then *again* through your depletion deductions. Why the *double* deduction when everyone else only gets one?

OILMAN: There is no double deduction. You see, the depletion allowance is to compensate a man for the fact that his oil is disappearing, and the intangible expenses you mention are to cover the cost of drilling and putting up a well and getting it into production once the oil pool has been found.

TAXPAYER: Well, the Supreme Court doesn't agree with you. It ruled that depletion is supposed to cover both, and another court ruled that the "intangible" deduction is a "special favor."

OILMAN: You know, you keep harping on this "special treatment" theme, but all depletion does is put us on the same footing as everybody else. You see, when I find new oil, I'm creating *new* capital, and when I sell it, all I'm getting is a "return of capital." Other people don't pay taxes on that—why should we?

TAXPAYER: Well, it seems funny to me that when you tell your *stockholders* about your oil sales you list the proceeds as income and profits. But all of a sudden, when you're telling the *tax collector* about them, they are magically transformed into a "return of capital." Some companies even keep two sets of books —one for their stockholders, showing the same kind of "original cost" figures that all other industries use, and another for the government. In fact, the Internal Revenue Service reported that in 1964 the petroleum industry showed after-tax profits of $1.7 billion, *for tax purposes*—yet *on their own books of account* those same companies showed after-tax profits of $5 billion—*nearly three times as great*! In 1966 their books of account showed after-tax profits twice as large as what showed up on their tax returns. That's quite a difference, wouldn't you say?

OILMAN: But that's done—sometimes *required*—in many industries. Besides, you people always forget the terrific risks we run when we look for oil and the fantastic money it costs us. And it's getting more expensive all the—

TAXPAYER: Let me stop you right there. Surely you're not suggesting that oil is the only risk-taking business. As a matter of fact, from one point of view, oil is one of the safest. The figures on business failures in *Dun's* magazine show that in every year from 1925 to 1954, oil had about the lowest rate of failures. In the mid-Fifties, the failure rate per 10,000 businesses was twenty in food, fifty in apparel, eighty-six in construction, over four hundred in retailing—*and only four in oil, gas and mining*!

OILMAN: Now I've heard it all. Are you saying oil is a "safe" industry?

TAXPAYER: No, I'm not denying there are risks in oil, just as there are in every business. But if the oil industry is going to get a tax concession on the basis of its risks, then the only fair thing would be for the government to try to measure the exact amount of risk in *every* industry—in fact, every individual business—and give a tax concession to everybody to compensate for his risks.

You know, you oilmen talk a lot about free enterprise. Why aren't you willing to rely on free enterprise to take care of the risk factor? Other industries assume that if risk is high, prices and returns on investment will reflect it. Why can't the oil industry stand on its own feet? How come it needs a government subsidy?

OILMAN: What are you trying to do, make me mad or something? We oilmen are individualists. We get no subsidy; we want no subsidy.

TAXPAYER: Frankly, I don't see what else you can call it when U.S. corporations as a whole paid about 40 percent taxes in 1971, while five major oil companies paid about 5 percent—for a tax saving, compared with other corporations, of two and a half billion dollars, for just five companies in a single year!*

OILMAN: I still can't seem to get you to realize the extent of the risk we take. In "wildcat" drilling, for instance, when you're exploring in a brand-new field—eight out of nine tries turn out to be dry holes. It's true that drilling near proven oil pools, only one out of four is a dry hole. But where else—other than in wild-catting—do you get eight-to-one odds against you?

TAXPAYER: You admit there are different risks involved in different kinds of drilling. Yet why does everybody get the same depletion allowance—whether his risk is high, low, or even zero?

As a matter of fact, most of the depletion deductions don't go to the small wildcatters, who are really risking their financial necks. They go to the giant corporations, who take much smaller risks.

OILMAN: You'll have to prove that one to me.

TAXPAYER: All right. The latest available government statistics on the subject show that in 1967 nearly 92 percent of all depletion deductions were taken by the most colossal corporations in the country—those with assets of more than a quarter of a billion dollars.

And about $99.70 out of every $100 went to companies with assets of a million dollars or more—that's still a pretty big company. So how much did the smallest companies get? *Thirty cents* out of every $100 of depletion deductions!

OILMAN: All right, everybody. All together. Let's all hiss the giant corporation and weep for the little fellow. Touching, very

---

* See table, p. 229.

touching—but I didn't hear one statistic that had anything to do with the *riskiness* of an oil investment.

TAXPAYER: On the contrary, my statistics were right to the point. In the first place, one of your most ardent Senatorial supporters has said that the big oil companies do very little wild-catting. They buy a lot of their new oil *from* wildcatters as proven wells—so there's no risk there.

Secondly, the drilling they do is fairly conservative, and highly successful. Take the five largest oil companies. In 1958, they hit 3,447 *productive* wells against only 868 dry holes. That's a four-to-one ratio. Even the *worst* record among the forty top oil companies was 105 successes to 96 dry holes—a far cry from the eight-to-one odds you were talking about.

OILMAN: But depletion isn't for risk alone. Everybody's capital—the big fellow's just the same as the little guy's—is disappearing as the oil gets pumped out. But since you're talking about risk, let's concentrate on the small wildcatter, the guy who's *really* taking the risks. If you cut down on the depletion allowance, he just won't go out looking for new oil. He'll sell out to the major oil companies.

TAXPAYER: Now maybe we're getting somewhere. If it's the small wildcatter who's taking the risks and needs the help, let's by all means give it to him. *But let's make sure the help really goes to him,* and not to a lot of people who take no risk and need no relief. The trouble with a tax deduction is that it's absolutely no good to the really small, hand-to-mouth wildcatter who doesn't have the outside income to offset against the deduction. Besides, why give a tax concession to a man who simply leases his *land* to an oil company, *risks nothing,* and then sits back and collects royalties? Or what if I buy an interest in a *proven* well? Where's my risk? And yet I may get more of a tax break than the wildcatter who risked his shirt.

OILMAN: But the oil industry is still less profitable than a lot of other industries, even *after* taxes, which proves there's no gouging or profiteering. So if you cut down on the depletion allowance, first, oil and gas prices will rise sharply, and secondly, how are we going to attract the capital to go on drilling for new oil?

Besides, what if there's a war? What if we get caught like Europe after Suez—suddenly deprived of our foreign oil supplies, just by the whim of some dictator?

TAXPAYER: Well, if we're going to give tax concessions to one industry solely on the ground that it's "war-essential," we ought to give it to all of them—airplane companies, electronics and missile companies—there'd be no end to it.

Secondly, if the object is to make sure we have plenty of oil here at home in case of a war, percentage depletion is just one hundred and eighty degrees wrong.

OILMAN: What do you mean? Why?

TAXPAYER: Because percentage depletion doesn't give you a single penny's benefit for *discovering* the oil. You only begin to get the advantages *when you begin drawing the oil out of the ground*—that is, when you begin using up the oil we might need in a war.

Anyway, if we need every drop of our oil for defense, why do we limit the imports of foreign oil? Why not do just the reverse: rely mainly on foreign oil now and conserve our domestic supplies in case of a war?

OILMAN: Oh, sure—and shut down the American oil industry! Where do you think we'd get the skilled hands to start up our industry again if war did break out?

TAXPAYER: You seem to want it both ways. First you tell me we need lots of domestic oil in case of war, and then you say we should use up our oil here at home to keep our industry going.

Besides, if, as you say, all this foreign oil is going to be cut off from us in time of war, why give it *any* depletion allowance? What sense does it make to subsidize foreign oil, and then deny ourselves the use of it by import quotas?

OILMAN: You mean grant depletion on *domestic* oil but not on *American-owned* foreign oil? Why, Congress would never discriminate that way.

TAXPAYER: I beg your pardon, sir. Congress has done precisely that. In the case of some thirty-five minerals, it has drawn a clear distinction between the domestic and the foreign production. It could do the same with oil.

OILMAN: I think we'd better wind this up. Let me make two final points. First, the depletion allowance has become as much a part of the oil industry as the rotary rig. You wouldn't dream of depriving us of that important tool; don't deprive us of depletion.

Second, the depletion allowance has worked. Since it's been in effect, we've had fabulous discovery of oil, we have lower prices to the consumer on oil and gas—lower, in fact, than in 1926, when depletion began, despite huge cost increases since then. We have one of the greatest oil industries in the world. Why rock the boat? Why experiment with something you don't know will work? I say you can't argue with success.

TAXPAYER: Despite that last admonition, let me put in my final two cents.

Success? Yes. Discovery? Yes. But how much of it is due to the depletion allowance? After all, not a penny of the depletion allowance *as such* (leaving aside the "intangible" deductions) helps new *discoveries*. And most of it goes to people who are doing little or no *high-risk* exploration.

Let me remind you of the study commissioned by the Treasury Department that concluded that the billion and a half dollars of annual tax subsidies to the oil industry was resulting in only $150 million of new oil exploration outlays—which, with only a 10 percent return, means that the oil tax subsidies are 90 percent waste!

That's one of the main troubles with a tax subsidy: so often it is extremely poorly aimed at its target objective. So if—and I emphasize "if"—the oil industry (or any other mineral industry) needs special government help because of the risks of exploration, let the help come directly out of the Treasury. Let Congress appropriate the funds every year, as they do with the farm subsidy and other kinds of subsidies. That way, we could start from scratch and design a new subsidy that would be tailored to help the *real* risk-taker: the explorer, the discoverer of oil. But as long as the subsidy is embedded in the tax laws, the billions lost to the Treasury will be unseen, unquestioned, and uncounted—until it's too late to retrieve the wasted money. A directly appropriated subsidy *would bear an annual price tag.* What's more, it would automatically be reviewed and debated every year.

You say we should continue depletion because it's always been there (which it hasn't) and has become part of the industry. Well, child labor and the twelve-hour day were also once part of American industry, but we abolished *them.* Besides, the premises behind the original depletion program have now been turned upside down: whereas once there was a shortage of oil, now the world supply is more ample. Whereas once depletion helped the *discoverer,* at this moment it mainly benefits the *non*-discoverer.

In the annual debate that would take place if the oil subsidy were directly appropriated, there would be a chance to ask questions, such as: Does it make sense to give tax windfalls to people who risk little or nothing—such as those who buy *proven* oil reserves and the landowners who let others take the risk but reap the tax benefits? Does it make sense to spend billions to stimulate the search for more oil, when we are deliberately curbing oil imports—and when studies indicate a 90 percent waste factor in the present tax subsidy?

I think the public deserves an airing of those questions.

LENGTHY AS THIS DEBATE HAS BEEN, it has not depleted the curiosity of our heroically persistent and inquisitive Taxpayer. Having fathomed the Oilman's arguments on behalf of percentage depletion, he longs to inquire how they apply to the one hundred-odd other minerals that now bask in the warmth of the depletion provisions.

He reflects on the "national defense" argument advanced on behalf of oil. But try as he may, his imagination does not perceive any connection between the defense needs of the nation and, say, flowerpot clay or ornamental stone or table salt, all of which are accorded percentage depletion.

What about the high-risk argument? His mind drifts back to the beaches of his summer vacation, with their limitless stretches of rolling sand dunes, and he wonders what unusual risk is involved in the finding and removal of sand, another depletion-favored mineral.

And what of that troublesome "wasting asset" concept? An alarming thought overwhelms him as he reflects on Congress's decree that oyster shells and clam shells are an exhaustible and irreplaceable asset. Could it be that Congress has been secretly warned of an imminent end to the procreative faculties of the oyster and the clam?*

---

* Be not alarmed; as you will learn in Chapter 14, Congress, in granting depletion to oyster and clam shells, was simply rendering "equity."

12

The World-Wide
Game of
"Beat the Tax Collector"

THIS CHAPTER is the story of how the Congressional tax-law writers have made Uncle Sam into "Uncle Sap."

If that sounds harsh or extreme, ponder the following actual news story that appeared in the Washington *Daily News* of March 30, 1972:

U.S. STEEL PROFITS SWELL
VENEZUELA'S TAX COFFERS

U.S. Steel Corp., the nation's largest steel producer, paid about four times as much income tax to Venezuela last year [1971] as it did to the United States.

According to private sources, the company—the 12th largest in the country—in 1971 paid about $45 million in taxes to Venezuela and between $10 and $13 million to the U.S.

A visitor from Mars, viewing a law under which the nation's twelfth largest corporate citizen pays four times as much to a foreign government as it does to its native land might conclude that the authors of such a law were positively un-American!

But that's not the whole story. The news account continues:

The firm [U.S. Steel] has operations in several foreign countries,

252

including Canada, Brazil, Spain, Italy and the Bahamas. In the Bahamas, U.S. Steel has a cement plant. . . .

A cement plant in the Bahamas? Why there? Why not here at home? There may be many reasons, but certainly U.S. Steel is not *dis*couraged from opening a cement plant there by the fact that the Bahamas impose no corporate income tax. This opens up what company officials euphemistically call "tax opportunities," of which, according to the news account, U.S. Steel took full advantage. Read on:

Late in 1971, according to private sources, the company brought back to the U.S. substantial dividends from the Bahamian operation (which helped swell U.S. Steel's 1971 profits). . . . But *U.S. Steel reportedly paid no U.S. income tax on those repatriated Bahamian dividends because it already had paid foreign taxes* on those earnings.* [Emphasis added.]

Again, the payment of the *foreign* taxes came first. Again, "Uncle Sap" wound up short-changed, receiving not a penny's share of profits earned by its twelfth largest corporation from furnishing jobs to Bahamian rather than American cement workers. (How does one explain *that* to the nearly five million unemployed Americans?)

Compared with Standard Oil of Ohio, U.S. Steel was positively generous to the U.S. government. At least U.S. Steel paid *some* tax—not much, but *some*. According to Cleveland Congressman Charles Vanik, on the other hand, in 1971 Standard of Ohio (Sohio) paid foreign governments some $7,500,000 in taxes, *but paid not a penny of income tax to its own government.* Not that Sohio lacked the "ability to pay" U.S. taxes: it enjoyed profits, in 1971, of $54,600,000. So there was enough money to pay $36,000,000 of dividends to its shareholders, but *not* enough, it seems, to pay any U.S. income tax. And not only that: because of $50 million of "unused tax losses," Representative Vanik doubted that the company would pay any income taxes to the U.S. Treasury in the near future.

---

* Since the Bahamas impose no tax, the foreign taxes referred to must have been paid to other countries. You will soon see (pp. 263 ff.) how those taxes could be used to shelter the Bahamian profits from any U.S. tax.

The U.S. Steel and Sohio stories are by no means isolated instances of "America last." Other examples:

• The celebrated International Telephone & Telegraph (ITT), in 1971, paid less than $5 million in taxes to the U.S. government, compared with nearly $139 million to states and foreign governments—mostly the latter.

• As the Sohio example illustrates, huge American-owned oil and mining companies pay enormous royalties and "taxes"* to foreign governments and sheikdoms, but there's precious little, if any, left over to pay to the government of the land of which they are, after all, corporate citizens. (The tax returns of several very large mining companies operating in Latin America reflected taxes of just a few thousand dollars *on net profits amounting to $150 million!*)

• American-owned shipping companies that register their ships in tax-free Liberia and Panama contrive to live in a tax limbo in which they pay no tax whatever to the United States (or, for that matter, to any government anywhere in the world). The globally tax-free status of this exotic industry has reportedly created several *billion*aires. Not millionaires. Billionaires.

CLEARLY, massive tax advantages await the company that can reach across the seas and place part of its operations beyond the immediate reach of Internal Revenue. And, as you might expect, the corporate colossi of America have responded eagerly to the tax lures, in rapidly growing proportions. In just ten years (between 1960 and 1970), American investment abroad showed a 240 percent growth (from $32 billion to $78 billion). In 1970, that investment resulted in an annual output of $150 billion and profits of $17.5 billion—*one-fifth of all U.S. corporate profits*. To many companies, those foreign-earned profits are becoming increasingly important. Of 175 firms canvassed by the editors of *Business International* magazine in mid-1972, more than half derived 25 percent or more of their profits from their overseas activities, and for a fifth of those companies more than half their profits were foreign-earned.

---

* "Taxes" is put in quotation marks here because, as you will see (pp. 281–283), many of them are really oil *royalty* payments *disguised* as taxes—to the joy and profit of everyone concerned, except, of course, poor "Uncle Sap."

But the factor that has shown the most explosive growth of all —and the factor of greatest interest to the American taxpayers— has been the amount of taxes U.S. firms have paid to foreign governments. In 1954, the amount (as reported to Internal Revenue) was only $630 million. By 1960, the amount had nearly doubled (to $1.1 billion). Ten years later, in 1970, that amount had nearly quadrupled—to four billion dollars: a 660 percent increase over 1954! Why are those foreign taxes of concern to the American taxpayer? Because, the way the U.S. tax law is written, *every dollar paid to a foreign government is a dollar less for the U.S. Treasury.* To put it another way, the U.S. tax law in effect permitted $4 billion of taxes to be diverted away from the American Treasury and into the treasuries of foreign governments.

Evidently, in the aggregate, foreign countries tax business profits more gently than does the United States. In 1970, the foreign subsidiaries of U.S. companies paid *nine hundred million dollars* less in taxes than they would have paid under U.S. tax rates.

W H E N Y O U E N T E R the realm of international tax manipulation, you step into a world that is, in many respects, about as real (or, if you prefer, about as much sham) as a Hollywood movie set or the legendary "Potemkin villages" of the Russians.* What could be more Potemkin-esque than the Nassau "branch" of the Fidelity Bank of Philadelphia, which in 1971 made loans of $120 million and profits of $1,300,000—yet consisted of but one tiny room described as "no bigger than a walk-in closet," with one desk, one file cabinet and a telephone? According to the *Wall Street Journal*, "there are no tellers' windows. And you never see any customers." Why? Because all the transactions are handled by Fidelity employees in the United States. The actual transfer of funds takes place in New York, with all transactions relayed to and dutifully recorded by a part-time bookkeeper in Nassau in order to "maintain the fiction" that the broom closet is "a fully operating branch bank." In reality, the *Journal* says, the Nassau "branch" is nothing but a "shell," opened by Fidelity just to have a foreign address. Not only does that free Fidelity of cer-

---

* Consisting solely of fake building fronts, with nothing behind them, to lead Catherine II and her entourage, passing by on railroads, to believe that the villages really did exist.

tain U.S.-imposed restrictions on loans to foreign concerns; it also allows the "branch"—and its profits—to bask in the totally tax-free atmosphere of the Bahamas.

Fidelity's "branch" is far from unique: as of mid-1972, some eighty such "shells" had "popped up" in Nassau since 1959, and had "several *billion* in loans outstanding." (Emphasis added.)

Nassau is by no means the only financial "Potemkin village" in the world. Take, for example, the tiny principality of Liechtenstein, an Alpine neighbor of Switzerland, which has 20,000 people, 7,000 cows and no less than 15,000 "foreign legal entities"— meaning, for the most part, businesses that maintain legal addresses in Liechtenstein but are little more substantial than Fidelity's Nassau "branch."

At least some of those "foreign legal entities" are doubtless attracted not only by Liechtenstein's taxlessness but by its tradition of maintaining absolute secrecy about the activities—and even the identity of the owners—of the "entities,"* so that an Internal Revenue agent would be hard-pressed to track down a tax avoider taking advantage of the Liechtensteinian confidentiality.

Astoundingly substantial businesses operate out of modest offices. Billionaire shipping magnate Daniel Ludwig (of whom you will learn more presently) is said to own ships "through a number of tax-haven companies" which share "sparse headquarters staffed by one full-time director and a part-time secretary." *Fortune* magazine reports that the Barracuda Tanker Corporation, created in a New York investment banking house and incorporated in Liberia, "has its registered headquarters in a filing cabinet" in Bermuda. Similarly, in 1971, the *Wall Street Journal* described the burgeoning of so-called "captive insurance companies" in Bermuda, created and owned by major U.S. corporations to insure their overseas activities. According to the *Journal*, these companies "exist largely on paper that's housed in file cabinets in [Bermudian] law offices."

Sometimes, in high international finance, the transactions them-

---

* When a Bavarian industrialist, Fidel Goetz, managed somehow to spirit $4 million out of the treasury of Penn Central (a fact that only came to light when that company went bankrupt), he put the funds into a trust company in Liechtenstein. According to the New York *Times,* the "daring" financial manipulation" whereby Mr. Goetz and his advisers extricated the $4 million from Penn Central and got it to Europe "caused comment even in Liechtenstein, where fancy financial maneuvers are a tradition."

selves, rather than the physical facilities, take on aspects of sham or fiction. For example, in 1970 ITT sold some company stock that soon found its way into the portfolio of a nearby American investment fund with which ITT already had a relationship (the fund held some ITT pension money). You would think that the natural way to handle such a transaction would have been for ITT to sell the stock directly to the fund. But that was not the way it was done. Instead, ITT sold the stock to a foreign bank, which promptly turned around and resold the selfsame stock to the investment fund. Why did ITT go through all those gyrations? Representative Vanik ventured an explanation: it was all "motivated by the desire to increase [certain] foreign tax credit [benefits]." For more on this, see page 266.

At other times it's the *location* of a company's overseas affairs that have a certain artificiality. Ordinarily, for instance, it might not seem natural to you for an American-owned business to establish offices on the island of Efate (have you ever even heard of it?) in the far Pacific, 1,000 miles east of Australia—hardly an easy flight from the financial nerve center of New York. Of late, however, a growing number of American corporations have been responding to the enticing invitations extended by this island in the New Hebrides. Yet it is not the "oceanic tropical" climate, "freshened by Southeast Trade[winds]," that these companies have found attractive, but the tax climate: the islands have "no income or corporation taxes, no capital gains tax, no estate duty, and no land taxes."* What could be more ideal for a profitable American firm than to set up a special New Hebrides company "through which the parent company shuffles papers and profits, thus avoiding or delaying taxes at home," as the *Wall Street Journal* put it. (For example, the *Journal* said, an American company with an overseas plant can send the profits to the New Hebrides and then reinvest them elsewhere in the world when the opportunity arises, free of the hefty U.S. corporate tax that would be levied if the profits were brought home.)

---

* Moreover, the come-on literature assures the prospective corporate citizen that the natives are not unduly restless: "The islands also have great political stability. . . . The rural life led by most of the indigenous population has changed little over the centuries. There is therefore little likelihood of a change in the New Hebrides' sleepy political climate for at least a generation."

The whole thing does have a Hollywood movie-set aura—even down to hiring locals as "extras" to play financial "bit parts." One of the few annoyances of forming a special company there is the requirement of an annual meeting of a board of directors. But that problem is easily solved: the "directors are often local people who merely follow the instructions that are mailed to them." Thus, says the *Journal,* the directors' meetings "tend to be casual affairs."

All a New Hebrides company must exhibit to the public is some kind of nameplate on a door. The Melanesia International Trust Co. building in Vila (the principal city—population 8,000 persons, 700 businesses) boasts no less than 200 such nameplates bearing such actual names as "Ixion, Ltd." and "Nostalgia Ltd."

For companies who do not wish their affairs aired in public, the New Hebrides assures that "strict secrecy can be maintained with regard to all the company's affairs." And they mean it: "Breach of this secrecy can entail a fine of $1,000 or imprisonment for up to twelve months." Thus, as with Liechtenstein, inquisitive Internal Revenue agents might as well save their air fares to this distant land.

The islands are what might be called "hetero-national": they offer prospective business residents the choice of operating under either French or British law, according to which "it is possible to form almost any entity or combination of entities that can be imagined. . . ."

Moreover, despite its sparse population (just 80,000), the New Hebrides already boast several branches of international banks, so that "dividends, interest, commissions, trading profits and capital gains can be received as easily . . . as anywhere else on earth." But nowhere else on earth will they be taxed more gently. So come one, come all. Don't be square and headquarter your tax-saving company in tired old Bermuda. Come to the New Hebrides. It's only six thousand miles from home.

WHAT USEFUL FUNCTION could possibly be served by a company that exists largely "on paper"? The case of U.S. Gypsum Export, Inc., is edifying, in part because it illuminates the intricacies (if not the absurdities) of the world-wide game of "Beat the Tax Collector."

U.S. Gypsum Export, Inc. (Export, for short), was not exactly what you would call a normal company. Up until 1956, at least, it had only two employees. It did none of its own accounting, billing or secretarial services; made out none of its bills of lading; made out none of the customs papers that you might ordinarily expect an export company to do. *Yet, in 1957 and 1958, it had profits of over a million dollars in each year.*

What did Export do to earn such handsome profits?

To understand, visualize a scene on a wind-swept shore of Nova Scotia. A seemingly ordinary industrial process is under way. The good ship *Gypsum Prince* is tied up to a special jetty, awaiting her cargo: gypsum rock, the stuff of which wallboard, plaster and other building materials are made. A conveyor belt reaches across the jetty and over the ship. As the rock, mined by a Canadian company named Canadian Gypsum, reaches the end of the belt, it is claimed by the laws of Isaac Newton and tumbles into the hold of the ship. Simple. Efficient. Nothing extraordinary.

But all is not as simple as it appears. For, at the instant each piece of rock reaches the end of the conveyor belt, a sale takes place: ownership of the rock passes from the mining company, Canadian Gypsum, to Export.

But Export, it seems, has only the briefest use for the rock, for, the instant it hits the hold of the *Gypsum Prince*, Export sells the rock it acquired no more than a blink of an eye earlier—at a profit of 50 cents a ton—to U.S. Gypsum, Inc., the major American gypsum company.

And that is the sum and substance of what Export does (or did) for its million-dollar-a-year profit: it held paper ownership of a couple of million tons of gypsum rock during the fleeting instants of its fall from conveyor belt to ship hold. Period.

Why this legal sleight of hand? Why should U.S. Gypsum (which we'll call USG, for short) pay a million dollars a year to Export when it could easily have bought the rock directly from the mining company? It *sounds* like an exceedingly poor business deal . . .

. . . until you learn that Export is wholly owned by U.S. Gypsum, so that USG is, in effect, paying the million dollars to itself. The mystery unravels further when you discover that Export qualifies, under U.S. tax law, as a "Western Hemisphere trade corporation" (known, in the tax trade, as a WHTC) whose profits are taxed at a substantially lower rate than those of its parent, USG (see page 280). Approximate tax savings during 1957 and 1958: $300,000. No wonder USG didn't mind paying the million-dollar profit to an empty corporate shell for doing nothing.

But that was not the limit of the tax-saving possibilities inherent in the situation at the Nova Scotia jetty, which was a cozy all-in-the-family affair. Export was not USG's only "corporate child." The Canadian mining company was also a "child." And so was the good ship *Gypsum Prince*—or, to be more precise, the Panamanian corporation (Panama Gypsum, Inc.) that owned the *Gypsum Prince*.

Why a Panamanian corporation? Because, as noted, friendly, generous Panama imposes no taxes whatever on the profits of corporations, a happy circumstance that netted USG another handsome tax abatement. It was all a financially incestuous arrangement: over a four-year period, USG paid its *wholly owned* shipping company (Panama) $17,684,823 to carry gypsum from its *wholly owned* mines in Nova Scotia to its *wholly owned* processing plants in the United States. Now just suppose that USG chose to pay Panama something "extra" (above the lowest competitive shipping rate) for doing that—as the U.S. government alleged in a court action against USG. The government contended that the overcharge amounted to between 25 and 60 percent—but if the "extra" amounted to just 10 percent, the effect would be to reduce by nearly $2 million the profits of USG (taxable at the American 48 percent rate) and to increase by $2 million the profits of USG's corporate offspring, Panama, *which are not taxed at all*. Approximate tax saving during 1957 and 1958: about half a million dollars.*

O B V I O U S L Y , American corporations do not go to the trouble and expense of setting up these complex networks of overseas subcompanies just to avoid idleness and sloth among their lawyers. There is, as you would guess, another motive: to abate the taxes they owe the United States of America.

What are the tax savings that flow from setting up subsidiary companies overseas?

Advantage Number One: General Motors manufactures Chev-

---

* Technically, the law prohibits the payment of such "extras" between related companies. But, especially in a field as complex and volatile as shipping (where the rates, largely unpublished, often fluctuate from week to week and even from contract to contract), an "overcharge" of 10 or even 20 percent (which in the Gypsum case would have meant tax savings of a million dollars in four years) is extremely difficult to prove, as the U.S. government found out in its unsuccessful two-and-a-half-year effort in Federal court to establish such proof. This is discussed further on p. 280.

rolets in Ohio and Opels in Germany (through a wholly owned subsidiary company that we'll call GM–Germany). In both cases, a corporate income tax must be paid; for simplicity's sake, let's say that in each case the tax amounts to $100. In the case of the Ohio tax, the U.S. law treats that just as it does any other cost of doing business and allows GM to *deduct* the $100 from its otherwise taxable profits. At the current corporate tax rate of 48 percent, that $100 deduction reduces GM's tax by $48.

But since 1918 the U.S. law has treated the $100 tax paid to Germany far more generously: rather than a tax *deduction*, it permits GM a tax *credit* (see Glossary) on the $100, which means that GM can reduce the amount of taxes owed the United States *by the full $100*. Thus, from GM's point of view, the *credit* for foreign taxes (which reduces its tax by $100) is more than twice as desirable as a *deduction* (which lowers its tax by just $48). The point of view of the U.S. Treasury (i.e., all the other taxpayers) is quite the opposite: the credit is about twice as "expensive" as a deduction would be. The overall difference is very substantial. It reduces Federal tax collections from corporations by $3 *billion* a year!

Two arguments are advanced in defense of allowing the tax *credit* instead of a tax *deduction*. First, it is said, the credit puts U.S. companies on a par with companies with which they are competing abroad (i.e., it puts the GM's Opel plant in Germany on an equal footing with the VW plants there). Second, if only a deduction were allowed, the combination of the high tax levied in many foreign countries (e.g., it amounts, in effect, to 57 percent in Canada) plus the U.S. tax would constitute unwarranted "double taxation." It would also be prohibitive, and all U.S. manufacturing operations in such high-tax countries would come to an abrupt halt. For example, if the foreign tax were merely deductible, a hypothetical "General Motors–Canada" making a $1,000 profit would have to pay a $575 tax to Canada and a $240 tax to the United States* for a total of $815 in tax. That is, the total tax rate would be 81.5 percent. The after-tax "keeping money" on $1,000 of profits would amount to just $185.

Thus, it is argued, the tax rates in most industrialized foreign countries are so much higher than those imposed by most states within the United States that it is not valid to analogize the two.

---

* See Notes and Sources.

If states' corporate tax rates were to rise to near the level of the *Federal* corporate rate, Congress would almost surely allow a credit there, too, just as is now permitted on *foreign* taxes.

In 1972, the American labor movement mounted a major campaign to repeal the foreign tax credit and to replace it with a tax *deduction* for foreign taxes paid, on the ground that the credit is an excessive inducement to the export of American capital and, with it, American jobs. Many tax reformers, however, believe that, given the virtually prohibitive combined effect of foreign plus U.S. taxes, the principle of allowing a tax credit rather than a deduction is, at the least, plausible, and that the attention of tax reformers can be more fruitfully focused on the manner in which the credit can be manipulated by American corporate giants (see pages 263–267), as well as on other benefits enjoyed by U.S.-owned foreign companies.

Advantage Number Two: When an American corporation such as General Motors, or any of its subsidiaries within the United States, makes a profit, that profit is subject to U.S. tax *in the very year in which it is earned*. But U.S. tax law takes a much more kindly view toward profits earned by American-owned companies abroad. Those firms are allowed to keep those profits, free of any U.S. tax, just as long as they don't bring the money back into the States and pay it to the corporate "Godfather." (When the profits *are* brought home, of course, they are subject to U.S. tax—lessened by whatever foreign tax has already been paid, under the foreign tax credit concept just discussed.)

To the extent, then, that the foreign taxes are *less* than the U.S. tax rate, profits earned overseas enjoy an enormous advantage over profits made "back home in Alabammy" (or any other state) because the foreign-earned profits may be reinvested abroad without being diluted by U.S. Internal Revenue. For example, in a country where the tax rate is 30 percent a U.S.-owned company would have 70 cents out of every profit dollar to reinvest, whereas the parent company, operating here at home, would only have 52 cents to reinvest. And, of course, where it can be arranged to have the profits either earned in or funneled to a taxless country like Panama or the New Hebrides, 100 cents out of every dollar remains available for reinvestment overseas—quite a difference from the poor back-home firms.

This is usually referred to as a mere "deferral" of the U.S. tax (since that tax must be paid if and when the profits come home). If you have dutifully read Chapter 8, you are onto the true meaning and value of merely *postponing* a tax. But to the extent the foreign-earned profits are plowed back into factories or other "fixed" assets abroad (and most of them are), Uncle Sam must bid permanent bye-bye to *those* tax dollars. Factories being rather inconvenient to transport, *those* particular reinvested profits "ain't never gwine come home."

Judging from the above two advantages conferred upon the foreign offspring of American firms, one might conclude that the tax-law writers in Congress somehow lost sight of the fact that the corporate parents are, both legally and in fact, citizens of the United States of America. Advantage Number One costs the U.S. Treasury $3,300,000,000 a year.* Advantage Number Two represents $900,000,000 of yearly "tax welfare" for U.S. corporations with foreign subsidiaries. Thus this advantage offers a $900,-000,000 incentive for American-owned firms to plow back their foreign-earned profits overseas, rather than bringing them back home (which hardly helps the U.S. unemployment picture). From the U.S. point of view, it would make more sense to tax foreign-earned profits in the same way as "home-grown" profits—namely in the year they are earned, especially where the foreign firm is largely or wholly owned by an American parent.†

Advantage Number Three is among the most crucial of the tax favors conferred by American tax-law writers on the multinational corporation. It involves allowing those companies to lump together, for certain vital tax calculations, the profits and foreign taxes paid on *all* of their overseas subcompanies, instead of treating them on a country-by-country basis.

The resulting blessings fall into two categories. The first has to do with the extent to which subcompanies in high-tax countries can exploit the foreign tax credit to the detriment of Uncle Sam.

A moment ago, you learned that this credit allows a $100 reduction in the tax owed Uncle Sam for each $100 paid in taxes to a foreign government. But there's a ceiling on that: the credit

---

* That's the estimated yearly revenue loss from having a tax *credit* rather than a *deduction* for foreign taxes paid.

† In 1966, in the case of four-fifths of all overseas assets, the American parent owned more than 95 percent of the foreign affiliate.

stops at the point where it cancels out the U.S. tax that would be due. Now, that presents a slight dilemma for the hypothetical International World Widget Company (IWW), which owns a subsidiary widget company in Canada. For if IWW–Canada wants to send profits back to its parent in the United States, it must pay what amounts to a 57½ percent tax—greater than the U.S. corporate tax of 48 percent. So on, say, $10 million of taxable profit, the tax paid to Canada comes to $5,750,000—$950,000 more than the tax due the U.S. Treasury on that amount of profit (and hence, under the ceiling just described, $950,000 more than the allowable foreign tax credit).

What happens to the extra $950,000? If IWW's tax calculations had to be made on a country-by-country basis, the excess $950,000 would, in effect, be a wasted tax credit, one of the penalties the American parent voluntarily chose when it placed its corporate "child" in a high-tax country such as Canada.

But it would be surprising if a Congress that is in that many other respects so sensitive to corporate needs would allow any tax advantages to go thus unused. And, as you would expect, Congress *did* provide a means whereby the more mammoth of the international corporate giants—those that operate in several countries at once—can make use of "excess foreign tax credits," such as the $950,000 in the above example.

How? By allowing such multinational companies to calculate their taxes on a world-wide basis, rather than on a country-by-country basis, which permits them to "pool" the taxes they pay in high-tax countries with those they pay in low-tax countries. For example: a company as large as IWW (and to picture its size, think of a company like General Motors) derives its overseas income from many countries. Let's say that in a given year IWW has $10 million in profits earned in Canada, and $10 million earned through a Swiss corporation (on which the tax rate is no higher than about 10 percent). The total of taxes paid to the two governments on the $20 million amounts to $6,750,000.* But that is well below the $9,600,000 U.S. tax that would be due on $20 million of profits, so that now International World Widget no longer finds itself bumping its corporate head against the foreign-tax-credit ceiling that was so bothersome when we were looking at its Canadian operation alone.

* $5,750,000 to Canada plus a million to Switzerland.

That "pooling" rule also confers another tax saving, since were it not for that rule (i.e., if IWW had to reckon things on a country-by-country basis and treat the Swiss tax separately), then when IWW brought the Swiss profits home it would have to pay the U.S. Treasury the difference between the American tax of 48 percent and the Swiss tax of 10 percent.

For certain kinds of multinational companies, this world-wide method of computing their affairs is less advantageous than doing so on a country-by-country basis. Especially is this true of large oil and mining companies, which would lose some of the advantages of percentage depletion on their overseas operations if they used the world-wide basis of figuring things. Fortunately for those companies (although not so happily for the rest of the U.S. taxpayers), Congress has adopted a most obliging attitude: it has permitted the mineral companies (and all others) to choose whichever method—world-wide or country-by-country—results in their paying the *least* tax to their own native land. That one option (which American companies did not enjoy from 1921 to 1960) saves these multinational American corporations—and deprives their native government of—an estimated *quarter of a billion dollars a year*. This has prompted some Congressional tax reformers to suggest that these corporations would fulfill their obligations to the United States more appropriately if the option were reversed —that is, if the corporations were obliged to make their calculations on either a world-wide or country-by-country basis, *whichever would be more favorable to the U.S. Treasury*.

The law does contain a ceiling on the amount of "excess foreign tax credits" a company can absorb through the world-wide pooling-of-profits device, a ceiling whose height depends, in part, on *the proportion of the company's world-wide income that comes from "foreign sources."* That is, if 50 percent of a company's profits are classified as "foreign-source," the ceiling on its use of foreign tax credits is higher than if, say, only 30 percent were labeled "foreign-source." But here, too, Congress has been helpful. It has bestowed legislative approval on certain techniques whereby a company can, in effect, inflate its "foreign-source income" and thereby boost its capacity to absorb "excess foreign tax credits."

To illustrate, take the so-called "title passage" device, one that has been used, for example, in exporting Hammond organs from the United States: Hammond Organ sells its products to a specially created and wholly owned company, which is careful to arrange to "pass title" to its foreign customers after the organs have left the United States—perhaps on the high seas, perhaps when they land on the dock at their port of destination, in a foreign land. The profits that special subsidiary makes when it resells the instruments contribute to Hammond's "foreign-source income."

Sometimes, the items whose "title passage" takes place overseas don't even remain abroad but are quickly returned to the United States, as in the case of the stock that ITT sold to a foreign bank, which immediately resold it to an investment fund in America. Yet, since legal ownership of the stock was transferred outside the United States, that "three-cushion shot" sufficed to add to ITT's "foreign-source income" and to elevate its tax-credit ceiling.

But is that reasonable? After all, the main justification for the foreign tax credit is to avoid prohibitive and unfair "double taxation" (i.e., a U.S. tax imposed *on top of* a foreign tax). Yet, in the above illustrations, the only "events" that took place outside the United States were paper transactions, *not enough to cause the imposition of any foreign tax.* (In fact, lawyers advise their company clients to be careful to have "title passage" occur at sea, or in some "tax haven," but *not* within any foreign country that might try to impose some annoying local tax.) So why should a mere legal fiction be allowed to elevate the foreign tax credit available to a company? Some tax reformers say the "title passage" rule should be revised to require that in order for income to be considered "foreign-source," there must be at least enough overseas activity to generate a tax *actually paid* to a foreign government.

One expert knowledgeable in the ways of international tax avoidance says that in many large companies with considerable export sales, if the company's tax adviser foresees the firm bumping its head against the foreign tax credit ceiling, he solves the problem with a single phone call to one of the company's department heads. Logic might lead you to suppose that the call would be to the head of the export department, urging him to redouble his efforts to sell more goods to foreign customers, so as to generate more "foreign-source income" and raise the company's foreign-tax-credit ceiling. But no such drastic effort is called for. Instead, the call goes to the head of the traffic department—the unit that handles the mechanics of shipping goods—and the request is simply that for the balance of the year, the traffic department arrange *the paper work* so that "title passes overseas" on all remaining exports. Beyond this mere paper change, no other alteration in company practices is needed.

W E T U R N N O W to the second manner in which worldwide tax calculations confer tax benefits on the huge multinational corporations. You will recall how the "pooling" of profits from a low-tax country like Switzerland made it possible to use, rather than having to waste, the "excess foreign tax credit" generated in high-taxing Canada. But what if a company doesn't have any factories or outlets in Switzerland (or other low-tax countries)? Answer: it creates special companies in such countries, and then goes about finding ways of channeling some of the company profits through them.

For example, the Pittsburgh Plate Glass Company had a great many customers in neighboring Canada. It could have sold to them directly. But it chose a different route: it sold the glass to a wholly owned subsidiary in Switzerland, which then resold the glass, at a profit, to Canadian customers. The Swiss company never handled the glass; it was shipped directly from PPG in the States to the Canadian customers. IRS attacked the arrangement as a tax dodge, but the Tax Court ruled that the Swiss company's sales efforts entitled it to the profits paid it by PPG. You can see, however, that by separating its "sales profits" from its "manufacturing profits," PPG succeeded in channeling income into low-taxing Switzerland.*

Sales profits are but one kind of corporate income that lend themselves to separate treatment of that kind. Clearly, with taxless countries such as the New Hebrides or the Bahamas or Panama extending a beckoning finger, it would be Foolishness Personified for an astute parent corporation not to create special offspring to receive *each* separable variety of income and sprinkle these corporate children in taxless oases throughout the world. Thus, International World Widget might take all the dividends and interest it

---

* Page 279 describes how there is, at the least, an incentive for closely related companies (such as PPG and its wholly owned subsidiary) to enter into artificial pricing arrangements that serve to channel the maximum amount of income into the lowest-taxed company—and how some companies, at least, have succumbed to that incentive, notwithstanding a prohibition in the tax law.

receives on its overseas investments and channel them into a Bahamian company. If any widgit patents are involved, they are almost sure to be owned by a special company established in, say, Curaçao, so that the patent royalties will escape bothersome taxation. And the widgits en route to Africa or some other far-off land must be insured, mustn't they? What better way than through IWW's own "captive insurance company" (headquartered in a desk drawer in Hamilton, Bermuda—which has shown the greatest hospitality toward the "captive" companies). And, of course, the huge international oil companies may do much of their actual drilling in the oil-soaked Middle East, but you can be sure that they carefully farm out the drilling operations (and the profits therefrom) to their wholly owned subsidiaries headquartered in some tax-free sunny island, far from the unfavorable tax climate of Kuwait or Saudi Arabia.

Until 1962, American companies were free almost without limit to divvy up their profits in the above manner, channeling them to special companies scattered among the various tax havens around the world. Often the sole function of such firms was to invoice the sales of other wholly owned subsidiaries of the common parent, for which they would collect a handsome profit (just as U.S. Gypsum did for briefly holding paper ownership of the tumbling rock for a split second).

In the late Fifties, tax havens were springing up, mushroomlike, and American companies were making ample use of them for tax-avoidance purposes. This prompted President Kennedy, in 1961, to call upon Congress to curb the "use of the tax haven device anywhere in the world." Congress did enact a law—not nearly as rigorous as Mr. Kennedy asked, but aimed, nonetheless, at putting a damper on the tax-haven operations. Under that law, certain kinds of income* channeled into a tax-haven company were considered "tainted." That had most unpleasant consequences: namely, the "tainted" income became subject to immediate U.S. tax, whether or not it was actually brought home and paid to the American parent.

Yet something must be amiss, for now—a little more than a decade after the enactment of the 1962 law—tax havens, rather than being on the wane, are on the increase. Corporate tax law-

---

* Principally dividends, interest, royalties and profits from sales or service operations with related companies.

yers receive a steady stream of enticing literature (you had a glimpse of it, regarding the political placidness of the New Hebrides natives, on page 257) glorifying the tax (and political) climate of some new island or territory. (For your information, at this writing the Cayman Islands in the Caribbean are the chic place to locate your new tax-haven company.)

Clearly, American corporations must be succeeding in "untainting" a significant amount of tax-haven profits that, under the 1962 law, were supposed to be "tainted" and hence subject to Mother Country taxes. How do they arrange it?

First of all, the big-hearted American tax law disregards the "taintedness" of 30 percent of any tax-haven company's gross income,* as long as the other 70 percent is "untainted." That is, if General Motors structures GM–Switzerland (with, say, $10 million of gross income) in such a way that $7 million of that is from manufacturing operations (which is taint-free), the other $3 million can enjoy the virtual taxlessness accorded by the Swiss without running afoul of the 1962 law. (Shipping operations lend themselves especially well to this device. See page 274.)

More important, however, is the way that law allows corporate giants like GM to bunch together the profits and the foreign taxes paid by *all* their foreign subcompanies—lumping those in high-tax countries together with the tax-haven companies. The formula is complex,† but its net effect is to permit an American company to enjoy as much as a 10 percent saving on the tax it would otherwise have to pay the U.S. Treasury. In 1967, for Standard Oil of New Jersey, that might have meant a tax bounty of about $30 million!

As is true of most corporate loopholes, wriggling through the "minimum distribution" escape hatch is vastly easier for the giant multinational corporations, which have operations in both high- and low-tax countries, than it is for the small and struggling companies trying to enter the international market and therefore far more in need of tax relief.‡

---

* Which means gross sales minus the cost of the goods sold.

† For an example of this so-called "minimum distribution" formula, see Notes and Sources.

‡ *Fortune* magazine has also noted that the high cost of the legal and accounting fees connected with "cutting a path through the legal thickets" has deterred many small- and medium-sized U.S. corporations from exploiting tax havens, even though "these are precisely the companies that need tax-haven benefits the most. 'The small company ought to generate a greater tax-free cash flow for reinvestment because it doesn't have such easy access

For certain companies, use of the world-wide method of reckoning their affairs does not provide the maximum "shelter" for tax-haven income. An understanding Congress has ministered to their plight. Such companies are permitted to reckon their foreign tax activities on the basis of special groupings of their overseas subcompanies, which they can arrange and manipulate with considerable flexibility. That is achieved by arranging these subcompanies and sub-subcompanies into "groups," "chains" or (would you believe it) "single first-tiers," each grouping made up of firms strategically mixed between high- and low-tax foreign lands, and each permitted its own averaging-out calculation that results in a maximum "un-tainting" of tax-haven profits.

Congress also provided a special way by which large multinational oil and other mining companies could shelter tax-haven income.* This special provision allowed those companies, in computing their so-called "minimum distribution" formula, to engage in a most convenient fiction, making believe that the percentage depletion deductions that are generously allowed under *American* tax law (see Chapter 11) are also permitted in figuring their *foreign* taxes—which of course is not the case. The effect of this make-believe was to permit the oil and mining companies to use the fictional depletion allowances to "un-taint" (i.e., shelter from tax) an equivalent amount of tax-haven profits. In 1969, Congress enacted a new provision designed to curb this benefit, but some experts believe that there are ways the mineral companies can wriggle through this law.

IN 1971, the President and the Congress jointly concluded that it was unseemly and unnecessary for the titans of the corporate world to be establishing dummy companies in unlikely places like the New Hebrides or Curaçao or the Cayman Islands. Instead, said the President and the Congress, firms should be

---

to long-term capital as the large company,' says a partner in [a New York] international accountancy firm. . . . 'And when it can borrow, the small corporation usually has to pay more for its money.' "

* Those familiar with Congress at the time this special exception was enacted will not be surprised by the fact that it was ingeniously maneuvered into the law by the late Senator Robert S. Kerr of Oklahoma, who seldom, if ever, allowed the fact of his own heavy ownership of oil and gas properties (e.g., the Kerr-McGee Corporation) to hinder his open efforts for legislation from which he and his companies would benefit handsomely.

allowed to form their own tax-haven subcompanies right here at home. As is so often the case, these new corporate creatures have been endowed with a fancy name, complete with an acronym: they are called "domestic international sales corporations," or "DISC's." Into these domestic tax havens, American companies can channel from 50 to 100 percent of their export profits, and be spared any *immediate* U.S. tax on half of that. Tax attorneys, recalling the jokes of the early Sixties about the "Banana Republics" that American companies were then using as tax havens, say the DISC legislation has turned the United States of America into a mini-Banana Republic—very undignified for the most potent industrial nation in the world. (In the eyes of many foreign nations, the DISC law was more than undignified: it was an outright violation of international trade agreements, of which the United States was a part, that forbid participating countries from unilaterally instituting export subsidies without the agreement of the other countries, and formal complaints have been lodged against the United States on that ground.)

A DISC is a truly remarkable corporate creature, inasmuch as Congress was kind enough to relieve it of almost all of the requirements ordinarily asked of a corporation. Under the law, a corporation is usually expected to have a respectable number of employees, a headquarters office and a certain amount of capital, and to be actively engaged in business. Not a DISC. Other than being required to have the magnificent sum of $2,500 in capital, a bank account and its own books and records, a DISC can be nothing more than the paper on which its tax-wise lawyers draw up the necessary documents. (The Treasury Department has even issued a ruling that confirms that a DISC does not have to be more than a paper entity.)

Congress has also considerately and explicitly exempted DISC's from another annoying requirement of the law—namely, that pricing arrangements between corporate parents and their wholly owned offspring be made on an "arm's length" basis (i.e., as if the two were not related). You may recall how the government alleged that U.S. Gypsum had permitted its wholly owned shipping company to overcharge it, as a means of shifting profits away from high-taxing America and into tax-free Panama. Well, companies setting up their own DISC's need not worry that such a charge will be leveled against them, for the new DISC law not only permits the DISC and its parent to make whatever cozy pricing arrangement they like; it even allows the two to make an after-the-fact adjustment of their pricing schedules in order to "obtain the most favorable allocation of [profits] permitted" by the special DISC pricing rules.

Still another usually applicable foreign-tax-law rule is waived in the case of DISC's. As noted, foreign subcompany profits are subject to U.S. tax if they are brought into the United States and paid to the parent. Ordinarily that same rule applies when the "child" *lends* rather than pays the money to the parent company. But under the DISC law, a DISC is free (within certain limits) to lend its tax-deferred profits to the parent, without subjecting the parent to the usual tax. Not only that; the loan turns out to be, in effect, interest-free to the parent. That handy result comes about in this ingenious way: in one clause, the law requires the parent to pay its DISC "child" interest on the loan, but then, in another clause, that same law encourages (virtually to the point of requiring) the DISC "child" to pay the interest right back to the parent.* If you could only develop a like arrangement with your own bank, think how much less painful borrowing would be!

The supposed purpose of the DISC legislation is to stimulate an increase in exports from the United States. To that end, Congress has, in effect, asked the American taxpayers to approve roughly a fifth of a billion dollars a year in "tax welfare" to U.S. corporations—for that is the estimated amount of annual "tax expenditures" resulting from the DISC legislation. Critics of the DISC law ask several questions about that $200 million annual "outlay":

First, was it necessary? Most trade experts feel that any stimulus to exports the DISC might provide is bound, at best, to be minuscule in comparison with the shot in the arm resulting from a devaluation of the dollar (as that taking place in 1971). Such a devaluation has the effect of lowering the price of all U.S. goods to everyone in the world (and didn't Adam Smith tell us that lower prices are supposed to result in increased demand, all other things being equal?). Currency devaluation, of course, is a lot cheaper, in the sense that it involves no "tax expenditures"; more-

---

* There is one slight drawback to borrowing money in this fashion: the parent must forgo the usual tax deductions on the interest it pays the DISC "child."

over, complain DISC critics, the Administration insisted on pushing the DISC concept into law without even waiting to see what stimulative effect devaluation would have.

Second, will the DISC law be *effective* in stimulating exports? The critics contend that the Administration never presented "hard" evidence that it would; they also argue that there is no valid way of measuring the effect of the DISC as time goes on, to see whether the $200 million annual "expenditure" of the taxpayers' dollars is actually paying dividends.

That weakness underscores what DISC critics say is the worst feature of the new law: namely, that the DISC benefits are not conditioned upon increases in a company's exports, or even upon increases in its *efforts* to expand its exports. On the contrary, DISC benefits are fully available to a company whose export efforts and/or results remain the same, or even *decline*—in which case, of course, the company enjoys a windfall tax benefit, and the rest of the taxpayers get nothing for their "tax expenditure."

As far as stimulating non-exporting firms to enter the field, the DISC law is thought by many to be virtually useless. It is so complex (recent Treasury regulations interpreting just one section of the law covered no less than fourteen closely printed pages) that the smaller, relatively unsophisticated businessman is probably incapable of dealing with its intricacies on his own, and, on the small volume of exports he can anticipate, the DISC benefits will be more than wiped out by the expense of hiring an expert lawyer to help guide him through the legal maze. In fact, that is precisely the advice that one such lawyer was obliged to give a small, would-be exporter whom he found struggling to decipher the Treasury regulations.

So, if the $200 million of "tax welfare" is not going to small, struggling businessmen, who *is* getting the DISC benefits? By now, the answer should be familiar to you: it is the corporate giants, already well established in the export field. According to one prediction, from 50 to 90 percent of the DISC benefits will go to just 125 of the nation's largest corporations. And, as noted, they need do nothing new or extra to get this "tax welfare." Indeed, to some Washington tax lawyers who are expertly aiding their corporate clients in the formation of DISC's, the whole device is laughable. When they ask their clients whether they intend to do anything different in the way of export efforts (other than save taxes), their clients respond with an "Are you kidding?" Indeed, what some clients ask for is advice on how to get the maximum tax saving from the DISC *without disturbing their business operations.*

Even so staid and solid a source as the *Wall Street Journal* has labeled the DISC a "tax gimmick" whose disappearance from the tax law would "be no great loss."

WE COME, NOW, to what might best be described as the Shangri-la of taxation—for there is something of Shangri-la's magically sheltered atmosphere about the total taxlessness in which the major international shipping magnates and corporations bask. It is not just that the American-owned shipping ventures are exempt from U.S. tax. They are generally exempt from paying *any* tax to *any* country *anywhere* in the world.

How does that come about? Very simply. If you own a ship that plies the seven seas, you will find it to your advantage to register it in Panama or Liberia, for those countries, considerately enough, do not subject corporations to *any* national taxes. Ordinarily, profits earned in such tax-haven countries are subject to being labeled "tainted income," and a U.S. tax is imposed as if the profits had been brought home, even if they are left abroad. But Congress, by legislative fiat, has simply declared that shipping company income is "untainted." Thus every bit of it can be left in Panama or Liberia, tax-free.

The statutory "un-tainting" of shipping income can be immensely useful to a corporation that wishes to shelter tax-haven income from "taintedness" by virtue of the "70-30" provision (whereby if 70 percent of a company's gross income can be classified as "untainted," that automatically cleanses the other 30 percent). Such a corporation would arrange to acquire and operate a ship which, by its nature, throws off an enormous amount of gross income, every bit of which Congress has declared usable to establish the requisite 70 percent cleanliness. Thus, in addition to carrying cargo, the vessel also serves as an "income un-tainter."

Congress's considerable appetite for enacting special exceptions for shipping companies does not stop there. For example, when other kinds of foreign corporations (e.g., banks and insurance companies) do part of their business in the United States, they must pay U.S. taxes on that part of their profit. The vessels of many foreign shipping companies, of course, put in at American ports, so under that general rule those companies should pay some U.S. tax. The calculation of just what part of the firms' profits should be taxed can be especially complicated as regards shipping companies; but the ever-resourceful Congress found a convenient answer: exempt those companies entirely from American taxation, so that no one need bother with the calculation. Simple. Also costly to the U.S. Treasury.

One tax advisory service lays out the simple steps leading to the tax-free build-up of a small fortune in the shipping business. It portrays the financial saga of one John Smith, a fictional "U.S. individual" whose name may not win any prizes for originality but who incorporates a new company, Ocean Shipping Corp., under the laws of Liberia (God forbid he should use the laws of his own native land). Smith receives all the stock of the new company "in return for the minimum cash required" to satisfy the business needs of the transaction. Then his company enters into a fifteen- to twenty-year "charter party" (which sounds like one hell of a long festivity, but is the technical name for a charter *agreement*) with a "substantial United States oil company" for a Liberian-flag vessel to be built to the oil company's specifications. On the strength of that "charter party" (really on the strength of the oil company's impeccable credit rating), John Smith's company borrows the several million to get the ship built—*outside* John Smith's own U.S. of A. (for if it were built at home, it would have to fly the American flag—which of course would not do at all). Upon completion, the vessel begins to ply the seas, transporting "black gold" between the United States and some foreign ports, netting sufficient profits to service the huge loan and to pay a small profit to Ocean, on which that worthy company "*pay[s] no U.S. tax and little or no foreign taxes.*" (Emphasis added.) These profits the company invests in "interest-bearing U.S. bank time deposits" on which it again "pay[s] no U.S. tax" on receipt of the interest. And, of course, the story has a deliriously happy ending: after ten years or so (but in any event before the charter agreement expires), Our Hero, John Smith, sells his stock in Ocean Shipping and realizes a gently taxed capital gain (and, we must assume, lives happily ever after—although tax advisory services are not ordinarily given to such conclusions).

Incidentally, John Smith's lightly taxed capital gain is the result of another act of definitional generosity on the part of the Congress. Ordinarily, certain of the profits on the sale of a U.S.-owned foreign corporation such as Ocean Shipping would be subject to taxation at the regular income tax rates, not at the special capital gains rate. But in the case of shipping companies, Congress has seen·to it that American owners who hold on to their stock for ten years or more will get capital gains treatment on the entire profit. The lawmakers did this by simply decreeing that shipping companies can be classified, when it suits them, as "less-developed country corporations" (LDCC's) to which the above capital gain rule applies—even though, in most cases, those shipping companies don't come anywhere near meeting the usual requirements of an LDCC. That is, ordinarily, in order to meet the objective of encouraging American companies to establish a business *within* a "less-developed country," at least 80 percent of the company's assets and activities have to be placed and occur within that country. But, in the case of a shipping firm, the company's only presence in, say, Panama or Liberia may be the registration papers of the ship. The vessel may never even put in to a Panamanian or Liberian port. Nonetheless, Congress, in its Alice-in-Wonderland way, has said that these companies are to be treated, for certain tax-saving purposes, as LDCC's.

Given sagas such as the above, it is not surprising that the world-wide taxlessness enjoyed by the shipping industry has created several *billion*aires—not millionaires, not multimillionaires, but billionaires. Some of the names—Onassis and Niarchos—are familiar. But who has heard of C. K. Tung or Y. K. Pao (the "Y. K." standing for Yeu Kong, which means "solid jade") ? The complexity of Pao's corporate empire suggests the advantages of the tax havens (his World Maritime Bahamas, Ltd., has nine Hong Kong subsidiaries and twenty-four Liberian subsidiaries; his Eastern Asia Navigation Co., Ltd., has twenty-three Hong Kong subsidiaries, fourteen Liberian subsidiaries, a Bahamian subsidiary and a Panamanian subsidiary; his World Shipping Investment Company . . . and so it goes).

Despite his far-flung holdings, Pao received only a so-so rating in an intriguing *Forbes* magazine speculation as to who among the world's shipping tycoons qualifies as a genuine billionaire. In 1970, *Forbes* surmised that while Pao might make the grade "a few years from now," at the moment he had to be content with "the more humble, but not painful [classification] of semi-billion-aire or demisemi-billionaire."

Yet one American shipping magnate has apparently come close to becoming a *multi*-billionaire. *Forbes* cites a London bank study that lists the total worth of shy New Yorker Daniel K. Ludwig as being closer to $2 billion than $1 billion. Even that made him, in 1970, only the fourth wealthiest man in America (after J. Paul Getty, H. L. Hunt and Howard Hughes).

But it isn't just the individual entrepreneur who benefits from the global taxlessness of shipping. Most large American corporations that have big shipping needs own their own fleets (which, of course, carry what are called the "flags of convenience"* of Panama or Liberia). The oil companies, for example, take care of about 85 percent of their own shipping needs with their wholly owned fleets. U.S. Steel has two shipping subsidiaries in the tax-free Bahamas which, as of 1969, were operating some thirty ships —sailing, of course, under the Liberian flag.

Then there is the Barracuda Tanker Corporation, mentioned earlier, with its filing-cabinet headquarters in Bermuda. Conceived and created by the major New York investment banking house of Dillon, Read (whence came John F. Kennedy's Treasury Secretary, C. Douglas Dillon), it involved some twenty-seven investors' putting up the meager total of $20,000 to organize the company. The firm then proceeded to borrow $51 million and to buy three tankers, which it leased to Union Oil. Over a twenty-year period, the leasing fees paid for the ships and still left a $1 million profit— not a bad return on a $20,000 initial outlay.†

Of course, all those valuable ships and their cargoes have to carry insurance. Shipowners have a happy answer to that problem —which also carries with it the encouragement of the U.S. tax laws: they form "captive insurance companies"—wholly owned subsidiaries that issue all the necessary insurance (and collect the

---

* This is the term the industry itself coined—until it came under fire for building and operating ships outside our own shores; whereupon industry spokesmen began referring to them, emphatically, as "flags of *necessity*."

† That profit was realized despite the mishap to Barracuda's most re-nowned (or notorious) ship—the *Torrey Canyon*, which split apart off the coast of England in 1967 and soaked the English beaches with oil. But since the *Canyon* itself was fully insured, the Barracuda company probably ended up losing far less than the seashore residents of Great Britain.

attendant profits)—tax-free, naturally, when organized in such havens as the Bahamas.* (According to *Fortune*, Daniel Ludwig uses the "captive" technique to insure all his vessels.) After all, why let an outsider get the profits when you can pay them to yourself? Like the shippers, U.S.-owned insurance companies abroad are immune from immediate U.S. taxation on the insurance they write on overseas risks, and, while they can't bring the money back into the States without paying tax, they can usually find lots of ways to invest the tax-free dollars overseas.

HOLD ON TO YOUR HAT, your seat, or your stomach, for now that you are a budding expert on foreign tax credits, DISC's and shipping, you are about to be exposed to the way in which Congress seems to have combined the three so as to make your old favorite, Uncle Sam, into a prime Uncle Sap.

Step One: Many U.S. banks own ships that they charter out for use abroad. What with accelerated depreciation and the investment tax credit, during the early years of the charter the ship throws off enormous "tax losses." That reduces the bank's domestic taxes, which is Very Good. But since the ship is used abroad, these large minuses have the disadvantage of reducing the bank's "foreign-source income" which, as you know, also reduces its advantages from the foreign tax credit. That is Very Bad. Prior to 1971, the banking industry (and other similar shipowners) was unhappy. It appealed to Congress.

Step Two: Congress, as usual, was sympathetic and in 1971 wrote a law saying, in effect, that where it does not suit the purposes of a shipowner to list the result of a ship's operation as "foreign-source," he may elect to list it instead as "domestic-source." That, of course, was strictly out of *Alice in Wonderland,* since the ship generates the income abroad just as much as ever; thus only the label changes.

Supposedly, Step Two wasn't *too* damaging to the U.S. Treasury, for when the tax losses ran their course and the ship began showing a tax *profit,* two things were supposed to happen: first, the shipowner's U.S. tax on that profit would begin to make up for his early-year tax savings; and second, because he had had to make a virtually irreversible choice of having the ship's operations la-

---

* As of this writing, Internal Revenue is taking a skeptical look at these "captive" companies.

beled "domestic-source," the owner would have to forgo classifying those later-year profits as "foreign-source" income and thus forgo using them to elevate his foreign-tax-credit ceiling.

So, at first glance, Step Two didn't appear too egregious—except for the fact that, as part of the same 1971 law, Congress enacted

Step Three: the DISC—which cancels out much of the painful effect of the supposedly irreversible choice the shipowner has made, and allows him to have the cake *and* the eating of it. That happy result comes about this way: before he enters into the shipping charter, he foresightedly forms a DISC and makes an agreement with the DISC that the minute the ship begins showing a tax profit, half of that profit will be funneled into the DISC. Under the DISC law, half of *that* will be exempt from immediate tax. Thus, in the very years that the owner is *supposed* to be replacing the tax "divot" created by the early-year tax losses, along comes the DISC and its tax-deferral privileges.

But that's not all: even though the owner has supposedly given up the use of those later-year profits to generate helpful "foreign-source income," the DISC comes to the rescue here, too. For, under the law, half of all DISC profits are automatically classified as "foreign-source," although the benefits of this are limited.

That may all sound very complicated—but if you have deduced from the above account that Uncle Sam gets "taken" at every turn of the road, you have gotten the essential meaning.*

REMEMBER THE IMAGE of the gypsum rock owned by Company A falling off the conveyor belt, to be owned, for a fleeting instant, by Company B, until it landed in the hold of a ship owned by Company C? In that one scene are compressed two of the devices that are used to save taxes in the international field.

Device No. 1 is the use of artificial pricing arrangements between related companies so as to shift profits into the ledger books of the most gently taxed of the companies. In the gypsum case, as you may recall, the government argued—although the judge was not persuaded—that the parent company, U.S. Gypsum, had paid too much to its tax-free Panamanian shipping "child" for

---

* Since the 1971 law has not been on the books very long, there is no public evidence that the above has actually been tried and tested, and it is possible that if (or possibly even before) that happens, the Treasury Department will take steps to prevent it.

transporting gypsum from Canada to the United States. The government also charged—and persuaded the judge—that U.S. Gypsum had paid unwarranted profits to its wholly owned dummy company whose sole function, you'll remember, was to hold legal ownership of the rock for those few seconds.

As mentioned, the tax law prohibits artificial profit-shifting of that sort, but it is one thing to prohibit it and quite another to prove it (as shown by the government's unavailing two-and-a-half-year effort to do so in the shipping aspect of the Gypsum case). Usually, modest "overcharges"—some say even *im*modest ones— can be gotten away with. But in the case of huge corporations doing multi-million-dollar shipping or insurance business, even minor overcharges can bring handsome tax savings. One thing is clear: huge companies with wholly owned foreign subsidiaries have the *incentive* to fudge their prices in favor of shifting the profits. One company that seems to have done so flagrantly enough to be slapped down by a Federal court was the Eli Lilly company, which sold its drugs so cheaply to its wholly owned subsidiary, Eli Lilly Pan American Corp., that Pan American received between 93 and 97 percent of the profits on Lilly's drug sales in the Western Hemisphere. The parent company's share of the profits ranged from .67 percent to 5.65 percent.*

Over the years, the short-staffed IRS has found it difficult to devote sufficient staff to sniffing out and—even more complicated—developing the proof of artificial pricing arrangements, and many feel that until recently enforcement has been, at best, spotty, and, at worst, virtually nonexistent. Today, most large exporting corporations need worry little about the pricing prohibition, for. they can easily run their exports through a DISC which, as noted, is exempt from that stricture.

The incentive for U.S. Gypsum to shift profits into the Panamanian shipping company, which was wholly tax-free, is plain enough. But why did Gypsum go to the trouble to create a special company to take legal title to the rock in midair? And why did Eli Lilly sacrifice so much of its own profits to its Latin-American subsidiary? The answer lies in Device No. 2: both subsidiary companies were "Western Hemisphere trade corporations" (WHTC's), whose profits are taxed at a rate fourteen percentage points lower than the generally applicable U.S. corporation tax rate.

---

* The balance went to a third subsidiary.

The WHTC's came into the tax law in 1942 when certain American companies operating in Latin America were experiencing financial difficulties. Their troubles, they told Congress, were exacerbated by the steeply rising U.S. tax rates necessitated by World War II defense expenditures.

Congress responded in a Good Neighbor gesture of great magnanimity: it provided for the creation of the WHTC's. To qualify for the favorable tax rate, at least 95 percent of a company's income had to come from other countries in the Western Hemisphere (that is, Canada or Latin America).

The tax benefits flowing from this provision are considerable: for a WHTC deriving $10 million in taxable profits, the tax saving is $1,400,000.

Because the companies whose plight prompted Congress to enact this dispensation had actual operations in Latin America (railroads, mining, etc.), many conclude that Congress had in mind encouraging other American companies to sally forth and do likewise (invest in and begin operations in Latin America and Canada). But over the years, the WHTC has been put to quite a different use. Today, it is used mainly by companies who invest little or nothing overseas, do all their manufacturing here at home, and merely *export* to Latin America, as clearly illustrated in the Eli Lilly case (as well as the Hammond Organ example cited on pages 265–266).

Even Congress, when it undertook a sweeping revision of the tax law in 1954, recognized that the WHTC provision had produced some "anomalous results"; but the lawmakers decided to leave untouched this windfall to exporters, "in order to avoid any disturbances at the present time to established channels of trade."

The WHTC privilege currently costs U.S. taxpayers (i.e., saves U.S. corporations) roughly $75 million a year. Many critics have difficulty discerning whether the benefits of this "tax expenditure" flow to anyone other than the corporations whose tax payments are substantially reduced thereby.

FAR MORE COSTLY to the American taxpayers is the manner in which the oil-rich Middle East sheikdoms and kingdoms* disguise, behind an Arabian "tax veil," what really amounts to royalty payments. It's a ploy that works superbly for the sheiks

---

* As well as certain mineral-rich Latin-American countries.

and kings, and well for the American oil companies, but dismally for the U.S. taxpayers.

Under U.S. tax law, payments to the owners of mineral lands for the privilege of extracting the minerals are termed royalties and, like other expenses, are deductible, thus saving a corporate royalty-payer 48 cents on the dollar. But in the countries in question, all subsurface oil and other minerals belong to the sovereign government, regardless of who owns the land under which they lie. Thus, in such countries, all royalty payments are to governments, rather than to individuals. But what are taxes, if not "payments to governments"? Therefore, in these countries, the line between a "tax" and a "royalty" becomes very thin.

Before 1950, the Middle East sovereign owners were content to receive royalties of about 15 percent.* But in the late Forties, they began to look enviously in the direction of Venezuela, which had worked out a far more favorable arrangement with the American firms, and they began to press for a better deal for themselves. What particularly titillated them was the fact that Venezuela had hit upon a scheme whereby the American companies could pay far more for the oil, *and whereby Uncle Sam's help eased the pain of the increase.* The device was simple: label the extra payments "taxes" instead of "royalties." That would entitle the American companies to reduce what they owed the U.S. Treasury by the amount of the "tax," *thus saving 100 cents, rather than just 48 cents, on the dollar.* In this manner, the companies could afford to double their payments, and still end up no worse. The difference would be footed by the American taxpayers.

The Middle East governments made no bones about wanting to stick the U.S. taxpayers with the bill. Here is the way the Chairman of the Board of the Arabian-American Oil Company (Aramco) described it to a Senate committee:

They [the Saudi Arabians] wanted more. They asked as early as 1948, "Isn't there some way in which we can get a greater take?" and a little later than that they said, *"Isn't there some way in which the income tax you pay to the United States can be diverted to us in whole or in part?"* [Emphasis added.]

---

* Required to be paid, once annually, in Mecca, in gold crowns—which often placed a strain on the American companies to lay their hands on enough gold crowns to make the payment in the prescribed manner.

And, of course, there was. The Saudis imported a tax expert from Washington* to advise them just how to go about it, and on December 27, 1950, the Saudi Arabian government issued a royal decree, stating that henceforth the Saudi government would be a fifty-fifty partner in all Aramco oil extractions, and that the difference between that and the old 20 percent royalty would be called an "income tax."

And so it came to pass that the Saudi government prospered mightily. In 1956, for example, Aramco's "royalties" amounted to just $80 million, but its "income taxes" came to roughly $200 million.

And it came to pass, too, that the United States Treasury suffered mightily. In 1949, Aramco—which is a full-fledged corporate citizen of the United States, chartered in the state of Delaware—was paying more to the United States than to Saudi Arabia. But, as of 1956, after the imposition of the "income tax," Aramco's chairman told the Senators, the U.S. Treasury hadn't *"received any taxes* [on Aramco's Saudi Arabian operations] *for I don't know, two or three years now, I guess."* (Emphasis added.)

AT FIRST GLANCE, *Fortune* magazine—that staid and deadly serious publication for super-busy executives—may not seem the most logical place for a full-page advertisement extolling the joys of an Irish holiday. *The New Yorker,* perhaps, or *Vogue* —but *Fortune?*

The choice of publications becomes clear, however, when you discover that the appeal is not for a fun-filled tour of the Emerald Isle (bring your whole family), but for quite a different kind of holiday: a *tax* holiday (bring your corporation—if you happen to own one).

To any sensible businessman, a tax holiday ought to offer great allure. It is a period of total tax forgiveness to new businesses by the host country, designed to create a hospitable financial atmosphere in which new corporate seeds can be planted and sink

---

* There are differing views as to the identity of that "expert." Some believe no such person existed, and that the talk of such an expert was merely to create the impression that Saudi Arabia was pushing the new arrangement down the throat of the oil companies. Others, however, have a much more intriguing notion: that the "expert" in question was none other than Harry Dexter White, the Treasury Department aide later accused by Senator Joseph McCarthy of being a Russian spy.

their initial roots. As it works out in practice, at least in the case of the Irish tax holiday, it amounts to an ideal invitation to American business to transplant its facilities—and the jobs that go with it—to Eire. Here's how it works:

The hypothetical Amalgamated Buttonhook Company (ABC), wooed and lured by the Irish, dismantles one of its less modern factories and ships the buttonhook machinery to Ireland. There, it sets up a *branch* of the American company—*not* a separate subsidiary corporation (you'll see why in a moment). During its initial years of "start-up" operations in Ireland, while it is developing a renewed European taste for buttonhooks, the new company naturally suffers losses. Since it was carefully set up as a *branch* (rather than a separate subsidiary) of Amalgamated Buttonhook, American tax law permits those losses to be deducted from ABC's U.S. profits, and thus to reduce ABC's tax payments to Uncle Sam. The effect is that the U.S. Treasury underwrites part of the cost of starting up the Irish buttonhook company.

Now comes the real twist. After a time, the Europeans become as passionately fond of buttonhooks as their grandparents had been, and the new company begins to make a profit. Now inasmuch as Uncle Sam had been, in a sense, a contributing partner to the business during its unprofitable early years, it would seem only fair that he ought to share in the company's prosperity, and if the company were still in America, that would be the case: part of the profits would be paid in taxes to the U.S. Treasury.

But not in this instance, for just at the moment the Irish "branch" begins to make a profit, presto chango, the "branch" is, with the magnanimous assent of put-upon Uncle Sam, transformed into an Irish *subsidiary* of Amalgamated Buttonhook, and embarks on its Irish tax holiday. Result: its profits are not taxed at all, in either Ireland *or* the United States.* Once again Uncle ends up holding the bag. All the United States gets for its troubles is the loss of the American jobs that once belonged with the domestic buttonhook factory.

There is one more grain of salt to be rubbed into Uncle's open wound. Let's say the European buttonhook mania grows to such a degree that the Irish company finds a buyer for its old buttonhook machinery at a generous price. Remember that Uncle Sam has

---

* Assuming ABC does not bring the profits home, but leaves them in Ireland so as to take advantage of the tax-free funds to expand the business.

borne a part of the cost of depreciation on that machinery (because of the depreciation deductions against U.S. taxes). If the machinery were sold for a profit in the United States, the profit would be taxed at the full corporate tax rate, not the special capital gains rate. But in this case, the United States exacts no tax from the Irish company—not even the low-low capital gains tax. Once again, Uncle Sam is the fall guy.

A SIMILARLY ONE-SIDED tax arrangement accounts for one of the most intriguing but useless tidbits of information I picked up in the course of writing this book: namely, that most American brassieres are now made in Puerto Rico. The exodus of this industry from the continental United States does not stem from the American Woman's growing disenchantment with bras. It stems, instead, from Section 931 of the Internal Revenue Code, which has spawned a creature known as a "possessions corporation."* This creature enjoys all the tax advantages of Amalgamated Buttonhook's Irish operation—and then some. A budding brassiere company can, for example, set up a Puerto Rican operation, deduct all the start-up losses and reduce its U.S. taxes. Once it becomes profitable, the Puerto Rican company suddenly claims treatment as a "possessions corporation." As such, it is spared both U.S. *and* Puerto Rican taxes for a time. The U.S. parent company can also, after a time, liquidate the Puerto Rican firm and bring the untaxed profits it has earned back into the United States without *ever* paying a dime of taxes.

IT WOULD NOT DO to end this discussion of "The World-Wide Game of 'Beat the Tax Collector'" talking about brassiere companies, for, while such minor firms may get in on one of the minor side aspects of the game, they are distinctly unrepresentative of the serious players in this game. Those who play for major stakes, those that come off real winners, are no cross section of American businesses. Half of all U.S. direct investment abroad in 1970 fell into just two categories: manufacturing and petroleum.

No, the players in this particular game are decidedly *not* Main Street, U.S.A. They are the colossi of the American corporate world.

---

* A misnomer as regards Puerto Rico, which is *not* a U.S. possession.

Lest you have any doubt about that statement, reflect on these facts:

- *Half of all U.S. exports come from just ninety-three companies.*
- *Four-fifths of all the taxable dollars earned abroad by corporations in 1966 went to corporations with assets of a quarter of a billion dollars or more.* They constituted just six one-hundredths of one percent of all U.S. corporations.
- Nine-tenths of all such foreign-earned dollars went to corporations with assets of $100,000,000 or more. They make up just one one-hundredth of one percent of all U.S. corporations.
- Firms with assets of less than $25,000,000 got just 5 percent of the taxable dollars earned overseas. Those with less than $5,000,000 of assets (still a substantial size) represented nearly 98 percent of all corporations, yet received only about two and a half percent of the total foreign-earned dollars.

AS NOTED at several points in this chapter, this is not a game for any but the sophisticated firms that can afford to hire expensive and expert lawyers, for the rules of the game are as complex as any in the tax field.

And so the big winners in this game are the ITTs and the Standard Oils and the U.S. Steels of the world, who end up paying far more to foreign governments than to their own.*

One thing is certain: in this particular game, Uncle Sam most decidedly does *not* end up a winner. And in this book, as you know, Uncle Sam means The U.S. Taxpayers.

---

* In the case of those three firms, short-changing their government on income taxes (in a perfectly legal way, of course) has not inhibited them from appealing to that government for help—help in preventing the election of (and/or subverting) a foreign regime; help in persuading foreign governments not to raise their taxes; help in walling off the United States from foreign goods that might compete with (and lower the price of) those companies' products—help, in short, to further increase their profits, whether or not it also increased the national well-being of the United States.

13

Timber — Ideal for Your "Tax Shelter"

IF SOME UNEXPECTED great good fortune should befall you (like winning the Irish Sweepstakes or receiving a $10 million bequest from a distant and dimly known relative) and you should find yourself in need of a "tax shelter," you might as well build it out of timber as anything else. For timber is one of those happy industries that has found favor in the eyes of the tax-law writers.

And a handsome favor it is: it bestows some $175 million in annual "tax welfare" upon the owners and growers of the nation's timber. As usual, this "tax welfare" can hardly be said to be directed toward America's needy; statistics show that most of the tax advantages go to corporations and upper-bracket individuals. And, also as usual, the lion's share of the corporate tax bounty goes to just five companies—presumably the Big Five of the industry: International Paper, U.S. Plywood, Weyerhaeuser, Boise Cascade, and Georgia-Pacific. Those five corporations alone receive "tax welfare" estimated at nearly $60 million a year—and that emanates from just one (although the principal one) of the three tax advantages those corporations enjoy.

All told, the tax advantages enjoyed by these huge timber and paper companies may be far greater than the $60 million suggested above, if we compare the portion of their profits they paid in taxes in 1969 with that paid by U.S. corporations as a whole:

Company	Before-Tax Profits	Percent of Profits Paid in Taxes.	Approximate Tax Saving to Company*
International Paper	$188,714,000	26.5%	$25,500,000
Boise Cascade	$111,541,000	15.4%	$27,400,000
Weyerhaeuser	$185,192,000	19.4%	$38,150,000
Georgia-Pacific	$121,220,000	17.5%	$27,250,000
U.S. Plywood	$107,686,000	33.0%†	$7,540,000
Total	$714,353,000	22.3%	$125,850,000

    * Difference between what company *did* pay in taxes and what it would have paid had it paid what corporations as a whole did (about 40 percent).
    † This seems to have been an unusually high-tax year for U.S. Plywood. In the following year, 1970, the company paid only 19 percent taxes.

That $175 million of "tax welfare" to these corporations and wealthy individuals is one-fourth the total direct expenditures by the entire Federal government for the care and preservation of the nation's forests.

THE FAVORABLE TAX TREATMENT of timber should inspire a feeling of some pity for that vanishing breed of American, The Man with the Hoe (the American farmer). Allow yourself, if you will, to be a trifle old-fashioned and picture one of the few remaining "family farmers": that hard-working soul plants seed, then nurtures and cultivates it with Tender Loving Care (and a lot of backbreaking work), and if, at the end, he realizes a profit for all his labors, he must pay taxes at the regular income tax rates, which can ascend as high as 70 percent.

The identical process is carried on by the timber grower, only with much less day-to-day care than nature requires of the farmer. Yet when, in the end, he sells *his* product, his tax is, at most, only half as great as that of the farmer. Why? Because Congress has decreed, in effect by fiat, that the profits from growing trees, unlike the profits from growing wheat and barley, are classified as "capital gains," and thus are taxed at the special rates that apply to such "gains" (see Chapter 5).*

    * When Congress enacted this fiat in 1943, at the height of World War II, President Roosevelt cited it, in a veto message, as one of the provisions that provided relief "not for the needy but for the greedy." He went on to say, "As a grower and seller of timber, I think that timber should be treated as a crop and therefore as income when sold." His veto message mightily angered his friend and Senate floor leader, the eloquent Senator Alben W. Barkley of Kentucky, who told his fellow Senators: "I do not know to what extent the President is engaged in the timber business. I do know that he

That is by far the greatest single source of the handsome tax savings enjoyed by the Big Five corporations in the lumber industry: more than nine-tenths of their taxable incomes, during the Sixties, consisted of low-taxed capital gains. And the share of capital gains being reported by just five companies in the timber industry is on the increase—up from 51.3 percent in the early Sixties to 57.3 percent, as indicated by the latest available figures (for 1968).

The comparison with—and the unfairness to—farmers is particularly striking with respect to Christmas trees* for they, even more than the longer-lived timber, resemble the crops raised by farmers. Not only are their lives shorter (generally a little more than six years), but they require more constant tending, pruning and shaping than do trees grown for lumber. And they are a highly specialized crop: the requirements for Christmas trees are just the opposite of those grown for lumber, where knot-causing branches should be kept to a minimum; with Christmas trees, the effort is to foster the maximum number of branches from which to hang the traditional baubles.

So much do Christmas trees resemble a farmer's crop, in fact, that at one time an Internal Revenue ruling denied them the capital gains advantage that Congress conferred on timber generally. The ruling naturally provoked not only the jealousy but the vocal outcry of Christmas tree raisers, and, as noted earlier in Chapter 5, this prompted Congress, in 1954, to pass a new legislative decree according the more favorable tax treatment to Christmas trees (as eloquently described in tax-law verbiage—if you missed it, be sure to see page 104). In 1969, the Christmas tree industry was potent and vocal enough to abort a short-lived effort to repeal this decree.

The tax laws governing the timber industry often involve one-sided "heads-the-timber-owner-wins, tails-the-U.S.-taxpayers-lose" propositions. One is that when a top-bracket timber owner pays the tax-deductible *expenses* of bringing a timber stand to maturity, Uncle Sam must bear as much as 70 percent of the burden. But when it comes time to receive the *profits* resulting from those

---

sells Christmas trees at Christmas time. . . . But . . . to compare those little pine businesses with a sturdy oak, gum, poplar or spruce . . . is like comparing a cricket to a stallion."

* Senator Barkley, in his retort to President Roosevelt's veto message, thought the comparison apt, remarking that Christmas trees "are no doubt of easy growth and short life, and I have no doubt that the income from their sale constitutes [ordinary] income. . . ."

expenses, Uncle receives no more than 35 percent of the "take" (even though his early-year contributions should have entitled him to a 70 percent share). In the case of corporate timber owners, Uncle is a 48 percent partner in the unpleasant part (paying the expenses), but receives only a 30 percent* share of the resulting profits. It is a lousy business deal for Uncle Sam (which is to say the U.S. taxpayers) but it is a highly rewarding arrangement for the owners and growers of the trees, in whom the Congressional tax-law writers seem to have a greater interest.

Due to another one-sided tax provision, timber growers and owners are one jump ahead of the usual capital gains recipient. Ordinarily, if a person is unfortunate enough to suffer some capital *losses* (e.g., if he has to sell his AT&T stock at less than he paid for it), he can only offset those losses against his capital *gains* for that year. That seems only just; if a capital gain is going to cost him no more than 35 cents on the dollar, a capital loss should not save him more than that. But timber owners are exempt from that common-sense rule: a top-bracket timber baron, while never having to pay more than 35 percent of his timber sale *profits*, is nonetheless permitted to save up to 70 percent of his timber *losses* (since he can offset those losses against his regular income, which is taxed at the 70 percent rate). Happy timber baron.

Timber growers receive still a third basic tax advantage that is unavailable to most other industries and companies. Generally, as you learned in Chapter 9, the tax deductions for business outlays that will produce income and profits over a period of years (rather than immediately) have to be spread out over that profit period, so that there is an approximate matching of the deductible outlays and the profits they generate. That is, if the National Widget Company buys a $10,000 machine that is expected to produce widgets for ten years, it is not allowed to deduct the full $10,000 the year it buys the widget machine but must space out the deductions over the "useful life" of the machine.

In the case of the timber industry, however, even though it takes years, often decades, to bring a timber stand to the point where it can be sold—that is, to the point where there are taxable profits—many of the expenses† involved in bringing about that

---

* The corporate capital gains tax rate is 30 percent.

† For such things as taxes, interest, fire insurance and protection and disease prevention.

happy moment do not have to be spread over a many-year period but may be fully deducted in the year of the outlays. So if, say, Boise Cascade were to have $2,083,333 of deductible expenses in Year One of developing a forty-year stand of Douglas fir, it would enjoy a tax saving, that year, of $1,000,000 (48 percent of the outlay), and it can keep that million dollars, as an interest-free loan from munificent Uncle Sam, for another thirty-nine years before the timber has reached maturity and any taxable profits are received. The value to Boise Cascade of enjoying that million-dollar, thirty-nine-year loan on an interest-free basis comes to the staggering total of a little over $41 million.*

If anyone doubts that the immediate deductibility of these expenses represents a tax preference, he should waste no time in consulting with the accountants for the timber industry who, in a supposed effort to convey to company managers and shareholders the *true* cost-and-profit picture, spread many of those costs over the "life" of the timber stands. Thus, the earnings and profits that the companies report to their shareholders (and to the Securities and Exchange Commission) reflect the cost-spreading rather than an all-in-one-year outlay.† It is only to Internal Revenue that the expenses are reported in the all-income-year manner, in order to get the advantage of the tax-free loan from the U.S. Treasury.

The combination of these preferences—the full and immediate deduction of growing expenses plus the delayed and favored taxation of the resulting profits—produces dramatic advantages for the owners and sellers of trees. One analysis shows that, in theory at least, the various preferences, when put together, lower the proportion of taxes paid on timber profits from 50 percent to 7 percent, and nearly double the after-tax rate of return on investment in timber properties (increasing it from 3 percent to 5.6 percent).

THE GIANT "INTEGRATED" timber companies—i.e., those companies that not only grow and sell trees but also

---

* Assuming a 10 percent return, compounded. That is conservative: most corporations expect at least a 12 percent return when they have idle cash to invest.

† While the accountants adopt this practice in order to reflect the true economics of the situation, cynics might suspect that company managers are happy to follow it in their annual reports since the result is to puff up the apparent earnings and profits, which does nothing to tarnish their managerial performance in the eyes of grateful shareholders.

fabricate them into lumber, paper or other wood products—can squeeze some extra advantage out of the favorable capital gains treatment of timber sales by the curious device of charging themselves too much for the trees they grow.

For example: let's say, hypothetically, that the Universal Paper Company has a stand of pulpwood trees on which the original cost and the growing expenses total $12 million, and on which the "true" value,* at the time of sale, is $20 million. But if the *Timber Division* of Universal Paper sells the trees to the *Paper Division* of that same company not at its "true" $20 million value but for, say, $25 million, the result would be to reduce by $5 million the profits of the Paper Division (which are subject to a 48 percent tax) while at the same time bestowing an added capital gain of $5 million to the Timber Division, on which the tax would be only 30 percent. Tax saving to Universal Paper: 18 percent† of $5 million, or $900,000.

The tax law is supposed to prohibit such inflated-price arrangements among the siblings of a single corporate parent, but, although Internal Revenue employs no less than twenty-five timber experts, they are usually at an acute disadvantage in proving such schemes. By the time they are called on to judge the question (usually two or more years after the timber stand has been cut down and ground into pulp), the evidence has long vanished, and they have no reliable way of judging such critical pricing factors as size and straightness of trees, presence or absence of knots, etc.

WHAT ARE THE ARGUMENTS in favor of the tax preference for timber?

First, it is contended, the pre-1943 situation discriminated against those timber owners who either cut their own timber or had it cut under contract (and whose profits were taxed at the regular rates) and in favor of those who sold the timber, uncut, with or without the land beneath it (to whom the capital gains rate applied). One corrective solution would have been to class all timber as a crop, and tax all timber profits at the regular rates. But that would have gone against Congress's path-of-least-resistance

---

* This assumes that there is a Jovian, or absolutely "true" value to a given stand or lot of timber. In fact, timber valuation is not that precise.

† The difference between the 48 percent regular corporate rate and the 30 percent corporate capital gains rate.

way of correcting "inequities" in favor of the least-taxed (described in Chapter 14).

Second, it is argued that the capital gains treatment of timber encourages conservation-minded ownership of timber stands. The pre-1943 tax law (i.e., pre-capital gains law), it is argued, gave an incentive to "clear-cutting" (reducing a given forest area to mere stumps) rather than selective cutting, leaving some trees standing. This latter practice is supposedly (although not provably, some say) better from a conservation viewpoint, since the nudity of the land resulting from clear-cutting permits more land erosion. Supporters of the tax preference point to an increase in private forest planting and forest management expenditures since the capital gains provision was enacted in 1943. But opponents cite other factors that almost surely were major, if not exclusive, causes of those increases (such as greater demand for new housing and the lumber that goes into houses, the disappearance of old-growth timber supplies and sharp price increases for timber). Moreover, say the capital gains critics, the favored tax rates are accorded to *all* timber owners, *whether or not they follow model conservation practices.* If conservation is the goal, it would be more effectively promoted by limiting the tax favors to those timber owners who follow specific conservation practices or increase their forest management outlays.

Third, the defenders of capital-gains-for-timber argue that other natural resources (e.g., all those that are accorded percentage depletion—see Chapter 11) receive tax favors, and that since timber is a natural resource it should not be discriminated against. (Farmers might argue with equal persuasiveness that wheat is also a natural resource and hence deserves the more gentle tax treatment.)

Finally, the industry argues that it would be unfair to tax, at the regular rates and all in one year, the profits that had accrued over the many-year period of the trees' growth. But the answer to that is not a favored rate but an averaging device, similar to that currently permitted authors, movie stars and others whose income tends to come in spurts (see page 113).

THERE ARE MANY QUESTIONS to be raised about the tax favors to the timber industry.

First, since the giant corporations derive more benefit than the small ones,* is it sensible to put them in a position to outbid the small ones and to tend to concentrate timber ownership in fewer and fewer hands?

Second, is it sensible to give a tax incentive to the cutting of new timber stands rather than the recycling of paper and other wood products so as to conserve forest resources?

Finally, is it sensible (and fair) to oblige non-timber-owning taxpayers to bear the cost of paying $175 million in annual "tax welfare" payments, mainly to distinctly non-needy giant corporations and well-to-do individuals—both highly unlikely candidates for conventional "welfare"?

---

* The very small companies—those with taxable incomes of $25,000 or less—get no benefit from the capital gains treatment (since the 30 percent corporate capital gains rate is higher than their 22 percent regular tax rates). Moreover, the giant "integrated" companies (those that produce paper as well as lumber) can squeeze the added advantage described on p. 293.

Old Loopholes Never Die,
They Just Get Bigger

ON OCTOBER 9, 1942, Stalingrad was under Nazi siege, and American heavy bombers were staging their greatest daylight raids in Europe and striking hard at both ends of the Pacific fighting line. In the Senate of the United States, Robert La Follette was waging his own battle to prevent the Senate from "extending special [tax] privileges in time of war." "Apparently," he said, "the Senate . . . wants to see that everyone comes through the war entirely whole, except the poor devils who have to go out and fight."

His target in this instance was an effort to add "ball and sagger clay"* to the list of tax-favored minerals enjoying a percentage depletion allowance. "We are vesting interests which will come back to plague us," he warned the Senate. "If we are to include all these things, why do we not put in sand and gravel?"

At the time, granting percentage depletion to encourage exploration for these two relatively plentiful and easy-to-find minerals must have seemed as ridiculous as Senator La Follette sought to portray it. (As one Senator later put it, "You only have to stub

---

* A type of clay used especially in the manufacture of porcelain. Lest anyone doubt its essentiality, Tennessee's Senator Kenneth McKellar assured the Senate that it was "very essential. Every time we eat a meal we have to use cups and saucers and other kinds of crockeryware." He then added that small amounts of the clay were also used by one Tennessee firm to make porcelain used in military radios.

your toe to find gravel.") Yet a bare nine years later, depletion for sand and gravel was not ridiculous; it was the law of the land. Not only that: oyster shells and clam shells had joined the depletion family. Senator Hubert Humphrey was horrified. "How far shall we go? Where shall we draw the line?" he asked the Senate. "If we are to give depletion allowances to sand and gravel and oyster and clam shells I do not see any reason why we should not give depletion . . . to anything that can be taken from the earth."

Three years later, Congress came perilously close to making his intended exaggeration into a prophecy by awarding depletion to a long list of new minerals. As noted in Chapter 11, so swollen did the depletion list become that Congress felt obliged specifically to *exclude* "soil, sod, dirt, turf, water, mosses, minerals from sea water, the air or similar inexhaustible sources."

But the chain did not end even there. In 1963, a Federal district court ruled that cost depletion could even apply, in certain circumstances, to *water*. And, in 1969, the Tax Court ruled that underground steam from natural geysers was entitled to the same generous depletion allowance accorded to oil and gas, on the theory that underground steam was "a gas." Dissenting Tax Court judges, perhaps of the belief that the steam was more the product of God's ingenuity than of man's dollar, characterized the decision as "depletion run riot."

IF ANYONE IS SURPRISED or indignant about these apparent absurdities, it is merely because he does not fully apprehend the principle of "equity" in taxation. Judging from Congressional behavior, one can almost imagine this principle, as perceptively worded by Louis Eisenstein, framed in a sampler on the wall of the Ways and Means and Finance committee rooms:

EQUITY IS THE PRIVILEGE
OF PAYING AS LITTLE
AS SOMEBODY ELSE.

That is, once a tax concession has been granted to one group, it becomes inequitable to deny the same favor to anyone else who can successfully claim to be "similarly situated."

As soon as this principle is properly understood, the case for percentage depletion for sand and gravel ceases to be ridiculous; it becomes irrefutable. Consider the argument presented to Congress in 1951 by the National Sand and Gravel Association. That group's witness noted that (a) percentage depletion had already been granted to many nonmetallic minerals; and (b) sand and gravel are nonmetallic minerals. Therefore, the witness concluded, "it seems to us an unreasonable discrimination against our industry to continue to be denied the benefit of a taxation policy already extended to other members of the nonmetallic minerals family." Q.E.D.

This line of reasoning seemed eminently sensible to the Ways and Means Committee, which concluded that the then-excluded nonmetallics "have just as good a claim" for percentage depletion as those already enjoying this favor. (Senator Douglas of Illinois had the unkindness to point out that the Committee "does not say they have a *good* claim. It says they have *just as good* a claim as those which [had] been [favored]."

In 1951, therefore, sand and gravel were awarded a 5 percent depletion allowance. But equity had still not been achieved. Just three years later, the Sand and Gravel Association was back before Congress, asserting that since sand and gravel are sold in competition with such products as limestone, which enjoys a 15 percent depletion allowance, the 5 percent rate was clearly inadequate to "eliminate this competitive inequality."

Limestone, in turn, had come to be honored with a 15 percent depletion rate when the two Senators from Texas pointed out that it competes directly with such 15 percent road-building materials as rock asphalt. And how had rock asphalt ascended to its favored position? Thereby, as the saying goes, hangs a tale which helps illuminate our guiding principle that "Old Loopholes Never Die. . . ."

Go back to October, 1942, in the United States Senate. Senator Elmer Thomas of Utah had run into heavy weather in his effort to confer percentage depletion on rock asphalt as well as ball and sagger clay. He resorted to the ultimate Senatorial weapon. To "clarify the issue," he told his brethren that if the clay-asphalt amendment should be defeated, he intended to propose the repeal of percentage depletion for *all* minerals save the sacred oil and gas. Then, glowering at his critics, he began to lash them with the list of depletion-favored products in their own states: timber in La Follette's Wisconsin, copper and iron mines in Senator Prentiss Brown's Michigan. Apparently the lesson was not lost on other

Senators, for rock asphalt and ball and sagger clay were voted into the pending tax bill, war or no war.

The next round of depletion-blessed minerals, approved in 1943, gave a stirring demonstration of the imperishability of tax preferences. The 1943 law explicitly provided that these members of the depletion "club" were being granted membership solely because of, and "for the duration" of, World War II, and that the membership card expired automatically with the end of the fighting. When peace came, Congress quickly (and with little opposition) extended the membership privilege for the 1943 list—and even added a few new minerals just for good measure. Today these "temporary" depletion war babies are thirty years old, and show no signs of fading.*

Since 1942, the list of tax-favored minerals has become all-encompassing, and there is likely not a single state without its own built-in pro-depletion lobby. Thus, by meticulously hanging together,† the beneficiaries of depletion have brilliantly avoided hanging separately.

In the case of oil and coal, the spreading of equity (and Federal largesse) reached a state of exquisite logic. On the one hand, Congress gave the oil and gas industry a massive injection of percentage depletion to spur exploration and development, but this proved to have an unhappy side effect: the expansion of the industry and the prodigious use of oil and gas for fuel and energy drove the coal industry into a state of chronic illness. To Congress, the prescription was clear: simply double the dose of depletion for coal.

IN THE FIELD OF CAPITAL GAINS, the rendering of equity has also tested Congress's ingenuity, but the lawmakers have proved themselves up to the test. During World War II, for example, supposedly to induce businessmen to replace used

---

* The same durability was exhibited by the tax deduction for personal medical expenses. When it was initially enacted, in 1942, it was supposedly to last no longer than the duration of the "emergency." Not only has it survived; like all good tax preferences, it has been expanded. Annual revenue cost today: $1.3 billion.

† In asking for a 15 percent depletion allowance, for example, the Sand and Gravel Association went to repeated pains to emphasize to the Senate Finance Committee that "we do not wish to be regarded as asking, here, any reduction in the percentage depletion rate [for other minerals] provided for in the bill which passed the House."

machinery and equipment, Congress enacted the so-called "one-way street," which operated in an inventive manner: a machine sold at a *profit* was considered a "capital asset," and the profit was taxed at the favorable 25 percent capital gains rate. But if the selfsame machine were sold at a *loss*, it suddenly ceased to be a "capital asset," so that the loss could be deducted at the much higher regular income tax rates (then up to 82 percent for individuals and 31 percent for corporations). One Senator called this the "heads-I-win-tails-you-lose" provision.*

Some years later, a dispute arose between Internal Revenue and the courts as to whether sales of livestock "held for draft, breeding or dairy purposes" were entitled to capital gains treatment. In 1951, in order to end all doubt, the Senate Finance Committee herded all such livestock into the warm shelter of the "one-way street" provision and, always on guard against unfair discriminations, carefully included turkeys in the definition of "livestock." On the Senate floor, Minnesota's Senator Edward Thye sought a broader justice: if turkeys were worthy, why not chickens? There followed this exchange:

SENATOR DOUGLAS: Would the Senator from Minnesota consider the possibility of adding ducks, angora cats and dogs to his amendment?

SENATOR THYE: There would be some justification for adding the ducks, though ducks are not equal in importance to either turkeys or chickens with respect to the national income. The senator has an argument there, but when one goes too far down the ladder . . . he may get into a category which causes someone possibly to look upon the proposition as ridiculous.

---

* One facet of the "one-way street" allowing banks the "heads-I-win-tails-the-Treasury-loses" treatment on their purchases and sales of government bonds was enacted in 1942 at the outset of American involvement in World War II under the rationale of encouraging banks to buy war bonds. That is, it was supposed to have been solely a wartime measure, and, as two tax experts have observed, there was "no justification for continuing it after the war." For one thing, say these experts, it encouraged banks, in postwar years, to manipulate their bond portfolios in such a way as to reap handsome tax benefits without really changing their overall holdings of government bonds. But, as with other "temporary" tax savers, this one proved durable enough to remain in effect for more than two decades after the end of World War II. It was not until 1969 that Congress finally repealed it.

Finance Committee Chairman Walter George apparently also feared the Senate was on the brink of the ludicrous. "I certainly cannot [accept] the chicken amendment," he told the Senate. "Turkeys were included somehow, I do not know how. . . . I cannot conceive that Congress ever had in mind [according capital gains treatment] to assets which are purely transitory." Senator Williams of Delaware quickly jumped to Senator George's aid with an amendment to deny capital gains treatment to livestock which, he said, were clearly "transitory." But he apparently overstepped the bounds of helpfulness, for Senator George ungratefully rebuffed his proposal. "It would be a dangerous thing indeed," he intoned, "to say that the whole [livestock capital gain] section should be impaired" by so lowly a creature as a chicken or turkey. The turkey amendment, incidentally, perished at the hands of a heartless House–Senate conference committee, but the livestock provision remained securely in the law, bringing tax joy to many a movie star and other top-bracket taxpayer (see pages 187–199) until its repeal in 1969.*

Still another chain of dispensations sprang from Congress's rectifying a supposed inequity regarding timber. Prior to 1943, if Timberland Owner A caused his trees to be cut and *then* sold them, he paid regular income tax rates while his neighbor, B, who sold the timber without cutting it, paid only the favorable 25 percent capital gains tax—a clear discrimination against A. So Congress proceeded to apply the customary and approved remedy: lower A's taxes to the level of B's. (So disturbed were the lawmakers about this particular discrimination that they made the remedy retroactive some thirty years—back to 1913.)

Later, in 1951, Congress felt a need to bestow tax relief on coal royalty recipients whose contracts had unforesightedly neglected to tie the royalty payments to the rising price of coal. The chosen *form* of tax relief for this "hardship" was to confer the special capital gains rate on coal royalty income. The chosen rationale: coal royalties would simply be receiving "the same treatment as timber royalties." Sidelight: although the alleged

---

* Obviously, the author, in entitling this chapter "Old Loopholes *Never* Die . . . ," has been caught exaggerating. As the demise of the cattle provision shows, there are occasions when loopholes do succumb. But most of them have shown great durability, if not immortality; so perhaps the expository license will be indulged.

"hardship" was suffered only by past royalty contracts, the remedy was made available to *future* contracts as well. To discriminate between the two would, of course, have been inequitable.

In granting capital gains treatment to coal royalties, however, Congress had created still another inequity which cried out for correction: it had denied comparable tax treatment to iron ore royalties. The Kennedy Administration perceived the discrimination and proposed the unorthodox remedy of repealing the favorable treatment enjoyed by coal royalties. But this did not accord with the Congressional sense of justice; in 1964, instead of repealing the coal provision, Congress simply extended it to cover iron ore.

In 1951, Congress decreed that crops standing on farmland at the time it is sold should, like timber, be shaded by the capital gains umbrella. Thus, a farmer can set the sale of his land just before harvest time and have the proceeds of his year's work taxed at the favorable capital gains rate instead of his regular tax rates.

The last link in the chain (to date, at least) came in 1954, when Congress corrected an apparent ambiguity: as we saw in Chapter 13, capital gains for timber, the law now assures all and sundry, definitely *includes* the sale of "evergreen trees which are more than 6 years old at the time severed from the roots and are sold for ornamental purposes"—i.e., Christmas trees.

IF THE SPECIALLY TAILORED Louis B. Mayer amendment (page 41) struck you as an unwarranted tax favor, it was only because you had not been properly indoctrinated in "the new equity," under which it would have been heartless and unfair to treat Mr. Mayer any other way. It may be recalled that rather than waiting for the year-by-year share of MGM profits to which he was entitled after leaving the company, Mr. Mayer wished his money all in one lump. In asking that Mr. Mayer be spared the tax consequences of this wish (via being permitted to pay only a 25 percent capital gains tax on the lump-sum settlement), his attorney appealed to precedent and to Congress's sense of fairness: "The justice of this approach," attorney Alvord pointed out, "has already received congressional approval" in permitting capital gains taxation of lump-sum *pension* pay-outs. Judging from the way the Mayer amendment was finally tailored (see page 41), there was just enough merit in Mr. Alvord's argument to cover Louis B. Mayer, but no others.

ONE GUIDING PRINCIPLE of taxation seems to be that one good tax favor deserves another. Social Security and railroad retirement benefits, for example, have always been tax-free, but the pensions of Federal, state and local employees are taxable. "Discrimination!" cried the teachers, the policemen and firemen. "Discrimination!" answered Congress in 1954, by enacting the retirement income credit (page 353). Current annual cost to the U.S. Treasury: $200 million.

In 1971, the Treasury Department proposed deferral privileges for domestic U.S. corporations engaged in exporting direct overseas (see the description of DISC's, pages 271–274). How did the Treasury defend this proposal? You guessed it: on the ground that it would merely put these domestic companies on a par with other firms that had for years been enjoying comparable tax-deferral privileges by operating overseas through subsidiary companies. Therefore, the Treasury maintained that the DISC idea was not a novel concept. It was simply an "effort to cut through all this maze of complexity" involved in setting up a foreign subsidiary and to provide the same privileges, "in a forthright fashion," to domestic corporations.

In 1948, as you learned in Chapter 6, the blessings of income-splitting were bestowed on married people, but plainly the chain of tax concessions could not end here. What, for example, of the bachelor supporting his mother, brothers and sisters—is he not entitled to tax relief? Of course he is, Congress was compelled to conclude, although only half as much as, say, a less burdened childless married couple. And what about the suddenly bereaved wife or husband—did Congress really intend to add to the blow by abruptly withdrawing the marital tax dispensation? Clearly not, and so they were given a two-year cushion to soften the impact.

Just a short decade ago, in writing about the Congressional favoritism toward the married, I wondered, "Might we one day witness a Bachelors' March on Washington in search of single 'tax equity'?" That statement proved prophetic, for today there *is* a march of sorts on Washington, under the acronym CO$T (Committee of $ingle Taxpayers). Although in 1969 Congress reduced by half the discrimination against the unmarried, CO$T members remain unsatisfied: they want Congress to go the whole way and reduce their tax rates so they will be on a par with the married. And, being large in number as well as ably represented in Washington, these $ingle Taxpayers had, as of 1972, succeeded in enlisting no fewer than 181 Congressmen and 44 Senators to their cause. That year they persuaded the House Ways and Means Committee to hold hearings on their proposal, but the Committee took no action. There were, of course, no voices at the hearing calling for curing the "inequity" by *raising* the tax rates of the married to match those of single taxpayers, as suggested on page 128—a move that would raise the oppressive total of $21.5 billion in added Federal revenues, mainly from well-to-do taxpayers.

In any event, as long as Congress fails to tax all persons on a uniform basis, regardless of their marital status, the $ingle Taxpayers have an irrefutable case. They are, in fact, discriminated against—and past experience leaves little doubt that one day, perhaps soon, Congress will once again achieve "equity" in the approved manner: by lowering the taxes of the $ingles to match those of the Doubles.

WHAT IS A DOCTOR or lawyer or small-business owner to think when corporations are permitted tax-deductible contributions to employee pension plans but the self-employed are denied comparable tax deductions in providing for their old age? Ask the spokesmen for the American Bar or Medical associations or for groups as diverse as the National Funeral Directors Association or the Society of American Florists and Ornamental Horticulturists—groups which for years besieged Congress with cries of "discrimination." In 1962, at long last, they prevailed in part (see page 362). But, as with most "creeping preferences," the country has not heard the last of this one, for many self-employed groups are not covered by the 1962 measure. "I have no doubt," said Senator Smathers of Florida, principal Senatorial sponsor of the bill, "that sooner or later we are going to make this type of [tax-deductible] pension program available to anyone who is not otherwise in a position to get into such a program. . . . In my opinion, it is a matter of time before this goal is achieved." But the 1962 measure permitted the self-employed to take tax deductions only on a maximum of *10* percent of their income, to set aside for their later years, whereas corporations may deduct up to 25 percent of their executives' earnings for that purpose. There was, as you can see, a clear discrimination—but professional men, rather than waiting for Congress to correct the inequity, have taken matters into their own hands. With the cooperation of the various state legislatures and the aid of nimble tax attorneys, they have begun transforming themselves into corporate executives. How? They have simply incorporated themselves. That is, your friendly neighborhood doctor or dentist, rather than having a mere M.D. or D.D.S. on his shingle, is likely now to be Doctor Herman A. Stethoscope, Inc., or, perhaps, Horace B. Toothpuller, Inc. (Some patients may wonder whether the incorporated physicians have persuaded their attorneys to write into their corporate charters an absolute prohibition against house calls.)

This recent rush toward incorporation represents a marked change of heart on the part of the medical professional associations, which, not long ago, were staunchly opposed to permitting their members to don the corporate cloak, generally on the ground that to interpose so impersonal an entity as a corporation would diminish the personal nature of the doctor-patient or lawyer-client relationship. Apparently, however, the prospect of an additional 15 percent retirement-fund tax deduction melted their prior philosophical reservations, and, encouraged by the doctors' and dentists' new-found enthusiasm, every state legislature has enacted laws permitting professionals to incorporate.* As a result, the number of professional corporations has mushroomed in recent years. Sometimes the doctors incorporate in duos, in threesomes and foursomes, but often they incorporate alone. One tax lawyer, who has helped several clients envelop themselves in a corporate shroud, sees in this the ultimate tax-induced absurdity: an annual shareholders' meeting at which the question arises as to whether the Corporation's principal employee (the doctor) is entitled to a raise in salary. The Chairman of the Board (also the doctor) asks for (and receives, from the lone shareholder) a motion to grant a handsome 25 percent increase. The shareholder extols the virtues of the Corporation's employee—his diligence, kindliness,

---

* The last entity to join the movement was the District of Columbia, largely because Congress, not trusting the nation's capital to pass its own laws and reserving this function to itself, took some time to enact a statute for Washington. At one point, before Congress gave D.C. the nod, one tax-conscious psychiatrist actually moved his office and couch a few blocks into neighboring Maryland, which had a law hospitable to his desire to become Sigmund Saynothing, Inc.

generosity, wisdom, brilliance and, above all, his modesty. The shareholder calls for the vote; the Chairman of the Board puts the question, and it is approved by acclamation.

AND SO IT GOES, with each tax concession containing the seeds of still others, in a process that is strikingly unidirectional. As Senators Long of Louisiana and McCarthy of Minnesota once put it, "the principle seems to be that if inequity is *extended*, justice is achieved." And Senator Albert Gore of Tennessee has commented: "It seems never to occur to some that provisions of law can be equalized by *taking away* some benefits. . . ." (Emphases added.) (Such a thought did occur, briefly, to the Ways and Means Committee when, in 1961, it tentatively voted to repeal a tax deduction enjoyed by life insurance but not casualty insurance companies. But the displeasure of the life insurance companies was such that the vote was later reversed. The Senate Finance Committee's thinking was more in keeping with tradition: it voted to extend the tax deduction to casualty *as well as* life insurance companies. This happy solution was postponed, however, pending further study.)

Where will the process end? Already, imaginative pleas have been entered for the enlargement of the percentage depletion family. The National Patent Council, for example, has suggested that depletion be bestowed on inventions since patents "can last only 17 years," after which inventions, like oil wells, are depleted of their value. In California, a seventy-six-year-old lawyer, Fred Heisler, requested that he and his wife Briedy, seventy-two, be granted depletion allowances on their bodies. Attorney Heisler somehow managed to have his plea heard by the United States Court of Appeals, which straight-facedly observed that the Heislers' "bodies and skills are not among the 'other natural deposits' for which the Internal Revenue Code allows a deduction for percentage depletion." Actress Gloria Swanson told the Ways and Means Committee that aging actresses should get depletion allowances just like Texas oilmen. The Jockeys' Guild of America has made what one Senator called a "rather strong case" for granting depletion to racing jockeys "since their capabilities are in part physical, their average riding life is less than four years" and, therefore, "their assets deplete."* In 1963, the President of the National

---

* This was a facetious characterization by Senator Eugene McCarthy of Minnesota.

Football League Players' Association appealed to the Senate Finance Committee to grant some tax concession to the professional athlete "who depletes his natural resources of physical ability and muscular strength while earning a high income on which he is heavily taxed." Illinois Senator Paul Douglas sympathized, saying it would be reasonable to grant that depletion allowance but warning that this might oblige Congress to extend the same privilege to movie stars, TV actors, poets and others. That stimulated Kansas's Senator Frank Carlson to suggest that depletion be granted to United States Senators.*

Outlandish? Far-fetched? Senator La Follette apparently thought that percentage depletion for sand and gravel was far-fetched. And what would he have said if someone had suggested to him, in 1942, that depletion would be granted in a few years to oyster shells and clam shells—and even water—or that turkeys would come within a feather of joining the capital gains family?

Randolph Paul, the eminent tax authority, once observed that "most of the inequities in the tax structure . . . are men who came to dinner and do not mean to go home."

Even since he wrote those words in 1955, the dinner table has become considerably more crowded.

---

* Senator Douglas demurred to this suggestion: mindful of his many ex-colleagues receiving lucrative fees for lobbying among their former Senatorial associates, he observed that often a Senator's earning power increases, rather than declines, upon his retirement.

15

Tax Handouts Behind Closed Doors

IMAGINE AND APPRAISE for yourself the fairness of a courtroom trial that proceeds as follows:

The judge enters. Before him, there is only one lawyer's table instead of the usual two. No press or members of the public are permitted.

A lawyer for just one of the opposing factions, whom we will call Lawyer A, rises and argues his case. Having heard but one side of the case, the judge declares the trial ended and retires to deliberate the matter. There is no Lawyer B to develop and argue the other side. That task falls to the judge, who thus is thrust into the awkward role of being both judge and advocate.

As the judge ponders the questions before him, Lawyer A makes repeated private visits to his chambers, pressing him with further arguments, rebutting any doubts he seems to have.

When the judge ultimately reaches and issues his decision, it, like the trial itself, is not open to the public but is kept confidential, known only to himself and to Lawyer A.

If the decision is unfavorable to Lawyer A, he can appeal it to a higher court. But if it is favorable to A, no one else, no matter how aggrieved by it, may appeal it. And so it stands, as final as a Supreme Court decision (until and unless the Congress of the United States sees fit to change it).

The preceding is perhaps oversimplified, yet it is a surprisingly precise parallel to the manner in which the Internal Revenue Service hears and decides questions put to it about the tax law tens of thousands of times a year. These questions emanate mostly from business concerns, often seeking an in-advance-of-the-fact ruling about how IRS would apply the tax law to a transaction they are about to undertake. Many of the requests for rulings are routine. But, as you will see, others involve tens, if not hundreds, of millions of dollars.

In theory—that is, technically speaking—rulings are available to any taxpayer who knows about them and submits a request. But most average taxpayers are not even aware they can ask for an in-advance-of-the-fact ruling (how many readers of these words know about them?). By contrast, rulings are well known to—and hence mainly used by—businesses, especially major companies advised by experienced and handsomely paid tax attorneys. The contrast could well give rise to the following two types of situations:

FOR JOHN AND ESTHER HALE, the letter from Internal Revenue seemed not far removed from disaster. It had to do with their tax return of two years earlier, and, in particular, with the sale of their house for considerably more than they had originally paid. John was aware of the disadvantage of having his profit on the deal taxed all in one lump in the year of the sale (which would push him into a much higher tax bracket) and thought he had carefully worked things out so that the transaction would be treated as an "installment sale"—i.e., so that he could, in calculating the tax, spread out the profit over the five-year period of the mortgage pay-out. But apparently he had run afoul of some technicality in the law, and Internal Revenue was taxing the whole profit in the year of the sale. The upshot was that the Hales had to pay a "deficiency" of a little more than $4,000, and if they didn't pay it before the end of the year, they would have to start paying the government 6 percent interest on the $4,000.

Surprised and puzzled, John telephoned Internal Revenue. The IRS agent, while firm that John would have to pay the deficiency, was sympathetic, since, he said, a minor change in the transaction could have saved the Hales the extra tax. "It's a shame," he said, "that you didn't come to us with your contract beforehand. We could have told you that it wouldn't qualify for the installment sale and, probably, how to change it to fit the regulations."

That was all very nice, but it didn't suggest to John Hale how he was going to come up with four thousand dollars before the end of the year.

I N 1 9 6 6 , the Continental Oil Company had a tax problem of considerably greater magnitude than that of John and Esther Hale. It was, to be precise, a $175 million tax problem. But because Continental had the advantage of being counseled by influential and experienced tax lawyers, the company knew that it could go to IRS to seek advance approval of what it sought to do.

Boiled down to its simplest terms, Continental Oil wanted to borrow some $460 million in order to buy up one of its major energy-source competitors, Consolidation Coal—the largest coal company in the United States. For some years, oil companies wishing to borrow in order to buy additional oil properties had been using an ingenious three-party device known as an "ABC" transaction.* That intricate triangular transaction had an enormous advantage: it enabled the companies to pay back the borrowed money with *untaxed* dollars instead of having to use after-tax dollars, as most taxpayers do when they repay loans. If Continental could employ such an arrangement to buy Consolidation Coal, that would mean a tax saving of about $175 million. But while the "ABC" device had been successfully used in buying *oil* properties, it was unclear that IRS would approve such an arrangement for the purchase of "hard" minerals like coal. Without IRS approval, Continental would have to make just about twice as many dollars of profits† to repay the mammoth $460 million loan; thus, before any banks would put up the money, they insisted on knowing in advance whether IRS would give its blessing to the "ABC" deal.

Accordingly, the highly prestigious New York law firm of Simpson, Thacher and Bartlett was engaged to present the facts of the "ABC" transaction to IRS with a request for a binding in-advance-of-the-fact ruling. And in due course, on August 18, 1966, a piece of paper assuring Continental of its $175 million tax

---

* See Glossary.

† That is, if IRS approved and the loan could be repaid with untaxed dollars, it would require only one dollar of profit to repay a dollar of the loan. But if IRS disapproved the arrangement and the loan had to be repaid with *after-tax* dollars, it would require roughly *two* dollars of profit to repay each dollar of the loan, since about one dollar of the profit would go to pay taxes.

saving went forward from IRS—a "letter ruling" approving the "ABC" transaction.

Thus was the way paved for the buy-up of the nation's largest coal company by what was then the nation's tenth largest oil company.

Thus was the precedent set, and the path made easier for other oil companies to buy up other coal companies—as in fact subsequently happened (see page 312).

Thus was the $175 million tax saving assured the Continental Oil Company.

Thus it was that the shifting of this $175 million burden to the other taxpayers of the United States was also assured.

IRS's $175 MILLION LETTER of August 18, 1966, was but one of roughly 30,000 such "letter rulings" issued every year. While most do not involve such prodigious sums as in the Continental Oil case (about 14,000 of them merely approve changes in accounting methods), they often involve substantial amounts—occasionally far more than was at stake in Continental's case. For example:

• On July 24, 1964, General Electric, Westinghouse and the other major electric companies—whose 1960 conviction of price-fixing in criminal violation of the antitrust laws subjected them to treble-damage claims by customers who had been overcharged—were granted IRS approval to treat their treble-damage payments as tax-deductible "ordinary and necessary" business expenses.* That is, not only would the general public have to bear the burden of any overcharges on the monopolistically priced electrical equipment, but, under the ruling, the public was also required to bear about half the cost of the companies' damage payments to aggrieved parties.† As of 1971, it was estimated that this one ruling had cost the American taxpayers $400 million—about $250 million of that

---

* The ruling applied to all antitrust violators, not just the electric companies.

† That effect comes about this way: Assume that, with the damage payments *non*deductible, Company A's taxable income is $10 million and that, for simplicity's sake, its tax is $5 million. If, as a result of the IRS ruling, damage payments of, say, $1 million are deemed tax-deductible, Company A's taxable income is suddenly $1 million lower. At the 48 percent corporation tax rate, that means its tax is reduced by $480,000 (48 percent of $1 million), so now its tax is only $4,520,000. The rest of the taxpayers must, one way or another, pay for Company A's $480,000 tax saving, in the form of either higher taxes, higher Federal deficits or reduced Federal spending.

probably having been saved by the electric companies alone.

    • On January 10, 1972, an IRS ruling permitted the Anaconda and Kennecott Copper companies, plus a few others, a tax treatment of the losses they sustained when the Chilean government expropriated their assets that saved those companies between $75 million and $175 million. Some tax experts who have studied the ruling, while acknowledging that the law on the question was close, feel that IRS did some stretching of past law and practice in arriving at the ruling favorable to the copper companies.

    • On December 29, 1966—just two days before a New Year's Eve deadline, an IRS ruling letter saved the United States Steel Corporation the discomfort of having some $60 million of "excess foreign tax credits" (see page 264 and Glossary) expire, unused. As if that $60 million tax saving weren't enough, U.S. Steel also asked for—and Internal Revenue generously granted—permission to whipsaw the U.S. Treasury into further losses in future years.*

    BUT THE IMPORTANCE of IRS rulings often goes beyond the dollar tax savings assured the various companies. For while the rulings supposedly revolve around highly technical interpretations of the tax law, they can also decide very large policy questions.

    For example, in ruling that treble-damage payments by antitrust violators were "ordinary and necessary" business expenses, and therefore tax-deductible, IRS in effect made it just half as expensive to be caught violating the antimonopoly laws of the land. To put it another way, the IRS ruling had the effect of amending the antitrust laws themselves, so as to provide that the kind of violations of which the electric companies were convicted are punishable by out-of-pocket damage payments not of 300 percent but of only 150 percent. From the companies' point of view, the effect of the IRS decision was no different from the result if Congress had in fact changed the basic antimonopoly laws in just that manner.† Yet IRS could, and did, make that vital change, in 1964, without seeking or obtaining Congress's assent.

    IRS's facilitation of Continental's Oil's "ABC" buy-up of Con-

---

    * Those who are intrigued with the ingeniousness and inventiveness that sometimes characterized these tax-saving transactions may find the details of this one spelled out in the Notes and Sources section.

    † Ultimately (but only after the passage of five very expensive years), Congress concluded that the 1964 IRS ruling had been wrong as a matter of policy, and partially reversed it. (See below.)

solidated Coal also involved important antitrust policy considerations. For one thing, as mentioned, Consolidation Coal, the nation's largest coal company, was one of Continental's major competitors in the field of selling energy (which is what coal and oil both ultimately produce); to that extent, the merger of the two into a single company lessened competition in the energy field.

For another, also as noted, the ruling in the Continental case paved the way for other companies to take over other coal companies, using the lucrative "ABC" device: Kennecott Copper later "ABC'd" the Peabody Coal Company, the nation's second largest; and Occidental Petroleum followed suit, buying up the Island Creek Coal Company via an "ABC" transaction. By 1972, there were only two major independent coal companies left in the United States, and five of the top ten had been gobbled up by oil companies.

Lest there be any doubt that the IRS rulings can involve questions of high policy, in the case of both the treble-damage and the "ABC" rulings Congress subsequently concluded that Internal Revenue had been wrong, as a matter of policy, and enacted laws reversing them. In 1969, Congress saw fit to unmask the legal intricacies of the "ABC" transactions and to pass a law taxing them for what they are: pure mortgage loans, which any other taxpayer must repay with *after*-tax dollars. In that same year, Congress decreed that where criminal antitrust violations are involved, two-thirds of the damage payments are no longer deductible. Unhappily, in both cases, Congress did not act until the major horses had already fled the barn (the bulk of the electric company treble damages had already been deducted and the important "hard" mineral "ABC" takeovers had already been consummated.

THE VARIOUS RULING LETTERS mentioned above were just fine for the companies that requested and received them, for they assured* tens or even hundreds of millions of dollars of

---

* The word "assured" is carefully chosen, for the reader should be aware that even if IRS were to rule against the company, that concern could appeal the matter to the courts, where it might win some or all of the tax savings it sought—the question of what "the law" is being, in almost all these cases, a close one. So it would be wrong to assume that an IRS ruling opposite to those just described would automatically have deprived the companies of all the tax savings indicated above. On the other hand, an IRS ruling *favorable* to such a company, being unappealable, spares subjecting the question to court test, and thus "assures" the company the tax saving indicated.

tax savings for General Electric, Westinghouse, U.S. Steel, Anaconda Copper and the others.

But were they equally fine for the general public, for the rest of the U.S. taxpayers who must suffer the consequences of what amounts to changes in the antimonopoly laws?

Alas—and this is the crucial defect in the process—there is no opportunity for advocates on behalf of those "rest-of-the-U.S.-taxpayers," the "general public," to argue their side of the case, *either before or after the ruling is issued.* There is no provision for public hearings on these rulings—even when matters of high policy are involved (such as in the treble-damage ruling).* On the contrary, not only does the decision-making process take place in private; often the general public does not even know the process is taking place. And, what is even more remarkable, in most cases (e.g., in the cases of Continental Oil and U.S. Steel), *the ruling letter itself is not even made public.* It is known only to three parties: IRS, the company requesting the ruling and its attorneys. (More about this later—page 314.)

Even more striking—and more serious—is the one-sidedness of the process *after* the issuance of the ruling letter. For if IRS's decision is unfavorable to the requesting company, it can proceed with its intended course of action and contest the IRS position in a court of law. But if the ruling goes the other way—that is, if it *favors* the requesting company and thus assures shifting a major tax burden onto the rest-of-the-taxpayers—they have no corresponding right to challenge the ruling in court. In that sense, Internal Revenue is, in effect, the Supreme Court. If IRS throws in the legal towel, the matter is settled (until and unless Congress enacts a corrective law which, as we have seen, is unlikely to happen with any promptness).

Look at the treble-damage ruling in that light. Obviously, there were legal arguments to be made on both sides of the question, and IRS's chief lawyer advised his superiors that "our chances of

---

* Prior to issuing the treble-damage ruling, the Commissioner of Internal Revenue did take one step to "get a feeling of the outside terrain": a private, closed-door meeting in his office, at which the only nongovernment persons present were members of large law and accounting firms (e.g., the immense New York law firm of Cravath, Swaine and Moore and the equally immense accounting firm, Price Waterhouse) of whom, it was later admitted, "obviously some . . . may have been representing one of the parties [companies] in the [electric antimonopoly] case." That hardly qualifies as a broadly representative public hearing.

success [in a court test] would be questionable." Yet, from the
general public's point of view, there was everything to gain and
nothing to lose from IRS's ruling against deductibility of the
damage payments* and risking a court test. Even if such a test had
ended up in the companies' favor, IRS and the rest of the taxpayers would have been no worse off than they were the day after
Internal Revenue issued its unappealable ruling in favor of the
companies.†

WHEN LAWYERS want to know what previous court
decisions have held on any given question, they have comparatively little difficulty finding out, for not only are court opinions
made public but they are meticulously indexed. Thus, attorneys
for both sides have equal access to past court interpretations of
the law and can invoke them, as they see fit, to bolster their respective positions.

But in the case of IRS rulings, taxpayers and their attorneys
cannot so easily discover the prior decisions in IRS rulings, for, as
mentioned, the vast majority of them, rather than being made
public, are known to only three parties: the IRS, the requesting
company and its attorney.‡

Confidentiality is not *supposed* to be a problem, for in 1952, at
the urging of a Congressional investigating committee, Internal
Revenue issued instructions that all rulings "of general interest"
were to be made public, a commitment which it reaffirmed in

---

* And in 1961 IRS attorneys had been convinced that was the correct
legal stance.

† IRS later defended its ruling in part because of its limited legal staff
which it couldn't "fritter away on cases [where] we do not have a heck of a
lot of chance to win." But IRS has had the staff for court tests of questions
such as whether elm disease qualifies as a casualty loss deduction, or whether
termites strike with sufficient suddenness to qualify for that same deduction.
If IRS can litigate questions such as those, it is nonsense to suggest that it
would lack the staff for a court test of the treble-damage case in view of
the policy issues involved, not to mention the hundreds of millions of tax
dollars, and especially considering the one-sidedness of the appeal procedures.

‡ Some contend that the rulings' confidentiality confers a special and
unwarranted advantage not only on the company but on the tax lawyer who
coaxed the ruling from IRS, for he alone knows not only the precise set of
facts that made the ruling possible but also which aspects of it troubled the
IRS and which ones met little resistance. Thus, it is argued, the lawyer who,
say, puts through the first major "ABC" oil ruling is in a particularly
advantageous position to attract clients who hear about it through the
inevitable grapevine and desire similarly kind treatment from the IRS.

1960. Yet over the decade of the Sixties, out of roughly 30,000 rulings issued each year, an average of only 480—about 1½ percent—were formally published by IRS,* even though informed persons estimate that fully a third of the rulings involved matters of general interest and importance. In 1972, three practicing attorneys in Chicago were able to list some thirty major rulings that had been of sufficient "general interest" to have rated mention in legal periodicals, yet had never been formally published by Internal Revenue. "This list amply demonstrates [IRS's] lack of adherence to the formal commitment to Congress to publish [precedent-setting] rulings," said the attorneys.

The enactment of the Freedom of Information Act in 1966 was supposed to have a salutary effect, for, on its face, that law required agencies such as the IRS to make public all actions of "precedential" value (that is, rulings that might be used as a precedent for decisions in subsequent cases).† But IRS found an ingenious means of circumventing that requirement: it merely obliterated the word "precedent" from all the rulings thus categorized in its files, and reclassified them as "reference"—a term not mentioned in the Freedom of Information Act. In 1972 a legal action was filed to compel IRS to make public not only the unpublished rulings but IRS's confidential card index of rulings and related correspondence in the percentage depletion field. As of this writing, that action is pending in the courts.

IRS's exclusive possession of that card index places in the hands of government attorneys a one-sided weapon that they can use effectively against private taxpayers whose lawyers are in the dark about unpublished rulings. An example: a court suit entailing more than $3,400,000 of taxes supposedly owed by Allstate Insurance Company, in which the judge noted, in his opinion in the case, that "the government placed in evidence a number of private letter rulings of the Internal Revenue Service over a 12-year period" to bolster its position. Before the Allstate suit was filed, though, only the government's attorneys were privy to those

---

* There is, naturally, an active grapevine among tax advisers, and some of the unpublished rulings are even "summarized" by two Washington reporting services. Yet that is no substitute for formal publication. Lawyers and laymen alike would consider it unthinkable if the opinions of judges in courts of law were communicated in such haphazard fashion.

† One of the Congressional explanations of that law seems to exclude IRS rulings from that requirement, but the wording of the law itself does not.

private rulings; Allstate's lawyers had no way to know of their existence.

The exclusive distribution of the unpublished rulings can sometimes work against the government. On one occasion, when the Treasury Department issued a tentative regulation that was not to the liking of the china clay industry, a private attorney who had long represented the industry fished out of his files an unpublished ruling given by IRS to one clay company fifteen years earlier that was directly contrary to the new Treasury proposal—a letter of which not even Treasury was aware. (As a result, the proposed new regulation was withdrawn, and the letter version, far more favorable to the china clay companies, prevailed.)

THE ABOVE PORTRAYAL of the IRS ruling process is, admittedly, a partial one that highlights what seems to me its defects and may suggest that the process is wholly without merit or utility.

Of course, that is not the case. With a law as complex as the Internal Revenue Code, there is ample room for doubt about its meaning, and there are bound to be cases where companies would be paralyzed without advance knowledge of how IRS will treat a given transaction. In a system that relies on citizen honesty (since it is the taxpayer, not the government, who makes the initial calculation of taxes owed), it is important that the system meet taxpayer needs where it legitimately can. Moreover, to the extent these in-advance rulings avoid time-consuming and expensive court contests, they can benefit the government as well as the taxpayer. (The government also contends that the ruling requests offer helpful information as to what questions are causing problems of interpretation or enforcement.)

Yet, while useful, the procedures for issuing rulings do suffer major defects that were suggested by the hypothetical court proceeding that began this chapter: the process takes place in excessive privacy and thus invites unseen and potentially improper pressures. It provides for only one-sided advocacy (by the requester of the ruling), and, because there is no public notice that the deliberation is even taking place, it offers no opportunity for comment by disinterested parties.* Moreover, it thrusts the IRS into the dual role of both advocate and judge.

---

* There is recent evidence that when such an opportunity is afforded, at least on major issues, there is no lack of disinterested experts willing to

But perhaps the most serious aspect is the one-sidedness of the process *after* the ruling is issued (with an adverse ruling being appealable to the courts by its requester while a favorable ruling cannot be appealed). If IRS declines the requested ruling, it risks a court challenge; if it grants the request, all will be tranquil.* Under those circumstances, the only party that can look over IRS's shoulder with any "clout" is the company requesting the ruling, since it alone is in a position to lodge an effective protest.

WHAT SHOULD BE DONE to improve the rulings procedures?

Students of the problem have widely varying views, but many believe that the following changes would make the process far more open and balanced.

First, require that all IRS rulings be made public.

Second, provide opportunity for public comment before major rulings formally take effect.

Third, broaden the right of citizens to challenge particular rulings in court.†

---

expend considerable effort in commenting on important tax questions. In 1971, "Taxation with Representation," a self-styled "public interest tax lobby," as well as Ralph Nader's Public Interest Research Group, solicited comments on the legality of effecting the "asset depreciation range" (ADR) system (pp. 219–227) by administrative action (in that case by Treasury regulations, rather than by rulings) without Congressional approval. Some thirteen separate papers, many of them involving substantial legal research, were submitted by legal scholars and experts throughout the country.

* Once in every several thousand cases, there may be a one- or two-day Congressional hearing on a given ruling (as occurred in the case of the treble-damage ruling and of one other involving the court-ordered sale of General Motors stock by DuPont shareholders in the wake of an antitrust action. But such events occur so rarely as to be a negligible risk; and, at worst, they are only temporary annoyances.

† In addition, some are concerned over the fact that the rulings process lacks any explicit authority in Congressionally approved statutes, and hence suffers from vague standards (such as "the good of the [Internal Revenue] Service." As those students see it, a fourth urgent need is for Congress to enact a law laying down definite criteria and guidelines, as well as explicit authority, for the issuance of rulings.

Others contend that most, if not all, of the problems connected with the rulings procedure also arise in IRS *audits* of tax returns, especially those of large corporations. The same elements are there in an audit: close questions of interpretation; large sums of money at stake; broad IRS discretion in deciding close questions; lack of opportunity for public comment, etc. So why not impose the same reforms on the audit process? Perhaps some of those reforms would be appropriate to audits. But there is one major

As to making all rulings public, it has been objected that such a step would result in disclosure of legitimate business secrets and would render the rulings process useless in the very cases where an in-advance ruling is most needed, namely, those involving delicate and confidential business negotiations (e.g., mergers of two companies) where publication of the facts would (or might) blow up the entire negotiation.

The answers offered to those objections are many. First, as Columbia law professor George Cooper has observed, where large public policy questions and/or large dollar amounts are involved, these ruling decisions are "not a 'private' matter in any but the most technical sense." Second, those who request rulings are asking for what, in a court of law, would be a declaratory judgment, to obtain which would require public disclosure of all the facts involved. Third, in the case of mergers or acquisitions involving publicly held companies, the details of the transactions are ultimately given to the shareholders (and hence made public) anyway. Moreover, all rulings dealing with charitable foundations are made public, without apparent public harm. Why not apply the same rule across the board? Doing so would make IRS more careful in its issuance of rulings that would have to stand the light of day; would promote more even treatment, as among various taxpayers; and would put all taxpayers on an equal footing, both with each other and with government attorneys, in having full knowledge of the precedents on which they can rely.*

As to the second proposal, many protest that requiring (or even expanding the opportunity for) public hearings would overtax IRS and Treasury personnel, and would so bog down the ruling process as to render it useless. That need not be the case if all rulings were to be made public on a tentative basis, to take

difference that warrants giving priority to reform of the rulings procedures: namely, that there is more likelihood that a ruling will have broad effect (i.e., on a whole class of taxpayers) than is true in the case of a single-company audit.

* Another objection to making all rulings public is that this would lock IRS in to mistaken rulings—that is, if it gave an overly generous ruling to one taxpayer, public knowledge of that fact would lead all similarly situated taxpayers to insist, in fairness, on the same generous treatment. But if there were opportunity for public comment before rulings became generally applicable, as suggested in the next proposal (see especially the refinement suggested in the footnote), this would serve as a check against such unduly generous rulings.

formal effect in, say, thirty or sixty days* unless a hearing were requested by a given number of individual taxpayers, the number to be set sufficiently high so that frivolous or harassing hearing requests would be minimized while still providing for public comment in cases of broad importance.

Finally, as to broadening the right of citizens to bring court challenges against particular IRS rulings, it will doubtless be objected that this would open the floodgates to trifling, pestersome suits. That is a standard specter, traditionally raised by those who dislike the unpleasantness of public spats, but the reality is rarely as fearsome as the prediction. For example, the Freedom of Information Act conferred broad rights upon citizens to bring legal actions in order to extract information from the government. Yet in the first six years that law was in effect, not more than 100 court suits had been brought. Moreover, the expenses involved in bringing and sustaining a major court action usually dampen the ardor of those whose motives are purely frivolous.

Harassing legal actions are not inconceivable; yet common sense and experience say that they are remote, rather than imminent possibilities. And does that danger outweigh the disadvantages of the present one-sided nature of the post-ruling legal challenge?

THE RULING PROCESS has its usefulness. Open it up and let in some fresh air (and even a little public argument and debate), and it can become a more balanced process, fairer not just to the one taxpayer requesting the ruling but to all of those nameless (and, heretofore, voiceless) rest-of-the-taxpayers as well.

---

* One sensible refinement that has been suggested would establish two "waiting periods": after, say, thirty or sixty days, in the absence of a hearing request, the ruling would take effect for the one taxpayer who had requested it; but it could not be relied on as a precedent for other taxpayers until, say, another thirty or sixty days had elapsed. Such a plan would increase the opportunity for public comment on a ruling that might have very broad application, and hence greater public importance.

16

Death May Be Inevitable, But Death Taxes Sure Aren't

T A X L A W Y E R Joseph Prentice shook his head as he pushed away from the breakfast table to make the morning paper more maneuverable. "Incredible!" he said.

"What's incredible, dear?" asked Mrs. Prentice as she plugged in the coffeepot.

"Well, there's a story here about a college chemistry professor who thought up some fantastic invention, and made himself a ten-million-dollar fortune. He died recently, and it seems he's going to pay about six million in estate taxes."

"What's so incredible about that?" asked his wife, placing bacon strips in the frying pan.

"Why, nobody in his right mind pays estate taxes like that," replied Mr. Prentice. "But this poor fellow had some fetish about doing all his own research and he tried to look up the law by himself, without a lawyer. When he saw that the rates called for a six-million-dollar tax on a ten-million-dollar estate, he figured there wasn't anything he could do about it—left the whole ten million to his daughters and told them to take care of their stepmother. Can you imagine anyone taking those rates seriously?"

"Why shouldn't they?" asked Mrs. Prentice as the toast disappeared into the toaster.

"Why, with all the ways of getting around them, anyone's a fool to pay those rates."

"Well, I must say," said Mrs. Prentice, "*that's* a fine attitude for a lawyer to take. Don't you have any respect for the law?"

"Of course I do. It's all perfectly legal. Why, just by adding one simple sentence to his will—'I hereby bequeath half my worldly goods to my wife'—his tax could have been about three and a half million dollars less."

Mrs. Prentice turned away from the sputtering bacon with a new interest. "Three and a half *million*! You mean a man can save that much by leaving money to his wife? I must say, I think *that's* a pretty cute law."

"Cute, nothing," said Sam Prentice, their vacationing college freshman son, who had just walked into the room. "It's nothing but a big rip-off for the rich." (Sam, long of hair, beard and radical beliefs, was a zealous member of the campus Revolutionary Society.)

"Why, Sam Prentice. What a thing to say," said his mother, as the first curls of smoke rose from the forgotten bacon.

"It's true. How are we ever going to break up the big concentrations of wealth when a man with a hundred million dollars can leave fifty million of it to his wife, tax-free?"

"Of course, Son," said Mr. Prentice, "he would have to be a pretty trusting husband to do a thing like that. After all, his widow might run off with some handsome gigolo and cut off the children without a penny. But, of course, you wouldn't do a thing like that to our Sam, would you, dear?"

"Oh, I don't know," said Mrs. Prentice, lifting the charred remains of the bacon from the pan. "With fifty million dollars and an attractive man, I might get pretty reckless."

"Now if the professor had come to *me* for advice," said Mr. Prentice, "I probably would have advised him to leave some of his money to his grandchildren instead of his children—that could easily have saved him around six hundred thousand dollars in taxes."

The Revolutionary Society was momentarily forgotten as Sam perceived a threat to his own position in the Prentice will. "What? And by-pass his own children?"

"Well, he wouldn't need to by-pass them completely. They could have all the *income* from the stocks and bonds as long as they lived, and when they died the stocks and bonds themselves would pass to their children tax-free."

"You mean you can skip a whole generation of taxes?"

"Why limit it to one generation?" said Mr. Prentice. "A good many really wealthy people leave their money to their great-grandchildren and skip *two* generations."

"What a steal," said Sam.

"Then again," said Mr. Prentice, "I could have saved the professor another million by advising him to start giving his money away to his children during his lifetime."

"Speaking as your son," said Sam, "*that* plan interests me. As a member of the Revolutionary Society, however, I am appalled. How can he save a million dollars that way? Wouldn't he have to pay a gift tax?"

"Not necessarily," said Mr. Prentice. "But even if he did, the gift tax rates are a lot lower than the estate or death tax rates. Of course, I wouldn't advise the professor to start making big gifts unless he looked pretty healthy."

"Why not?" asked Mrs. Prentice, who was now starting the second batch of bacon. "What could his health possibly have to do with his taxes?"

"Well, if he died within three years of making the gift, the government might claim he had only been trying to avoid taxes and take away his tax saving. But if he survived three years, the government couldn't question his motives—even if, when he made the gift, he had been firmly convinced he was on his death-bed."

"Man," said Sam. "That really *is* the end. But you said he wouldn't necessarily have to pay *any* gift tax. Don't tell me there's a way of getting out of *that*, too!"

"Well," said Mr. Prentice, "together, the professor and his wife could give six thousand dollars a year tax-free to as many people as they wanted. So if they started early, and gave six thousand dollars each to the three daughters and the nine grand-children, in ten years they could give seven hundred and twenty thousand dollars without paying a penny of tax on it."

"Father," said Sam, "I don't remember your giving *me* six thousand dollars a year."

"Son," countered Mr. Prentice, "I don't remember *making* ten million dollars."

"Look, Dad. The way you describe it, the estate tax rates *look* tough—but nobody pays what those rates seem to call for."

"That's about what it comes down to," said Mr. Prentice.

"Well, why did Congress bother to put the rates in there in the first place?" asked Sam.

SAM'S QUESTION is more than rhetorical. Upon casual inspection the estate tax rates—a severe 77 percent at their highest—appear to be the act of a Congress as devoted as the most ardent Revolutionary Society member to breaking up huge fortunes as they pass from one generation to another.*

But, as with the income tax rates, all is not what it might seem, as the following table shows:

Gross Estate Size	Tax per Rate Schedule*	Actual Tax†
$500,000–$1,000,000	29%–33%	17.3%
$1–$2,000,000	33%–38%	21.0%
$2–$3,000,000	38%–42%	23.5%
$3–$5,000,000	42%–49%	25.6%
$5–$10,000,000	49%–61%	25.7%
$10–$20,000,000	61%–69%	26.8%
$20,000,000 and over	69%+	26.8%

* What would be paid if the rate schedule. in the tax code applied to the entire gross estate.

† The *actual* average tax before credits in 1969 (latest available data). Both columns indicate tax as percent of gross estate.

The above table shows vividly that the Congress of the United States has provided ample escape routes for those to whom the estate and gift taxes supposedly apply. In doing so, Congress has demonstrated as clearly as with any tax loophole its tender solicitude for the wealthy. If that seems an extravagant statement, bear in mind, as you look at the table and read about the many gaping loopholes, that the death and gift taxes with which this chapter will deal are paid "almost exclusively [by] families with annual incomes of over $20,000"—which is to say, *the top 5 percent of the population.*

That will give you an idea of which group in the population has benefited from the astounding fact that Congress has left the estate and gift tax rates wholly unchanged for more than thirty

---

* After a less casual look at the rate schedule, which you will experience in a moment, you may conclude that even on their face, leaving aside the escape routes, the rates are far less "revolutionary" than that top 77 percent rate we imply.

years. They are precisely the same today as they were in 1941, just prior to U.S. entry into World War II. In the ensuing few years after 1941, in order to finance that war effort, virtually every American was called upon to make sacrifices and pay higher taxes. At the lowest end of the economic scale, the poorest Americans saw the personal exemption cut back from $750 to just $500 for each taxpayer (and from $400 to $350 for each dependent) —and largely as a result of that* the *income* tax was transformed from a class tax (with just 4 percent of the population covered in 1939) to a broad, mass tax, which now encompasses more than half the population. By contrast, Congress did not reduce by so much as a dollar the large *sixty-thousand-dollar exemption* for wealth transfer taxes, so that the estate and gift tax "club" remains highly exclusive. As noted, only the top 5 percent belong.

But the contrast between the income and estate taxes doesn't end there. In addition to lowering the income tax exemption in order to finance the war, Congress also more than doubled the lowest-bracket income tax rate (from 10 percent prewar to 23 percent at the height of the war). In sharp contrast, Congress stubbornly held the lowest *estate* tax rate at just 3 percent—and that mild rate applies only when an estate exceeds $60,000. Even today, the lowest-bracket *income* tax rate (to which every American taxpayer is subject) is nearly five times higher than the lowest death tax rate (to which only the richest 5 percent are subject).

What's more, the income tax rates rise swiftly, even for those with moderate incomes. For example, when a single person's taxable income reaches just $14,000, he must part with a little more than thirty cents out of every added dollar he earns. But in the case of death taxes, that tax rate only applies to estates of *more than a quarter of a million dollars*. To show another comparison: the income tax takes about half of each added dollar from a bachelor with a taxable income of just $32,000. But that misfortune does not befall any estate of *less than two million dollars*.

There is much sympathy for (and much popular apprehension about) the supposedly "confiscatory" top death tax rate of 77 percent. But perhaps one's tears will be stemmed somewhat by the knowledge that the 77 percent tax rate only applies when a person

---

* And of the fact that for more than twenty years after the war, Congress insisted on keeping the personal exemption at $600. Not until 1972 was the exemption returned to its prewar level of $750.

is foolish enough (as our hypothetical Mr. Prentice put it) to subject to taxation *an estate of ten million dollars* (twenty million
dollars for a married person taking full advantage of the "marital
deduction"—see page 327). As you will soon see, a person can
have an estate vastly larger than that without subjecting it to the
unpleasantness of a death tax. A prime example in that regard is
the late Ailsa Mellon Bruce, descendant of the fabled Andrew
Mellon, who died in 1969 leaving wealth valued at $570,748,725
—well over half a *billion* dollars. Of that colossal sum, only
$6,565,527 (a little over one percent) was actually subject to the
death tax (see page 339).

Congress's solicitude toward the leavers of wealth is not confined to establishing a gently rising scale of death and gift tax
rates and leaving those rates absolutely unchanged through three
decades of war and peace. On top of that, Congress has, in those
thirty years, opened up new means by which the transfer of wealth
could be shielded from those rates.

As a result, the share of Federal revenue furnished by the
richest 5 percent of Americans through the death and gift taxes
has fallen sharply—from 7 percent prewar to about 2 percent
today. If those transfer-of-wealth taxes were simply asked to bear
the share of the burden they bore before the United States entered
the war, estate and gift taxes would amount to about $13 billion.
As it is, they come to about $3.5 billion. That's a tidy difference,
considering it is enjoyed by just the top 5 percent (and suffered
by the other 95 percent).

NEITHER THE ESTATE TAX nor the means of avoiding
it can properly be appraised without taking into account its supposed purposes which, in the tax history of the United States, have
been two: first, to raise revenue and second, to curb the passing
on from generation to generation of great wealth and the economic
power that goes with it.

Prior to the twentieth century, the revenue-raising aspect was
paramount: a death tax was sporadically enacted when war crises
demanded added tax collections, but invariably the tax would
fade with the crisis. Theodore Roosevelt was the first president to
expound the wealth-leveling purpose of an estate tax. "No
advantage comes," he said in 1907, "either to the country as a
whole or to the individuals inheriting the money by permitting

the transmission in their entirety of . . . enormous fortunes." A graduated death tax would, he thought, "preserve a measurable equality of opportunity for [future] generations."

Twenty-eight years later, another Roosevelt spoke in a similar vein: "Inherited economic power," said FDR in 1935, "is as inconsistent with the ideals of this generation as inherited political power was inconsistent with the ideals of the generation which established our Government."

This view of the estate tax has not been confined to the political progressives. No less a conservative than Herbert Hoover viewed the tax as a means of striking at the "evils of inherited economic power" and of "thaw[ing] out frozen and inactive capital and the inherited control of the tools of production." And Andrew Carnegie, the self-made steel magnate, must have sounded like a traitor to his class when, in 1889, he asked, "Why should men leave great fortunes to their children? If this is done from affection, is it not misguided affection?" "Observation teaches," he said, that "generally speaking, it is not well for the children that they should be so burdened." The "thoughtful man," said Carnegie, would as soon leave to his sons "a curse as the almighty dollar."

This was hardly the view of most persons in Mr. Carnegie's income bracket. Most prominent foe of the estate tax was Treasury Secretary Andrew Mellon, who during the 1920's led a one-man campaign for the repeal of the tax, predicting that as things were going, it might be "only two or three generations until private ownership of property would cease to exist." And when, in 1924, Congress raised the estate tax rates, the Under Secretary of the Treasury, Garrard B. Winston, darkly prophesied that "we shall have more golf players and fewer Henry Fords and Thomas Edisons."

Congress itself has seemed to suffer a certain ambivalence about the estate tax, for despite the apparently stiff progressive rate schedule in the law, the estate tax laws are, in practice, more Mellon than Roosevelt.

AS NOTED, in contrast to the income tax, the estate tax has remained a distinctly elite tax. This is due principally to Congress's decision that the first $60,000 of anyone's property left at death should not be subject to tax.* Thus, most people don't even have to file an estate tax return; and even among the 133,944 who *did* file returns in 1969, about 30 percent of their wealth was placed beyond the reach of the tax collector by reason of the $60,000 exemption.

This exemption is, of course, most helpful to the smaller estates. Vastly more important to the larger estates is the so-called "marital deduction," the privilege of leaving half one's property tax-free to one's wife or husband—which Louis Eisenstein has characterized as "an exemption which is felicitously called something else." It is, of course, available to all estates, no matter how large. In fact, the larger the estate, the larger the exemption (causing great anguish to adherents of the "ability to pay" school of taxation). For the married, then, the top 77 percent rate does not apply to estates of over $10 million, as the rate schedule in the law seems to indicate, but to estates of over $20 million. At the lower end of the scale, the marital deduction has the effect of doubling the $60,000 exemption and enabling a married person to leave property of $120,000 tax-free.† All told, in 1969, it removed from Internal Revenue's reach more than $5½ billion of wealth—about a fifth of the total wealth reported on estate tax returns that year.

Defenders of the marital deduction point out that it does not offer a *permanent escape* of tax on the amount left to the wife, but merely a *temporary postponement* until the unhappy day when she too passes on. But, in fact, there is a considerable *net* tax saving. In the case of the hypothetical chemistry professor and his $10 million estate, without a marital deduction the tax would be $6 million at his death. But the marital deduction permits splitting the estate into two separately taxed bundles, on which the total tax is only $5 million (twice $2½ million of tax on each bundle), *for a net saving of one million dollars.*

Moreover, the very postponement of the tax on the wife's share is not to be sneezed at, since as long as she lives, she can enjoy the use of the $3½ million that otherwise would have been

---

* Other deductions (e.g., for bequests to one's spouse or to charity) also contribute to the exclusivity of the estate tax "club."

† The first $60,000 because of the exemption, another $60,000 via the marital deduction.

swallowed up by the U.S. Treasury at the time of her husband's death. Assuming, conservatively, that this money would earn the professor's wife a 6 percent return if she outlived him by ten years (as more than half of surviving spouses actually do), the delay in paying the tax on her half of the estate would be worth *over six and a quarter million dollars.*

As our imaginary tax attorney, Joseph Prentice, pointed out, however, it takes a trusting husband to make full use of the marital deduction, since under the law his wife must be given a no-strings-attached power to dispose of his bequest when she dies. On the other hand, the incentives for a trusting attitude on the part of a man with a $10 million estate are considerable: a $3½ million immediate (though temporary) saving, a $1 million permanent saving.

The adoption of the marital deduction in 1948 lowered estate tax revenues by about a third. According to President Truman's unavailing veto message, the annual quarter of a billion dollars this cost the Treasury redounded to the benefit of "only about 12,000 of the most wealthy families."

The marital deduction has its roots in the distinction between the "common law" states and the so-called "community property" states, to which you were introduced in Chapter 6 (page 124). Under "community property" laws (which are of French and Spanish descent) half a husband's property legally belongs to the wife. Thus, in "community property" states, only *half* a husband's property was subject to tax at his death.

In 1942, Congress in effect overrode the "community property" principle and ended the death tax advantages previously enjoyed by citizens of the eight "community property" states. A few fringe discriminations remained, but some experts feel these could have been solved by minor changes in the 1942 law. Nevertheless, in 1948, along with marital income-splitting (see Chapter 6), Congress enacted the estate tax marital deduction. Thus, the eight-state tail wagged the forty-state dog, but since this resulted only in lower taxes for those in the lucky forty, and no increase in the remaining eight, taxpayer complaints were handily avoided. The only injured party was the United States Treasury, which lost roughly $2 billion from income-splitting plus the quarter-billion dollars via the marital deduction.

The estate tax has never recovered, either as a revenue raiser or as the purported leveler of wealth, from the body blow of the marital deduction. Ordinarily, it would be natural for the Treasury Department to recommend tightening or eliminating such a vast truck hole in the tax law. But the latest Treasury recommendation, formulated in 1968 under the Johnson Administration, surprisingly went in the opposite direction, proposing that a person be allowed to leave his (or her) *entire* estate (rather than just half) tax-free to his (or her) spouse. Why? The Treasury, viewing the impact of subjecting half the estate to taxation at the husband's death (as under existing law), looked pityingly at the plight of the widows "where the estate is *modest in size*" and of widows "whose husbands leave *smaller* estates." (Emphasis added.) It is indeed a touching thought—until one discovers that when the Treasury talked of "smaller estates," it was apparently referring to instances where husbands leave less than *half a million dollars* to their wives.* Under that definition, most Americans may be disposed to dry away the tears the Treasury sought to evoke.

YOU MAY RECALL HOW, at the beginning of this chapter, Tax Lawyer Prentice threw a temporary scare into his "revolutionary" son by talking of the advantages of "generation skipping"—which means leaving your wealth to your grandchildren or great-grandchildren instead of to your own offspring. For example, the naïve college professor of whom Lawyer Prentice spoke might have saved nearly a million dollars by skipping two generations of estate taxes, using just $3 million of his $10 million estate.† The method of achieving this would be to leave the $3 million in the hands of a trustee (perhaps a bank or trust company) with instructions that the *income* from the $3 million was to be paid to his children during *their* lifetime, then to the grandchildren during *their* lifetime. At the grandchildren's death, the $3 million itself‡ would pass to the great-grandchildren. An estate tax *would* be

---

* The Treasury's point was that in half of those "smaller estate" cases, husbands were leaving their wives more than the 50 percent marital deduction allows—hence the alleged hardship and the arguments for increasing the marital deduction.

The Treasury also argued that to tax transfers between husbands and wives violated the usual sense of marital property being "ours," and that it made for complex will-drafting problems.

† The other $7 million being judiciously left, tax-free, to his wife and to charity.

‡ Assuming no rise in the price of the stocks left in trust.

paid at the time of the professor's death, but none would be paid either at his children's or at his grandchildren's demise. The tax savings (assuming the $3 million passes, each time, to an only child): $622,000 by skipping one generation, nearly a million by skipping two generations. Looked at another way, the use of the "trust" device would leave the great-grandchild more than twice as much wealth—i.e., $1,768,000 instead of $787,000.*

That is all very well for the grandchildren and the usually as yet unborn great-grandchildren, but it is a rather heartless way to treat your own children *unless* the wealth you are leaving is so large that it produces ample income for them during their lifetime. Since that requires huge amounts of wealth, however, it is not surprising that, as with so many tax-saving devices, this one is for the primary use and benefit of the very rich. According to a survey of 1957–1959 estate tax returns, those with estates of more than a million dollars left nearly three times as much of their wealth in "generation-skipping" trusts as did those with estates of less than $300,000. Nonetheless, "generation skipping" is a widely used device. In 1957 the president of one of the largest trust companies in the United States, noting the dramatic growth of "generation-skipping" trusts in his own company, told *Fortune* magazine, "Uncle Sam *isn't* taking the big estates" these days.

Tax experts believe that estate tax revenues could be increased by $200 million a year if the United States were to tax each generation-to-generation transfer of wealth, as the British do.

But, some ask, suppose a father chooses to leave his property to his grandson, in effect by-passing his son: is it proper, in that event, to impose a tax, when the son dies, on the transfer of property *he never really owned?*

Advocates of the British system have a twofold answer. First, they say, to an important extent he *does* own the property. He has complete enjoyment of one of the most vital aspects of ownership (the use of the income), and, especially if he serves as a trustee of his own trust, he may have an important, if not controlling, voice in how the property itself is managed and used during his lifetime. Hence, it *is* fair to impose some tax when he dies.

Second, property left "in trust" is, traditionally, conservatively managed. Therefore, it is argued, from the point of view of foster-

---

* Assuming, again, for simplicity's sake, no price rise and no use made of the $60,000 exemption.

ing a dynamic economy through venturesome investment, the tax system should discourage rather than encourage "trust" arrangements. To do so (perhaps by a tax on each generation-to-generation transfer) would admittedly present technical problems, but experts believe these would not be insurmountable ones.

Here again, it is not just the traditional liberals who look askance at "generation skipping." Herbert Hoover's voice may once again be summoned, warning, as it did in 1932, that "fortunes have become so large and lawyers so cunning that they can freeze them into trusts extending over more than three generations."

B UT THERE IS REALLY NO NEED to go to all the bother and legal expense of creating "trusts" and leaving money to as yet unborn grandchildren. Substantial savings are to be had simply by giving money away during one's lifetime—so great in fact that *with a $2 million gift, our hypothetical chemistry professor could have saved $1,400,000 in taxes.**

What accounts for this enormous saving? For one thing, the gift tax rates themselves are one-fourth lower than the estate tax rates. But because of a vital difference in the way the two taxes are computed, the tax advantage is actually greater than one-fourth. For a man in the top estate tax bracket (77 percent) and the top gift tax bracket (57 percent), for example, a $157 out-of-pocket outlay (including taxes) toward his son *during his lifetime would mean less than half the tax and would leave his son with nearly three times as much after taxes* as the identical outlay, by will, would after his death. It works out this way:

	Gift During Lifetime	Gift After Death
Total out-of-pocket outlay	$157	$157
Tax	$57	$121
Tax as percent of total outlay	36%	77%
Amount left for son after tax*	$100	$36

* The difference is that the 57 percent gift tax applies to the gift alone, *not including the tax,* whereas the 77 percent estate tax applies not only to the transfer itself, *but also to the tax on it.*

* This is merely the estate tax saving. In addition, there are substantial income tax savings to be realized—via the glories of income-splitting—by giving money in trust to children.

The *Journal of Accountancy* has published an illustrative example of a $5 million gift wherein the gift tax would be only *one-fifth* as large as the estate tax on a like amount bequeathed after death.

Tax savings from lifetime (rather than "deathtime") gifts also stem from the fact that each has its own separate rate schedule. A multimillionaire Rockefeller, Mellon or Whitney, for example, is bound to have the "top dollars" of his gigantic estate subject to a 77 percent tax (unless he leaves the whole thing to his wife and/or to charity). But to the extent he can bring himself to part with his wealth during his lifetime, he removes the given dollars from the 77 percent tax bracket and, for the first $30,000 of gifts, allows them to escape wholly tax-free (under the $30,000 gift-tax exemption allowed every taxpayer). Even then, his gifts are subject to the lowest gift tax rates, which begin at 2¼ percent. As with "generation skipping," this device is more popular with the hugely endowed (who can more comfortably part with portions of their wealth during their lifetime) than with the more modestly wealthy. (The Treasury Department found that over half of those with "large" estates had taken advantage of the savings of lifetime giving, compared with just 10 percent of those with "small" estates.)

Despite the attendant savings, though, human nature apparently rebels against parting with property during one's lifetime. The special 1957–1959 Treasury survey showed that "living gifts" amounted to no more than 5 percent of transfers at death. Even the wealthiest, who presumably had most to gain, made gifts during their lifetime equal to just 12 percent of their bequests at death.*

Nevertheless, recognizing the clear temptation to avoid taxes through "living gifts," especially among the ill or morbid to whom death seems imminent, the law has always held that gifts made "in contemplation of death" should be subject to the higher estate tax rates.

But when a person makes a large gift, how can it be established whether or not he is "contemplating" his demise? What was the state of mind, for example, of one Oliver Johnson who,

---

* This is thought to understate the amount of *actual* lifetime giving, since it does not include the large amounts that can be given free of any gift tax under the astonishing annual $6,000 per-couple-per-recipient-per-year "exclusion" about which you will read momentarily.

at the advanced age of ninety years and four months, gave his children $200,000 in real estate? The Tax Court, apparently impressed with his ability to make "a large percentage of ringers" in horseshoe pitching and, more particularly, with his practice of jumping "into the air and click[ing] his heels together two or three times before descending to the floor," ruled that death was not on his mind when he made the gift.

In 1950, even while acknowledging that "undoubtedly many gifts have escaped the estate tax" due to the government's inability to prove tax-avoidance motives, Congress eased the path of tax saving through "living gifts," in order, it was said, to end the previous legal uncertainties. Under the 1950 law (still in effect), for any gift made more than three years prior to death, the government is precluded from claiming "contemplation of death," even in the most flagrant circumstances (e.g., a donor's believing he was on his deathbed when he made the gift). As the law is now worded, a wealthy person has everything to gain and nothing to lose by making substantial "living gifts" in his later years. If he survives for three years, handsome tax savings are his beyond challenge. Even if he dies within three years and his gift motives are successfully challenged, there can still be huge assured tax savings—to such an extent, in fact, that the guardians of a member of the DuPont family were emboldened to approve a gift by their ward of no less than $36 million, though the donor was eighty-six years of age and legally incompetent at the time (he died within two months of the gift). Even under those circumstances, so strongly suggestive that death was near at hand and that the nature of the gift would be challenged, the guardians could be sure that their swift $36 million action, and the immediate payment of a $21,100,000 gift tax, *would save the DuPonts a minimum of $16,100,000* in estate taxes.* Why? Because, under the law, the payment of the $21,100,000 lessened the old gentleman's estate by that amount, thus reducing his death tax by $16,100,000.

There are two ways of solving this thorny problem of gift v.

---

* If, notwithstanding their ward's advanced age, the guardians made a claim that the $36 million gift had not been made "in contemplation of death" and prevailed in that claim, then the lower gift tax rates would have applied to the gift, and an additional saving of $7,100,000 in transfer taxes would have been realized—bringing the total savings to the impressive sum of $23,200,000.

estate taxes. One would be to weld the two into a single tax, with one rate schedule (the property left at death being considered the last in a chain of "lifetime gifts"). Under such a plan, the size of the transfer would no longer depend on whether the transfer occurred before or after death.

A simpler solution—for this and other gift and death tax-avoidance devices—would be to impose the tax not on the giver or the bequeather but on the recipient of the wealth, as suggested on page 339. Under such a plan, the tax would, as with the income tax, depend on the amount received, no matter whether by gift or bequest.

THE TAX LAWS enhance the "joys of giving" in two other respects: first, for a married person, the initial $60,000* of "living gifts" is exempt from taxation. More important, every married couple is also permitted to give $6,000* a year tax-free to as many people as they choose. Thus, one as blessed with wealth, longevity and direct descendants as John D. Rockefeller (who had thirty-seven living children, grandchildren and great-grand-children when he died at age ninety-seven) could, if still married, make tax-free gifts of $222,000 a year without even going outside the immediate family. Few, of course, are as amply endowed, with either wealth or descendants. But it would not be surprising to find an affluent couple with three children (and their three spouses) and nine grandchildren, on whom a total of $90,000 of gifts could be lavished, tax-free, each year.

Yet the annual tax-free gifts need not be made to family members, or even, for that matter, to human persons—a fact that was exploited to the hilt by rich donors to both political parties during the 1972 Presidential campaign. It's a time-honored prac-tice: donors who wish to give more than the tax-free limit simply split up their largesse into lots of $3,000 (or $6,000 when a married couple's political views are in sufficient harmony to permit them to join in making the gift together) and then sprinkle their gifts among the seemingly numberless special committees that each party sets up to receive such emoluments.

But in 1972, according to an enterprising piece of reporting by Jerry Landauer in the *Wall Street Journal*, the Republicans added

---

* This, incidentally, is another tax incentive to matrimony, for a bachelor or spinster may give only the first $30,000 and $3,000 a year tax-free.

a special wrinkle. First of all, they used the special-committee device to beat the April, 1972, deadline for the stricter reporting of campaign contributions, pursuant to a newly enacted law. In February of that year, Landauer reported, "a group of imaginative financiers sat down in secrecy to dream up fancy titles for a batch of phony organizations." The names would not have won any prizes for originality: there was the Better America Council, and Loyal Americans for Effective Government, Dedicated Volunteers for Reform in Society, etc. But the names didn't matter; what did matter was that there were fifty separate receptacles for the generosity of Republican donors which received the money and deposited it in four banks prior to the April 7 deadline—and then all fifty groups vanished.

It would seem that the name-inventing of the Republicans was severely tested, for, according to the Washington *Post,* Pittsburgh millionaire Richard Mellon Scaife, in giving the astounding sum of $990,000 to the Nixon reelection effort prior to April 7, acknowledged writing no fewer than 330 separate checks of $3,000 each—presumably to avoid the gift tax and presumably, therefore, to 330 separate "committees."

But the really new wrinkle came in the form in which the Republicans asked that the funds be given: not by cash or check (as is customary) but in corporate stocks that the donor had acquired at low prices and that had subsequently risen sharply in value. That is, the contributor would hand over the stock and then the Better America Council or the Loyal Americans for Effective Government would sell it and deposit the proceeds. Why go to all that trouble? Because, while the point has never been formally tested in the courts, political parties and committees are thought to be nontaxable entities—*so that these dummy committees could cash in the contributor's profit without paying any capital gains tax.* How much nicer for all concerned than having the donor sell the stock, which would mean he'd have to pay the tax (and, presumably, have less to contribute to the Grand Old Party). As the *Wall Street Journal* put it, if that concept is affirmed in law, "couldn't stock-receiving politicians run for public office partly at Treasury expense?"*

The *Journal* reported that McGovern fund-raisers also exploited gift-splitting and the creation of special committees (as

* See Notes and Sources.

many as 350 of them).* In the case of both parties, though, the circumvention of the gift-tax law is transparent. There is no question that the donations were to be funneled to a single cause, as the Republicans' spring solicitation makes clear: the appeal for "sacrificial commitments to the President's reelection," of which Mr. Nixon would be "personally" apprised. In fact, the instructions to would-be donors as to how they could avoid both the gift tax and the capital gains tax contemplated that there would be a single gift, with a letter to whoever actually received the stock authorizing him to "divide this stock into certificates with values of $3,000 each. . . ."

Since in reality there was but a single recipient, weren't the dummy committees merely a subterfuge? It seems the Chairman of the Republican National Committee, Senator Robert Dole, thought so. Apparently unaware of the fifty-committee caper his own party had used in the spring, he charged that the proliferation of committees by the McGovern campaign was "illegal."

The total avoidance of the capital gains tax also seems of questionable legality. After all, a profit was realized on the sale of the stock but neither the donor nor the recipient paid any tax on it. For tax purposes, it had simply vanished into thin air. Absent any specific sanction in the law (such as exists in the case of gifts of stock to charitable organizations), is such a disappearing act legal? Are the political committees really tax-exempt?† The Republicans displayed a highly expensive eagerness *not* to have that question formally raised; having collected some $10 million prior to the April disclosure deadline, the Committee to Reelect the President allowed that huge sum to lie idle in the banks rather than have it earn interest—which would have meant the Committee would have to report earned income (thus raising the tax question). The price of that sacrifice: "perhaps $100,000" in interest that would otherwise have been earned, according to the *Journal.*

---

* With two distinct differences from the Republican setup: "the McGovern committees weren't set up secretly and didn't quickly disappear." They were registered with the Federal government and their donors were publicly listed.

† On September 11, 1972, the *Wall Street Journal* put that question to Internal Revenue. As of September 27 (the day the *Journal* published its story), Internal Revenue had not responded. As of this writing, no answer has yet been issued.

IT MIGHT HAVE OCCURRED TO YOU to wonder *why* it is necessary or wise to permit the super-rich to give up to $6,000 per-couple-per-recipient-per-year without paying the gift tax called for in the law. You would doubtless agree (if only from your own selfish point of view) that there should be *some* tax-free gift privilege so as not to burden either you or the government with the task of accounting for every fountain pen or handkerchief or necktie bestowed upon a loved one or friend. But $6,000 per couple would take care of a hell of a lot of handkerchiefs or neckties; it would even neatly accommodate the gift of quite a fancy automobile. So why was the limit set that high? The answer suggests the extent to which Congressmen have the super-rich uppermost in their minds when they write the tax laws, for their official explanation was that a $3,000* gift tax exemption was essential "to cover *in most instances,* wedding and Christmas gifts." (Emphasis added.) The italicized words indicate a Congressional doubt that even the $3,000 would not always be enough to cover wedding and Christmas gifts—a doubt that most American families would not feel applied to them.

AS ANY ENTERPRISING life insurance salesman will be glad to tell you, at the drop of his hat on your desk, one of the best ways to use your tax-free gift privilege is to pay $6,000 a year in life insurance premiums and give the policies to your children, since the proceeds will go to them tax-free when you die. Louis Eisenstein once estimated that if you started such a program at age forty, you might easily leave each of your children $900,000 of insurance, totally untouched by the tax collector. Ordinarily, a taxable estate of $900,000 would pay $288,700 in taxes. If you have three children, you can thus engineer a tax saving of $866,100.

Prior to 1954, such an arrangement was barred by the so-called "premium payment test," under which, if you paid the premiums, the insurance proceeds could not pass tax-free at your death, even if you had given your children complete ownership of the policies. But, said some, there is no estate tax on other property completely owned by an heir—why discriminate against insurance? Congress, persuaded by this reasoning, abolished the "premium payment test" in 1954. (The insurance industry was not slow in seizing on

---

* That explanation was given prior to 1948, when joint-return filing was instituted, and the per-couple exemption was doubled to $6,000.

this new selling point in promoting greater insurance purchases. As early as November, 1954, a scant three months after the passage of the 1954 tax law, Eisenhower Administration officials were reportedly "annoyed with the life insurance industry" for so "strenuously 'selling' the new provision"—which had had the Administration's blessing—and driving up the revenue cost to the Treasury.)

Opponents of this change contend that life insurance is not like other property; by its very nature it bestows wealth on a loved one, after a person's death, and in that sense it is essentially no different from a bequest left in the person's will. If, say these critics, Father wishes to give the $3,000 or $6,000 to his wife or children and leave to *them* the decision of whether or not to buy insurance, that's one thing. But if Father makes the decision himself, and simply buys the policy for them, he is merely providing for their welfare after his death and should pay estate taxes accordingly.

PRIOR TO 1969, the law permitted a select few super-rich taxpayers an option that many a less affluent person might have considered enviable: namely, the choice of paying no tax whatever to the United States government and, instead, of funneling what would have been their tax money to causes of their own choosing. In 1969, however, Congress concluded that, however laudable charitable gifts might be, they should not lead to *total* tax avoidance. Accordingly, Congress repealed the so-called "unlimited charitable deduction"—but for the living only. A parallel provision (adopted in 1918 without debate) remains steadfastly in the estate tax laws today, so that anyone with a genuine antipathy to taxpaying (and with enough wealth so that he can otherwise provide for his loved ones) continues to enjoy the option of paying no death taxes, and of directing his wealth to the charities totally of his choice—*including* his (or her) family-controlled private foundation. Here again, Congress has failed to extend to the estate tax area a policy decision it reached in the income tax field. In 1969 Congress wrote into the law an expressed preference for gifts to "public" charities over gifts to "private" foundations,* which are often controlled, in whole or in part, by the giver of the money. But when it comes to the estate tax,

---

* By allowing more liberal income tax deductions for gifts to "public" charities than for gifts to "private" foundations.

bequests to private foundations are fully as deductible as those to "public" charities. Thus, the late Ailsa Mellon Bruce (already mentioned) was able to leave all the $12,500,000 of her $570,-748,725 estate to public and charitable causes, most of it to the Andrew W. Mellon Foundation started by and named after her celebrated father.

THE DEFECTS in the estate and gift tax listed above are serious. But the basic trouble with the present system is that it springs from the wrong concept (or, at any rate, from a concept wholly at odds with the idea that underlies the income tax). That is, the present system imposes the tax on the giver/bequeather rather than on the recipient of the wealth. Yet who can doubt that a dollar that a person inherits or receives as a gift endows him with just as much "ability to pay" for necessities, luxuries—or taxes—as a dollar earned by the sweat of the brow or a dollar made in a stock market bonanza? If the criterion of "ability to pay" is a fair basis of taxation where *income* is concerned (and I know of no fairer basis), what reason is there for wholly abandoning that yardstick when it comes to estates and gifts?

What's more, correcting the defects of the present system (the $60,000 exemption, the marital deduction, the gift v. estate tax and "contemplation of death" problems) has proved immensely difficult under the existing notion of imposing the tax on the giver rather than on the receiver. Abandon that concept in favor of a receiver-paid tax, and the solutions, while far from problem-free, become much simpler.*

Shifting to a receiver-paid tax also offers the possibility of substantially increasing Federal revenues from transfers of wealth (which could, if desired, open the way for reducing income taxes). When Senator George McGovern proposed such a system, in January, 1972 (including a 100 percent tax on wealth transfers of more than $500,000), he said that a "conservative estimate would indicate the doubling of present receipts" on wealth transfers— which, he said, would mean an added five billion dollars of revenue in 1973.

---

* This discussion of estate tax reform omits mention of the zero tax rate now permitted on the profits on securities that are transferred at death. That loophole, and the urgent need for its reform, are fully discussed in Chapter 5.

THE CONTROVERSY over estate taxes is of ancient vintage. Pliny the Younger, for example, complained that the death tax was "an 'unnatural' tax, augmenting the sorrow of the bereaved." A similar lament was heard two thousand years later, when Senator William V. Allen of Nebraska wondered, in the United States Senate, whether it is "right . . . to stand with the widow and children at the graveside of a dead father to collect a tax."

In recent decades, it has become more customary to assail the estate tax because of its supposed effects on the incentives and productivity of the living and, hence, on the private enterprise system. Andrew Mellon was a prime exponent of this viewpoint, decrying the tax for forcing the liquidation of securities, depressing stock prices and "destroying" capital. The breaking up of large estates, he believed, would violate the "theory upon which the country was founded . . . equality of opportunity."

It is precisely here that Mellon collides head-on with the advocates of a steep estate tax, who picture large inheritances as not only perpetuating but magnifying economic inequalities. According to one economist, such inequalities are caused by three main factors: unequal ability, unequal luck and unequal inheritance.

Philosophers as well as economists have argued for a steep estate tax. John Stuart Mill—like Andrew Carnegie after him (see page 326)—favored a death tax that would set a limit on "what anyone may acquire by the mere favor of others without any exercise of his faculties." If "he desires any further accession of his fortune," said Mill, "he shall work for it." That concept should kindle a flame of enthusiasm in the bosoms of the most ardent disciples of the Work Ethic (i.e., those who are most insistent that the poor work for their welfare grants). So far, however, they have not clamored for reforming the wealth-transfer tax to accord with the preachments of John Stuart Mill.

Adding a political note to the controversy, Roger Babson expressed inability to "see why the control of ten or twenty thousand men should descend by inheritance through the death of some manufacturer, any more than the control of a city or a state should pass on to the son of a mayor or governor."

Congress, for its part, has apparently had difficulty choosing between the philosophy of the Carnegies, the Roosevelts and the Babsons on the one hand and that of the Mellons and the Plinys on the other. Thus confronted, it has chosen both: a Rooseveltian rate schedule largely vitiated by Mellon-sized loopholes.

17

Some Moral Preachments of Our Tax Laws

THE FOLLOWING IS AN ATTITUDE TEST. Do you agree or disagree with these statements?

	Agree	Disagree

1. Repairing a dented fender is more important than fixing a broken arm.
2. Living in sin should be rewarded as more praiseworthy than legally sanctioned marriage.
3. People should not try to educate themselves for a better job, but should be content with their present job.
4. The boy working his way through college is less deserving than the football star on an athletic scholarship.
5. People should be penalized for continuing to work beyond age sixty-five.
6. People should be encouraged to go into debt rather than to live within their means.
7. Machines are more important than people.
8. The inventor of, say, a new pretzel-bender is more important than the writer of a new book, play, poem, song or symphony.

341

Agree   Disagree

9. A blind person deserves financial help, but
   a paralytic does not.
10. People who work for a living are less
    deserving than those who don't.
11. The work of money is entitled to a greater
    reward than the work of people.

If you disagree with eight or more of the above statements, it
is not time to see your doctor—but it may well be time to see your
Congressman or Senator and ask him a few questions about our
tax law.

Why? Because every one of the above statements is reflected
in that law. Of course, you won't find them stated in just the way
they were in the attitude test; nor, in most cases, did the writers
of the tax laws *intend* to make such value judgments when they
framed the tax code. So there they sit, even though many of them
don't coincide with what a preponderance of Americans believe.

Most people probably aren't even aware these judgments exist.
Even now, for example, you may be highly dubious that the tax laws
really do draw the conclusions on which the attitude test was
based. Where, it might occur to you to ask, does it say that repairing a fender is more important than fixing a broken arm? Well,
Section 165 (c) (3) of the Internal Revenue Code provides that
all so-called "casualty losses" above $100—and these days a
dented fender can easily cost more than $100 to fix—are tax-
deductible, whereas Section 213 (a) (1) (B) states that *medical*
expenses that come to less than 3 percent of your income are *not*
deductible.

Those who see the Congress of the United States as the valiant
protector of our Age-Old Moral and Sexual Virtues will be surprised, if not shocked, to learn that this selfsame Congress of the
United States has enacted into law a financial reward for cohabitation. In 1969, Congress created an incentive to certain happily
married couples to dissolve their legal union and continue their
relationship illicitly. This phenomenon occurs in cases where both
Mr. and Mrs. are gainfully employed—and the incentive to con-
cubinage reaches its maximum when Fem Lib triumphs and Her
earnings are identical to His.

For example, when each partner has taxable income of $14,000, as long as they are married they are obliged to pay $7,100 in taxes on their combined $28,000 of income, whether they file jointly or separately. If only they were unmarried, however, they could enjoy the advantages of the single-person rates on their respective $14,000 incomes, in which case He and She would each pay $3,210, for a total of $6,420. Thus, Congress has provided a $680* annual incentive for them to divorce and continue their relationship without the blessing of the law.

AMERICANS schooled to revere the shimmering virtues extolled by Horatio Alger will also be shocked to learn that the tax law discourages initiative, self-advancement and the quest for knowledge. Consider the case of Nora Payne Hill, a Danville, Virginia, schoolteacher very much in the Horatio Alger tradition. Although Miss Hill could have fulfilled her state teaching requirements right in Danville, she chose to journey to New York to attend Columbia University summer school, in the belief that "she could do a better job in Danville by so doing." But the Tax Court sternly disallowed the deduction of her $239.50 of summer school expenses, applying the accepted rule of law that educational expenses incurred in the pursuit of a higher position are *not* deductible. The expenses of standing still—yes, those are deductible; but not those devoted to moving ahead in life. "However commendable [Miss Hill's] conduct may have been," the Tax Court found, her journey to the fount of knowledge was not necessary to maintain her present position. Besides, the court observed, "she said she loved to go to summer school."

Happily, a higher court reversed the Tax Court decision as "unreal and hypercritical" and allowed Miss Hill her $239.50 deduction—but only because it exonerated her of the sin of trying to elevate herself to a higher station. Had the Appeals Court suspected her of such a sinister motive, it would have upheld the Tax Court, for the rule against self-advancement must be maintained.† A group of research chemists, for example, was not allowed to deduct the costs of attending law school in order to become patent chemists;

---

* The $7,100 of tax as a married couple minus the $6,420 if unmarried.

† The rule is defended on practical grounds: unless some line is drawn to define what educational costs are "ordinary and necessary" business expenses, it is argued, *all* educational outlays would have to become tax-deductible, and the drain on the Treasury would be formidable.

and a psychiatrist was denied a deduction for the expenses of his own psychoanalysis, a prerequisite to his advancement to the status of a qualified analyst.

Now that being born in a log cabin has gone out of style, a modern equivalent for the aspiring politician is the claim of having worked his way through college—preferably by waiting on table. While such industriousness thus appears to enjoy great public approbation, the law takes a more critical view: it taxes the hard-earned income of the college waiter, but leaves untouched the athletic "scholarship" which enthusiastic alumni bestow upon the football hero (and which the law treats as a gift).

In order to ease what are commonly called the "twilight years," Congress has compassionately conferred on those over sixty-two a tax credit on the first $1,200 of their income from pensions, dividends or other investment income. But the elderly are encouraged to suppress any desire to supplement that income (and to keep busy) by working, for the moment they earn more than $1,200 a year, the tax credit begins to fade away. When their earnings reach $3,248, it vanishes entirely. Their *unearned* income, however, can rise to any height without penalty; so long as all remunerative work is meticulously avoided, the tax credit retains its full glory. Once they have safely reached age seventy-two, they may once again join the ranks of the gainfully employed without adverse tax consequences.

Poor Richard's Almanack and similar fountainheads of wisdom are replete with admonitions about the evils of borrowing and the virtues of living within one's means ("He that goes a-Borrowing goes a-Sorrowing . . . The Borrower is a Slave to the Lender"). Benjamin Franklin would doubtless, therefore, be horrified by the manner in which the tax laws make the government of the United States an active partner in encouraging people to stray from the balanced family budget. For, after all, since interest payments are tax-deductible,* Uncle Sam bears a part of the cost and makes borrowing less expensive. Modern-day economists, to be sure, might well applaud the ample use of credit; but Poor Richard could never condone the concomitant erosion of fiscal virtue.

Judging from the tax law, the inventors in our midst are

---

* Subject to a very generous ceiling that Congress imposed in 1969 (see p. 367)—a limit that won't affect you unless you are borrowing more than $400,000. So most readers of these words can relax.

clearly to be revered over our authors and composers, for while Section 1235 specifically confers a tax blessing upon the fruits of the inventor's imagination, Section 1231 (b) (1) (C) just as specifically denies that tax favor (the special 25 or 35 percent capital gains rate) to authors, composers and artists. In the eyes of the tax law, it appears, *any* invention—whether it be a new kind of radar or a new pretzel-bender—contributes more to the well-being of society than, say, a Faulkner or Hemingway novel, a Robert Frost poem, an Aaron Copland symphony, or, perhaps, a Rodgers and Hammerstein Broadway musical.

As to the preference shown the blind, the story is simple: Congress has sympathetically conferred an extra $750 exemption upon those to whom sight is denied, but this expression of compassion for the handicapped mysteriously began and ended there. Those afflicted with multiple sclerosis, muscular dystrophy or any other crippling malady have not attracted comparable Congressional sympathy.

And who, reading the tax law, can doubt that machines are more important than people? After all, when a businessman invests in a machine he is entitled to take tax deductions on the cost of that machine over its useful life. But the tax law gives him no comparable merit points for investing in his son (by sending him to college).

Moreover, the tax law is most understanding about the aging of machines: as indicated above, a year-by-year allowance is made as machines lose their zip and zest and approach the age of retirement. But leaving aside the minor concessions made at age sixty-five (pages 352–354), the tax laws sternly forbid any recognition of the gradual aging of human beings—except, perhaps, in one instance: the professional baseball and football players who are bought and sold precisely like indentured slaves, and whose initial purchase price may be "depreciable." But do not rejoice for the players, for they derive no benefit. Only the purchaser of the ball club is thus blessed.

A N Y Y O U N G S T E R reading the biographies of the titans of America's past (the Franklins, Jeffersons and Lincolns, the Lewis-and-Clarks, the Andrew Carnegies and the Henry Fords) cannot escape the deeply held American precept that it was heroic personal effort—hard work—that made these men and their country great. *Poor Richard's Almanack* confirms this wisdom ("Diligence is the Mother of good luck . . . Idleness is the greatest prodigality"). Yet in many respects the tax law seems to frown upon those who work for their living—or, at least, to smile warmly upon those who don't. Some of these respects have already been mentioned: the comparative penalty, for example, suffered by those who work beyond age sixty-five or who wait on table to get a college education. Wives, moreover, may be said to be discouraged from remunerative activity, since this reduces the tax advantage their husbands derive from matrimony (see Chapter 6). Those on welfare who have the temerity to work may be subject to a tax rate of 67 percent* on their earnings (that's almost as high as the rate applicable to multimillionaires with more than $200,000 income).† If those families are also eligible for food stamps to help feed their families, they may be subject to an additional 30 percent tax, so that the effort to satisfy the American idolatry of work may be greeted with a 97 percent tax. One would be hard-pressed to devise a more effective deterrent to hard work and self-help.

But these are not the only comparative penalties imposed on work; there are other dramatic preferences accorded *unearned* income over earned income. The sons and daughters of the well-to-do may, without lifting a finger, inherit great wealth (even after estate taxes)—wealth generated not by their efforts but by those of their forebears—*and pay not a penny of tax when they receive it.* Moreover, those blessed with large holdings of corporate stock derive their dividend income through the efforts and talents of others; yet they receive that dividend income (as well as interest from their bondholdings—also unearned) undiluted by any tax withholding such as diminishes a workingman's weekly pay check. In addition, of course, they have the privilege of enjoying the first $100 of dividend income ($200 if they're married) tax-free (see pages 89–92).

---

* Prior to 1969 this tax rate was 100 percent.

† The 67 percent tax rate comes about because when welfare recipients earn more than a certain amount, the law provides that they lose $2 of welfare for every dollar they earn. To the hard-pressed welfare recipients thus deprived, this is indistinguishable, in its effect, from their having to pay a $2 tax on every $3 of income, which would be a 67 percent tax rate. While that high "tax rate" is not imposed by the Internal Revenue Code, by coincidence the welfare laws in which it is written are the responsibility of the same Congressional committees that write the tax laws.

But by far the greatest advantage enjoyed by unearned income is the special capital gains tax rate, which openly proclaims that the work of money is entitled to a greater reward than the work of people. Lawyers (and other high-paid professionals such as doctors or engineers), it is said, live well but die poor. Why? Because they perform the work of *people*, and for their prodigious efforts they are taxed at the regular income tax rates, ranging up to 50 percent. Others, however, who have the means to put their *money* to work, are favored with a tax rate that rises no higher than 25 percent for most people, but in any event no higher than 35 percent.

This is not to deprecate the value of capital, an essential ingredient in society. But capital without human effort counts for little; in fact, it is the addition of human effort and ingenuity that brings capital to life.*

These and many other value judgments are scattered throughout the tax law. Few are as overtly stated as Section 152 (b) (5), which expresses a deeply engrained American attitude toward mistresses (it denies their benefactors the right to claim them as dependents). Most are subtly buried in the inscrutable legal verbiage of the Internal Revenue Code. But, as the Duchess said, "Everything's got a moral—if only you can find it."

---

* In times past, the American tax laws sought to favor this human factor through a preferential "earned income credit." But human effort requires no such preferential recognition. What is wrong with simple equality, which can be effortlessly achieved by taxing the work of money and the work of people according to the same rates?

The Slightly-Privileged Many

BY NOW, you may be feeling somewhat left out. You have no stock options, no tax-free bonds. Perhaps you own a few shares of corporation stock, but not enough to make much difference. Nary an oil well, nor office building, nor brood cow do you possess.

"Where's *my* tax gimmick?" you may be asking.

You've got your tax gimmicks, I reply. Lots of them.

"Not me!" you say. "I just figure up my income, take my deductions—just like everybody else—go to the regular tax table and find out how much I owe. How can *I* have any gimmicks working for me?"

Well, here are a few questions.

Are you over sixty-five? If so, whether you're rich or poor, you're automatically entitled to one special tax favor, and if you're not working, to a second. Your neighbor, who won't turn sixty-five until next year, doesn't get either favor.

Do you own your own home? Have you ever compared notes with your neighbor, who rents his? Try it. You may be surprised about the gimmicks you have working for you. (See pages 355–359.)

Did you serve in the armed forces? Maybe you were too excited to notice when you got out, but when you received your discharge ("mustering out") pay, you paid no tax on that. And

348

you pay no tax on your veteran's pension, or your disability benefits, do you?

Are you getting Social Security benefits? Did you declare them on your tax return? Of course you didn't. Social Security benefits (being nonreportable to Internal Revenue) in effect bear a zero tax rate, just like the interest on state and local bonds, or the capital gains on stocks and bonds you hold till your death.

Perhaps your son or daughter has a scholarship. Is anyone paying taxes on it? And what about the interest your life insurance premiums are drawing? There's no tax on that income, either. Not only is that particular interest *income* tax-free; all your interest *payments* are tax-deductible.*

"But," you protest, "my interest deductions just amounted to a few dollars last year—hardly saved me anything on my tax bill. Why make such a fuss about it?"

Because your "few dollars" of interest deductions, along with those of nearly 30 million other Americans, added up to nearly $24 billion in 1970—and cost the Treasury over $4 billion!

The provisions we're talking about here are far different from stock options and capital gains and tax-free bonds, which bring massive doses of tax relief to a comparative handful of taxpayers. By contrast, the tax favors in this chapter are more like aspirin: they bring a little relief—but to millions or tens of millions of taxpayers.

These favors bite deeply into the public coffers. Give a $100 annual tax saving (just $2 a week) to 10 million taxpayers and you've lost $1,000,000,000 of revenue in a single stroke.

In all, the tax favors described in this chapter—for the elderly, for veterans, home owners, factory workers and the like—*cost the Treasury nearly $50 billion a year.* Repeal them all tomorrow, and there could be an immediate 25 to 30 percent cut in all tax rates.

Therefore, while you may have a personal or ideological attachment to one or another of the tax preferences for the Slightly-Privileged Many, don't forget that each has its price tag. And, just as with every government *spending* program, everyone has to pay that price through higher taxes—a full $50 billion higher, considering all the Privileged-Many tax preferences together.

---

* The 1969 tax law placed a mild limit on the amount of deductible interest on loans the proceeds of which are used to produce investment income (see p. 367).

Congress boasts of great frugality with public moneys, and often spends hours debating appropriations of a few million (or even a few hundred thousand) dollars. In striking contrast, however, most of the multi-billion-dollar dispensations to the Slightly-Privileged Many have been enacted with little or no debate. Year after year, they dwell comfortably in the tax law, their security only rarely disturbed by some meddling questioner inquiring: *Why* a special tax exemption for the blind—and for no other handicapped persons? *Why* no tax on Social Security benefits or veterans' pensions or mustering-out pay? *Why* tax relief for the wealthy, non-needy aged, as well as the poor? Why permit deductions for interest costs, but not various other personal expenses? Is the charitable deduction the best and fairest way of fostering philanthropy?

Other general questions arise, relevant to *each* of these tax favors—questions such as: Is the price right? Do the original reasons for enacting it still hold true? And, most important of all: Is the provision really tailored to give aid and comfort to those who need it most? Or are large portions of these humanitarian "tax welfare" payments actually going, unseen, to rich (or comfortably-off) people who have but a scant need for assistance?

For example, take the basic personal exemption allowed for each taxpayer and each of his dependents. This is a tax feature of universal popularity, since it is of some assistance to every adult American. As a result, it is, politically speaking, Virtue Personified, and is rarely subjected to critical questioning. After all, shouldn't every person be spared taxation on some minimum amount of income?* Indubitably. But if the object of the personal exemption is to provide untaxed "survival money" for those who live closest to the survival margin, it is a poorly tailored device indeed, for it accords just $105 *per year* of tax relief for the lowest-bracket taxpayers but five times that much—$525—for the multimillionaires in the top bracket. Even the Gettys, the Whitneys and the Rockefellers would probably admit that is not a very sensible way of handing out $30 billion of taxpayer money (for that is the approximate annual "cost" of this tax feature).

---

* My secretary, Miss Irene Saunders, has some rather caustic questions about the adequacy of the personal exemption in her letter to Congressman Mills and Senator Long (see p. 373). But for purposes of the present discussion, the *level* of the exemption is a separate question.

According to one analysis, less than one-fourth of the benefits goes to those with "adjusted gross incomes" of less than $5,000. Turning that coin over, more than *three*-fourths of the $30 billion goes to those with incomes of greater than $5,000—and 40 percent of it goes to those making more than $10,000.

A far more equitable result would be achieved by allowing a flat tax *credit*—that is, a reduction of taxes owed—of, say, $150 for each taxpayer and each dependent. The way that would work is spelled out on page 406. Not only would that be far more equitable than the present $750 exemption, it would mean nearly $2 billion in added annual revenues, which could, if desired, be used to lower everyone's tax rate a trifle.

MUCH THE SAME CRITICISM can be leveled at the array (some might call it the disarray) of tax favors for the elderly.

While in other respects you may be dreading your sixty-fifth birthday, from a tax point of view it will be a red-letter day. You will suddenly find yourself entitled to an extra $750 exemption, more lenient taxation of your dividend or interest income, and tax-free Social Security benefits.

Why these sudden blessings? Chances are you look and feel much the same as on the day before your birthday; you may have no thought of retiring; you may be millionaire or pauper. No matter: the tax blessings are yours—because it's your sixty-fifth birthday.

As Congress sees it, the elderly, as a group, are deserving of these tax advantages because their incomes are, on the average, unusually low, "reflecting the fact that the group as a whole is handicapped in an economic, if not a physical sense," and because "unlike younger persons" they cannot supplement their meager incomes "by accepting full-time jobs." Hence, they suffer "with unusual severity" from rises in prices and taxes.

There is no denying that the aged, as a group, have shockingly low incomes. In 1970, about a fifth of those over sixty-five had incomes of under $1,500. One family in every eight, in this age group, actually took in less than $1,000! Where the head of the family was sixty-five or over, the median family income was just half that of families headed by a person under sixty-five.

But poverty is by no means the exclusive province of the

elderly; nor are they alone in their inability to take jobs and supplement slender incomes so as to combat rising prices. If low incomes and unemployability are proper reasons for granting tax concessions, then surely the humane tax legislator should not ignore those living in chronically unemployed or depressed areas such as in West Virginia or eastern Kentucky. Special dispensations should also go to the ill-educated and ill-trained, or the discriminated-against groups like Blacks and Chicanos, for whom jobs may be scarce—in short, to *all* the poor and underprivileged, *whether young or old.*

Look at the question from the point of view of "ability to pay": Is a *childless* couple aged sixty-six with $5,000 of income necessarily less able to pay taxes than a younger two-child family trying to live on the same $5,000? One government study, in fact, concluded that overall living expenses for the elderly are somewhat *lower*—some 10 to 15 percent lower—than a comparable budget (aimed at providing a "modest but adequate level of living") for a younger family.* To this extent, older people may be *better* able to pay taxes than the younger people *with the same income.*

Nonetheless, it is apparently a matter of national conscience to ease the lot of the elderly in every possible way: in part through direct-benefit programs such as Social Security; in part, too, through indirect means such as tax concessions. But the tax advantages *now* accorded those over sixty-five may be more effective in easing the national conscience than in actually *helping* the aged.

Consider the extra $750 exemption enjoyed by the elderly, one of the government's sixty-fifth-birthday gifts, bestowed on rich and poor alike.

Compassionate? Certainly.

Expensive? It costs the Treasury about $1 billion annually.

Effective? For nearly one-fifth of the elderly—those with incomes of less than $1,500—it provides no tax relief whatever.

Equitable? For those in the lowest tax bracket (14 percent), it means a saving of $105. Equally important, it ignores—in fact, it discriminates against—those who may be just as impoverished and needy, but who happen not to have reached the age of sixty-five.

---

* The survey comparison allowed for such factors as family size, child expenses and differing requirements for clothing, transportation and, above all, medical care.

THE ELDERLY, as noted, also receive all their Social Security benefits tax-free. For this favor, Congress may not claim credit (or blame): it resulted from a Treasury Department ruling in 1941 which doubtless had little impact on the Federal revenues at the time but today costs more than $6 billion annually,* now that Social Security benefits are running at the rate of about $37 billion a year.

Well, you may say, it wouldn't make much sense for the government to hand out Social Security benefits with one hand and turn around and tax them with the other. While this reasoning has the force of logic, it did not, over the years, salve the wounds of others—mainly teachers and state and local government employees—who, unlike Social Security recipients, had to pay taxes on their pension incomes. In 1954, Congress heeded their cries of anguish and enacted the so-called "retirement income credit" (see Glossary). As is so often the case with the spreading of tax preferences, this new provision went beyond correcting the discrimination against government employees' *pension* income; it also eased the taxation of the *dividend* and *interest* income of *all* the elderly, on the theory that those who had provided for their old age by virtue of their own frugality and savings should not be penalized as compared with pensioners and annuitants.

The thrifty were thus spared, but the industrious and energetic were penalized. Woe is the man or woman who goes on working beyond sixty-two† and earns as much as $3,248 a year if single ($3,736 if married), for he or she is wholly denied the benefactions of the retirement income credit. (Those over seventy-two may, however, work to their hearts' content without lessening the tax pleasure they derive from the retirement income credit.)

President Kennedy in 1963 proposed repealing the double exemption and the retirement income credit and substituting a flat $300 tax reduction for all those over sixty-five. Assuming you have accepted the *principle* that old age is, in and of itself, a good and sufficient reason for a tax favor, the plan proposed by President Kennedy has much to recommend it over the amalgam of tax preferences now accorded the aged. It would simplify the tax

---

* That estimate assumes no extra $750 exemption for the elderly as presently allowed.

† The age at which retired Federal, state and local government employees became eligible for the retirement income credit.

return and end the penalty against the industrious elderly who continue working (and one out of three does). All who benefit from it would receive equal dollar savings, so that a greater portion of its advantages would go to those with lower incomes who most need help. It also would lessen considerably the remaining preference enjoyed by Social Security recipients.

Improvement though it would be, the Kennedy plan (which Congress rejected) cannot escape the cardinal charge leveled at the existing concessions to the aged: it still fails to extend a helping hand to those who most need it—those whose incomes are so low as to be nontaxable. And, at best, an extra $300, while a minor help, is far from a solution when major illness strikes and medical bills pile up. To paraphrase one writer, "The income tax can avoid taking the shirt off a man, but it cannot provide a shirt for a naked man."

SOCIAL SECURITY BENEFITS are by no means the only government payments that are free from taxation. Also exempt are the following: *

Railroad retirement benefits	$2.0 billion
Public assistance payments	$10.8 billion
Veterans' benefits	$5.9 billion
Unemployment compensation	$6.2 billion
Workmen's compensation (for injuries, etc.)	$2.4 billion
Servicemen's mustering-out pay, combat pay, subsistence and rental allowances	$5.6 billion

* Figures are estimated *total* payments, some portion of which goes to persons whose incomes are so low as to be nontaxable.

All told, according to the Brookings Institution analysis, the tax-free status of these government payments (including Social Security) costs the Treasury roughly $13 billion in revenue every year. End the exemption and all tax rates could be cut about 15 percent without affecting Federal tax collection. Such a drastic change would, no doubt, evoke cries of anguish from aggrieved veterans, servicemen and others, which leads some to argue that Congress would feel compelled to increase government benefit payments to make up for the taxes, so that the Treasury would be no better off. Maybe so and maybe not, but the basic question remains: Isn't a dollar of, say, mustering-out pay exactly the same as a dollar of wages or salary in enabling a man to buy food and clothing or a present for his wife—or, for that matter, to pay taxes? If so, then why, under the principle of "ability to pay," should one be taxed and not the other?

Besides, under the prevailing practices of providing "equity" in taxation (more fully described in Chapter 14), once one government benefit has been freed from taxation, "equity" requires that other benefits be given similar tax-free treatment, and the leak in the Treasury grows and grows. All in all, then, it would be better, from the point of view of tax fairness and of preventing growing punctures in the tax system, to *tax*, rather than *exempt*, the billions of government benefit payments, even if Congress were to increase them to offset the taxes.

A T T E N T I O N   H O M E   O W N E R : Did you know that you and 39 million other home owners are enjoying nearly *$15.5 billion* of tax-free income every year?

Specifically, did you know that if you're living in a $20,000 house, you're enjoying somewhere around $800 of untaxed income a year? If your house is worth $35,000, your tax-free income is about $1,400. For a $150,000 home, the untaxed income amounts to roughly $6,000 annually.*

What is all this supposedly "untaxed" income?

It is, in effect, the rent you don't have to pay because you own your home.

Now, you may feel you can't see or feel this "income," but it's there, all right. Just compare a few notes with your neighbor who *rents* his house, and you'll see how and why.

Let's say it so happens that you and your neighbor are alike in most respects. You both hold $10,000-a-year jobs, you're both married and have two children. You both managed, as of a year or so ago, to accumulate $10,000 of savings—but here you and he followed different courses. Your neighbor put his $10,000 into bonds and you put yours into buying your $25,000 house, on which you have a $15,000 mortgage.

Your taxes and mortgage interest come to $1,400 a year and your maintenance and repairs and insurance cost you $700 a

---

* Assuming each of the above-mentioned homes is owned free and clear, without a mortgage.

year. So you lay out $2,100 a year as the out-of-pocket cost of living in your home.

Your neighbor, on the other hand, has to pay $208.50 a month rent, or $2,500 a year, so you're ahead of him on housing costs.

One way of looking at it is that you and your neighbor both made investments. He happened to invest in stocks and bonds, and the return on his money is the 4 percent yield he receives on them. You happened to invest in a piece of real estate. If you had rented it out to someone else, you would have paid a tax on the net rental income (i.e., after your expenses). But, instead, you found another tenant—namely, yourself.

So what's the return on your investment in real estate? It's the $400 of housing costs your neighbor pays and you don't.

"But why should I pay taxes on that four hundred dollars?" you ask. "I can't see it or feel it—nobody *paid* me rent on my house. How can you call that 'income'?"

Your neighbor might answer your question with one of his own. He paid taxes on the return on his $10,000 investment. Why shouldn't you? Besides, your $400 return *is* real: you can see it, feel it, and spend it—for you, the $400 you *didn't* pay for housing made you end up with the same number of spendable dollars as your neighbor with his $400 of income from his bonds. The following chart makes this clear:

	You (*Home* Owner)	Your Neighbor (*Home* Renter)
Salary	$10,000	$10,000
Interest income from bonds	—	+400
Rent (or housing cost)	−$2,100	−$2,500
Spendable dollars remaining	$7,900	$7,900

It's your $400 return on your house investment, and like amounts enjoyed by the 39 million U.S. home owners, that make up the nearly $15.5 billion of untaxed income. If we were to tax that $15.5 billion—as the English did until 1963,* and as other

---

* The British government attributed the repeal of this tax to the increase that would result in an updating of real-estate valuations and to its characterization of the rent-equivalent as "notional income"—which the *Economist* branded "double talk." In abolishing the tax, the government was acting counter to the recommendation of a 1955 Royal Commission on Taxation.

countries still do—*the Treasury would gain $5 billion in revenue,* which would make it possible to reduce everyone's taxes.

But we haven't really finished·the comparison. Your neighbor (poor fellow) laid out $2,500 for his housing cost, *but none of it was tax-deductible.* By contrast, $1,400 of your out-of-pocket cost —the interest and taxes—*is* deductible. Result: Although you and your neighbor have the same amount of *spendable* income (and might expect, under a Utopian system of justice, to pay the same taxes), *you end up with $1,800 less taxable income*:

	You (Home Owner)	Your Neighbor (Home Renter)
Salary (assume all taxable)	$10,000	$10,000
Interest from bonds	—	+400
Deductions (for mortgage interest and taxes)	$1,400	—
Taxable income	$8,600	$10,400
Taxes	$1,512	$1,908

In other words, you're allowed to take tax deductions on your interest and taxes as if you were a landlord, but at the same time you're excused from paying taxes on your landlordly income. In the example above, having your cake and eating it too gives you a $396 tax advantage.

"Now, just a minute," you say a bit heatedly. "First you want to tax me on income I can't even see and now you want to take away my tax deductions on my home. Don't you think it's worth encouraging a man to own his own house?"

Well, I counter, worth how much? Worth a billion dollars? Or would *two* billion dollars' worth of encouragement be about right? After all, with two billion dollars a year, we could build a lot of houses for people who don't have any, or for people who live in slums—so this "encouragement price tag" is important.

The fact is that, today, we're paying not $2 billion but *well over $9.6 billion a year** to encourage home ownership—about six times what the Federal government was spending for *all* housing-assistance programs.

---

* Includes the cost of deductions for taxes and interest plus the cost of not taxing the "rental incomes" on owned homes.

Now, some argue that these billions are far better spent encouraging *private* home building and home owning than through a musclebound, bureaucratically run *government* housing program. The proof of this particular pudding, they may well say, is in the spectacular rise in home ownership in America—up well over 50 percent since 1940.

But, as discussed in some detail in Chapter 7, the existing tax incentives are a wasteful way to try to induce home ownership, since the greatest benefits go to those most likely to own their homes anyway—those least in need of encouragement. The higher your tax bracket and the more expensive your home, the greater your tax savings. All of that produces the nonsensical result of just 66 cents a year in tax relief to the neediest and poorest housed, contrasted with benefactions to the average mansion owner of 10,000 times that amount—well over $6,000 a year. Would any sensible architect of a housing-aid program, starting from scratch, ever draw up a plan like that?

Besides, it would be hard to prove how much of this remarkable increase in home ownership was due to the tax spur and how much due to other factors, such as sharply rising personal income and the greater availability of mortgage credit.

Taxing the equivalent net-rent value of owned homes presents two difficulties. One is the practical problem (that has apparently plagued the British) of keeping up-to-date appraisals of rental values. The other is the fact that the rent equivalent on your owned home is not the only kind of unseen "imputed" income you receive (owning a car spares you public bus expense, owning a washing machine saves you a laundry bill);* so why, it is asked, tax just one kind of "imputed" income, and not all the others? Where and how could one fairly draw the line?

Yet, say some tax experts, such as those at the Brookings Institution, it is legitimate to single out rent-equivalent income in part because of its immense size ($15.5 billion a year) and in part because it *is* feasible, in their view, to overcome the home-valuation difficulties that finally stymied the British and to tax this kind of unseen income on a reasonable basis. This could be done by having each home owner state on his tax return the portion of his

---

* There is also thought to be $14.4 billion of "imputed interest income" in the form of services provided free by commercial banks and other financial institutions in lieu of interest payments on deposits.

home he actually owns (his "equity" in the house—something almost every home owner either knows or can find out). That "equity" would then be treated, for tax purposes, just like any other kind of investment. That is, IRS would assume that it yielded the investor a certain amount of income (based on an "interest rate" or yield that could be changed from time to time, to reflect current reality). The assumed "investment income" would become part of the home owner's taxable income.

As mentioned, ending the various tax preferences enjoyed by home owners (but denied to renters) would bring in to the .S. Treasury added revenues of about $9.6 billion per year. the mind of man could devise ways of using that $9.6 billio solve America's housing problems in a fairer and more sensible way than handing out $6,000 a year to the richest but just 66 *cents* a year to the poorest families.

L E T ' S   S A Y you're a factory worker. Your taxes are taken out of your weekly pay check before you even see them. You rent your home; you take no special deductions; you file the short-form 1040* and that's the end of it. Chances are you're convinced you're the proverbial "forgotten man." No special tax favors for you.

But think carefully.

Is there, by any chance, a company health or medical plan? Or a company-paid group-term life insurance arrangement? Or a pension or profit-sharing plan?

If so, then you, sir (or madam), are the proud possessor of a tax preference. So don't look so glum. Smile.

A smile will suffice—a full-fledged grin would probably be overdoing it, since the dollars-and-cents savings to you are probably small. But to the U.S. Treasury, looking at these fringe benefits through the other end of the telescope, the theoretical revenue loss looks huge, since, in all, there is no current tax on about $30 billion—$24 billion of employer contributions† to various fringe benefits plus about $6 billion earned by pension trust funds.

That's the amount that is *theoretically* untaxed on a current

---

* Abandoned temporarily in 1968, but reportedly to be revived.

† There is no problem about the *employees'* contributions escaping tax-free since they were made with workers' *after*-tax dollars—i.e., were already taxed in the employees' hands.

basis. From a *practical* point of view, it would be difficult, if not impossible, to tax a great deal of it currently anyway. Still, it's worth listing some of the tax preferences enjoyed by those who receive fringe benefits:

• *Health and medical benefits:* Tax-deductible employer contributions to health plans total nearly $10 billion annually; yet the benefits of those plans are, by and large, untaxed when received by the employee. Trying to tax those benefits wouldn't produce as much revenue as you might theoretically expect (since employees in many cases could claim offsetting medical-expense tax deductions), and it would create serious administrative problems, both for employers and for the government. Nevertheless, anyone covered by a company health plan is getting, tax-free, benefits which others have to buy with after-tax dollars. Estimated annual cost to the Treasury: $2 billion.

• *Company-paid group-term life insurance:* This is another fringe benefit that most people have to pay for with after-tax dollars. Employer contributions to group life plans amount to about $2½ billion a year. Under pre-1963 regulations, there was no limit on the amount of company-paid insurance an employee could receive tax-free. The Kennedy Administration proposed limiting it to $5,000 of insurance, but in 1964 Congress set the limit at $50,000. Annual cost to the U.S. Treasury: $500 million.

• *Miscellaneous employee benefits:* These take a variety of forms—discount sales, free meals and lodging, low-interest loans, company-paid vacation facilities or transportation (especially significant in the case of airline employees and their families) and so on. The government estimates that the annual cost to the Treasury of tax-free meals and lodging alone comes to $170 million. While the total volume of these probably reaches into the billions, it would be impractical to try to tax most of them. Still, to the extent others are using already taxed dollars to buy these same pleasures, a tax preference exists.

One tax-free "fringe benefit" tinged with irony is the zero tax rate permitted the employee who gets sick and is paid up to $100 a week* in "sick pay" in lieu of salary.† This can result in the

---

* Up to $75 per week during the first thirty days of sickness each year.
† This tax-free sick-pay provision was enacted under the principle of "tax equity" described more fully in Chapter 14. Prior to 1954, sick employees covered by insurance contracts received tax-free sick benefits, but those covered by company-paid plans, as distinct from insurance plans, were taxable on their sick benefits. "Equity" was achieved, in the customary

anomaly of a man staying home with, say, a sprained ankle, savoring the thought of his $100-a-week tax-free salary substitute, while his co-worker who braves it to work despite a dizzying head cold is penalized for his conscientiousness by paying taxes on all his earnings. Before the $100-a-week limit was enacted in 1954, however, the abuses were far more imaginative. According to Dan Throop Smith, insurance companies, in a cozy arrangement with a closely held business (i.e., one mostly owned by one person or a few persons), would write a cost-plus policy providing generous sick-leave privileges for the company's owner-president—the cost of the policy being, of course, tax-deductible to the company. Result: the company president would take "a year or two of sick leave before retirement" which, with its wholly tax-free benefits, "could be more useful than an elaborate pension plan."

Even with the $100 limitation, the sick-pay exclusion has apparently been a highly popular and well-used tax favor, for it currently costs the Treasury an estimated $120 million every year.

• *Pension and profit-sharing benefits, plus earnings of pension trust funds:* These, in theory, are enjoyed only on a tax-*postponed* rather than a tax-*free* basis, since they are, supposedly, taxed when received upon retirement. But in practice the tax concessions granted those over sixty-five (the double exemption plus the retirement income credit) make it probable that a substantial part of these benefits is not, in fact, taxed on receipt but escapes taxation entirely.

Even if there were no side tax concessions to the aged and pension income were fully taxed when received, there would remain the advantage of tax postponement. After all, company pension contributions, like wages, are payment for services currently rendered (they're negotiated in the same bargaining "package")—but, unlike wages, they are not currently taxed. This postponement advantage is hard to avoid, since in most pension plans it is some years before an employee gets legal ownership (called, technically, a "vested" right) in his pension. Clearly, it would be unfair to tax him on something he doesn't legally own, and it is often extremely difficult to unravel the "vested" from the "unvested" pension contributions.

In all these cases, tax-deductible dollars are used to buy retirement and other benefits for certain employees that others must

manner, by extending the zero tax rate to company as well as insured sick benefits.

use after-tax dollars to buy. This point was a particular source of irritation among self-employed business owners and professionals (doctors, lawyers and so on) who pleaded for—and in 1962 won —tax deductions on certain of their own outlays for pensions, annuities and other retirement aids. At the time of its enactment, the 1962 measure was expected to cost the Treasury about a hundred million dollars annually. Since then, its cost has risen to a quarter of a *billion* dollars a year. And President Nixon has talked of expanding even further the retirement deductions for the self-employed.

E VEN I F , by some miracle, you are neither ex-service-man nor home owner nor over sixty-five, and even if you have no fringe benefits and have never drawn any unemployment insurance, Social Security or other government benefit, you may well be enjoying a tax preference.

How? By virtue of your various tax deductions—for interest, taxes, medical expenses, charity gifts and so on.

"Not me," you say, "I'm a standard deduction man myself."

Well, if that's the case, you're simply getting the benefit of what really amounts to Congress's decision that it had set the rates too high and that they ought to be eased—for that's really all the standard deduction comes down to.

But you're barely in the majority these days. Nearly half the taxpayers now itemize their deductions—*and they cost the Treasury about $17 billion dollars every year. If we eliminated all the itemized deductions, all tax rates could be cut about 20 percent without costing the Treasury a cent.*

Considering the fact they open up a $17 billion leak in the U.S. Treasury, these personal deductions ha e enjoyed an almost total immunity from public criticism or debate. How often do you hear questions asked such as: Why give more favorable tax treatment to the repairing of a car fender than to the setting of a broken arm?* Is it right that if a millionaire and a drugstore clerk should find themselves side by side in church and each puts money in the plate, the millionaire should be out-of-pocket as little as 30 cents on the dollar but the clerk 86 cents? Or, if the millionaire's Cadillac and the clerk's Volkswagen collide on the street, is it fair for the government to pay up to 70 percent of the cost of fixing

---

* See p. 342.

the Cadillac but only 14 percent of the VW repairs? Is this how we really want to spend $17 billion of our taxpayer dollars of Federal revenue?

Now, *business* deductions are fairly easy to understand and defend: if you incur some costs in getting your income (travel, office rent and the like), it is generally accepted that those should be deductible and not taxed. But the same reasoning doesn't apply to strictly *personal* deductions, where moneymaking is not involved.

Why, then, allow them? Their purposes fall into three main categories:

• to stimulate (some might say "subsidize") a "socially worthy" activity—e.g., charitable giving or home ownership.

• to ease the blow of extraordinary, uncontrollable and unexpected expenses—e.g., unusually high medical expenses or losses from fire, collision and so on.

• to avoid the possibly confiscatory—and emotionally grating —effect of imposing a "tax on a tax," which explains the deductibility of most state and local and some Federal taxes.

Commendable ends, perhaps, but do the means suit the ends? Put a bright spotlight on the personal deductions, and defects begin to appear—serious ones.

Some of the flaws have already been suggested. If we wish, in all compassion, to cushion the financial shock of an illness, why use a device that wholly by-passes those who most need succor— those whose incomes are so low as to be nontaxable? And if incentives to worthy activity are the order of the day, why give a 70 percent encouragement to a rich man (who probably needs it least) and only a 14 percent encouragement to the least prosperous taxpayers?

The spotlight also reveals a practical shortcoming. Because ours is a self-assessment tax system, the initial claim for the deduction comes from the taxpayer, and if he abuses or misunderstands it, the burden is on the government to catch the error and to challenge it. With more than 74 million tax returns to review, that presents Uncle Sam with a major enforcement headache, compounded by the fact that taxpayers seem especially prone to mistakes on their deductions, whether accidental or deliberate. A 1948 survey disclosed that one out of three itemized-deduction returns contained major errors in the claimed deductions.

Ordinarily, Congress is very chary about, if not downright hostile to, granting open-end spending authority to the President or a Cabinet officer. Yet the lawmakers have, in effect, extended just such carte blanche authority to each taxpayer, who is permitted to decide (sometimes within limits, sometimes not) just how much revenue he wishes to drain from the Treasury for his own private purposes. Over the years, the practice has become an increasingly expensive fad among taxpayers, as the following table eloquently demonstrates:

Type of Deduction	Amount Deducted			Percent of Increase 1950–1970	Estimated 1971 Revenue Cost
	1950	1960	1970		
	(In billions)				(In billions)
Taxes	$2.0	$10.5	$32.0	1600%	$8.0
Interest	$1.5	$8.4	$23.9	1600%	$5.0
Charitable gifts	$2.3	$6.8	$12.9	560%	$3.5
Medical expenses	$1.4	$5.2	$10.6	760%	$1.9
Miscellaneous	$2.0	$4.4	$8.6	430%	$1.8
Total	$9.2	$35.3	$88.0	960%	$20.2

It was this prodigious growth in the use of these deductions, and the drain on the Treasury, that prompted the Kennedy Administration to propose a 5 percent cutback (by means of restricting a taxpayer to deductions in excess of 5 percent of his gross income). This 5 percent "floor" (which would at that time have added $2.3 billion to Treasury revenues) loosed a tidal wave of protest upon Congress and got nowhere. But perhaps it achieved its aim: it focused Congressional attention on the problem and resulted in the first cutback in personal deductions in many years ($520 million of deductions for state and local taxes were disallowed in the 1964 tax law).

HEADING THE LIST in the amount drained from the Treasury are the deductions for taxes paid—not *all* taxes, just some. State income and sales taxes and property taxes *are* deductible. Federal income and excise taxes, death taxes and local improvement taxes are not.

These deductions are allowed in part because of the supposed objections to imposing "a tax on a tax." Evidently, however, this is not a matter of inflexible moral principle; if it were, then Congress should logically allow deductions for *all* taxes paid. Surely, too, these deductions cannot be defended on the ground that the payment of taxes reduces a person's "ability to pay" (the time-honored philosophic base of the U.S. tax system)—for why do we not permit a deduction for by far the heaviest tax of all: the Federal income tax?*

If most state and local taxes stand justly accused of pressing more heavily on the poor than the rich (thus flouting "ability to pay"), their deductibility for Federal tax purposes compounds the felony. To "ability to pay" devotees, a flat sales tax (i.e., one that imposes the same rate on rich and poor alike) is heresy enough; but when the effect of Federal taxes is included in the calculation, the poor man actually ends up paying a higher rate of sales tax on what he buys than does the rich man.

Picture, for example, two cars drawn up on either side of a gasoline pump in New York City. On one side a millionaire's Rolls-Royce, on the other a day laborer's fourth-hand Chevy. On each gallon of gasoline, there is an eight-cent state tax, devoted to the care and building of public roads. Yet, after deducting this at their respective Federal top-bracket rates of 70 and 14 percent, the millionaire ends up paying, out-of-pocket, a little less than two and a half cents per gallon as his contribution to the public highways, while the day laborer pays nearly seven cents a gallon out-of-pocket.

Now suppose that when the millionaire and the day laborer pull away from the filling station, both proceed, by sheer coincidence, to a local appliance store where each shells out $150 (the day laborer gets a black-and-white TV set; the millionaire an electronic, computerized martini-mixer). City sales tax: ostensibly $6 for the millionaire, $6 for the laborer. Yet, after Federal tax deductions, the worker finds himself out-of-pocket more than $5 for the sales tax, the millionaire only $1.80—clearly a cause for hand-wringing and tooth-gnashing among "ability to pay" adherents.

Some argue that state *income* taxes, but no others, should be deductible for Federal tax purposes, on two grounds. First, without the deduction it would be possible, in the case of the 70 per-

---

* That tax was, in fact, deductible during the first four years of the American income tax, from 1913 to 1917.

cent Federal taxpayer, to have more than 100 percent of his "top dollars" taken from him by piling a state tax on top of his Federal tax. Second, in the case of so-called "consumption taxes," there is an element of choice (if you don't want to pay the tax, don't buy the item). But a state *income* tax is compulsory and therefore should be deductible.

INTEREST DEDUCTIONS are next on the list of Treasury-drainers, amounting to $23.9 billion in 1970 and costing roughly $5.0 billion in revenue.

Interest outlays for personal (as distinct from business) purposes have been deductible ever since the first Federal income tax law of 1913. But why, critics ask, should they be? After all, they say, interest is only a part of the cost of buying things—for example, on many installment purchase loans the interest payments are not even considered separately, but simply melt into the weekly or monthly installments. Why, therefore, should the interest cost be treated differently, for tax purposes, than the price of the refrigerator, TV set, or car itself?

In reply, one practical reason is often advanced: namely, that it is simply not feasible to separate, for tax purposes, the interest on *business* loans (i.e., loans made to generate profits or income) from the interest on personal loans. Let's say a man borrows $5,000 to buy some shares of stock, rather than delving into his savings account. Yet really all he did was to make $5,000 of his savings available to buy that new car he'd been eying. So what was the *real* purpose or effect of the loan: to help him buy the stocks (tax-deductible) or the car (nondeductible)? Since no one can ever be sure (the argument runs), equity and simplicity demand allowing deductions for *all* interest costs.

But there *is* a way of, in effect, separating business from personal borrowing at least in an approximate way. In many if not most cases, when a person uses the proceeds of a loan for a business purpose, he will expect this to produce income that will at least equal his cost of borrowing the money.* To the extent that's the case, interest deductions exceeding a taxpayer's investment

---

* If that's not the case, the loan makes no business sense, for the cost of borrowing the money and making the investment is greater than the return. There is one exception to that rule: where the investment is expected to result in a long-run capital gain, rather than immediate income (see next paragraph).

income can be presumed to be related to personal rather than business loans. The way to disallow nonbusiness interest deductions, then, is to limit the deductions to a person's investment income.

Such an approach was tried, half-heartedly, in the 1969 tax law, in order to counter an ingenious use of the interest deduction by the super-rich in such a way as to transform high-taxed "ordinary income" into low-taxed capital gains. The device was used to a fare-thee-well by Taxpayer C, a Treasury Department case study to whom you were introduced on page 75. Mr. C evidently borrowed about $10 million, and thereby incurred fully deductible interest costs of $587,000. He used these interest deductions to offset, and shield from taxation, $587,000 of "ordinary income" which otherwise would have been taxed at the regular rates, up to 70 percent. If he put the borrowed $10 million into a "growth stock," such as, say, Xerox, the return on his investment would come not in the form of high-taxed dividend income, but in the form of large capital gains when Xerox skyrocketed in price. Thus, the cost of borrowing to make the investment was fully deductible, saving him up to 70 cents on the dollar; but the capital gains profit was taxed (at the time) at no more than 25 cents on the dollar.

To curb such a practice, Congress, in 1969, tied interest deductions to investment income but, as usual, wrote in some highly generous loopholes. First of all, there is a flat $25,000 exemption under which anyone has a right to deduct at least $25,000 over and above his investment income—which is to say anyone has a right to borrow at least $415,000,* either for personal or for capital gains purposes, on a tax-deductible basis. But that was just for openers. In addition, half of all interest outlays in excess of investment-income-plus-$25,000 are also deductible. It all results in the most gentle and generous treatment for the super-rich, as illustrated by the case of a hypothetical Mr. Greenjeans who takes $100,000 of interest deductions but has only $20,000 of investment income. Under a formula that limited such deductions strictly to investment income, as suggested above, $80,000 of his interest outlays would be nondeductible. But under the exceptions that Congress wrote into the law, only $27,500 of the deductions

---

* Assuming a 6 percent interest rate, $25,000 of interest payments would support a loan of a little over $415,000.

is disallowed.* The remaining $72,500 is still fully available to reduce Mr. Greenjeans' taxable income.

NEXT IN ORDER OF MAGNITUDE is the deduction for gifts to charity, limited in general, since 1969, to 50 percent of a person's income,† and generally regarded as among the most unarguably worthy provisions of the tax law, clearly worth every penny of the $3½ billion it costs the Treasury annually.

Yet there are some who view the present charitable deduction with less than total enthusiasm. Even leaving aside certain fancy wrinkles in charitable giving that are available only to the rich (you'll find an example on page 71, fn.), some critics find basic fault with the charitable deduction as it is presently structured. Why, they ask, should 70 percent of a wealthy man's generosity but only 14 percent of an unmoneyed taxpayer's be financed by Uncle Sam? (See page 141.) Is it sensible to permit some $3.5 billion of public revenues to be strewn broadcast, with little sense of order or priority, for such varied causes as Allied Cat Lovers International, or the International Footprint Association Scholarship Foundation or the Genealogical Research Society of New Orleans (all actually enjoying official Internal Revenue approval to receive tax-deductible charitable gifts)? Is it right, they ask, that your neighbor be allowed to divert some of *your* tax money‡ to support a cause that might not rank very high in your schedule

---

* It works this way:

Investment interest		$100,000
Amount allowed as deductible:		
Exemption	$25,000	
Investment income	$20,000	
½ of $55,000 (i.e., amount by which the $100,000 of investment interest exceeds the $45,000 of exemption-plus-investment income	$27,500	
Total deduction allowed		$72,500
Interest deductions disallowed		$27,500

† Prior to the 1969 law, a few taxpayers were eligible to take unlimited charitable deductions. Under the phase-out of that provision enacted in 1969, those taxpayers may still be allowed to deduct more than 50 percent for charitable gifts until 1975, at which point the 50 percent ceiling will apply to everyone.

‡ After all, you have to pay higher taxes because of your neighbor's—and everyone else's—charitable deduction privilege.

of preference—be it the Loving of Cats or the Training of Footprint Scholars—and to which, in fact, you may be violently opposed (if, for example, you are allergic to cats or, perchance, to footprints)? In answer to the preceding two questions, some argue vigorously that variety is the spice of democracy as well as of life, and that privately financed good works can often achieve what government spending via centralized decisions either could not or would not.

It has come to be unquestioned dogma that without the incentive of the charitable deduction, philanthropy would wither, and museums, colleges, churches and other worthy institutions would fade or die on the vine. It was predicted, for example, that when the standard deduction was introduced in 1942 and millions stopped taking advantage of the particular itemized deductions, charities would suffer. The pessimism proved unwarranted. Moreover, even though the lure of a 20 to 50 percent allowable deduction has been dangled before the taxpayers, the attraction has only been powerful enough to induce those who itemize to give about 2.9 percent of their income to charity.* In 1970, those with "adjusted gross incomes" of more than $100,000 gave only about 7 percent of their incomes to charity. Even more striking, perhaps, is the fact that among 1,106 taxpayers with "adjusted gross incomes" of a million dollars or more in 1968, nearly 40 percent gave less than 1 percent of their income to charity, and two-thirds gave 10 percent or less. Two years later, the only available information, while less detailed, suggested that the pattern continued: more than a third of those with incomes of a million or more gave less than one percent to charity. I had thought that the prize for uncharitableness would go to an actual taxpayer, cited in a Treasury Department study, who enjoyed a total income of $1,284,718 and whose charitable gifts for the year came to just $463! But those gifts, small as they were, seemed Generosity Personified when I ran across the cases of two super-hyper-ultra-rich oilmen, mentioned in Chapters 1 and 11, who, between them, one year enjoyed income of nearly four and a half million dollars—*yet did not see fit to share so much as one dollar of it with charity!*

Some have suggested that charitable gifts should be tax-

---

* The percent of income going to charity has remained constant over the years, even while tax rates (and hence, theoretically, the tax incentive to philanthropy) have risen and fallen.

favored only to the extent they exceed, say, 2 or 3 percent of income (similar to the existing medical deduction). This is based on the philosophy that citizens might reasonably be expected to give a small share of their income to public causes without tax inducements, and that a tax concession should be reserved for *unusual* generosity—over and above the norm. This, it is argued, would substantially reduce the revenue loss from the charitable deduction yet would have comparatively little effect on total volume of philanthropy, much of which even now comes from small contributions (especially to churches) by those who use the standard deduction.

Many strongly urge, moreover, that the tax incentive should be in the form of a uniform tax *credit* (e.g., for every dollar donated, a dollar could be subtracted from your taxes, up to a reasonable limit) rather than a deduction, so that for a particular gift, those with modest means would get the same tax benefits as the well-to-do.

Still another suggestion that combines the above two notions, but with the focus on aiding the charity rather than the taxpayer, would be to have the government match the donor's contribution with a direct gift of its own to the charity in question. That is, if Citizen John Doe gives $10 (or $100 or $1,000) to the Red Cross, Uncle Sam would pay the same amount to the Red Cross. But, under such a plan, Citizen Doe would have to find his satisfaction not in a tax deduction for himself but in the knowledge that he has doubly aided the Red Cross. To reward unusual generosity or sacrifice if Citizen Doe gave more than a certain *percent* of his income to charity, the government would match his donations on more than a dollar-for-dollar basis. Such a plan, were it in effect, would put to the test the motives of American charitable donors: is it mainly true charity that they have in mind? Or is the *self*-help motivation of a tax reduction the prime mover?

THE FINAL MAJOR CATEGORY of personal deductions is that for medical expenses, introduced into the tax laws in 1942 as a means of relieving the burden of extraordinary and unexpected medical expenses. Originally, only those medical expenditures in excess of 5 percent of income could be deducted. Today, this "floor" stands at 3 percent for medical expenses, 1 percent for medicines and drugs.

The weaknesses in the medical deduction have already been suggested (page 354): the greatest help is accorded those who need it least, and none goes to those who need it the most.

Basically, the income tax system is a poor instrument for accommodating extraordinary and uncontrollable expenses of this sort. At best, its help is minimal, and it cannot place in a family's hands the dollars it needs to pay the often ruinous hospital and doctors' bills that come with major illness. Only health insurance, private or public, can do that.

WHERE WILL IT ALL END? That is the question that troubles Treasury officials when they consider the range, magnitude and cost of personal deductions now permitted by the tax laws. Moreover, the pressures are strong for *expanding* the list of tax-deductible outlays. In past years, bills have been introduced, for example, to make the cost of fallout shelters tax-deductible. And, as of 1972, no fewer than 170 Senators and Representatives had introduced bills to permit tax deductions for the expenses of sending children to college. Annual cost to the Treasury: about a billion dollars. And if college expenses become deductible, why not private school expenses? Or outlays for vocational training? Or for correspondence courses or night school college courses for inquisitive adults? (Both Presidential candidates in the 1972 campaign endorsed the concept of tax credits for private school tuition.)

As Chapter 14 demonstrates, once the procession of tax favors begins, it picks up momentum and becomes increasingly difficult to stop. Not only do inequities grow, but as a smaller and smaller part of Americans' income is subject to tax due to the larger deductions, higher and higher rates are required to raise the necessary revenues. Reverse the trend, however, start with a clean slate, as suggested in Chapter 21, and you pave the way for tax rates ranging from, say, 7 to 44 percent in place of the 14 to 70 percent rates in effect in 1973. But let the present trend continue . . . and who knows how the rates might have to rise? Or, perhaps even worse, who knows what alternative measures might be adopted to raise needed revenues—measures such as a value added tax (see Glossary) or a national sales tax, either of which would bear more heavily on the poor than on the well-to-do?

Every taxpayer, therefore, would do well to join in pondering the question, Where will it all end?

Letter from
an Indignant Taxpayer

The Honorable Wilbur Mills
Chairman
The House Ways and Means Committee
The United States House of Representatives
Washington, D.C.   20515

The Honorable Russell B. Long
Chairman
The Senate Finance Committee
The United States Senate
Washington, D.C.   20510

Dear Congressman Mills and Senator Long:*

I am the overworked, underpaid, long-suffering and deeply exploited secretary to Philip M. Stern, the author of this book. He pays me $150 a week, which comes to $7,800 a year, and last year I paid $1057.50 in Federal income taxes (which I figure—with the aid of my boss's handy calculator—means I paid nearly 14 cents out of every dollar to Uncle Sam) .†

---

* This letter was actually sent to Messrs. Mills and Long on August 9, 1972, inviting them to make whatever comment they would like to see included in this book. Neither chose to comment.

† See Notes and Sources.

372

In the course of helping him with this book, I have learned one hell of a lot I hadn't known about the tax law, and since you two, as chairmen of the tax-writing committees of the Congress, play a key role in deciding what that law should be, I have a lot of questions for you. For instance:

Why do you make me pay 14 percent taxes while you let a huge company like U.S. Steel or Alcoa pay none at all—even while they're making huge profits and paying enormous dividends to their shareholders?

Why do you make me pay 14 percent taxes while you let three families get dividends *averaging* nearly two and a half million dollars each—and yet pay no tax?

Why do you make me pay 14 percent taxes while you let billionaires like H. L. Hunt and Jean Paul Getty get away with paying just a tiny fraction of their huge incomes in taxes?

In short, why don't you give "average" taxpayers like me the same tender and gentle treatment you give rich people like Hunt and Getty and big corporations like U.S. Steel?

Since I started pounding my fingers to the bone on the various chapters of this book, I've learned about lots of ways the tax law discriminates against people like me and in favor of the Rich and Powerful.

Take, for instance, the question of tax exemptions. I've found out, in working on this book, that for the rich, the word "exemptions" can mean a great many things; but down in my tax bracket, it means just one thing: the personal exemption. I don't need to tell you that it's *supposedly* meant to give every taxpayer enough untaxed income to get by on. But I wonder whether you people in Congress really look at it that way. If you did, you wouldn't have let it stay at just $600 for more than two decades (from 1948 to 1969) while the cost of living was going up by half. By rights, just to keep up with the cost of living you should have raised it to $900.

Yet when, in 1969, some Congressmen proposed raising it to just $800, that was too much for you. $750 was all you'd go.

What I want to know is this:

Why, that year, wouldn't you give people like me a lousy *eight-hundred*-dollar exemption when you gave the richest people in the country a *fifty-thousand*-dollar exemption from a capital gains increase you passed?

Why wouldn't you give "average" taxpayers like me an eight-hundred-dollar exemption when you were perfectly willing to give the millionaires a *thirty-thousand*-dollar exemption from the "minimum tax" that was supposed to stop them from paying zero taxes?

You didn't see anything wrong in giving a twenty-five-thousand-dollar exemption to "tax farmers" (the rich doctors and lawyers and stockbrokers who use farms just as "tax shelters")—yet you wouldn't give the average person like me a measly $800 exemption. Why?

And can you imagine how I felt when I found out that you let rich couples give $6,000 every year, to as many people as they like, without paying any gift tax? What kind of an exemption is that? I nearly flipped when I found out the *reason* your predecessors gave for putting the gift-tax exemption that high: so as not to tax "wedding and Christmas gifts"! It makes me wonder who you people have in mind when you pass tax laws like that. The Rockefellers and the Vanderbilts, maybe. But certainly not people like me. I should live so long as to *get*, much less *give* $6,000 wedding and Christmas presents!

For instance, in that same year you turned down the $800 exemption for people like me, you gave a hefty tax cut to rich lawyers and doctors and corporate executives by lowering the top rate on salary income from 70 to 50 percent. I guess the people you were taking pity on were people like the head of ITT, Harold Geneen, and the former head of General Motors, James Roche, both of whom have made more than *eight hundred thousand dollars a year* in salary and bonus. Your display of pity for gentlemen like that, I might add, meant shifting a $100 million tax burden off the shoulders of the Roches and the Geneens and onto the shoulders of us average taxpayers.

But what really got me was the reason you gave for lowering the taxes of the Geneens and the Roches. You said you thought that with lower tax rates, all those rich people wouldn't spend so much time and energy looking for the loopholes and thinking up fancy "shelter" deals to escape paying taxes. But it seems to me there was a much simpler—or at any rate a much *fairer*—way of solving that problem: namely, close up all the loopholes, so there wouldn't *be* any escape hatches to look for.

If you did that, those rich people would be more nearly in the same boat as I am every spring, when I make out my tax return, because you've got people like me pretty well boxed in. What have I got going for me? I take my $750 exemption and my $1,300 standard deduction (it isn't worthwhile for me to itemize my deductions), I figure up my tax, and that's it. No loopholes (to amount to anything). No "shelters." No maneuvering room. Like I say, I'm boxed in.

So are millions of others like me. The government figures prove it. Down in my lowly tax bracket, about 70 percent of us pay just about the same portion of our incomes in taxes—within 5 percent of one another.

But up where the Rockefellers and the Vanderbilts live, a lot of people seem to be able to write their own ticket. Some of them pay no taxes at all. Like the oil investors with their so-called "intangible" deductions. I notice you were careful to make a special exception for *them* when you passed the so-called "mini-mum tax," so they can go on paying zero taxes. So you box us "average" taxpayers in, but you let rich people manipulate the tax system to their own liking.

It's not just that there's so little I can do about the taxes I pay; worse still, I don't even get to *see* or *touch* my tax money. You've got it so my boss holds it back from my pay check and sends it directly to the government. You insist on that rule for the wages and salaries that people like me *earn* (supposedly to make sure I pay my taxes), but you've been equally insistent on keeping in the law different rules for people who own corporate stock and who get dividends, or for people who can buy bonds and get interest. No tax withholding for them—even though they don't report about six billion dollars of their dividends and interest on their tax returns every year. I'm sure you know that costs the Treasury about a billion dollars a year. That's a billion dollars we wage earners have to make up in taxes. And please. Spare me the routine about all the "widows and orphans" who depend on their dividends and interest to make ends meet. You and I both know that stocks and bonds are owned mainly by the rich. (I just hap-pen to know that the figures are laid out on pages 62 and 89.)

Not only do you spare the rich the "pay-as-you-go" withholding rules; you also let them play games with their tax money, by investing in things like the "Mexican vegetable roll-over" and other gimmicks that let them postpone their taxes, sometimes for years. I hadn't known, before I read and typed Chapter 8, that when rich people and big corporations can delay their taxes and invest the tax money, that amounts to an interest-free loan, paid for by people like me—with the taxes you insist on whisking away from us before we even see them.

And I've noticed that you people in Congress are very up-tight about giving "welfare" to poor people (at one point, Senator Long, you even suggested that some people be *fingerprinted** in order to get their welfare). You get especially nervous about welfare going to poor people who don't *work* for it. For instance, Senator Long, you once talked about the "filthy neighborhoods" in which many poor people live, and you said that "a minimum for people on welfare ought to be that they be required to do at least some public service work" to clean up those neighborhoods.

But you don't seem to have any hesitation in handing out billions of "tax welfare" to the giant corporations and to the rich without asking that they lift a finger in order to get their "tax welfare." For instance, take the billions you handed to companies like General Motors and IBM with the investment credit. They get that even if they just do "business as usual," without investing a dime more than they would have anyway. And what about the billions of capital gains "tax welfare" you hand out to rich investors who make a killing when the price of their stock soars— not because of any work *they* did, but because of the work *others* did to make the company and its stock prosper. Or even if the stock shot up because of a stock market boom or by sheer good luck—you give them the "tax welfare" anyway. And all those banks and super-rich people who buy tax-free state and local bonds—what work do *they* have to do to get their tax bonanzas? Answer: none. And yet you want poor people to clean up their "filthy" neighborhoods—or even get fingerprinted—to get their welfare pittances. Do I detect a hint of a double standard?

There seems to be a dual standard, too, when it comes to imposing higher taxes. For the Rich and Powerful, you seem to take great pains to cushion the blow. For instance, before 1969, you were allowing the commercial banks to deduct *twelve times* too much for their so-called "bad debt" reserves—which was saving the banks at least a quarter of a billion dollars a year. When

---

* See Notes and Sources.

you finally decided, in 1969, that that particular form of "tax welfare" should end, you gave the banks *seventeen years* to get used to taking the same kind of deductions that other businesses are allowed. Seventeen years! I wish I were a bank.

By contrast, though, my parents have told me about the time in 1950 (I'm too young to remember this) when the Korean War broke out and you Congressmen voted an across-the-board tax increase—with heavier increases for the poor than for the rich. You didn't give us "average" taxpayers any seventeen years to adjust to that blow. Zap—one *week* after the President signed that tax increase into law, the tax increase took effect. No one bothered to ask us whether that would disrupt our plans (you're always worrying about disrupting businessmen's plans), or whether that was going to interfere with our buying a new home or a car we'd counted on or anything like that. You just went ahead and zapped us with the tax.

But your nervousness about disrupting business plans seems to apply only to *closing* loopholes, not to opening them. As I say, when you closed up that bad-debt loophole, you gave the banks a seventeen year "transition period." But when it came to handing out three and a half billion dollars of "tax welfare" to corporations through so-called "ADR," there was no "phase-in," no "transition period." No, sir. Here, General Motors; here, IBM—here's your billions, right now. No need to wait.

What it looks like to me is that when you deal with the Rich and Powerful, you open the loopholes with a bang, but close them (if at all) with a whimper.

Everybody, I suppose, has his own pet hate among the things the government spends our tax dollars on. For a lot of people who have worked hard for every cent they ever made, it gives them a knot in their stomach to think that their tax dollars are being spent to support people on welfare, whether they work or not. As for me, it makes me sick when I think that my money is buying napalm and fragmentation bombs that our planes drop on innocent Asian women and children who never did me or anyone else a bit of harm. All of us, I guess, would dearly love to withhold the taxes that support the programs we hate; we'd like to refuse to pay those taxes and divert them to a cause that suits us (like, maybe, building hospitals to heal those burned children in Vietnam).

But we "average taxpayers" don't really have that privilege. If we refuse to pay a part of our taxes, the law you've written might get us thrown into jail.

But you've given that privilege to the rich. A few years ago, John D. Rockefeller, III, told Congress how he could, if he chose, divert *all* of his taxes to his favorite charities. (As it happened, he told Congress, he paid 5 to 10 percent of his income in taxes (*less than I do, you'll note*)—but only because he *chose* to; not because he *had* to). Since then, you've cut back on that particular privilege: in a few years, John D. and I will only be allowed to divert *half* our income from Uncle Sam to charity. But of course Mr. Rockefeller can *afford* to part with half his income; I can't. To say that we're equal is like saying that rich and poor alike are welcome to sleep under bridges when it rains.

Mind you, it's not that John D. isn't a public-spirited man; I understand he does some wonderful things with his philanthropy. But I think I'm pretty public-spirited, too. Shouldn't I have the same choice as Mr. Rockefeller?

I mentioned before your lowering the top tax rate on salaries from 70 to 50 percent. I admit that 70 percent is a steep tax, but it's a hell of a lot steeper for a welfare mother than it is for the head of General Motors or ITT. Yet you and your colleagues don't seem to mind socking that kind of rate—and even higher— on the poorest and neediest people in this country.

That high tax rate for the poor isn't in the tax law. It's in the welfare law—the one for families with dependent children— which your committees pass on, just as they pass on the tax laws. And that law says that for every dollar a welfare mother *earns,* over and above a certain amount, *she loses 67 cents from her welfare allowance.* So she earns a dollar and sacrifices 67 cents of it to the government. Maybe *you* can see a difference between that and a 67 percent tax rate; I must say, I can't.

Actually, the "tax rates" on the poor can go even higher than that. If a welfare mother is also eligible for food stamps, for every dollar she earns she is likely to have to pay 30 cents more for the food stamps. So that puts her in a 97 percent bracket! That's higher than the 70 percent Nelson Rockefeller might pay on his dividend income, and just about twice as high as the top rate you permit James Roche and Harold Geneen to pay on their huge salaries. It is also twice as high as the 48 percent tax rate that applies to General Motors or ITT or IBM or any of the other corporate giants.

I'd like to hear you explain the justice of *that* to a welfare mother. Or to me.

One of the reasons I pay as much tax as I do is that I happen to be single. I always knew that we unmarried people got the short end of the tax deal, but when I read that chapter "Your Wife May Be Worth a Million" I really saw red! I never knew before that the tax break for married people was such a sop to *rich* married folk—and that it does nothing for the genuinely impoverished people who really *need* a break. I figured it out: a movie star like Raquel Welch with something like twenty-five times my income would get a tax break of something over $12,000 a year. As for me, in my tax bracket, I'd save about $105—about one one-hundredth as much as Raquel. A hundred and five dollars a year comes to two miserable dollars a week.

There have been times, Mr. Mills and Senator Long, when there has been something special that I've wanted to buy and I've done some moonlighting to pay for it. But usually that pushes me into a higher tax bracket, so I think twice before I do it. A lot of my friends' wives work to help make ends meet—but of course that makes them pay more to Uncle Sam, too.

I can understand that in a way (even though I don't enjoy it). I think it's right that taxes ought to be based on "ability to pay," and as people's incomes get bigger they *are* able to pay more, because they've got more left after taxes.

What I want to know is: if that principle is OK for people like me, why don't you people who write the tax laws apply it across the board—to *all* taxpayers? Why, when a Whitney or a Vanderbilt or a Rockefeller gets $100,000 or a million dollars or *ten* million dollars in "capital gains," does his tax rate stay the same? Why do you let those people ignore half of all their capital gains when they make out their tax returns—as if the money didn't exist? For that matter, why do you let the super-rich people and the banks who buy up all the state and local bonds pretend the interest income doesn't exist, so they don't even have to report it on their tax returns? You make people like me report every penny of income, but in 1969 you were so solicitous of those rich bond-holders you wouldn't even make them declare their tax-free bond interest on their tax returns.

And if you insist that *my* tax rate go up as I earn more money, why don't you apply the same rule to corporations? Why do General Motors (with its nearly three-and-a-half-billion-dollar profit) and ITT and IBM have the same tax rate as a chain of hardware stores in a small town? And why does that tax rate stay the same whether they make a million or a billion dollars? Mine doesn't. Why should General Motors'?

Well, Mr. Mills and Senator Long, I've gotten a lot off my chest, and I've meant every word I've said.

I like to think I'm a good citizen. I've always made out my tax return as honestly as I knew how, and I've always turned it in promptly. Naturally, I've never exactly enjoyed paying my taxes—but I never minded it all that much, either, because I had the feeling that everybody else was in the same boat. But working on this book has taught me otherwise. It's taught me that often you Congressmen and Senators who write the tax laws (and I know you're not the only two) have one set of rules for us "average" taxpayers, and another for the rich and for the big corporations. And it makes me see red when I read about Internal Revenue zeroing in on some poor guy because he got in a bind and couldn't pay his taxes when I know you Senators and Congressmen are letting rich people and corporations get away with a thousand times as much—all perfectly legally—through the loopholes.

From where I look—from far nearer the bottom than the top of the heap—the tax laws surely don't look fair, or even-handed.

What would be wrong with scrapping the existing tax law and starting over—taxing "incomes, from whatever source derived" (just like the Sixteenth Amendment says), on a uniform basis for everybody?

That way, I wouldn't be so mad, in April, when I sit down, without the help of any tax lawyer or accountant, and without the hope of finding any special "shelters" or loopholes, and make out my Form 1040.

Respectfully but indignantly yours,
Irene Saunders

Why the Wealthy Few
Win Out
over the Un-Rich Many

Fact: There are roughly 60 million American taxpayers who would benefit if the personal exemption were raised to $800.

Fact: There are only about 30,000 American taxpayers who earn enough to benefit from lowering the top-bracket rates on salary income.

Fact: The former group outnumbers the latter group by *two thousand to one.*

Mystery: Why, in 1969, did the Congress of the United States —elected by the people of what is *supposed* to be a one-man/ one-vote democracy—so stubbornly deny the 60 million and, with equal stubbornness, insist on satisfying the 30,000?

Fact: Of the 75 million taxpayers in the United States in 1970, only 1 in 10 had *any* income in the form of capital gains profits. That is, those who got *no* capital gains profits outnumbered those who got *some* by 10 to 1.

Fact: Of the 75 million taxpayers, only 1 in 100 got any substantial amount of capital gains income.* That is, those who got little or no capital gains outnumbered those who got a significant amount by *100 to 1.*

Mystery: Why does the Congress of the United States insist on taxing unearned capital gains only half as severely as hard-earned wage and salary income?

---

* More than $1,500 for the year.

Greater mystery: Why do virtually no candidates for the Congress of the United States—campaigning in a purportedly one-man/one-vote democracy—openly call for repealing this tax preference that is substantially denied to 99 voters out of 100?

Throughout this book—especially in Chapter 19—you've read one example after another in which the tax laws favor the wealthy few over the un-moneyed many. On the basis of sheer numbers of people affected, that makes no sense. Clearly, forces other than one-man/one-vote democracy are at work in shaping the U.S. tax laws.

The most potent such force—the undemocratic way American election campaigns are financed—gives the affluent few a disproportionate voice in the selection and election of the Congressmen and Senators who vote the tax laws. So, even before the legislators are sworn in, the deck is stacked in favor of the wealthy. Then other antidemocratic forces come into play: the rigid control of the writing of the tax laws by two tightly controlled Congressional committees, on which reform-minded legislators are carefully kept to a feeble minority; the unusual secrecy that shields the work of those committees from public scrutiny; and the grotesque complexity of the tax laws themselves, which renders the average legislator (and the general public) helpless and places everyone at the mercy of a few experts.

That's the thumbnail sketch; obviously, it needs to be filled in.

IN MY VIEW, the main reason that the tax laws favor the rich is the manner in which political campaigns are financed. It is the antithesis of one man/one vote. First, the bulk of political donations comes from the wealthy. Ninety percent of such contributions come from just one percent of the population, according to *Time* magazine. Second, and more important in its effect on the tax laws, every candidate for the United States Senate and virtually everyone who runs for the House of Representatives is dependent on contributions from the rich. He or she simply cannot finance an election without them. If campaign costs continue to escalate as they have been, that dependence will become more and more acute. The willingness of the wealthy to contribute will be an increasingly important factor in the selection* as well as the election of those who vote the tax laws.

---

* In political fund-raising circles there is increasing reference to the "cocktail party primary," in which a little-known aspirant to Congress journeys to New York or California to try to persuade wealthy political

Both major parties receive huge sums from rich donors. In 1968, they received the following:

	Republicans	*Democrats*
Officers and directors of the 25 largest corporations	$699,000	$132,000
Members of 12 prominent families	$2,581,000	$150,000
The Rockefellers	$1,701,000	$13,500
The Mellons	$279,000	$17,000
The Pews	$208,000	—
Officers and directors of the American Petroleum Institute	$429,000	$31,000
Individuals with wealth of $150 million or more	$1,021,000	$106,000
Bankers*	$478,261	$14,493

* Officers and directors of twelve banks having the largest holdings of tax-exempt bonds.

While the above figures are heavily weighted toward Republicans, the unhappy fact is that both parties depend greatly on rich givers. According to one study, "at least half, and perhaps more, of [Hubert] Humphrey's general election campaign expenses [in the 1968 Presidential campaign] were paid for through contributions and loans from about 50 individuals . . . reports filed with the Clerk of the House [of Representatives] show itemized loans totalling $3,125,000 from 43 persons." Of these, $1,040,000 came from persons whose business is listed as "real estate"; $391,000 from persons in "investment banking"; $222,000 from persons in "oil"; and $200,000 from persons in "transportation" industries.

In the six Presidential elections from 1948 through 1968, an average of three-fifths of all contributions from individuals to the Democratic and Republican parties came from contributors of $500 or more. What percent of American families have enough income so that they can afford to make a political contribution of $500?

---

givers, almost invariably gathered at the cocktail hour, that his effort to "knock off" Congressman X or Senator Y is worthy of financial support. Where the cocktail party proves a dismal failure, many such hopefuls have abandoned the race even before entering it—screened out of politics, in effect, by a handful of wealthy people for whom the hors d'oeuvre and cocktails were more appealing than the candidate and his program.

This dependence on wealthy contributors is even more acute on the level of Senatorial and Congressional races, especially as the cost of television boosts the expenses of mounting a political campaign. For example, according to the Washington *Post,* in the 1970 Tennessee Senatorial race the Democratic candidate, Albert Gore, raised and collected more than $500,000—more than five times what he had spent in his prior two election campaigns; but his successful opponent spent $1 million to $1,250,000—at least three times what any Republican candidate had spent in a Tennessee Senate race.

The most dramatic example both of soaring costs and of dependence on "interested" givers is the North Dakota Senate contest of 1970, between Republican Thomas Kleppe and Democrat Quentin Burdick—the same two who had opposed each other six years earlier. Burdick's 1970 spending was twice what he had spent in 1964; Kleppe's was *five* times greater. More important, according to the Washington *Post, from 85 to 90 percent of money spent by both candidates came from outside North Dakota.* The *Post* reported that Burdick's out-of-state money came mainly from "liberal anti-war groups and labor unions," and that "Kleppe's entire campaign was planned, financed and directed from Washington, D.C., by a team of professionals assembled by the White House." According to the *Post's* report:

Throughout the campaign the postman walked into [the] Bismarck law office [of Kleppe's finance chairman, Harold Anderson] with letters containing checks from wealthy individuals all over the country. Thirteen of the letters contained $5,000 campaign gifts and another 50 letters brought gifts of from $1,000 to $4,000. When money ran short, Anderson said he would talk to Republican officials in Washington and more checks would soon arrive. In addition, Kleppe received $30,000 from the Republican National Committee's campaign fund and $35,000 from various organized business and medical groups.

The fact that the better-heeled candidate doesn't always win (Kleppe lost his 1970 Senatorial race) is beside the point. The lesson of the North Dakota experience is that as one side raises the financial "ante," he obliges his opponent to do likewise, thus increasing the dependence of *both* candidates on "interested" givers,* mostly rich ones.

Campaign costs on the Congressional District level are sky-rocketing as well. Several of the 1972 Congressional *primary* campaigns had budgets of $125,000 or more. Where is a Congressional candidate to raise sums of that magnitude *every two years* without being heavily dependent on wealthy donors? And if he cannot do so, what is the probability of his advocating a tax policy likely to offend people he can't do without? Does that help explain why almost no candidate for Congress has openly espoused ending the preferential tax treatment of capital gains—a preference virtually denied to ninety-nine out of every hundred voters.

An incident from the 1970 Senatorial campaign in Connecticut suggests that this is more than a rhetorical question. The Democratic candidate, Joseph Duffey, proposed a tax-reform "package" in which he inserted, almost casually, a proposal to tax capital gains on the same basis as earned income. He was stunned by the reaction. The first result was the cancellation of a businessmen's fund-raising lunch on his behalf in New York City. Then some of his liberal-minded but wealthy financial backers began calling him, saying, in effect, "Good God, Joe, what are you trying to do to us?" This was not a question to bring joy to the ear of a candidate faced with raising $1,000,000 to run for the United States Senate.

How are campaign contributions translated into specific provisions of the tax law? Are the $156,000 of donations by officers of Litton Industries in 1968 related to the provision in a tax law a year later specially tailored for Litton executives and no others?† Is there a connection between the $208,000 donated in 1968 to Republican causes by members of the Pew family and the "pressure from members of the White House staff" exerted on behalf of a bill for the Pew Foundation, according to the New York *Times*?

Members of the Harvey family have been generous contributors to the Democratic party and its candidates, and the Harvey Alumi-

---

* The out-of-state "liberal anti-war groups and labor unions" who sent money to Democrat Burdick were just as "interested" givers—i.e., had just as much of an ax to grind and just as much hope or expectation that they would carry special weight with Burdick—as the "wealthy individuals" who contributed to Republican Kleppe.

† See p. 39.

num Company "man in Washington," besides giving $10,000 of company money to Senate aide Bobby Baker, once served as Treasurer to the Democratic Senatorial Campaign Committee. Did that help Harvey Aluminum to achieve the passage of a specially tailored $2 million tax amendment in 1966?

It is hazardous to speculate whether there is any cause-and-effect connection between campaign contributions and provisions that benefit one company or one foundation. There is more solid evidence for such speculation, however, when it comes to tax favors granted entire industries. The oil industry is the most notable example, for Congressional solicitude for that industry is apparent not merely in the percentage depletion provisions but almost everywhere that taxes and oil come into confrontation.* Surely the industry has generated no political enmity with

• the $429,000 in 1968 contributions to Republicans by members of the American Petroleum Institute;

• the $66,000 contributed by officers of the Atlantic Richfield Oil Company;

• the donations totaling $324,000 by four wealthy individuals associated with the oil industry ($105,000 by Max Fisher of Detroit, $95,000 by Henry Salvatore of Los Angeles, $62,000 by J. Howard Pew of Philadelphia and $62,000 by the late Richard K. Mellon of Pittsburgh).

But such conspicuous on-the-record contributions are only a small part of the story. Most oil money flows much more quietly and effectively, and reaches liberal Democrats as well as conservative Republicans. According to Richard Harris, writing in the *New Yorker* in the summer of 1971, oil money that had in the past been channeled through Finance Committee Chairman Russell Long was, instead, funneled through Senator Robert C. Byrd of West Virginia, who was contemplating challenging Edward Kennedy for the post of Senate Democratic whip. Kennedy was one of the first anti-depletion Senators to occupy a position of Senate leadership, and his defeat would certainly be welcome to the industry. According to Harris, "Throughout the fall campaign, Byrd carefully parceled out [oil] money to selected [Senate]

---

* For example, the provisions of the laws governing taxation of foreign-source income that are helpful to the Arabian-American Oil Company (p. 283), and to oil and mining companies in making good use of the "minimum distribution" escape hatch (p. 270).

colleagues who were up for re-election and then when the time came to challenge Kennedy, the following winter, Byrd called in his I.O.U.'s from those he had helped." After Byrd's defeat of Kennedy, Harris says, a legislative liaison man for the American Petroleum Institute, "the Washington spigot man for oil money, telephoned . . . [Senators] Harrison A. Williams, Jr. of New Jersey, and Gale W. McGee of Wyoming—to thank them for voting for Byrd. Both men ran for re-election last fall, both were in deep trouble, and both won." Senator Williams is generally regarded as a solid liberal Democrat, and an unlikely ally of the oil industry.

It is in mid-campaign that hard-pressed candidates are most susceptible to financial blandishments, for it is at this juncture (rightly or wrongly) that they smell victory if only they can get the needed funds. One mid-October, the media representative for several Democratic candidates in Western states received an offer of substantial contributions to any of the Democrats who would commit themselves to support the oil depletion allowance. Most of them resisted the temptation, but one or two succumbed.

It is rare that a contributor asks for such a specific quid pro quo. What most are after, and almost all receive, is assurance of *access* to the right Congressman or Senator at the right time. That (plus the ability to hire a skilled and highly paid Washington lobbyist* who knows just whom to approach, when and how) is an immense advantage that most citizens do not enjoy. Especially at the height of Congressional consideration of a major tax bill, the lobbyists are lined up several deep to see key Senators. Obviously all cannot be received. Who will be favored? Who cold-shouldered? It is at this moment that the political donor is likely to take a crucial step forward over the others—crucial because once the company vice-president or lobbyist has the legislator's ear, a plausible, if not a persuasive case can be developed for almost any tax provision (given the complexities of the law); crucial, too, because any but the most ungrateful Senator or Congressman will be disposed to listen with a receptive ear, wanting to accommodate if only he can be given reason

---

* These lobbying fees are, of course, tax-deductible to the corporations and rich persons who pay them. As a result, if the lobbyist succeeds in raiding the Treasury on behalf of his client, the rest of the taxpayers must not only pay more to make up for the lost revenue; they are also obliged to foot part of the bill for inflicting this pain upon themselves.

to. Even former Senator Paul Douglas—one of the most vigorously independent of Senators—once observed that he could not avoid "having a warm feeling in my heart" for those who had been generous to his campaign.

Finance Committee Chairman Long himself once took a hardheaded approach to the matter of campaign contributions in a Senate speech. "It would be my guess," he said, "that about ninety-five percent of campaign funds at the Congressional level are derived from businessmen . . . the government pays out many billions of dollars"—in various kinds of unwarranted benefits, including "all sorts of tax favoritism." The Senator went on to observe that "investments in this area can be viewed as monetary bread cast upon the water, to be returned a thousandfold." If that is true, then as the campaign costs mount and with them the dependence of candidates on "interested" contributors, there will be no dearth of such "interested" donors to fill the breach, expecting that "thousandfold" return on their investment.

It is the universality of this dependence that distorts the one-man/one-vote principle. Even the most "public-interest-minded" are not immune. One Washingtonian tells of receiving a telephone report on a financial planning meeting on behalf of a liberal Democratic member of the Senate Commerce Committee. "Oh, it went just fine—so-and-so agreed to take the airline industry and so-and-so said he'd approach the truckers and so-and-so will talk to the railroads. . . ."

As long as that is the way political money is raised, what hope is there for a one-man/one-vote tax system?

THE FACT that the rich tend to be disproportionately represented in the election of Senators and Congressmen does not mean a total absence of tax-reform-minded legislators. There are some, but by and large they find themselves on the outside trying vainly to look in on the tightly knit and highly exclusive Congressional Tax Establishment, consisting mainly of the two tax-writing Congressional committees: the House Ways and Means Committee and the Senate Finance Committee.

While Congress refers all legislative matters to specialized committees for study and approval and tends to defer to their recommendations, almost no other committees have such iron influence as the two tax committees. In the House of Representatives, this is assured by the almost invariable rule adopted when the full House considers a tax measure, under which no changes to the Ways and Means bill may be suggested by "outsiders," i.e., non-Committee members. That is, the only choice open to a non-member of Ways and Means is to vote "yes" or "no" on the Committee's recommended bill, which may contain several hundred pages and several thousand individual provisions. While the Senate has no rule of comparable rigidity, and "outsiders" have the privilege of offering amendments during Senate debate, only rarely does the Senate adopt such a change if the Finance Committee Chairman opposes it.

The tight committee control over tax legislation vastly simplifies life for opponents of loophole-closing as well as those seeking special tax favors, for it permits them to concentrate on a limited target. If they can win the favor of a few "swing" votes on Ways and Means, for example, they can, by and large, ignore the other 400-plus members of the House. The tenacity exhibited by the oil depletion allowance (which has suffered only one major change in forty-five years) is a case in point. When Congress is controlled by the Democrats (as it generally has been in recent decades), Ways and Means has fifteen Democrats and ten Republicans.* Over the years, it was generally assumed that depletion advocates could count on most, if not all, of the ten Republican votes, so that just a few Democratic votes were needed to carry the day. Since the Democratic leadership of the House generally decides who should fill Ways and Means vacancies, and since historically depletion states have been well represented in the House leadership,† the oil industry had little reason to be concerned.

One candidate for Ways and Means was "approached" (he declined to say by whom) for a commitment in favor of oil depletion and was told that all the other contestants for the seat had declared themselves pro-depletion, just as all prior-year candidates had. "If that's true," he replied, "the oil people certainly don't need *my* vote." He refused to commit himself one way or

---

* Ways and Means is one of three House committees that maintain a fixed party ratio—15–10 in the case of Ways and Means—no matter what the party line-up is in the House as a whole.

† For years, Texas's Sam Rayburn *was* the leadership; as of 1972, both the Speaker, Oklahoma's Carl Albert, and the floor leader, Louisiana's Hale Boggs (who was also a high-ranking member of Ways and Means), were from oil-rich states.

the other and was denied the Democratic leadership blessing he had hoped to receive

Former Congressional aide V. O. French states that lobbyists also play a role in shaping the membership to Ways and Means, plumping for those candidates they think will be receptive to them at a later date, and trying to prevent reform-minded Congressmen from winning the treasured seats. According to French, "One good reason why Congressman Don Fraser [a liberal Democrat from Minnesota] didn't get on Ways and Means was [lobbyists'] doubt about his solicitude for the special tax amendments."

Reform-minded Senators have had similar difficulty gaining membership on Senate Finance, which has been variously called "the citadel of conservatism" and the "happy hunting ground" for tax pressure groups. At times, such as the early Fifties, political "liberals" have had no representation on the Committee; at best, they have been an impotent and frustrated minority. This is not entirely accidental: two reformist windmill tilters, former Senators Albert Gore of Tennessee and Paul Douglas of Illinois, have both said they had great difficulty gaining their Finance Committee posts. According to Robert Engler, in *The Politics of Oil,* at one point in 1955 a Committee vacancy thought sure to go to Douglas (a leading critic of the depletion allowance) was preempted by Majority Leader Lyndon Johnson, who, later in the session, handed on the seat to former Vice-president Alben Barkley, again stymieing Douglas. It was only on Barkley's death that Douglas finally won his Finance Committee seat.

V. O. French has also noted that the usually rigid Senatorial adherence to seniority becomes unusually flexible when it comes to Finance Committee assignments. French reports that when liberal Montana Senator Lee Metcalf unexpectedly resigned from the Committee, within three hours a conservative quorum of the Democratic Steering Committee met and replaced Metcalf with Virginia's Harry Byrd, a comparative newcomer to the Senate.

Wisconsin's Senator Proxmire says he applied for the Finance Committee as soon as he got to the Senate in 1957, but found himself continually passed over in favor of Senators whose requests were submitted far later than his, such as McCarthy of Minnesota and Fulbright of Arkansas. Proxmire, although a sixteen-year veteran in the Senate, has never been named to Finance; yet Texas's Lloyd Bentsen very nearly won a bid for the Finance Com-

mittee after he had been in the Senate for just a matter of weeks
(he reportedly lost by only one vote). Thus, says French, it is no
accident that the voting records of members of the Finance Committee get an average rating of only 38.9 percent by the liberal
organization Americans for Democratic Action, in sharp contrast
to the average 71.7 percent ADA rating for members of the Senate
Labor Committee, giving the liberals what amounts to "overkill"·
voting strength on the Labor Committee while holding them to a
distinct minority on Finance.

THERE IS A THIRD ELEMENT in the Congres-
sional Tax Establishment: the House-Senate "conference committees" that are appointed to reconcile the differences between the
House and Senate versions of any given measure. These conference
committees play an extraordinarily important role in the legislative
process, for it is they who determine the final complexion of the
law, they who decide whether this or that provision survives or
dies. Woodrow Wilson, in fact, once observed that there are
three houses of Congress: the House, the Senate and the conference
committees.

By Congressional custom, when a tax bill is involved, the conference committee members are almost invariably drawn from
Ways and Means and Finance, so once again there is no danger
of interference from "outsiders." Even the selection of committee
members to sit on the conferences is not a random one. The Senate
conferees, for example, are, by custom, appointed on the recommendation of the Chairman of the Finance Committee and some,
such as the populist-minded former Senator Fred Harris of Oklahoma, have felt they do not properly reflect the philosophical
make-up of the Senate as a whole. On some occasions, loophole-
closing amendments have been voted by the full Senate, only to
perish at the hands of the conference committee. Senate liberals
darkly suspect conservative conferees of yielding too easily in
bargaining with the House. For example, in 1959, the Senate
repealed a major tax preference for corporate shareholders. When
that action failed to survive the House-Senate conference, even
though it had enjoyed a 47–31 Senate majority, Senator Douglas
was prompted to liken the fate of such loophole-closing actions
"to the fate of the two young princes of England who put their
trust in Richard the Third, who went into the Tower of London

under very good promises but were strangled by Richard the Third and never emerged from the Tower." Similarly, former Senator Albert Gore has told of how, in 1969, the Senate as a whole had voted to increase the personal exemption to $800, again with a substantial voting margin of 58 to 37. Yet, when the crunch came in the House-Senate conference, his Senate colleagues on the conference committee—even some who had voted for the $800 exemption during the Senate debate—would not side with him in insisting on the higher figure, and so the Senate's will was overridden and a $750 exemption prevailed.

THE FREEDOM of the tax-writing committees to enact special favors for this company or that industry is greatly enhanced by the ultra-secrecy with which they surround themselves once they get down to the business of actually drafting and approving tax measures. It is a secrecy unusual even in Congress. Not only are press and public barred from their bill-writing sessions; so are Senators' and Congressmen's personal staff members (Senate Finance is one of the few Senate committees to impose such a stringent rule). This leaves the legislators free to say, in closed session, that Provision X is for the Mobil Oil Company and its Joliet, Illinois, refinery (and therefore dear to Illinois Senator Everett Dirksen's heart); and that one is for Washington hostess Gwen Cafritz and her foundation. According to one Finance Committee member, the atmosphere is one of comradely mutual helpfulness, in which the tendency of even the reform-minded Committee member is to say, "Well, hell, this one will help out old Ev Dirksen, and what the hell, it will only cost a few million." Former Senator Fred Harris, who served on Senate Finance, is convinced that most of the privately tailored provisions would never be proposed if bill-drafting took place in *full public view,* and has proposed opening the Committee's now-secret sessions to the public. This would not be a Congressional "first": the House Education and Labor Committee has already taken that step, so that the public can see just who is doing what to (and for) whom. In no legislative field is this of greater interest to the public than the field of taxation.

The committees' closed-door procedures also assure a minimum of public accountability for each member's actions and votes. Although Congress itself enacted a law (the Legislative Reorganization Act of 1970) that requires publishing how each committee member votes on recorded yeas and nays taken in these closed sessions, the two tax-writing committees have solved that problem by taking very few recorded votes. The secrecy surrounding their deliberations is unusual, even for Congress. Only Ways and Means Committee members are allowed to read the written records of closed-door meetings of the Committee and, according to V. O. French, "such records are guarded with far greater care than any . . . record of a National Security Council meeting." But, the account continues, Senate Finance "offers the ultimate in document security—no records at all. There is no chance for an Ellsberg with a Xerox machine at Finance, because the committee keeps itself protected as man did before the advent of the printing press, through showing of hands and gutteral utterances. To go along with such strategic amnesia, until this year Finance had no rules of any kind.* Even now, the rules are so few and flexible that they hardly interfere at all with [Chairman Russell] Long's power."

Despite all the elaborate efforts to preserve the privacy of closed bill-writing meetings, the lobbyists seem to maintain a pipeline of sorts into the super-secret sessions. Journalists, who have no such pipeline, often wait for hours in cold Congressional corridors for the meetings to break up. But not the lobbyists. One veteran of such vigils marvels at how suddenly, just moments before the magic hour arrives, the lobbyists suddenly foregather outside the committee room, just in time to hear the committee announce its decisions. Obviously, says this reporter, someone within the *sanctum sanctorum* keeps the lobbyists currently informed on the committee's progress.

A FINAL ELEMENT that freezes out the average Congressman or Senator and tightens the grip of the Tax Establishment is the hideous complexity of the tax laws and the virtual unintelligibility of most of their provisions. How is the average member of Congress, much less the "average taxpayer," to deal with provisions such as this one (taken at random from the Internal Revenue Code):

---

* Chairman Long once observed to a Treasury official, "This committee doesn't have a single rule. We just make ourselves up as we go along. Why, we can vote on the time of the day if we want to."

For purposes of paragraphs (1), (2) and (4), the term "subsection (e) asset" means, with respect to property held by any corporation (i) property (except property used in the trade or business, as defined in paragraph (9)) which in the hands of the corporation is, or, in the hands of a shareholder who owns more than 20 percent in value of the outstanding stock of the corporation, would be, property gain from the sale or exchange of which would under any provision of this chapter be considered in whole or in part as gain from the sale or exchange of property which is neither a capital asset nor property described in section 1231(b)....

Or this one:

For purposes of paragraph (3), an organization described in paragraph (2) shall be deemed to include an organization described in Section 501(c)(4), (5) or (6) which would be described in paragraph (2) if it were an organization described in Section 501(c)(3).

Even so eminent and brilliant a jurist as Learned Hand was driven to observe that the words of a tax law "merely dance before my eyes in a meaningless procession . . . couched in abstract terms that offer no handle to seize hold of. . . . [They] leave in my mind only a confused sense of some vitally important, but successfully concealed purpose which it is my duty to extract, but which is in my power, if at all, only after the most inordinate expenditure of time." If the complexities of the tax law are so baffling and time-consuming to a Learned Hand, think how helpless they leave the average, super-busy Congressman, much less the average, man-on-the-street taxpayer.

Admittedly, many of the tax code's intricacies are inherent in the difficulty of its assignment: trying to foresee and deal fairly with the almost infinite variety of transactions that can take place (or that can be invented by ingenious legal minds in search of lucrative escape hatches). Nonetheless, this very complexity is an important obstacle to loophole-closing, for it endows the experts and the "insiders" with unusual powers, and robs even the most vigilant Congressman or newsman of his normal powers of scrutiny. What casual observer, for example, would be able to spot a provision in a 585-page tax bill innocuously headed "Certain New Design Products" and know that it was tailor-made to confer more than $20,000,000 in tax saving upon the Lockheed and McDonnell Douglas companies? And who could discern that a measure ambiguously entitled "A Bill to Amend Part III of Subchapter O of the Internal Revenue Code of 1954" was really a bill to provide substantial retroactive tax relief to the Hilton hotel chain* (and, potentially, nineteen other unsuccessful defendants in antitrust proceedings)?

The very complexity of the tax laws places an unusual burden on the most conscientious reform-minded legislator—even if he is a member of a tax-writing committee—and accentuates the importance of (and his dependence on) expert staff assistance. Imagine the problem confronting an intensely busy Finance Committee member like former Senator Fred Harris when the Finance Committee was drafting a major tax bill in 1969, with twenty-five to fifty separate provisions to be considered at each day's meeting. How was he to acquaint himself with the merits of each, or to know that one was tailor-made for Lockheed or another for the Litton executives? For this, he was totally reliant on a late-afternoon "skull session," on the eve of each Finance meeting, with a lone member of his personal staff, Fred Gibson (who had *his* hands full trying to gather information on the myriad intricate proposals). Had this not been the Finance Committee, Harris would not have been so utterly dependent on these frantic "briefing sessions," for under the rules of most other committees he could have brought Gibson to sit beside him in the bill-writing meeting. As mentioned, Finance is one of the few Senate committees that forbid this.

Unhappily for tax reformers, that is not the only unique characteristic of Finance (and its House counterpart, Ways and Means). Virtually every other major committee of the Congress divides its work among subcommittees. The Senate Judiciary Committee, for example, has fifteen subcommittees, each with its own expert staff† so that members can concentrate on a given topic and become at least semi-expert on such matters as antitrust and antimonopoly legislation, or immigration and naturalization laws or constitutional rights. Most Congressional hearings are held by these specialized subcommittees, which then shape the first draft of

---

* See p. 52.

† Even the House Administration Committee has a Subcommittee on Libraries and Memorials and a Select Subcommittee on Non-Essential Employees, and the Senate Rules and Administration is so finely subdivided as to have a Subcommittee on the [Senate] Restaurant.

a bill.* Only then does the full Committee consider it, deferring, in general, to the expertness of the subcommittee.

No other Congressional committees lend themselves more naturally to such a subdivided structure than Ways and Means and Finance, since they must deal not only with hideously complex *tax* legislation of all kinds but also with all laws concerning tariffs, Social Security, welfare, Medicare, Medicaid and the national debt. Yet they are the only major committees of Congress that have no subcommittees, and no subcommittee staffs.† All matters are handled by the full committee. All staff members are appointed by and answerable to the chairman—which is not to say they will not respond to requests for information from any committee member, but they are not likely to take the initiative in alerting a Senator or Congressman to the loopholes in a particular provision without the express or implied approval of the chairman. There is a world of difference.

Thus, when someone like Fred Harris attends a closed session of Senate Finance, armed only with as much knowledge as his lone assistant has been able to amass and convey to him in one hurried night-before meeting, he is truly at the mercy of the "experts." If another Senator or a Treasury official suggests a highly technical change in the language of this or that provision, he has little way to evaluate the new suggestion.

This dependence on experts is a significant roadblock to tax reform. It is one thing to *want* to close loopholes and reform the tax system; it is quite another to anticipate all the "what ifs" and to devise and draft a provision that will deal fairly with all the contingencies; and no reform proposal can be seriously considered until there is legislative language to effect it. Expertise and specific legislative proposals are available in abundance from those seeking or defending special tax favors. Tax hearings are dominated by witnesses representing such groups as the Clay Pipe Industry Depletion Committee or the New Jersey Associaton of Chosen Freeholders or the National Industrial Sand Association, and each

---

* In addition, these subcommittees and their specialized staffs often initiate inquiries and hearings in depth on certain subjects on which they seek more information.

† Among the thirty-six "standing" committees, aside from the tax-writing committees, only the Senate Committee on Aeronautical and Space Sciences and the House committees on Internal Security and on Standards of Official Conduct have no subcommittees.

lobbyist who approaches a Senator or Congressman comes prepared with one or more draft provisions and tightly argued supporting memoranda. Reform-minded legislators, on the other hand, must generally seek out and rely on the part-time volunteer services of far-flung law professors and other academicians* who may or may not be on hand at the crucial legislative moment to rebut industry arguments or draft a new compromise provision. It's an uneven battle.

Perhaps the most serious obstacle to tax reform is the failure of the media and of the educational system to penetrate the heavy fog of complexity and secrecy that enshrouds the tax-writing process—their failure to tell the public just who is doing what to whom. How many readers can recall seeing one article either in a newspaper or in a weekly news magazine or one mention on television of the specially tailored tax provisions such as those for the Lockheed Corporation or the Mobil Oil Company? How many Americans are aware of a provision that crept into the 1969 tax law almost entirely unnoticed, although it is predicted to save the oil shale industry (and to cost the American taxpayers) a *billion* dollars or more in taxes before the year 2000? And what civics textbooks describe the secretive way in which Congressional committees determine which citizens should be taxed how much (or how little) ?

Some years ago the most reform-minded member of the House Ways and Means Committee attributed conventional antipathy toward tax reform to the lack of public pressure for it: "You shouldn't blame Congress about what the American people don't want," he said, a bit regretfully. But how can the public be expected to care about something concerning which so little is told them? There are some signs, now, of public restiveness about the tax system's apparent unfairness. Tax reform stirs markedly more public response than it did ten years ago. The main question is, can genuine tax reform be achieved without some basic changes in American politics, especially in the way this country finances its political campaigns?

---

* Whose talents are being alerted and mobilized on a systematic basis, for the first time, by a Washington organization called Taxation with Representation, headed by former Treasury Department official Thomas F. Field.

21

What Should Be Done About Our Tax System?

WHAT SHOULD BE DONE about the preference-riddled American tax law?

I suggest abolishing all the preferences, or loopholes—for the un-rich many as well as for the wealthy few—and taxing everyone, uniformly, on the basis of his or her total income, *"from whatever source derived."* (This was the language the latter-day Founding Fathers used when they drafted the Sixteenth Amendment to the United States Constitution, so my suggestion, while seemingly "radical" at first blush, is really highly conservative, striving, as it does, to return to basic Constitutional principles.)

Such a preference-free tax system would fully express the notion that a dollar received, whether in the form of hard-earned wages, or from capital gains or municipal bond interest, or by gift or inheritance, endows its recipient with 100 cents' worth of "ability to pay" for food, shoes for the baby, yachts—or taxes.

Embodying that principle in the individual income tax law (leaving aside, for a moment, the corporate tax preferences*) would open up a wide variety of choices. Among them:

• *Lowering all existing tax rates by about two-fifths* (assuming it was decided to leave Federal tax *collections* at their 1972 levels). If that were done uniformly across the board (i.e., for all

---

* Suggestions for removing the major tax preferences enjoyed by corporations may be found in the footnote on pp. 403–404.

398

income levels), the individual income tax rates, which now (in 1973) range from 14 percent to 70 percent, would begin at 8 percent and rise no higher than 40 percent.

• *Raising upwards of $77 billion* in added Federal revenues* (assuming it was decided to leave Federal income tax *rates* at their 1972 levels). These added revenues could be used for any number of purposes. For instance, they could be devoted to meeting long-neglected public needs (e.g., making massive assaults on urban blight, hunger, malnutrition, health-care needs; formulating major programs to make air breathable and lakes and streams swimmable; acquiring and preserving open spaces for recreation; replacing disgracefully antiquated schools and hospitals, and building and manning day-care centers—the list is endless). This could be done either at the Federal level or through revenue-sharing grants to local communities.

• *Lightening the burden of present regressive taxes that bear most heavily on those least able to pay.* For example, the added Federal revenues could be used to help the states and localities finance activities, such as schools, that are now financed out of the harshly regressive property tax.† This might pose some difficult problems of state versus Federal jurisdiction in certain fields. But those problems have not prevented Congress from enacting a Federal revenue-sharing plan, which presumably could be adapted to embody the notion suggested here.‡

• *Any combination of the above.*

Or, as a further alternative, if the American people were to

---

* The $77 billion figure is based on 1972 income levels and would rise as national income grows.

† But this should not be undertaken unless and until the states and localities have reformed their property tax systems so as to ensure that everyone is paying his fair share—notably those large corporations and tax-exempt organizations that now, by one means or another, escape their share.

‡ In early 1972, the Nixon Administration was reportedly considering a "value added tax" (see Glossary) as a means of raising large additional amounts of Federal revenues, which presumably would be devoted, in the manner suggested above, to relieving the burden of the property tax. But most tax authorities see little difference between a "value added tax" (VAT) and a Federal sales tax (except that the VAT would be more hidden). Therefore, enacting a VAT to give relief from the property tax would simply mean enacting one "soak-the-poor" tax to replace another. What's more, since across-the-board loophole-closing, as suggested in this chapter, would raise vastly more revenue than has been contemplated under a VAT, what reason is there to resort to a VAT—at least until all the loopholes have been closed?

ask whether wealth and income are now fairly apportioned in this country and were to conclude that they are not, the tax system is one of the most effective means of correcting inequities. That question is discussed in more detail on pages 416–425.

H O W   W O U L D   a "Sixteenth Amendment tax system" operate?

Under such a system, making out your tax return would be far simpler and faster than it is today. It would, in essence, be a three-step operation. (See note at bottom of page.)

Step One: Add up all your income for the year—that is, everything you received that gave you an ability to buy things.[1] That would include not only your wages and salaries, but all your government benefits (Social Security, welfare, etc.) and any money you received by gift or inheritance.[2] If you are lucky enough to own any stocks or bonds, or if you have a savings account, you would include all your dividend and interest income[3] —including interest on state and local bonds.[4] You would also include 100 percent (rather than 50 percent, as under existing law) of any capital gains profits you happened to make on the sale of stocks or bonds or other property[5] (if you are among the fortunate few property owners).

Step Two: From the income you calculated under Step One, you would subtract:[6]

(a) a certain amount for yourself and each dependent—this amount to be set by Congress.[7]

(b) any business or investment costs you incurred in getting your income (just as you do now on your tax return).[8]

Step Three: Taking the above result (Step One minus Step Two), you would compute your tax in accordance with whatever rate schedule Congress might establish in the law.[9] Under a no-loophole system, though, you would be reasonably sure that all taxpayers, no matter how rich they might be, would also be computing *their* taxes not only on the basis of those same rates but also on the basis of *their* total incomes. No longer would a favored few be able to wriggle out of paying their fair share of taxes by using all sorts of exemptions, exclusions, special rates, delaying

---

Note: The footnotes applicable to the following description of those steps may be found on pp. 401–404.

devices and the rest. Not that the system would be airtight; not that the rich and their ingenious and well-paid tax lawyers wouldn't be hard at work trying to figure out ways around the system—they always have been (see page 410). But under this preference-free tax system, the number of escape hatches through which they could squeeze would be drastically reduced, and the tax system, while imperfect, would be enormously fairer and more honest than it is today.[10]

---

[1] The general criterion for what you should include as "income" under Step One is what economists call "control over economic resources." In order to satisfy that somewhat jargonish definition, you would include (in addition to the items listed in the text) interest on your life insurance savings plus those fringe benefits paid for by your employer and actually received by you (to the extent these can be practically and accurately measured on a taxpayer-by-taxpayer basis. Under that standard, some "income in kind"—for example, an occasional free meal furnished by an employer—would not be taxed; but employer-paid life insurance would be).

Strict, logical adherence to the criterion of "ability to buy things" would also require taxing such things as life insurance proceeds as they are received, as well as such income equivalents as the return on your investment in your home (or car), food that a farmer produces and consumes on his farm, the free services provided by your bank in lieu of interest payments on your deposits, and others. Most of these (e.g., bank services) are not susceptible to an accurate taxpayer-by-taxpayer measurement, and an effort to tax them would not be worth the administrative and compliance headaches it would cause. As to one important kind of income equivalent—the rent equivalent on owned homes (i.e., the return on one's investment in one's home), opinion is divided. Some say it is not easily measurable and hence would be difficult to tax, and they add that to tax it and not other kinds of "imputed" income (i.e., income equivalents) would be inconsistent. Others (including myself), however, maintain that it *would* be feasible to tax this kind of income equivalent (by basing the tax on the owner's "equity" interest in his home) and that this item is so large (it amounts to an estimated $15.5 billion per year and failure to tax it costs the Treasury $5 billion a year) that to leave it untaxed would be a major departure from the "ability to pay" principle.

[2] The income tax paid by the receivers of gifts and inheritances would replace the existing estate and gift tax.

[3] Which would be subject to a tax-withholding system similar to that now in effect for wages and salaries, to guard against taxpayer forgetfulness about reporting the bits and pieces of dividend and interest income that dribble in through the course of the year. As noted, an estimated $6 billion of dividend and interest income is now unreported on tax returns each year, resulting in an annual revenue loss of about $1 billion.

[4] Congress would probably want to accompany the taxation of this bond interest with a direct subsidy to state and local governments to keep down their borrowing costs. (See p. 66.)

[5] This would include increases in the value of property that a person owned at the time of his death. Where any capital gains came from property

you had held for a period of years, an averaging system similar to that in existing law would avoid the unfairness of having the tax figured as if all the gain had been earned in a single year. Of course, since capital gains would be taxed at your regular income tax rates, capital *losses* (to the extent that you had capital gains in that same year) would also be deductible at those same rates.

⁶ In adddition to the subtraction (i.e., deduction) items listed in (a) and (b) in the text, the new tax system might well make some allowance for *major* uninsured medical expenses and casualty losses (i.e., those in excess of, say, 5 percent of your income), on the dual ground that such expenses are irregular and therefore cannot be planned for in family budgeting, and that they uncontrollably deprive a taxpayer of much of his "ability to buy things." It should be remembered, though, that *any* kind of tax allowance—say, for catastrophic medical expenses—is no real answer to the problem. For no matter how generous the tax forgiveness, it does not enable a family to meet more than a minuscule portion of such expenses (and provides no assistance whatever to those too poor to pay taxes). The only real way to provide families with the wherewithal to bear large medical costs is a system of public health insurance.

There might also be a tax incentive to charitable giving, although on this question I am obliged to acknowledge both philosophical anguish and, in one sense, a "conflict of interest." Both are occasioned by my personal involvement and intense interest in charitable giving (I preside over two family foundations). This has led to a strong belief in the value of trying to meet public needs and probe public questions with other than government-controlled funds, as a result of judgments made by a large number and wide variety of decision-makers. I am convinced this country would be worse off if all expenditures of a broad public nature were made by the government, as a result of politically motivated decisions. If that were to come to pass, there would be little questioning of basic premises or of Conventional Wisdom in public endeavors. Granted, not many foundations show a penchant for basic-premise questioning, but some do; and there is more of it in foundation-supported endeavors than in government programs.

On the other hand, I am troubled by the thought of making an exception to the preference-free system with a tax concession for charitable giving. Experience shows (see Chapter 14) that if the tax tent is cracked an inch, a dozen (or more) camels' noses will instantly present themselves, each with a claim on the tax system to foster this or that publicly beneficial activity. (After all—to take one example—isn't home ownership as unarguable a virtue as charity?)

Other techniques for encouraging philanthropy should therefore be explored before invading the tax system for this purpose. My own preference would be for something along the line of the English system (as described on p. 370), whereby an individual's gift is matched by a gift from the government to the same charity. Thus the charity is benefited, but the tax tent remains tightly closed. (To avoid undue political interference with this process, the government's matching gift must be automatically forthcoming in the case of any charitable recipient that qualifies under the law—just as automatically as the present tax deduction allowed for gifts to any qualified charity under existing U.S. tax law.)

It will be said—probably with considerable reason—that such a system would result in a sharp decrease in donations to charity, because it would downplay, if not remove, the self-interest motivation in favor of the purely altruistic motivation for a charitable gift. Even if that should prove to be true, however, I would still choose that course over a loophole-riddled tax system, which I fear would be the result of leaving the tax concession for charity in the law, where it would serve as a rationale, if not an invitation, for other special tax preferences.

If the above approach is rejected as too idealistic, and a tax concession to the donor is deemed desirable, it should certainly be in the form of a tax *credit* (see Glossary) rather than a deduction, so that a like portion of each person's generosity, be he rich or poor, would be borne by the government.

[7] Many (including the author) believe that this allowance should also take the form of a tax *credit*, rather than an exemption, so as to give equal benefit to taxpayers at all income levels. As you will see in a moment, that would concentrate more of the tax relief among low-income taxpayers, which would be consistent with the purpose behind this allowance: namely, to accord each family, free of tax, a minimum level of income. To permit such a tax-free allowance for every family does not depart from the objective of a preference-free tax system in that it simply amounts to putting a zero bracket in the tax rate schedule. Any per-person allowance, however, has the added effect of taking into account differences in family size which, it is generally agreed, makes a difference in a family's "ability to pay."

[8] The return of your capital outlays would continue to be nontaxable as at present.

[9] Unmarried persons, now discriminated against under existing law, should note that, under the new system, all persons would pay the same tax regardless of their marital status. As described on pp. 128 ff. this could be accomplished without reverting to the pre-1948 discrepancy between the so-called "community property" and "common law" states. It would be done by establishing a separate rate schedule for married couples filing separate returns that would, in effect, permit couples from "community property" states to split their incomes (as if half belonged to husband and half to wife) but would take away the tax advantage of doing so. In that way, such couples would pay the same taxes as married people in "common law" states and the same as unmarried people in all the states.

[10] As to loophole-closing in the area of corporate and business taxation, under the preference-free tax system corporations would no longer enjoy the investment tax credit, nor the tax deferral privileges of DISC export corporations, and their depreciation deductions would be limited, as closely as possible, to their actual plant and equipment replacement practices. This could be effected by two measures: first, by restoration of the Reserve Ratio Test (see p. 222) which is designed to bring about adjustments in a company's depreciation deductions when they diverge from actual replacement practices; and second, by obliging corporations to limit their depreciation deductions to those they report to their shareholders. (See pp. 212–213 for a discussion of existing discrepancies between what corporations claim in the way of depreciation on their tax returns and what they tell their shareholders in reporting earnings and profits.)

In the case of mineral industries, depletion deductions would be limited to the amount originally invested in the mineral property. Deductions for "intangible drilling expenses," in the case of the oil industry, would be spread over the life of the property rather than being deductible all in one year.

Corporations would be taxed on their overseas profits in the year those profits are earned, and their international operations would be taxed on either a country-by-country or a world-wide basis, whichever proved better from the point of view of the U.S. Treasury. So-called "Western Hemisphere trade corporations" would no longer enjoy the preferential rate now available to them.

The corporation tax also would be reckoned not on the basis of total profits but rather on the basis of those profits *not* distributed to shareholders. That would create an incentive on the part of corporate managers to distribute a far larger share of the profits to shareholders and would have a dual advantage. First, it would oblige corporate managers to stand the test of the marketplace in making their decisions and in seeking the capital needed to implement them. Second, it would give the shareholders who own the corporation much greater control over the fruits of their ownership and would leave them free to decide whether or not they wanted to reinvest a part of all of their dividends in the corporation. Under the present system, that decision is, to all intents and purposes, made for the shareholders by the corporate managers.

The bad-debt-reserve deductions of all financial institutions (not just commercial banks) would be limited to their actual bad-debt experience. Real-estate depreciation deductions would be limited to a "straight-line" basis (see Glossary); and since capital gains would, under the new system, be taxed on a par with other kinds of income (with an averaging scheme to obviate the "bunched income" problem), there would no longer be the opportunity that now exists in many industries (e.g., real estate, timber, farming) to "alchemize" ordinary income into capital gains.

Taxpayers with significant amounts of non-farm income would no longer be privileged to use the accounting (and tax-delaying) methods that were designed for "real" farmers, and deductions for farming "development" expenses that are now immediately deductible would have to be spread out over a period of years so as to match up with the income that resulted.

OBVIOUSLY, with everybody's total income subject to tax, and with all except business deductions eliminated, if present tax rates were maintained Federal tax collections would rise hugely (by about $77 billion for individuals plus another $10 billion for corporations).*

The other side of the coin is that if it were decided that Federal tax collections should remain the same, it would be possible to reduce all tax rates substantially—by an average of 43 percent. Applying such a cut uniformly across the board would produce a schedule of tax rates ranging from 8 percent to 40 percent, instead of the present 14 to 70 percent range.

Tax experts Joseph A. Pechman and Benjamin A. Okner—the Brookings Institution economists whose computerized analysis of "tax welfare" was cited in Chapter 1—have suggested another rate schedule ranging from 7 to 44 percent that would lighten the load of the very poor more than the 8 to 40 percent rate schedule

---

* Assuming 1972 income levels. As mentioned, those amounts will rise as the economy grows.

mentioned above, in large part because, under their proposal, the "low-income allowance," or minimum standard deduction, would be raised from $1,300 to $2,000 per family. Thus, a family of four could have $5,000 of income* before the rate schedule even began to apply.

The following table will give you an idea of what your taxes would be under their suggested rates:

Illustrative Rate Schedule Under No-Loophole Tax System (1)

To compute your tax under this rate schedule, take total family income and subtract from that (a) $2,000 plus (b) $750 for each person in the family. Then find where the resulting figure fits in the left-hand column ("family's taxable income") and compute your tax.

If family's taxable income (see above note) is:	Then your tax would be:
Under $500	7%
$500–$1,000	$35 plus 8% of excess over $500
$1,000–$1,500	$75 plus 10% of excess over $1,000
$1,500–$2,000	$125 plus 11% of excess over $1,500
$2,000–$4,000	$180 plus 13% of excess over $2,000
$4,000–$6,000	$440 plus 14% of excess over $4,000
$6,000–$8,000	$720 plus 15% of excess over $6,000
$8,000–$10,000	$1,020 plus 16% of excess over $8,000
$10,000–$12,000	$1,340 plus 20% of excess over $10,000
$12,000–$14,000	$1,740 plus 22% of excess over $12,000
$14,000–$16,000	$2,180 plus 24% of excess over $14,000
$16,000–$18,000	$2,660 plus 26% of excess over $16,000
$18,000–$20,000	$3,180 plus 28% of excess over $18,000
$20,000–$22,000	$3,740 plus 29% of excess over $20,000
$22,000–$26,000	$4,320 plus 30% of excess over $22,000
$26,000–$32,000	$5,520 plus 32% of excess over $26,000
$32,000–$38,000	$7,440 plus 34% of excess over $32,000
$38,000–$44,000	$9,480 plus 35% of excess over $38,000
$44,000–$50,000	$11,580 plus 36% of excess over $44,000
$50,000–$60,000	$13,740 plus 37% of excess over $50,000
$60,000–$70,000	$17,440 plus 38% of excess over $60,000
$70,000–$80,000	$21,240 plus 40% of excess over $70,000
$80,000–$90,000	$25,240 plus 41% of excess over $80,000
$90,000–$100,000	$29,340 plus 42% of excess over $90,000
$100,000 and over	$33,540 plus 44% of excess over $100,000

---

* 4 times $750 exemption = $3,000 + $2,000 low-income allowance = $5,000.

Here are the taxes that would be paid by various families under the Pechman-Okner proposal, compared with what they must now pay (assuming that all the family income is in the form of wages and/or salaries).

Family Income	Tax Now*	Tax Then†	Percent Change
	Couple, with Two Children		
$5,000	$98	$0	−100%
$7,500	$484	$245	−49%
$10,000	$905	$580	−36%
$15,000	$1,666	$1,340	−20%
	Couple, with No Children		
$5,000	$322	$125	−61%
$7,500	$753	$440	−42%
$10,000	$1,190	$795	−33%
$15,000	$1,996	$1,640	−18%
	Single Person		
$5,000	$490.50	$212.50	−57%
$7,500	$994.50	$545.00	−45%
$10,000	$1,530.00	$907.50	−41%
$15,000	$2,508.50	$1,795.00	−28%

* Assumes that all families take a $750 per-person exemption; that those making $5,000 and $7,500 take the $1,300 minimum standard deduction; that those making $10,000 take the 15 percent standard deduction; and that those making $15,000 have itemized deductions amounting to 18 percent of their income (which is the present average for families in that income range).

† Using a $750 per-person *exemption* and a $2,000 minimum standard deduction.

As previously discussed, there is a basic flaw in the present system of granting a $750 per-person *exemption*: it results in upside-down "tax welfare," bestowing a $525 per-person benefit on top-bracket families that don't need the tax break, in contrast with a meager $105 per-person relief for the lowest-bracket families that sorely need every dollar they can get. It would, therefore, be fairer and more sensible to substitute, instead, a tax *credit* (i.e., a reduction in the amount of tax owed) of, say, $150 for each taxpayer and each dependent.* For low-income families, the $150 credit would provide markedly more tax relief than the $750 exemption. For more well-to-do families, it would produce slightly less than the present exemption. The results for various illustrative families (assuming the $2,000 per-family low-income allowance remained unchanged) would be as follows:

Family Income	Tax Now	Tax Then*	Percent Change
	Couple, with Two Children		
$5,000	$98	$290 *Refund*	−396%
$7,500	$484	$50	−90%
$10,000	$905	$420	−54%
$15,000	$1,666	$1,360	−18%
	Couple, with No Children		
$5,000	$322	$10	−97%
$7,500	$753	$350	−54%
$10,000	$1,190	$720	−39%
$15,000	$1,996	$1,660	−17%
	Single Person		
$5,000	$490.50	$160	−67%
$7,500	$994.50	$500	−50%
$10,000	$1,530.00	$870	−43%
$15,000	$2,508.50	$1,810	−28%

* Using a $150 per-person tax *credit* instead of a personal exemption.

Messrs. Pechman and Okner (or, more precisely, their computers) calculate that under their suggested rates (using the $750 *exemption* rather than the $150 per-person credit) a no-loophole system would result in tax *reductions* of more than $100 for about half of all families; about one-fourth would experience less than

---

* Under such a system, you would compute your tax from the rate schedule on p. 405 in the following illustrative manner (assuming a family of four with a total income of $10,000, and assuming a $2,000 per-family low-income allowance:

Total income	$10,000
Minus $2,000 low-income allowance	−2,000
Family taxable income	$8,000
Tax, per rate schedule, on $8,000	$1,020
Minus $150 per-person tax credit ($15 x 4)	−600
Tax due	$420

$100 change in the taxes they now pay, and the remaining one-fourth would find themselves with tax *increases* of more than $100. This latter group consists mostly of wealthy families (who now enjoy large amounts of tax-favored income—mainly capital gains) as well as upper-middle-income families who now take large personal deductions. In general, under the Pechman-Okner rates, families with $25,000 or more income would pay higher taxes; families with less than $25,000 incomes would generally get tax cuts. Here are the Pechman-Okner computer calculations on the *average* effect of a no-loophole system on the wealthier families:

Income Group	Average Family Income	Average Tax Under Present Law	Average Tax Under No-Loophole System*
(In thousands)			
$20–$25	$22,188	$2,685	$2,649
$25–$50	$32,015	$4,640	$5,006
$50–$100	$65,687	$15,467	$16,398
$100–$500	$165,998	$48,926	$55,222
$500–$1,000	$673,040	$204,416	$247,167
$1,000 and over	$2,316,872	$742,802	$938,333

* Using $750 per-person *exemption* rather than $150 per-person tax *credit*.

Before any reader weeps for the million-and-over group, he should note carefully that the *average* income for families in that group comes to $2,316,872. So even after paying the taxes suggested by Messrs. Pechman and Okner, the average stratospherically rich family would still keep $1,378,539 (or, in more commonly used terms, $26,510.37 of weekly "take-home pay").

Below you will find the facts about the after-tax "keeping money" that the more well-to-do families in the nation would retain, under the Pechman-Okner proposal:

Family Income	Average Family After-Tax "Keeping Money" Under Proposed Rate Schedule
$25,000–$50,000	$27,009
$50,000–$100,000	$49,289
$100,000–$500,000	$110,776
$500,000–$1,000,000	$425,873
$1,000,000 and over	$1,378,539

These figures may cause most readers to dry their eyes and might even prompt some to wonder, as they struggle to pay their taxes *plus* their monthly bills, whether any family really *needs* nearly $1,378,000 of spending money every year. That means $3,777 available to spend *every day, seven days a week, 365 days a year.* Such hard-pressed taxpayers may wonder, too, whether those super-rich families' "ability to pay" is fully reflected in asking them to share just 40 percent of their gargantuan incomes with "the community," while keeping 60 percent for themselves. Especially in light of the astounding figures on the distribution (or *mal*distribution) of wealth and income in the United States, as set forth more fully on pages 416–420, the Pechman-Okner rate schedule seems excessively gentle on rich taxpayers. I suggest an alternative rate schedule on pages 420–421.

THE ADVANTAGES of a simplified tax system, such as that outlined above, are many. It would mean a fairer tax system, in that everyone would pay taxes more nearly according to a uniform rate schedule. Naturally, the above-outlined plan does not claim to be flawless* or problem-free. No system of taxation can be expected to render Solomon-like justice for each of 74 million individual taxpayers. But tax experts have little doubt that a simplified preference-free system would work (they are much more troubled about winning Congressional acceptance than about achieving practical workability in such a plan). Moreover, any injustices resulting from a broadly based tax plan would surely not be as great as the existing discrimination against those whose income is wholly earned, or as flagrant as the spectacle of three families with $2,500,000 of dividend income paying no tax while five million taxpayers making less than $3,000 a year were obliged to share some of their meager incomes with their government.

Under a tax system that favored no industry or special group of taxpayers, there would, hopefully, be more disposition, where government subsidies are indicated, to search for ways of providing direct, out-in-the-open government aid, and less inclination to resort to hidden tax subsidies and to invade an otherwise preference-free tax system for that purpose—which, as we have seen (in Chapter 7), is usually clumsier and costlier anyway.

Finally, a simplified tax plan would mean a more *forthright* tax system, in which each citizen would have greater reason to

---

* It does not, for example, claim to tax every single item that contributes to a person's "ability to pay."

believe that the tax rates he uses when filing his tax return mean what they say and apply uniformly to others, not just to himself.

I DO NOT MEAN TO EXAGGERATE the happy effects that would flow from a simpler, more broadly based tax system. I have no illusions that America would overnight be transformed into a Utopian society in which every man shared Justice Holmes's pleasure in paying taxes in order to "pay for civilized society." Even if we took advantage of the no-loophole system to lower all tax rates substantially, the "tax angle" would still be with us, just as it has always been; high top-bracket rates are not its only raison d'être. There were massive tax preferences long before high rates were enacted.* Nor did the low tax rates of the Twenties (top rate, 25 percent) diminish the avidity with which tax avoidance was pursued. The very architect of those gentle rates, Andrew Mellon, when he resigned as Secretary of the Treasury, was careful to take with him, as his tax adviser in private life, the Treasury Department's top expert on tax-avoidance techniques.

While there is little reason to expect the future to differ markedly from the past, nonetheless, as things now stand, the very possibility of escape creates its own pressure. Block off the major escape routes (especially the capital gains route) and you tap much of that pressure.

ANYONE IN HIGH PUBLIC OFFICE who seriously proposes a no-preference tax system should be prepared for the air to be filled with black predictions of catastrophe. Without oil depletion (it would be said), oil exploration would come "to a standstill"; without mortgage interest deductions, home-buying would plummet; without a special capital gains tax, the sources of capital would wither; the economy would flounder and the Treasury, far from gaining revenues, would be starved for the dollars to run the government.

No one should minimize the economic impact of a major revision of the tax structure. There would be some dislocations as the tax supports now underpinning many areas of the economy were removed. Past history provides assurance that Congress would not

---

*Three of the most conspicuous tax favors—tax-exempt bonds, oil depletion, and the preferential capital gains rate—all became law when the top rates were comparatively low (7, 58 and 25 percent, respectively).

remove the crutches abruptly, but would provide a cushion of time during which the tax-supported industries could develop the muscles to stand on their own. Where that has been done, the adjustment has been successfully accomplished.* In any event, such changes would be in a direction that should be applauded by the United States Chamber of Commerce and the National Association of Manufacturers. There would be less government interference with private decision-making (via tax subsidies) and greater freedom for the free market forces. Perhaps there *would* be less building of apartments and offices in major cities if the fast-depreciation capital gains tax advantages of real estate were entirely ended. But with office-building vacancy rates growing in, say, New York, isn't there evidence that this tax subsidy has to some degree encouraged some *over*building? Wouldn't the economy be better off, in the long run, with a free play of market forces regulating the allocation of capital and resources—determining, for example, the level of oil exploration and real-estate construction? And shouldn't those who decry "backdoor" government spending rejoice in the elimination of tax subsidies—the most insidiously invisible of all drains on the Federal Treasury?

While taxes can have a profound effect on economic activity, there is a tendency to endow them with vastly more power—to heal as well as to injure—than they actually possess. For example, the low tax rates of the Twenties, which Andrew Mellon said would be the salvation of free enterprise, were followed by the greatest economic calamity in the nation's history. Conversely, from 1942 to 1964, the top income tax rate was as high as 94 percent, and never below 82 percent; yet those tax rates did not, as some might have feared, trigger any similar Great Depression.

There is also a tendency to underrate the resiliency of the American economy, which took in stride such fiscal shocks as a $7 billion tax increase bill in 1942 and, more significantly, a $94 billion drop-off of government purchases between 1945 and 1948. Surely an economy that withstood abrupt adjustments of that magnitude can withstand a rearrangement of the tax system that does not involve major overall changes in Federal tax collections (as is assumed in this book).

---

* By way of illustration, see p. 115 for a description of the manner in which both the stock market and the economy adjusted to the 1969 increase in the capital gains tax.

IF THE COMPARATIVELY MODEST tax reform efforts of the past have met, by and large, with dismal failure, what chance is there for the kind of "drastic" reform suggested here?

The answer may well be, "Far more chance than there has been with the half-loaf reform efforts of the past."

That may sound illogical. Yet one of the main reasons that tax reform has fared so badly has been the lack of public pressure on Washington. How explain that? Is it because the public doesn't *care* about taxes? Not likely.

More probably it's because tax reform debates have, by and large, been conducted in such a way that the public can't participate. The issues have usually been posed and debated in terms that mean little or nothing to the public. Taxpayers have never been given much reason to feel that *they* had enough to gain from loophole-closing to warrant a pro-reform letter to a Congressman.

By way of illustration, back in the early Sixties it would have been politically unthinkable to call for the outright abolition of the preferential treatment of capital gains, and so President Kennedy elected, instead, to try to nibble away at particular facets of that preference—for example, ending the capital gains treatment of coal royalty income.

Now suppose the Gallup Poll had asked an average taxpayer: *Do you think coal royalties should receive capital gains tax treatment?*

My guess is that the response might well have been something like this:

What is capital gains tax treatment?	*21%*
What are coal royalties?	*19%*
How should I know?	*60%*

Or the response might well have been, *"Why should I care?"* After all, closing that particular loophole meant, at most, a few cents a year on the average person's tax bill.

Suppose, on the other hand, Mr. Kennedy had tackled the capital gains preference head-on (as Senator McGovern sought to do in 1972), and suppose he had suggested that an average taxpayer compare the tax on his entire year's earnings—let's say

$10,000—with the substantially smaller tax on an identical amount his neighbor made by selling some stock at a $10,000 profit. Suppose the question were then to be posed to that taxpayer in this manner:

Dollar for dollar, your neighbor's $10,000 will do just as well as yours when it comes to buying food, or clothes—or a new car or a Florida vacation. Why won't it do just as well when it comes to paying taxes?

Why should he pay less taxes on his $10,000 than you do on your $10,000?

When a tax reform debate begins posing questions like that, then the public can join the discussion.

Similarly, most Presidents have thought it futile to suggest outright abolition of the oil depletion allowance, and so have confined their reforms to technical (but peripheral) changes. Thus they ruled out posing basic questions about the depletion allowance, such as:

Do you believe the oil industry should be allowed tax deductions for nonexistent investments?

*Do you support an exploration subsidy that costs $1½ billion but results in only $150 million of new exploration outlays—and thus wastes 90 percent of the taxpayers' money?**

Those, too, are questions a taxpayer can understand.

Tax reform might also spark greater interest on the part of the average taxpayer if he were told that an across-the-board loophole-closing program *could pave the way for a 43 percent cut in all tax rates.* Then, perhaps, he might feel there was something in it for *him.*

Unhappily, tax reformers have rarely posed such questions or offered such stakes. Most reform programs have, instead, been tailored to what was thought to be "politically possible." Yet that phrase must have a hollow and ironic ring to those who survey the wreckage of what they trimmed to fit the boundaries of political reality.

---

* This refers to the government-commissioned study that showed that the $1.6 billion depletion allowance stimulated added oil exploration spending of only $150 million. (See pp. 237–238.)

Those trimmed-back, "realistic" reform programs are like trying to patch a leaky tire—a halfway approach to the problem that
suffers two weaknesses in winning public and Congressional support: first, that appproach implies that there is nothing wrong *in
principle* with a leaky tire or with the punctures themselves; it's
just that some of them are a little too large. (Thus, the debate
centers around fringe technicalities, rather than basic questions,
and the public is left wholly bewildered.) Second, as long as we
cling to the leaky old tire—that is, as long as *some* groups continue
to enjoy tax favors, loophole-closing will have trouble winning
friends and influencing Congressmen. It is not surprising, for
example, that even a reform-minded Senator from the timber-laden
state of Oregon should have opposed a Kennedy Administration
proposal to end capital gains treatment for timber, as former
Senator Maurine Neuberger did in 1964. "How could I vote for
a tax crackdown on timber," she asked, "as long as the oil industry
still has its depletion loophole?" In a similar vein, AFL-CIO
president George Meany opposed ending the $100-per-week tax-
free "sick pay" provision (see page 360) on the ground that to
eliminate this tax concession "in the name of equity would hardly
be fair when so many glaring loopholes available to the wealthy
are still tolerated."

Apparently, then, if there is a "politically practical" way out
of the tax preference maze (and many believe none exists), it lies
not in the partial-patch approach but in starting afresh—with a
wholly new tire, of modern design.

I HAVE SUGGESTED in Chapter 20 that by far the
most serious obstacle to tax reform in the Congress of the United
States is the universal dependence, on the part of the Congressmen
and Senators who vote the tax laws, on wealthy campaign contributors. If I'm right, then a precondition of basic tax reform is
the elimination of that Congressional dependence on rich contributors. Naturally, any candidate who can be *assured in advance*
of the funds for a respectable campaign will be far more likely to
speak out against the tax havens for the wealthy than a candidate
who has to go hat in hand to those same wealthy people for his
political survival.

To my mind, the surest and fairest way to provide candidates
these assured-in-advance funds is through direct Federal assistance

to candidates for Federal office—for the Presidency, the House of Representatives and the United States Senate.* That can be achieved without undue Federal controls, and in a manner that would minimize the danger of taxpayers' dollars being used for the personal benefit of the candidate rather than being channeled into his campaign.†

In order to end the disproportionate influence now enjoyed by wealthy contributors, there must be a strict limit—of, say, $5 or $10, or at most $25—on the amount any individual could donate to a candidate in a given year. That must be coupled with a system for the prompt public reporting of all candidate expenditures,‡ for

---

* To assure candidates' independence at all stages of the election process, this Federal assistance should be available at the primaries as well as the general elections.

† This could be effected by setting up drawing accounts in the Federal Treasury for each candidate, based upon the number of votes cast for his office in previous elections. The candidates would avail themselves of these drawing accounts by sending to the Treasury approved invoices for campaign expenses (e.g., for TV and radio—assuming Congress did not oblige broadcasters to provide free air time to candidates as part of their public-service obligation—newspaper and billboard advertising, printing, posters, telephone, travel and the like). Upon receipt of these invoices, the Treasury would make payments *directly to the purveyors of these services*—i.e., to the printer, newspaper, radio or TV station, etc—*so that the money would not pass through the hands of the political candidate.* There would of course have to be stiff penalties against "kickbacks" to the candidates by the purveyors of the campaign services.

‡ That could be achieved, I believe, not only by requiring periodic reports by the candidates on their receipts and expenditures but also by requiring prompt reports *by the purveyors of campaign services,* listing all the services they have provided to each candidate. These reports by purveyors would be required within, say, three days of furnishing the service. Both the candidates' and the purveyors' reports must be promptly and publicly available at some convenient place *within the state or district in which the candidate is running.* (I would suggest that the candidates' reports be published in full in a local newspaper, at Federal expense, on the reporting day specified in the law. I would further suggest that the purveyors' reports be available for public inspection at, say, the office of the nearest U.S. District Court.)

Such a scheme would, I believe, for the first time make campaign spending ceilings respectably enforceable. First, it would call for reports on campaign spending by someone other than the candidates (i.e., by the purveyors of campaign services, who are in general at "arm's length" from the candidates and hence disinclined to jeopardize themselves by failing to render the reports). That way, if the total of the purveyor reports showed a candidate buying services far beyond his Federal drawing account plus his reported receipts from $5 and $25 contributions, there would be a clear inference that he had been receiving and spending unreported private funds, in violation of the law. To put it the other way, a candidate would find it difficult to spend large amounts of illegal or unreported funds without that fact showing

only with such a system would the ceiling on private contributions be enforceable.

Such a direct Federal subsidy would achieve genuine independence of political candidates more fairly than any system of tax incentives for political contributions (which, as I have said, excludes all those too poor to pay taxes). It would also be more effective than a "check-off" system (whereby citizens could designate candidates to whom Federal assistance should be given), for such a plan would likely result in uneven amounts of Federal help to various candidates. The direct-assistance program suggested here would not only provide equal public assistance to all candidates; it would also furnish the indispensable ingredient to candidate independence: *advance assurance* of the funds needed to carry out his campaign and the confidence that he (or she) will not have to rely on private donors at the emotional (often desperate) peak of the campaign.

How much would such a Federal-assistance program cost? I have calculated that an ample assistance program*—providing some (although a lesser) degree of support for candidates in primaries as well as in general elections—would cost each person of voting age in the United States about 69 cents per year. In my view, this is not an excessive investment in assuring *real* one-man/ one-vote democracy—a phenomenon that is thwarted by the present campaign-financing system and that is a precondition to a one-man/one-vote *tax* system.

BUT BEFORE DECIDING the nature and shape of the American tax system, there is another question that needs to

---

up in the purveyors' reports of services furnished him. Second, with these candidate and purveyor reports promptly *and locally* available, *it would be possible for each candidate to monitor the campaign spending of his opponent.* In this way, opponents could point publicly at (and perhaps file legal complaints against) any discrepancies between the purveyors' and the candidates' reports of spending, which, as noted, would suggest a violation of the law. With the candidates monitoring each other, no longer would enforcement depend totally, as at present, on politically protective officials of the Congress, or the politically cautious staffs of some other Federal bureaucracy.

* This suggested program would provide major party general-election candidates for the Congress and the Senate 50 cents per vote cast in previous elections, and 25 cents per vote for major-party presidential candidates. Candidates in primary elections would receive half that amount. New minor-party candidates would become eligible by petition for partial assistance; minor-party candidates with previous election records would be eligible for sliding-scale assistance, based on their previous vote received.

be asked. The question is this: *Are wealth and income in this richest of all nations fairly apportioned among its citizens?*

In arriving at your own judgment on that question, consider the following:

In 1968, measured by total* before-tax privately earned *income* (excluding government benefits)

- the richest *1* percent of Americans had three times as much income as the poorest *20* percent;
- the richest *5* percent had more than seven times as much as the poorest *20* percent;
- the richest one-fifth had *sixteen* times as much as the poorest one-fifth.

The concentration of *wealth* (as distinct from income) among the affluent is even more striking. Figures for 1962 showed that

- the richest fifth of the population owned 77 percent of personally held wealth;
- to put that another way, the richest one-fifth had three times as much wealth as the other 80 percent of the population;
- the richest one-fifth of Americans owned 97 percent of the personally owned corporate stock;
- in 1953, the wealthiest 1.6 percent of American families owned 82 percent of the personally held corporate stock, 90 percent of all corporate bonds and virtually all of the tax-free state and municipal bonds owned by individuals.

But perhaps the most meaningful perspective is the view from "the bottom of the heap." The 1968 figures showed that

- the least wealthy 40 percent of Americans (those earning less than $6,100 a year) received only 15 percent of all the income;
- the poorest 20 percent of Americans received just 4 percent of all the income.

Dwell on that last figure for just a moment.

These poorest one-fifth constituted about eleven and a half million American families and individuals.

Their total money income was *less than $3,150 a year*—just about $60 a week. And that is *before-tax* income.

How many readers of these words are raising their families on $60 a week? More than eleven million American families were faced with just that prospect in 1969.

---

* See Notes and Sources.

THE ABOVE FIGURES, you have noted, showed *before*-tax incomes. But what about the "progressive" Federal income tax—that purports to tax the wealthy more heavily than the poor? Doesn't it come to the rescue and correct the malapportionment?

As you have seen, because of the loopholes the Federal income tax is decidedly *not* as progressive, in actual operation, as the legal tax rates would indicate. That fact is borne out by the following statistics, for 1962, which show the almost unnoticeable effect the income tax has on the manner in which the income "pie" is sliced up:

	Before-Tax	*After-Tax*
Poorest fifth	4.6%	4.9%
Second fifth	10.9%	11.5%
Middle fifth	16.3%	16.8%
Fourth fifth	22.7%	23.1%
Richest fifth	45.5%	43.7%
Richest 5%	19.6%	17.7%

There are two other ways of looking at those after-tax figures. The first table below shows the view from the bottom of the economic heap, looking up; the second table portrays the aspect from the top of the heap, looking down:

THE VIEW FROM THE BOTTOM

This group . . .	*got . . .*	*this percent of all income*
The poorest 20%		4.9%
The poorest 40%		16.4%
The poorest 60%		33.2%
The poorest 80%		56.3%

THE VIEW FROM THE TOP

This group . . .	*got . . .*	*this percent of all income*
The richest 20%		43.7%
The richest 40%		66.8%
The richest 60%		83.6%
The richest 80%		95.1%

EACH FOURTH OF JULY, the orators tell us that "ours is the land of opportunity"; that it was founded on the notion "that all men are equal and that none are prescribed by birth to low status or high."

But is that the case? Take away the bands and the bunting and the red-white-and-blue rhetoric, and what are the facts?

The facts are that between 1947 and 1970 the nation's total output more than doubled. What more golden opportunity to put the lie to the notion that those born lowly are forever destined to remain lowly? Surely, in such an explosively expanding economy, there must have been *some* room for the poorest fifth to get more than just 5 percent of the economic "pie."

Alas, that does not seem to have been the case. In 1970, the share allotted to each fifth of the population was almost exactly what it had been twenty-three years earlier. At no time in that twenty-three years did the share allotted to the poorest fifth exceed 6 percent of the total. At times it was less than 5 percent.

The following figures may usefully be compared with the July Fourth oratory. They portray not only the distribution of income at various points in that period but also the amount by which the economy had grown since 1947—to indicate the *opportunity* that might have existed, in theory at least, for the lowly to improve themselves (and their share of the "pie"):

Percentage Share
of Before-Tax Money Income

Percent growth in total output* since 1947	—	+5	+44	+57	+71	+228	+232
	1947	*1950*	*1958*	*1960*	*1962*	*1968*	*1970*
Poorest fifth	5.0	4.5	5.1	4.9	5.1	5.7	5.5
Second fifth	11.8	12.0	12.4	12.0	12.0	12.4	12.0
Middle fifth	17.0	17.4	17.9	17.6	17.5	17.7	17.4
Fourth fifth	23.1	23.5	23.7	23.6	23.7	23.7	23.5
Richest fifth	43.0	42.6	40.9	42.0	41.7	40.6	41.6

* "Total output" is shorthand for "gross national product" (GNP)—the total of all goods and services produced in the United States in any given year.

It was figures such as those that doubtless prompted Yale professor James Tobin to comment:

There are limits to the contrasts of poverty and affluence that people will tolerate when they believe the credo of a society that proclaims that all men are equal and that none are prescribed by birth to low status or high. Today there is reason to believe that this country has transgressed those limits.

Those who find merit in Professor Tobin's observation will also see merit in enlisting the Federal income tax system to modify the apportionment of income in America and to eradicate—or at least lessen—the poverty and hunger that exist in this supposedly richest of nations on earth.

One way of achieving this would be to combine a no-loophole tax law, such as was outlined on pages 400–404, with a schedule of tax *rates* more steeply graduated than those suggested by the Brookings economists and set forth in the table on page 405. The following is illustrative of such a steeply graduated schedule of tax rates (calculated to produce approximately the same level of individual income tax collections as does present law, in accordance with the assumption consistently maintained in this book):

Illustrative Rate Schedule Under No-Loophole Tax System (2)

To compute your tax under this rate schedule, take total family income and subtract from that (a) $2,000 plus (b) $750 for each person in the family. Then find where the resulting figure fits in the left-hand column ("family's taxable income") and compute your tax.

If family's taxable income (see above note) is:	Then your tax would be:
Under $1,000	0*
$1,000–$1,500	6% of excess over $1,000
$1,500–$2,000	$30 plus 8% of excess over $1,500
$2,000–$4,000	$70 plus 9% of excess over $2,000
$4,000–$6,000	$250 plus 10% of excess over $4,000
$6,000–$8,000	$450 plus 12% of excess over $6,000
$8,000–$10,000	$690 plus 13% of excess over $8,000
$10,000–$12,000	$950 plus 15% of excess over $10,000
$12,000–$14,000	$1,250 plus 18% of excess over $12,000

* This has the effect of giving each taxpayer the equivalent of a $2,000 standard deduction.

If family's taxable income (see above note) is:	Then your tax would be:
$14,000–$16,000	$1,610 plus 21% of excess over $14,000
$16,000–$18,000	$2,030 plus 25% of excess over $16,000
$18,000–$20,000	$2,530 plus 28% of excess over $18,000
$20,000–$22,000	$3,090 plus 35% of excess over $20,000
$22,000–$26,000	$3,790 plus 40% of excess over $22,000
$26,000–$32,000	$5,390 plus 45% of excess over $26,000
$32,000–$38,000	$8,090 plus 50% of excess over $32,000
$38,000–$44,000	$11,090 plus 55% of excess over $38,000
$44,000–$50,000	$14,390 plus 60% of excess over $44,000
$50,000–$60,000	$17,990 plus 65% of excess over $50,000
$60,000–$70,000	$24,490 plus 70% of excess over $60,000
$70,000–$80,000	$31,490 plus 75% of excess over $70,000
$80,000–$90,000	$38,990 plus 80% of excess over $80,000
$90,000–$100,000	$46,990 plus 85% of excess over $90,000
$100,000 and more	$55,490 plus 90% of excess over $100,000

Another effective way to use the tax system to correct unfair distribution of income and wealth would be to couple the tax system with—or make it a replacement for—the existing welfare system, as suggested early in 1972 by Senator George McGovern. Such a move would consist, basically, of determining the minimum level of income below which no American family should be expected to live—say, for the sake of simple illustration, the $1,000 per person* suggested by Senator McGovern. Under such a formula, each family would, in effect, establish what would amount to a "line of credit" with the U.S. government amounting to $1,000 per person in the family ($4,000 for a family of four). Each year, at income tax time, the head of each family would add up all the family income† and compute the family's tax under whatever rate schedule Congress might establish. Then he would apply this figure against the family's $1,000 per-person "line of credit" to find out whether the government owed him money or vice versa.

---

* The flat per-person formula is suggested at this point for simplicity's sake, even though it results in giving disproportionately little to the single person and in some cases disproportionately much to the very large family. There are other formulations that can correct this, at least partially (e.g., more than $1,000 for the first person or two in the family; less than $1,000 for additional family members).

† Assuming a no-preference tax system as described in this chapter.

For example: assume an initial tax rate of 33⅓ percent. For a family of four, if the family income is $6,000, its tax would be $2,000 (33⅓ percent times $6,000). The result would be that the government would pay that family $2,000 (the $4,000 "line of credit" minus the $2,000 tax owed).

If that same family has an income of $8,000, the tax would be $2,667 (one-third of $8,000) and the government would pay $1,333 ($4,000 minus $2,667).

If the family's income is $12,000, its tax would be $4,000; its "line of credit" would also be $4,000, and neither the government nor the family would pay anything.

With a family income of $21,000, the tax before "credit" would be $7,000, and that, minus the $4,000 "credit," would leave that family paying $3,000 in taxes.

This system would, presumably, replace the existing programs of welfare, food stamps and housing assistance. That would eliminate not only the cost of the actual grants under those programs but also the cost—both in dollars and in red tape, and, often, in human degradation—of administering them.

At first glance, for each person in the country to be "entitled" to assistance from the U.S. government may seem a radical departure from present practice. In fact, it is not. It is no different in principle from the $750 per-person tax exemption, to which every American is "entitled"—i.e., receives as a matter of "right," no questions asked. But, as we have seen, the tax exemption is a nonsensical per-person benefit in that the richest are "entitled" to aid of $525 while the poorest get only $125. The flat $1,000 per-person "line of credit" would be far fairer and more sensible.

And the personal exemption is not the only way in which the present tax system bestows benefits on a widespread basis. All families are allowed either a standard deduction or itemized personal deductions. Thus, every person (or family) that pays state or local taxes, or owns a home or pays interest, gets a benefit from the deductions he or she takes in computing his or her Federal income tax—again, on the upside-down basis of the rich getting the biggest benefit and the poor the smallest. Sensible? Fair? Hardly.

IF THE TAX AND WELFARE SYSTEMS were combined in the manner just suggested, how would the "per-person entitlement" be paid for? It would (or at any rate could easily) be paid for in exactly the same way we now "pay for" the per-person benefits that are built into our existing tax system: by setting the tax rates at levels that will make the plan, in effect, "self-financing." For example, the existing $750 per-person tax exemption carries a price tag (rarely mentioned) of about $30 billion per year.* The various personal deductions that are permitted under present tax law "cost" an additional $20 billion. How do we "pay for" those two immensely costly tax features? Simply by setting tax rates at a level that gives us the total Federal tax collections we decide, as a nation, we need, taking into account the $50 billion cost of the deductions plus the personal exemption. That is precisely how we would "pay for" the "per-person entitlement." We would reckon its annual "cost" and set the tax rates at the level that would yield us the desired amount of Federal revenue.

Many may rebel at the thought of a "per-person entitlement" that would go to every person in the nation whether or not he or she did a lick of work. Well, that would not be the first time we gave "something for nothing" through our tax system. We bestow twenty-one and a half billion dollars of "entitlements" upon the wealthy married couples of this country (see Chapter 6) without asking them to do any work they weren't doing when they were single. We bestow billions of dollars in tax benefits upon corporations via the investment credit and ADR and DISC, and to the extent companies receive those benefits, even though they do nothing they wouldn't have done anyway (that is, to the extent they merely invest as usual or export as usual), that, too, is "something for nothing."

The real question to be asked is, Would we as a society, as a nation, benefit from such a program? Another way of putting the question is: What benefits are we, as a society and a country, deriving from leaving one-fifth of our people on poverty and sub-poverty incomes? Do we consider our slums a national asset? Are poorly educated people in poor health a "plus" on the national balance sheet? Do we benefit, in either human or economic terms, by leaving those millions of human beings with basic, if not desperate human needs unfulfilled? If we provided them with the

---

*That is, if there were no $750 exemption, Federal tax collections would be about $30 billion higher each year.

means of meeting those needs, wouldn't that generate a greater prosperity that would benefit us all? And can, or should, our national conscience tolerate the poverty we have today?

The need for a thorough overhauling of our tax system . . . is one of our most pressing national problems. . . . We should develop as soon as possible a long-range, integrated, well-balanced, equitable and simplified scheme of taxation.

—Statement by the Republican members
of the House Ways and Means Committee

We can no longer afford to defer serious, large-scale efforts to revise our federal tax system.

—Democratic Representative Wilbur Mills of Arkansas,
Chairman of the Ways and Means Committee

I do not believe we can continue much longer under our present tax structure. It is eroding faster every day.

—Republican Representative Thomas B. Curtis of Missouri,
third-ranking Republican member of that same committee

The first of those statements was made in 1943, the second two in 1958. Yet the years have rolled by, and the sweeping tax reform of which these Congressmen spoke so urgently is still a thing of the future. Meanwhile, as the late Randolph Paul, one of the most revered of modern tax reform proponents, put it, "the income tax . . . is a wasting asset of the Nation":

[The] process of erosion and patchwork amendment must stop somewhere; otherwise the statute, even now almost hopelessly complicated, will "approach the ridiculous," and taxpayers will spend more and more of their time and energy on the job of keeping their tax liability to a minimum.

Some will point out that America's is probably the most effective tax system in the world, that we collect the greatest revenues the most efficiently, with by far the greatest degree of voluntary compliance by taxpayers. This is all true, and no reader should conclude from this book that everything about our tax system is wrong.

Nor, however, should even the most impassioned Fourth of July orator be lulled into thinking that all is right with the system either, and the bill of complaint is a long one:

- the anomaly and inequity of three families receiving $2½ million of corporate dividends and paying *no* tax, while millions with but a tiny fraction as much income contribute a portion of their incomes to their government;
- the deceptiveness of a tax system that ostensibly calls for taking 60 percent of a multimillionaire's income but actually takes less than half that much;
- the discrimination against wage earners and professionals, whose earned income enjoys the fewest tax favors;
- the special dispensations to the Lockheeds and Uniroyals and Louis B. Mayers, whose principal claim for tax relief is their access to a lobbyist or a member of Congress;
- the effect of these anomalies and inequities on taxpayer compliance in a country where the government relies on each citizen to report his income honestly;
- the chain reaction of tax favors, whereby even the most "temporary" become permanently embedded in the system;
- the waste of energy and talent drained off in the frantic quest to "beat the tax game";
- the erosion, not only of the tax base but also of public morality, as "tax avoidance" becomes the norm and as each tax preference whets the appetite for more;
- *most of all, the helplessness of the uninformed public to understand the chipping away of the tax system that goes on behind an impenetrable screen of technicalities.*

We come full circle—to the appearance of James C. Carter before the Supreme Court in 1895, quoted, in part, in the first chapter. Describing the inevitable tendency of humans to "relieve themselves" from "the burdens of taxation," Mr. Carter said:

One class struggles to throw the burden off its own shoulders. If they succeed, of course, it must fall upon others. They also, in their turn, labor to get rid of it, and *finally the load falls upon those who will not, or cannot, make a successful effort for relief.* [Emphasis added.]

It is to this latter group that this book is addressed.

APPENDIX

ACKNOWLEDGMENTS

ONE'S INDEBTEDNESSES in the writing of any book are inevitably far greater than mere words can properly acknowledge. That is especially true when the book deals with a subject as complex as this one, where the layman's struggle for mere understanding of the subject, not to mention technical accuracy, often leaves him in prostrate dependence at the feet of the experts.

None have borne that dependence more stoically, helpfully and uncomplainingly than Drs. Benjamin Okner, Emil Sunley, Jr., and Joseph Pechman, all close at hand in Washington and all unfailingly willing to respond to my seemingly endless stream of questions, to which they always seemed to have the answers. So great has been my dependence on this trio that, in a just world, IRS would grant a special ruling permitting each to claim me as a dependent on his tax return. I am enormously indebted and grateful to each of them.

In Chapter 20, describing the many obstacles to tax reform, I mentioned the historic monopoly of tax expertise in the hands of those pleading for favored tax treatment and the virtual absence of vocal, mobilized technical know-how on the part of tax reformers outside the Treasury Department. No one person has done more toward redressing that imbalance than Thomas F. Field, who single-handedly spearheaded the formation of the organization Taxation with Representation and its educational counterpart, Tax

Analysts and Advocates. In addition to his personal research and writing, he has alerted and mobilized public-interest tax experts throughout the country, has opened the way for them to address themselves *promptly* to current tax issues, and has seen to it that their expert views and research were available to those who could make use of them. The taxpayers in general, and I in particular, have been the beneficiaries of his efforts.

It is doubtful I could have completed this book without the patient cooperation of a large number of Washington tax attorneys who helped me in the struggle to penetrate the complexities of the Internal Revenue Code and strove to save me from error. Naturally, they are not responsible for whatever errors may stubbornly have remained in the manuscript (despite my conscientious efforts to avoid them) or for the views expressed in this book, which are, of course, my own. Among those who gave generously of their time, patience and knowledge were Daniel Burt, Mortimer Caplin, Sheldon Cohen, Louis Diamond, Lester G. Fant, III, Joseph Guttentag, Robert Klayman, Jerome Kurtz, Barry London, Mitchell Rogovin, Stanford Ross, Norman Schwartz, Stuart Seigel, Walter Slocombe, Thomas Troyer, Stefan Tucker, Ronald West, the late Lester Uretz and Henry Zapruder. There are some others; they know who they are and I trust that they know of my appreciation for their help.

I am especially grateful to all of the above-mentioned for their understanding and tolerance of one of the most idiosyncratic (eccentric may be more precise) communication systems any modern-day author ever devised.

I have also received indispensable assistance from many experts in the Groves of Academe, among them Paul McDaniel, Reid Hambrick, Daniel Halperin, Meade Emory and, most especially, Charles Davenport.

My obligation to Stanley Surrey has many facets: his generosity in sharing with me some of his precious moments on Makonikey Heights; his many illuminating writings in the field; and, in particular, the remarkable and informative three-volume tax-reform study prepared by the Treasury Department under his leadership and cited frequently in this book. But great as was his direct and personal assistance, it might have been outweighed by the help for which he was indirectly responsible, for I have drawn enormous quantities of information, advice and wisdom from among the large number of gifted men who served under him during his eight years in the Treasury Department, learned from him and came to share his zeal for tax reform. Most of them, now, are in private practice, but it is clear that they remain among Stanley Surrey's steadfastly loyal disciples.

I am grateful to Donald Brown as expert guide in particular and unfailing friend in general. My thanks, too, to Gar Alperovitz; to Victor Honig; to Gerald Jantscher; to Lawrence Huntington and Peter Mills for responding cheerfully and effectively to pleas for help; and to the staff of the Treasury Department Library for their hospitality and cooperation.

I am indebted in a very special way to Senator Paul Douglas, in part because it was out of my great good fortune in serving on his Senate staff that I was first introduced to the injustices of the tax system, but in larger measure because of the example he set for, and the effect he inevitably had on, those who were privileged to be associated with him. I have never known, or known of, anyone in public life to match the combination of intellect, humanity, courage, scrupulous honesty and intolerance for injustice that has always dwelled within Paul Douglas. I doubt that any nobler man ever served in the United States Senate.

Book editors seldom get the credit due them; a very great deal is due Jason Epstein, not only for his counsel but for his friendship, both of which I value highly. Copy editors, too, are often unsung heroes, or heroines; heroine is just the right word for Lynn Strong.

My gratitude cannot adequately be expressed here to Irene Saunders and Anne Allen for their loyalty, patience and conscientiousness beyond any reasonable expectation in helping give birth to this book. Without Irene Saunders, there would have been no manuscript, no book—and, in all likelihood, very little remaining composure on the part of the author. Her gift for rescuing order from chaos, her toleration of her boss's idiosyncrasies and vagaries (as well as vagueries), her patience and good humor under stress (not to mention ten of the nimblest typing fingers on the East Coast) made her an indispensable part of this book. My appreciation, inadequately conveyed here, is enormous.

Mrs. Allen was the Sleuth Extraordinary in tracking down elusive information and assuring herself of its accuracy. If this book is factually accurate (as I hope it is) and if the source notes in the Appendix are helpful, the reader can be grateful for Mrs.

Allen's patience, resourcefulness and supreme conscientiousness. I know I am.

Finally, how does one go about thanking one's family? There are so many things to thank them for: their forbearance for a host of weekends and evenings of absence or abstractedness or sleepiness or grouchiness on my part—and so much more that has little to do with this book and so much to do with the quality of my life (as I tried to indicate in the Dedication). Of no one is that truer than Leni. Her special warmth and wisdom are blessings which, I'm sure, deserve more thanks than they receive, but not more than I feel, every day of my life.

PHILIP M. STERN

Washington, D.C.
October, 1972

GLOSSARY

"ABC" transaction—This refers to a triangular transaction, permitted prior to 1969 but barred by the 1969 "Tax Reform Act," under which oil companies were able, in effect, to borrow money to purchase new mineral properties or companies, paying back the "loan" with *un*taxed dollars, rather than with after-tax dollars as is the case in usual loan arrangements.

These were called "ABC" transactions because they involved three parties: A (the would-be seller of a mineral property), B (the prospective purchaser) and C (a helpful intermediary). Let's say A wished to sell an oil well for $100,000. If B were to put up $20,000 of his own and borrow the remaining $80,000 from a bank, intending to use the future income from the oil well to repay the bank, he would have to pay taxes on that income and be able to use only the diluted, *after*-tax dollars for the loan payment. But in an "ABC" transaction, A gets his $100,000 not by having B borrow the money from a bank, but by selling the oil well to B for a $20,000 down payment and at the same instant (that was a requirement under the law) selling (technically, transferring) to C, for $80,000, the right to $80,000 of the future income from the well. Under the pre-1969 law, B would fulfill that obligation by paying C the $80,000 *without having to pay any tax on it himself*. That way, B could repay with untaxed dollars rather than after-tax dollars. If B was a corporation (as was usually the case),

433

that meant the loan could be repaid with about half as many profit dollars as would have been the case if 48 percent of the profits went for taxes, leaving only about half of them to repay the loan. In 1969, Congress amended the law so as to treat these "ABC" transactions for what they really were: loan arrangements.

"Ability to pay"—As used in this book, "ability to pay" is a short-hand name for the basic philosophic concept underlying the graduated income tax (under which higher incomes are subject to stiffer tax rates than lower incomes).

This concept is based on the premise that as a person's income rises, he is "able to pay" to the government a greater share of each additional dollar of income. Thus, under 1973 tax rates, a married man need only pay nineteen cents of his four thousand and first dollar of taxable income, but on his four *hundred* thousand and first dollar of taxable income he is deemed "able to pay" seventy cents.

Accelerated depreciation—See *Depreciation.*

"Adjusted gross income" (AGI)—A taxpayer's income before taking his exemptions and personal deductions.

More specifically, it is, generally speaking, his total dollars received, minus (a) those items he does have to report on his tax return or include in computing his tax (such as interest on state and local bonds, Social Security benefits, etc.; (b) his business expenses; and (c) one-half of all his long-term capital gains (see *Capital gains*). Note that because of (b)—which can include very large deductions for such things as oil deductions or farm losses—and (c)—which can exclude large amounts of capital gains income—"adjusted gross income" can markedly understate a person's real total income.

Averaging—See *Income averaging.*

"Bunched income"—Refers, generally, to the uneven receipt of income—peaks in some years, valleys in others—in such a way that in peak years the taxpayer is pushed into an artificially high tax bracket.

Thus, he is obliged to pay more taxes than another taxpayer

who receives the same number of dollars spread evenly over the same number of years. In 1964, Congress wrote into the law a system of "income averaging" (see elsewhere in Glossary) designed to aid the person whose income varies greatly from year to year (e.g., the writer who sells his novel to the movies or, perhaps, the movie star who stars in his film).

Capital gains—Profits made on the sale or exchange of a share of stock, or a machine, building or other "capital asset" which a person has owned for more than six months (if owned for less than six months, there is no tax advantage) and which is not regularly used in his trade or business or held by him primarily for sale to customers. (There are some kinds of income which do not involve the sale of a capital asset—such as coal royalty income or lump-sum pension benefits—but which the law taxes as if they were capital gains.)

Only half a person's capital gains are included in his taxable income; the other half escapes tax entirely. For the first $50,000 of capital gains, the maximum rate on the included half is 50 percent—making the top capital gains rate 25 percent (50 percent tax on half the gain). But on that first $50,000 of gains each year, the capital gains rate may be less than 25 percent: if, for example, an individual's own top-bracket rate is 36 percent, then his capital gains rate is only 18 percent (36 percent tax on half the gain).

On capital gains above the first $50,000, the top rate on the included one-half is 70 percent, so that the maximum capital gains rate is 35 percent (70 percent on half the gain).

But note that in no event is the capital gains rate more than half as high as the rate on a person's "ordinary income."

Depletion; depletion allowance—A tax deduction that may be taken by the owners of oil and gas wells, minerals and other natural deposits.

There are two forms of depletion: "cost depletion" (limited to the original cost of the mineral property and similar to depreciation) and "percentage depletion," which is not based on, or limited to, original cost but is computed each year as a percentage of the gross income from the mineral property. It cannot, however, exceed 50 percent of the net (after-expense) income from the property. For example, oil and gas are accorded a 22 percent depletion allowance, which means that for an oil property with $100,000 of *gross* income per year, the depletion deduction would be $22,000. If, however, the *net* (after-expense) income from the property were $40,000, the depletion allowance would be limited to half that, or $20,000.

Depreciation—An annual tax deduction designed, in general, to recognize the wearing out of a capital asset such as a machine or building with the passage of time, and to permit the owner to recover, tax-free, his original capital investment in that asset over its "useful life." The "useful lives" of various kinds of assets are suggested by guidelines issued by the Treasury Department.

"Straight-line" depreciation consists of uniform deductions taken during each year of the asset's "life." For example, on a $100,000 asset with a ten-year "life," the annual deductions would be $10,000.

"Accelerated" depreciation may follow various formulas, but in essence it permits greater-than-average deductions in the early years of the asset's life, gradually shrinking until they become smaller than average in the later years. That is, in the case of the $100,000, ten-year asset referred to above, the early-year deductions would be greater than $10,000, the later-year deductions less than $10,000.

"Double taxation"—This usually refers to the fact that a dollar of corporate dividends is subjected to taxation twice: once in the hands of the corporation and again in the hands of the corporate shareholder. There are numerous other instances of "double taxation," such as the payment of an excise tax with dollars that have already been subject to an income tax.

Estate tax—The tax imposed on the transfer of property after a person's death. Only amounts above $60,000 are subject to this tax.

Exclusions—Income a taxpayer does not have to include in computing his tax.

This would include such items as various government payments (Social Security, railroad retirement and veterans' benefits), interest on state and local bonds, and all money received by gift or inheritance.

Gift tax—A tax that may be imposed on the giver when he transfers property to another person during his lifetime.

Each taxpayer is permitted to give $3,000 per year ($6,000 a year for married couples) tax-free to as many people as he may choose. Over and above that, each taxpayer is permitted to make $30,000 of tax-free gifts ($60,000 for married couples) during his lifetime.

Head-of-household—An unmarried person who supports a relative as part of his household, or who supports his father or mother even if they are not part of his household.

Heads-of-household are taxed according to special tax rates that lie roughly midway between the rates applicable to unmarried taxpayers and those applicable to married joint-return filers.

"Imputed" income—Income you   ceive in some form other than cash.

For example, your bank provides you certain services free, in lieu of paying you interest on your deposits. The value of those services is "imputed" income, as is the value of the housing you get from your owned home, over and above your expenses. Generally speaking, "imputed" income is not taxed in the United States, but in some countries the imputed rental income on owner-occupied homes is or has been taxed to the owner (see page 356).

Income averaging—A means of alleviating the so-called "bunched income" problem (described elsewhere in Glossary) by permitting a taxpayer, in effect, to smooth out the peaks and valleys of his income and compute his taxes as if the income had been received more evenly over a period of years.

For example, under the provision of the law enacted in 1964, anyone whose income has varied more than one-third in a five-year period could, in effect, lop off his above-average income in the fifth year and have it taxed as if it had been spread evenly over the prior four years.

Income-splitting—Refers to various means by which a given amount of income may be split up into smaller and separately taxed "bundles," thus avoiding the high tax rates that would apply if the income were taxed as a single "bundle."

The best-known and most widely used method is the filing of

a joint tax return by married couples, which permits the husband's income to be taxed as if it were two half-sized "bundles." For an example of how this operates, see pages 121–22.

"Ordinary income"—Income that is subject to the regular income tax rate schedules, as distinct from "capital gains," which are accorded special rates (see *Capital gains*).

Percentage depletion—See *Depletion*.

Retirement income credit—A provision easing the taxation of those over sixty-five.

Under this provision, an elderly person's tax bill may be reduced by an amount equal to one-fifth of his first $1,200 of pension, annuity, dividend, interest or royalty income. For example, it gives a person over sixty-five with $1,000 of pension income a $200 tax cut. However, the basis for the tax reduction is reduced by one dollar for every dollar (over $1,200) of either Social Security benefits or income earned from a job. Those over seventy-two may earn as much as they like without any reduction of their tax credit.

"Spin-off"—A device used for transforming a corporate dividend payment from "ordinary income" into a capital gain.

Stock option—The right granted a corporate officer or director to buy company stock at a fixed price within a certain period of time.

Example: An executive, given a five-year option (or right) to buy 5,000 shares of his company's stock at $25 per share, later exercises that right and still later sells the stock, whose market price has gone up to $50 per share. If his company's option plan meets certain requirements in the tax law, and if he has held the stock at least three years, his $125,000 profit is taxed at the special capital gains rate.

"Straight-line" depreciation—See *Depreciation*.

Taxable income—The amount left after a taxpayer has claimed all his exemptions and deductions; i.e., the amount actually subject to tax.

Tax Court—A special court made up of sixteen judges whose function is to resolve disputes between taxpayers and the Internal Revenue Service.

Although headquartered in Washington, individual judges hear cases all around the country. Tax cases may also be considered by the regular district courts of the United States and by the Court of Claims. Appeals from decisions of the Tax Court may be taken to the appropriate Federal Circuit Court of Appeals.

Tax credit—A subtraction from the amount of *tax* a person owes. (This is different from a tax deduction, which is a subtraction from the amount of a person's *income* that is subject to tax.)

A tax credit works this way: Suppose an elderly person has a $125 retirement income credit (see page 353). He figures up his tax bill, which happens to come out to $625, and then subtracts $125 from that. The tax he owes the government is thus reduced to $500. Under a tax credit, all taxpayers receive the same dollar advantages, no matter what their tax bracket—which is not the case with a tax deduction (see below). Examples of tax credits: the retirement income credit; the foreign tax credit; the credit for small political contributions.

Tax deduction—A subtraction that reduces the amount of a person's *income* that is subject to taxes.

Example: Suppose a taxpayer in the 58 percent tax bracket has $50,000 of income that would otherwise be taxable. If he takes a $1,000 medical expense deduction, his taxable income is reduced to $49,000. If he had not been permitted to deduct the $1,000 (if, say, he had bought a mink coat with it), $580 of the $1,000 would go to the government. *In this sense, Uncle Sam has paid $580, or 58 percent of the deducted amount.* The higher your tax bracket, the greater portion the government pays. For a person in the 26 percent bracket, for example, the government pays only $260 of a $1,000 tax-deductible medical bill.

"Tax shelter"—Generally speaking, any device or plan which shelters a person's income from the regular income tax rates.

Trusts—A legal—*and separately taxable*—arrangement with respect to property or wealth in which one or more "trustees" hold title to the property and manage it for the benefit of one or more beneficiaries.

For example, a father may put property in one trust—or several—for his minor son, to be managed by trustees until the son reaches a certain age. Since each trust is, in most cases, separately taxable, this offers the possibility of considerable tax savings through income-splitting (see elsewhere in Glossary).

Value added tax (VAT)—A tax imposed (and passed on) at each stage of the manufacturing-selling process and ultimately added to the price of the goods that the consumer pays at retail. To take a simplified example, under a VAT the manufacturer calculates the "value added" by him (by subtracting the costs of materials from the amount he receives from the wholesaler); the wholesaler, in turn, calculates the "value added" by him (by subtracting what he paid the manufacturer from what he receives from the retailer); the retailer calculates the "value added" by him (by subtracting what he paid the wholesaler from what he charges the consumer). At each stage, a tax is computed on the basis of the "value added," and that tax is immediately added on—by the manufacturer, in computing what he has to charge the wholesaler; by the wholesaler, in reckoning what he has to charge the retailer; by the retailer, in fixing the price he charges to the consumer. Thus, according to most analyses of the VAT, it is the consumer who ends up bearing the burden of the tax—and the VAT is nothing but a hidden sales tax. It is hidden in the sense that, unlike the sales tax, which is separately broken out so that the purchaser is aware of what he is paying when the cashier rings it up, the VAT is usually built into the price of the product.

NOTES AND SOURCES

EXPLANATION OF ABBREVIATIONS

Budget—The Budget of the United States Government, which sets forth the proposed expenditures in various Federal activities as recommended by the President in any given fiscal year (see *FY*, below). Available for purchase through the Government Printing Office, Washington, D.C.

Cambridge Institute Pamphlet—"Basic Facts: Distribution of Personal Income and Wealth in the United States," by Letitia Upton and Nancy Lyons. Published in May 1972 by the Cambridge Institute, a nonprofit research organization, 1878 Massachusetts Avenue, Cambridge, Massachusetts.

Compendium—Refers to "Tax Revision Compendium: Compendium of Papers on Broadening the Tax Base," a three-volume collection of papers on a broad range of tax policies collected and published by the House Ways and Means Committee in 1959. *2 Compendium 875* means Volume 2 of the Compendium, at page 875.

CR—Congressional Record; *100 CR 12312* refers to Volume 100 of the permanent, bound Congressional Record at page 12312. The notation "(Daily)" means the reference comes from the nonpermanent Record, whose page numbers are different from the permanent Record's.

Cum. Bull.—The Cumulative Bulletin, containing published Treasury Department and Internal Revenue Service regulations.

Dugger—Refers to "Oil and Politics," article by Ronnie Dugger appearing in the September 1969 issue of the *Atlantic*, pp. 66–90.

Economic Indicators—Monthly statistical publication prepared by the President's Council of Economic Advisors.

441

Eisenstein—Refers to *The Ideologies of Taxation* by the late tax attorney Louis Eisenstein (The Ronald Press, 1961).

Engler—Refers to *The Politics of Oil: A Study of Private Power and Democratic Directions* by Robert Engler (University of Chicago Press, 1967).

F.2d; F. Supp.—Federal Reports, Second Series; The Federal Supplement. A series of volumes reporting decisions of Federal courts. *220 F.2d 890, 895* means that the case quoted begins in Volume 220 of the series at page 890, but that the particular quotation in question appears at page 895.

French—Refers to "Why the Rich Shouldn't Worry About Tax Reform," article by V. O. French in the *Washington Monthly*, July 1972, pp. 29–36.

FY—Fiscal year, the government's accounting year, which ends June 30. *FY 1962* refers to the twelve months ending June 30, 1962.

H. Doc.—House Document. These frequently contain Presidential messages, including veto messages. *H. Doc. 43, 80-2* refers to House Document No. 43 of the Eightieth Congress, Second Session.

H.R.—Designates a bill introduced in the House of Representatives. Senate bills bear the prefix *S*.

H. Rep.—House Report: the report accompanying a bill issued by the committee of the U.S. House of Representatives that handled the bill. *H. Rep. 491, 81-2* refers to House Report No. 491 of the Eighty-first Congress, Second Session.

IRB—Internal Revenue Bulletin, a publication put out by the Internal Revenue Service that periodically sets forth IRS rules, regulations or interpretations of the law.

IRC—Internal Revenue Code, the basic tax law of the United States. *IRC Sec. 1237* refers to Section 1237 of the Code.

HWM—House Ways and Means Committee (the committee of the House of Representatives that deals with all tax legislation). *1969 HWM 456* refers to general tax hearings held by that committee in 1969, at page 456.

HWM Report—The report issued by the Ways and Means Committee containing the Committee's general and technical explanation of a given piece of legislation approved by it. *1969 HWM Report* refers to House Report 91-413, Ninety-first Congress, First Session. *1971 HWM Report* refers to House Report 92-533, Ninety-second Congress, First Session.

JCER—Congress's Joint Committee on the Economic Report. *1955 JCER 412* refers to page 412 of the collection of papers on "Federal Tax Policy for Economic Growth and Stability," compiled by the Joint Committee and issued November 9, 1955. *1955 JCER Hearings* refers to panel-discussion hearings on that same subject, also held in 1955. *1972 JCER Subsidy Papers* refers to "The Economics of Federal Subsidy Programs—A Compendium of Papers" submitted to the committee and issued in 1972 as Joint Committee prints. *1972 JCER Subsidy Hearings* refers to hearings held in January 1972 on the subject "The Economics of Federal Subsidy Programs."

Musgrave—Refers to "Tax Preferences to Foreign Investment," paper by Peggy B. Musgrave, in Part 2 of the 1972 JCER Subsidy Papers (see *JCER*, above), pp. 176–219.

PL—Public law. Refers to the number given each law that passes Congress and is signed by the President.

Pechman—Refers to writings by Joseph A. Pechman, Director of Economic Studies, the Brookings Institution, Washington, D.C. *Pechman, Federal Tax Policy* refers to his book by that name, published by Brookings in 1966, with a revised edition in 1971. *Pechman, "Rich, Poor"* refers to Brookings Reprint 168, containing Dr. Pechman's article "The Rich, the Poor and the Taxes They Pay," reprinted from *The Public Interest*, Fall 1969.

Pechman-Okner—Refers to "Individual Income Tax Erosion, by Income Classes," by Joseph A. Pechman and Benjamin A. Okner, referred to throughout this book, first at page 6. The paper may be found in two places: Part 1 of the 1972 JCER Subsidy Papers (see *JCER*, above), pp. 13–40, and Brookings Reprint 230, May 1972.

Regs.—Refers to regulations issued by the Treasury Department and the Internal Revenue Service, spelling out in detail the policies the Department and the IRS intend to follow in implementing a tax law enacted by Congress.

Rev. Rul.; Rev. Proc.—Refers to Revenue Rulings and Revenue Procedures, different forms of interpretations of the tax law issued from time to time by the Internal Revenue Service.

Rulings Compendium—"The Public and the Rulings Process," a 1972 compendium of papers submitted to the Treasury Department by Taxation with Representation, an organization describing themselves as "Tax Experts Representing the Public Interest" and headquartered in Arlington, Virginia.

Russkay and Osserman—Refers to *Halfway to Tax Reform*, by Joseph A. Russkay and Richard A. Osserman (The Indiana University Press, 1970).

SFC—Senate Finance Committee. *1971 SFC 179* refers to the hearings on a general tax bill held by that committee in 1971, at page 179.

SFC Report—The report issued by the Finance Committee containing the Committee's general and technical explanation of a given piece of legislation approved by it. *1962 SFC Report* refers to Senate Report 1881, Eighty-seventh Congress, Second Session. *1969 SFC Report* refers to Senate Report 91-552, Ninety-first Congress, First Session. *1971 SFC Report* refers to Senate Report 92-437, Ninety-second Congress, First Session.

SOI—"Statistics of Income," published annually by the Internal Revenue Service. Unless otherwise stated, reference is to volumes on individual income tax returns (separate volumes are published for corporations' and trust, gift and estate tax returns). *1960 SOI 34* refers to the 1960 "Statistics of Income" (for individual tax returns), at page 34.

S. Rep.—Senate Report (see *H. Rep.*). *S. Rep. 485, 84-1* refers to Senate Report No. 485 of the Eighty-fourth Congress, First Session.

Stat.—The General Statutes of the United States. *70 Stat. 43* refers to Volume 70 of the General Statutes, at page 43.

Sunley—Refers to "The Federal Tax Subsidy of the Timber Industry," a paper by Emil M. Sunley, Jr., appearing in Part 3 of the 1972 JCER Subsidy Papers (see *JCER*, above), pp. 317–42.

TC, TCM, USTC—Refers to decisions of the Tax Court of the United States. *25 TC 512* refers to Volume 25 of those decisions, at page 512. *TCM* refers to memorandum decisions of that court.

Tr.—Refers to "Tax Reform Studies and Proposals, U.S. Treasury Department," the result of extensive studies conducted by that department 1966–68 and published on February 5, 1969, by the House Ways and Means Committee and the Senate Finance Committee. *Tr. 413* refers to page 413 of those studies.

U.S.—The United States Reports, containing decisions of the U.S. Supreme Court. *215 U.S. 425* refers to Volume 215 of those reports, at page 425.

Westfall—Refers to "Revitalizing the Federal Estate and Gift Taxes" by David Westfall, Vol. 83, *Harvard Law Review*, March 1970, pp. 986–1,013.

Note: Figures on revenue losses from particular tax features have been derived from the Pechman-Okner analysis (see above); from the "illustrative tax expenditure budget" (pages 155-58); from a similar listing contained in a statement to the Joint Economic Committee by Treasury Undersecretary Edwin S. Cohen, July 21, 1972, Appendix D; and from official and unofficial estimates.

Page

vii   *Quotations:* Kenneth Lamott, *The Moneymakers* (Little, Brown, 1969), pp. 283, 281; *Clement Stone's $4 million donation:* Washington *Star*, Nov. 17, 1972 p. A1.

xvi   *Judge Learned Hand:* Commissioner v. Newman, 159 F.2d 848 (1947).

1. Uncle Sam's Welfare Program—for the Rich

6   *"Tax welfare" amounts:* Pechman-Okner, Table A-5, col. 4.
7   *Getty daily income: Esquire*, Oct. 1970, p. 146.
9   *Numbers of families, amount of "tax welfare":* Pechman-Okner, Table 8, col. 1 (numbers of families); Table 6, col. 3 ("tax wel-

fare"). *Note:* The figures on numbers of families in various income groups are based on *total* family income. They are therefore different from the statistics compiled by the IRS from tax returns (and cited elsewhere in this book), since the IRS figures are based on "adjusted gross income" (AGI). AGI excludes a number of income items that are included in the Brookings figures—such as income from state and local bonds and half of all capital gains.

9–10   *Federal outlays for various programs:* Budget, FY 1973, pp. 106, 144, 146, 292.

11   *Theoretical versus actual tax burdens:* Pechman-Okner. Theoretical burden may be derived by dividing Table 6, col. 1 by Table 2, col. 1. *Actual burden:* Table 2, col. 3.

11   *Average yearly income:* Pechman-Okner, Table 2, col. 1 divided by Table 8, col. 1.

13   *Capital gains "tax welfare":* Pechman-Okner, Table A-2, col. 2 divided by Table 8, col. 1.

14   *Numbers of non-taxpayers:* SOI. These figures are easily calculated by comparing the total number of returns in each income group with the *taxable* returns, usually in the first table in the given "Statistics of Income" publication.

14–15   *Examples of rich tax avoiders:* Tr. 88–94.

15   *Robert Short:* Washington *Post*, Dec. 19, 1971, p. D1, reporting on analysis by Benjamin Okner and Roger Noll, two Washington economists. According to the *Post*, in 1969 Short purchased a 90 percent interest in the Washington Senators baseball team (listing, at the time, a $9 million purchase price) for a cash outlay on his part of just $1,000. "The rest of the purchase price was made up of loans, some of them guaranteed by Short, and by the issue of preferred stock." The *Post* account also states that, at least in the first two years he owned the club, "Short vigorously refrained from pouring his own cash into the team—except as a loan, in the purchase, from one of his own companies, at a 9.75 percent interest rate." Nonetheless, his purchase of the team made him and/or his companies "eligible for tax reductions worth some $4 million, because of player depreciation over the next several years." In 1970 alone, he stood to realize "over half a million dollars in tax reductions" (provided his other business interests showed a sufficient profit). The *Post* noted that the average citizen who, say, won the Irish Sweepstakes, would have to invest no less than $7 million in AT&T stock to realize a return of $500,000. These tax savings resulted from reporting "bookkeeping losses" due largely to "depreciation" permitted under the tax law, principally of the value of the players' contracts. (Readers may note that it is Short who gets the tax benefits of the depreciation, not the athletes, whose prowess—and earning abilities—are inevitably declining with each year's passage of time.) In 1971, Short, complaining bitterly of the losses he had suffered in Washington (but not mentioning the tax savings he had enjoyed), won American League permission to move the Senators to Texas.

15   *Mrs. Dodge's $100 million of bonds:* Washington *Post*, Sept. 27, 1971, p. Bl.

Page

15   *Hyper-rich oilman:* 109 CR 24399, Dec. 12, 1963.

15   *2,200,000 "poverty line" taxpayers:* Tr. 3.

15   *20 million $100-a-week families:* 1969 SOI, Table 1.1, col. 6.

15   *Outgoing Treasury Secretary:* Statement by Joseph Barr before Joint Economic Committee, Jan. 17, 1969.

16   *Three families with $2,450,000 of dividends:* 1970 SOI (Preliminary), p. 36, cols. 11, 12 (comparing all returns with taxable returns).

16   *Other zero-tax families:* 1970 SOI (Preliminary), p. 24, col. 1.

16   *Groups 1, 2, 3:* Press release, May 7, 1972, by Rep. Henry Reuss of Wisconsin.

16   *Ralph Senters:* Washington *Post*, May 1, 1972, p. A1.

17–18   *Corporate non-taxpayers:* Industrial companies: 118 CR H6713–14 (Daily), July 19, 1972; oil companies: *Oil Week*, Aug. 21, 1972. *Dividends paid: Moody's Industrial and Utility Manuals,* 1971.

18   *Decline in corporate tax burden; Goldman Sachs quote: Wall Street Journal,* Aug. 2, 1972, p. 1.

18   *Decline in share of revenue provided by corporation income tax:* Pechman, *Federal Tax Policy,* Table C-3, pp. 288–9.

18–19   *$4–$6 billion dividend and interest reporting gap:* The Office of Tax Analysis, U.S. Treasury Dept., estimates that in 1966 there were $3.165 billion of interest payments that should have been reported on tax returns that were not ($17.715 billion reportable, $14.55 billion actually reported). As to unreported dividends, while there is considerable disagreement on the amount, national income figures reflect total dividend payments by corporations of about $21 billion annually, with roughly $15 billion reported on tax returns. While that would indicate a $6 billion gap, an estimated half of those dividends are paid to foundations and other nontaxable entities, which would indicate a $3 billion reporting gap for dividends. This, together with the $3 billion interest gap (see above), would mean a $6 billion dividend-plus-interest reporting gap. To reflect more conservative estimates of the dividend gap, the figure "$4–$6 billion" is used here.

20   *Senator Long on work requirement for welfare recipients:* Washington *Post*, Dec. 19, 1971, p. C4.

21   *Kennedy Administration re "discriminatory and inequitable":* 1963 HWM 51.

22   *Statistics on "un-preferenced" taxpayer:* 1969 SOI, p. 93, col. 8.

23–25   *Statistics on Social Security, property, state and local taxes:* Roger A. Herriott and Herman P. Miller, "Changes in the Distribution of Taxes Among Income Groups, 1962–1968" (mimeographed paper presented to Aug. 1971 American Statistical Association meeting, Fort Collins, Colo.), Table 2.

24   (Also footnote) *Increases in payroll taxes; Pechman on who bears burden:* Pechman, "Rich, Poor," p. 31.

25   *Total tax burden figures:* Roger A. Herriott and Herman P. Miller, "Who Paid the Taxes in 1968," Table 7. Paper published in the May 1971 *Conference Board Record* as "The Taxes We Pay."

26–7   *Taxpayers 1, 2, 3:* Tr. 90, 92, 93.

26   (Footnote) *Estimated stockholdings of Taxpayer 1:* Based on aver-

age stock yield of 3.5%, as is assumed wherever such estimates are made.

28   *Eisenstein:* p. 11.

28   *James C. Carter before the Supreme Court:* Pollock v. Farmers' Loan & Trust Co., 157 U.S. 429, 516 (1895).

3. How Would You Like a Special Tax Law, All Your Own?

34   *$3 million saving for Uniroyal:* 118 CR 37635 (Daily), Dec. 8, 1969.

36   *House repeal of investment credit:* H.R. 12290 (1969).

36   *Background of Uniroyal amendment:* 118 CR 37636 (Daily), Dec. 8, 1969; 1969 SFC Report, p. 279, third full para.; *Uniroyal sales: Fortune,* May 1972, p. 192.

38   *Lockheed, McDonnell Douglas amendments:* 118 CR 37635–36 (Daily), Dec. 8, 1969; 1969 SFC Report, p. 244, para. XIII.

38   (Footnote) *McDonnell Douglas testimony:* Hearings before Senate Finance Committee on H.R. 12290 (to continue the tax surcharge), July 8–15, 1969, p. 371.

39   *Mobil Oil, Litton, Cafritz amendments:* 118 CR 37635–36; see also 1969 SFC Report at p. 235, third full para. (Mobil), p. 124, fourth full para. (Litton), and p. 43, first full para. (Cafritz).

40   *At least 15 hand-tailored amendments:* 118 CR 37635, Dec. 8, 1969.

40   *WWL provision "no coincidence":* Wall Street Journal, May 27, 1970, p. 1.

40   *Senator Long's sense of humor:* Washington Monthly, July 1972, p. 31.

42–3   *Description of Mayer amendment background:* Eisenstein, p. 156. Inner quote from S. Rep. 781, 82-1, p. 50 (1951).

43   *Alvord appearance for U.S. Chamber of Commerce:* 1951 SFC 1451, 1478.

43   *Revenue loss "negligible":* S. Rep. 781, 82-1, p. 50 (1951).

43   *1954 reenactment of Mayer provision:* 1954 SFC 1985, 2002–3; S. Rep. 1622, 83-2, p. 115 (1954).

43   *The "Hollywood Rajah":* Taken from the title of Bosley Crowther's book, *Hollywood Rajah: The Life and Times of Louis B. Mayer* (Holt, Rinehart & Winston, 1960).

43–4   *Alvord amendment:* New York Herald Tribune, Jan. 19, 1964.

44–5   *Merrill provision:* Eisenstein, p. 159.

46–7   *Sanders case and provision:* Leo Sanders et al. v. Commissioner, 21 TC 1012 (1954); 255 F.2d 629 (1955), cert. denied 350 U.S. 967 (1956); S. Rep. 1941, 84-2 (1956); 102 CR 7795 (1956); H. Rep. 2253, 84-2 (1956), p. 5; PL 84-269, 70 Stat. 404.

48   *L. R. McKee:* L. R. and Lulu McKee v. Commissioner, 18 TC 512 (1952).

48   *Universal Oil Products:* Universal Oil Products Co. v. Root Refining Co., 328 U.S. 575 (1946).

49   *Clarence Cannon bill:* S. Rep. 1283, 84-1 (1955); 101 CR 12655, 1287 (1955).

49–50   *Fort Wayne Journal-Gazette, Owens-Corning Fiberglas provisions:* 5 National Tax Journal 58 (1952).

Page

49–50   *Budd, Sangamo Electric and Bridgeport Brass companies:* 98 CR 9072–76 (1952).

52   *No tax on $20 million of income:* 1961 HWM 107.

52   *$25 million yearly drain:* 118 CR 37635 (Daily), Dec. 8, 1969.

52   *Bill for DuPont-General Motors:* H.R. 8847, 87-1 (1961); PL 87-403 (1962).

52   *Hilton Hotels Corp.:* H. Rep. 1269, 85-1, p. 18 (1957); see also 109 CR 4172 (Daily), Mar. 18, 1963.

52   *Twin Cities provision:* 108 CR 17076 (Daily), Aug. 30, 1962. Previously vetoed bill: H.R. 8652, 87-1; S. Rep. 1101, 87-1; 107 CR 21552 (1961).

53   *Howard F. Knipp provision:* Knipp's Estate v. Commissioner, 25 TC 153 (1955); 244 F.2d 436 (1957); H. Rep. 632, 86-1; S. Rep. 1002, 86-1; 105 CR 8478 (1959).

55   *Sen. Kennedy naming 15 provisions:* 118 CR 37633–9 (Daily), Dec. 8, 1969; *Kennedy and Long interchange:* p. 37633.

55   *Father Jolley testimony:* 1969 SFC 1099–1109, Sept. 12, 1969.

56   *Sen. Kennedy quote:* 118 CR 37635–6 (Daily), Dec. 8, 1969; *Sen. Long quote:* 118 CR 37637 (Daily), Dec. 8, 1969.

56   *(Footnote) Sen. Williams quote:* 118 CR 37637 (Daily), Dec. 8, 1969.

58   *Sens. Humphrey, Lausche, Kerr:* 108 CR 17076 (Daily), Aug. 30, 1962.

58   *Prof. Walter Blum:* 1955 JCER 259.

59   *"It has been observed":* Harvard Law Review, May 1957, p. vii.

59   *William L. Cary:* 68 Harvard Law Review 745 (1955); 1955 JCER 264.

4. The Mightily-Privileged Few

60   *Percent of taxpayers in income groups:* 1969 SOI, p. 9, col. 7.

61   *Thomas J. Watson stock options:* IBM Proxy Statements, 1966–72.

62   *Ownership of tax-free bonds:* Figures based on Pechman-Okner data on the distribution of benefits to individuals from ownership of tax-free bonds. Additional information may be found in "Survey of Financial Characteristics of Consumers" (Federal Reserve Board), by Dorothy S. Projector and Gertrude S. Weiss, pp. 123, 151.

62   *Rep. John Byrnes quote:* Speech before National Conference of State Legislative Leaders, Honolulu, Dec. 6, 1968.

63   *Equivalent yields on taxable bonds:* Assumes taxpayers are married, and filing a joint return.

63   *"Daily Investor" column:* Washington Daily News, Apr. 20, 1972, p. 16; *New York Times ad:* Apr. 9, 1972, p. F7.

64   *Tax savings, benefits, from tax-free bonds:* Pechman-Okner data.

64   *Non-riskiness of tax-free bonds:* Russkay and Osserman, p. 273; also "Daily Investor" column (see above).

64–5   *Tax-free bond ownership by particular banks:* Chase Manhattan Corporation 1970 Annual Report, p. 26; First National City Corporation 1971 Annual Report, p. 24.

65   *Opposition to tax-free bonds by Coolidge, Carter, Mellon, etc.:* Russkay and Osserman, p. 97.

Page

66   *Federal revenue loss twice gain to states; subsidy proposal by Sen. Nelson:* 118 CR S4288 (Daily), Mar. 21, 1972.

66   (Footnote) *States would pick up $180 million:* Ott and Meltzer, "Federal Tax Treatment of State and Local Securities" (Brookings Institution, 1963), p. 7; 1 Compendium 726. *State per-capita debt:* 118 CR S14683 (Daily), Sept. 12, 1972.

67   *Joseph Barr:* See note, p. 15, above; *number of taxless families:* SOI for each year cited (see note, p. 15, above).

67   (Footnote to table) *Examples of rich taxpayers:* Tr. 94, 92.

68   *Number of taxless families in 1970:* 1970 SOI (Preliminary), p. 24, col. 1 (comparing all returns with taxable returns); also press release of Rep. Henry Reuss of Wisconsin, May 7, 1972.

68   *Three taxless families:* 1970 SOI (Preliminary), p. 24, col. 1; dividend information at p. 32, cols. 32, 33 (comparing all returns with taxable returns).

68   *Senatorial pronunciamento:* 1969 SFC Report, p. 112.

69   *Groups 1, 2, 3:* Press release by Rep. Henry Reuss of Wisconsin, May 7, 1972.

69   *Ralph Senters:* Washington *Post*, May 1, 1972, p .1.

70   *Amount of "tax-favored" income:* Reuss press release, May 7, 1972 (see p. 69, above). Reuss differentiated between "non-favored" income (such as corporate dividends) and "tax-favored" income (such as from capital gains, or from oil ventures qualifying for percentage depletion deductions, etc.). According to Reuss, families in Group 3, for example, averaged about $1 million in "non-favored" income and about $703,750 in "tax-favored" income.

70   (Footnote) *Senate Finance favored 5% minimum tax:* 1969 SFC Report, p. 112.

71   *$30,000 exemption from "minimum tax":* IRC, Sec. 56(a)(1).

71   *Exemption for capital gains on charitable gifts:* IRC, Sec. 170(e); see also Sec. 17(b)(1)(D) and (E).

71   *Average $50,000 income from tax-free bonds:* based on Pechman-Okner data.

73   *December 31, 1970 law:* PL 91-614, Sec. 501(a).

73–4   *Sen. Nelson re "love tap":* 118 CR S4289 (Daily), Mar. 21, 1972.

75   *Mr. C:* Tr. 92.

75   *Tax advantages from "double-dip":* Tr. 147.

77   *$100 million saving for 30,000 executives:* 1969 SFC Report, p. 333.

77   *Congress's reasoning:* 1969 HWM Report, pp. 208–9; also "General Explanation of the Tax Reform Act of 1969" (Joint Committee on Internal Revenue Taxation), pp. 224–5.

77   *Harold Geneen salary-plus-bonus: Gallagher President's Report,* Apr. 19, 1972.

78   *Average salary of 215 executives:* Lent and Menge, "The Importance of Restricted Stock Options in Executive Compensation" (mimeographed, Amos Tuck School, Dartmouth College, 1962), p. 8.

78–9   *IBM stock options:* 1962 IBM Proxy Statement, p. 10; 1971 IBM Proxy Statement, pp. 24–5.

78–9   *Thomas J. Watson salary:* IBM Proxy Statements, 1966–70.

79   *Harold Geneen stock options:* ITT Proxy Statement, Mar. 23. 1971.

79   (Footnote) *Geneen's salary/bonus increase:* ITT 1972 Proxy Statement.

Page

79   *Confidential letter: Gallagher President's Report,* Apr. 19, 1972.
80   *General Motors stock options:* 1971 GM Proxy Statement, pp. 9, 45.
80   *Continental Airlines stock option:* 32nd Annual Report, Corporate Democracy, Inc. (published by Lewis D. and John G. Gilbert, 1971), p. 144.
81   *"The Supreme Court has held":* Commissioner v. LoBue, 351 U.S. 243 (1956), in which the Court "held that the 'proprietary interest' test had no basis and that all employee options resulted in taxable compensation" (1963 HWM 466).
83   *Overall stock prices, 1950–63:* 1963 HWM 482.
83   *38 matched pairs:* 1953 HWM 483.
83   *Sen. Albert Gore:* 1961 SFC Stock Option Hearings, p. 96.
86   *Allied Chemical, John Connor; Xerox; Ford: Dun's,* June 1971, p. 40.
87   *"Cornucopia of lesser perquisites": Dun's,* Apr. 1972, p. 120.
89   *10 separate steps required: Dun's,* Apr. 1972, p. 50.
89   *110 out of 120 corporations: Dun's,* Apr. 1972, pp. 44–9.
89   *Ownership of corporate stock: Inequality and Poverty,* ed. by Edward C. Budd (W. W. Norton, 1967), p. xxii.
90   *Distribution of benefits from dividend exclusion:* Based on Pechman-Okner data.
91   *Eisenhower re 100 taxes on an egg:* Jacksonville, Fla., Sept. 2, 1952; also Warsaw, Ind., July 15, 1962.
92   *Reps. Daniel Reed and Joseph Martin:* 96 CR 9238, 9386 (1950).
92   *Dividends received in 1970:* 1970 SOI (Preliminary), p. 30, col. 33.

5. The Great Capital Gains Trial

94   *Capital gains "tax welfare":* Pechman-Okner, Table A-3, col. 2 divided by Table 8, col. 1.
95   *Who receives capital gains:* 1969 SOI, p. 40, col. 4.
96   *$6 million capital gains on $9 million income:* 1963 SFC 279.
96   *Percent of group receiving capital gains:* 1969 SOI, p. 40, col. 3 divided by p. 9, col. 6.
96   *Percent of incomes from capital gains:* 1969 SOI, p. 40, col. 4; p. 9, col. 8.
98   *Mr. C:* Tr. 92.
99   *Charles Stewart Mott wealth: Fortune,* May 1968, p. 156.
100   *$10 billion escapes tax; $4½ billion revenue loss:* Pechman-Okner data; revenue loss in Table A-4, col. 2.
100   *Ailsa Mellon Bruce: Wall Street Journal,* Dec. 24, 1971.
101   *Nixon veto of education bill: Congressional Quarterly Almanac,* 1970, p. 226.
101   *Super-rich paying just 25%:* 1963 SFC 279.
102   *Million-and-over families paying 32%:* See note on table, p. 11.
102   *Capital gains the biggest single factor:* This is graphically portrayed in Pechman-Okner, Fig. 1, which shows on a chart the elements, at various income levels, that account for the difference between what the legal tax rates call for a person to pay and what he actually *does* pay. I have often called this "the whale chart," because as family income rises, the gap between "theory" and "practice" caused by capital gains yawns wider and wider, like the mouth of a whale.

Page

103   *Situation No. 1:* Compare IRC Sec. 1221(3) with IRC Sec. 1235. In 1964, Congress permitted authors and others whose income comes in uneven "spurts" to average out several years' income, but they are still denied capital gains treatment of that income.

103   *Congress's reasons for capital gains for inventors:* S. Rep. 2375, 81-2, p. 44 (1950).

105   *General counsel of Ford:* William T. Gossett; from *Fortune,* Dec. 1958, p. 202.

107   *Tax code on "collapsibles":* IRC Sec. 341.

107   *Tax code on "spin-offs":* IRC Sec. 355. See also Regs. 1.355-1.

108–9   *Capital gains tax history:* National Tax Journal, 1949, pp. 12 ff.

112   *51% tax on $25,000 gain taxed in a single year:* the gain would make his taxable income for that year $65,000, on which his tax would come to $24,970—$12,830 more than his tax would have been without the gain. The additional $12,830 of tax is 51.3% of the $25,000 capital gain.

114   *Three Harvard Business School professors:* Walter W. Heller, at 1955 JCER 389, summarizing findings of Butters, Thompson and Bollinger, *Effects of Taxation: Investments by Individuals* (Harvard University, 1953).

115   *Joseph Pechman on effects of 1969 capital gains tax increase:* New York *Times,* July 5, 1962.

116   *Corporations derived only 1.5% of capital from stock issues:* Economic Report of the President, Jan. 1972, p. 284. Over the decade of the Sixties, corporations derived just $12.8 billion out of $824.9 billion of capital from stocks.

118   *Brandeis quote:* By Merle Miller at 1958 HWM 2321.

6. Your Wife May Be Worth a Million

119–20   *Figures of wife's worth:* Calculated in accordance with the method described on pp. 121–2, based on 1973 tax rates. All calculations assume a standard deduction of either $1,300 or 15% (whichever is more favorable) on incomes up to $25,000; itemized deductions of 18% of income (which is the approximate actual average) on incomes greater than $25,000. For the sake of simplicity and clarity, the calculations omit the effect of the added $750 exemption the new bride would bring.

120   *Three million men with incomes under $3,000:* 1970 SOI, p. 24, col. 9.

120   *$21.5 billion cost of marital income-splitting:* Pechman-Okner, Table A-1. Note that this assumes that the advantages now enjoyed by heads-of-household as well as married joint-return filers (as compared with single people) would be ended. This estimate also is based on this being the first change made in the tax law (i.e., the revenue effect has been calculated assuming that no other change in the law, such as abolition of the preferential capital gains tax rate, has taken place).

120   *97% of benefits went to top 5%:* Eisenstein, p. 45; Treasury Dept. release, Apr. 14, 1948.

121   *Couple A gets 97 times benefits of Couple B:* A couple with $150,000 income enjoys a tax saving of $9,567 compared with a saving of just $99 for a couple taking in $7,500.

7. The "Treasury Papers" Episode
or *A Dollar Lost Is a Dollar Spent*

owners, as well as the cost of home owner deductions for taxes and mortgage interest.

144   *Six times direct Federal housing assistance:* Special Analyses, Budget, FY 1973, pp. 202–3.

145   *1968 oil depletion study: Tax Reform Studies and Proposals,* U.S. Treasury Dept. (joint publication of Senate Finance Committee and House Ways and Means Committee, March 11, 1969, Part 4), described as "the final report of a study of the potential effects of changes in the special Federal tax provisions relating to the oil and gas industry on the level of domestic petroleum reserves" (p. ii). The study is summarized at Tr. 426–8.

146   *"Tax expenditures" one-third Federal budget:* The $77 billion is what the Pechman-Okner computer study concluded would be collected under a comprehensive tax system, over and above 1972 Federal tax collections. That does not include the effect of any tax preferences to corporations. The one-third figure is based on the 1972 Federal expenditures of $236.6 billion (Budget, FY 1973, p. 15).

146   *"Tax expenditure" concept originated with Stanley Surrey:* 1968 Annual Report of the Secretary of the Treasury, pp. 326–40.

147   *Tax credits and deductions for political contributions:* IRC Secs. 41 and 642(a)(3) (tax credit) and Sec. 218 (deduction).

148   *One-fourth of population too poor to use political tax credit:* Statement of Stanley Surrey, 1972 JCER Subsidy Hearings, p. 51.

148   *Purpose of personal exemption to meet "minimum living costs":* Appendix to 1947 Treasury Dept. study, "Function and Purpose of Individual Income Tax Exemptions," quoted at S. Rep. 91-552, 91-1, p. 343 (1969).

149   *John Connally told Congress:* 1971 HWM 10.

150   *Wall Street Journal on subsidies:* Editorial, Sept. 30, 1971, p. 22.

150   *New York office building vacancies: Fortune,* Feb. 1971, p. 118.

151   *How DISC's might be used to avoid estate and gift taxes:* One such scheme might go like this: Mr. A, the sole owner of Company A (which does a lively export business), rather than have his company form a DISC, arranges for his children to do so—not an arduous feat for them, since, as you will see on p. 271, a DISC can be merely a "paper" company, and all the children have to put up, among them, is $2,500. The children's DISC proceeds to enter into an agreement with Papa's company whereby a portion of Company A's export profits will be channeled into the DISC. Half of *those* profits will, under the DISC law, be subject to *no* immediate tax; the other half will be taxed to the children (who are likely to be in low tax brackets) rather than at Company A's 48% tax rate. The estate tax saving comes about because some of the export profits that had been going to Company A have been diverted to the DISC, thus producing a less rosy profit picture, thus lessening the value that IRS places on Company A when Mr. A expires, thus lessening his estate tax. While there is no evidence that such a scheme has actually been tried, the possibilities of using the DISC for estate tax avoidance have stirred Mr. Robert L. Weiss to write an entire article about it (see "DISC: An International Dimension for Estates," *Trusts and Estates,* Aug. 1972, pp. 606–9.

8. A Dollar Delayed Can Be Many Dollars Saved

9. Running for Shelter

Page

176–7   *Deductions permitted on borrowed element of real estate:* IRC
        Secs. 1012, 1016; see Crane v. Commissioner, 331 U.S. 1 (1947).

177   *Refinancing of real estate:* See Woodsan Associates v. Commis-
        sioner, 198 F.2d 357, 2nd Circuit (1952).

178   (Footnote) *Promoters believe challenges can be fended off:* See
        Martin Gage, *Journal of Taxation,* Nov. 1972, p. 312.

179–81   *Ocean Towers project:* Preliminary prospectus, dated Nov. 8, 1971,
        for Ocean Towers, Ltd.

182   *Treatment as partnership, not corporation; IRS regulations permit
        corporate advantages:* Rev. Proc. 72-13 (1972-2 IRB, p. 26); Regs.
        Sec. 301.7701-2.

183   *1960 REIT law:* IRC Secs. 856–8.

184   *Skirting of bank lending restrictions:* For examples, see Helvering
        v. F. & R. Lazarus & Co., 308 U.S. 252 (1939) and Paul W. Frenzel,
        22 TCM 1391 (1963).

185   *Dan Throop Smith: Federal Tax Reform,* p. 157, quoted at Tr.
        446n.

187   *"I'm a rich cowhand":* Wall Street Journal, Mar. 19, 1969.

188   *Taxpayer K:* Tr. 94.

188   *2,400 affluent "tax farmers":* Tr. 158.

190   *Cattle eligible for investment credit:* IRC 48(a) (6).

190   *Top-bracket notables: Rodgers, Marx, Harriman, Rockefeller: Wall
        Street Journal,* Aug. 19, 1968; *Jack Benny: Time,* Aug. 30, 1968.

190–1   *Musician-conductor, chain link fence manufacturer:* 1963 HWM
        456, 457.

191   *Pamphlet in ersatz Western lingo:* Prentice-Hall Executives' Tax
        Report, Feb. 4, 1963.

191   *Black Watch Farms: Wall Street Journal,* Sept. 21, 1970, and Apr.
        6, 1971.

195   *1969, 1970 rules re citrus and almond groves:* IRC 278 (citrus);
        PL 91-680 (almond groves).

195   *Cash accounting for farmers:* Regs. Sec. 1.61-4 (as exception to
        Regs. Sec. 1.446-1(c) (2) (i), providing that, as a general rule,
        accrual accounting must be used where the taxpayer keeps inven-
        tories of goods on hand.

197   *U.S. Dept. of Agriculture study:* cited in "Lure of the Land," *Wall
        Street Journal,* Aug. 19, 1968.

197   *Sen. Metcalf bill:* S. 500, 91st Cong., 1st Sess.

197   (Footnote) *Taxpayer J:* Tr. 94.

198   *Charles Davenport on the 1969 "reform":* "Farm Losses Under the
        Tax Reform Act of 1969: Keepin' 'em Happy Down on the Farm,"
        12 *Boston College Industrial and Commercial Law Review* 319
        (Feb. 1971), at 349–50.

198   Newsweek *description:* Aug. 19, 1968, p. 56.

198   *1969 farm "reforms" "not as severe as anticipated":* "Tax Sheltered
        Investments," Arthur Andersen & Co., May 1970, p. 29.

199   *Securities and Exchange Commission oil shelter prospectuses: Oil
        Daily,* Aug. 29, 1969, p. 4.

200   *Oil Daily:* Aug. 29, 1969, p. 4.

201   (Footnote) *IRS restrictions on oil-drilling funds:* See Rev. Proc.
        72-13, 1972-2 IRB, p. 26.

203   New Yorker *account:* Oct. 17, 1970.

214   *Tax savings from investment credit for General Motors, U.S. Steel:* 1971 SFC 197.

214   *Congress on ITC "combating inflation":* 1971 HWM Report, p. 6.

215   *57% of ITC benefits to 260 corporations:* 118 CR H6709 (Daily), July 19, 1972, citing a Library of Congress report on corporations using the ITC in 1965.

215   *Original ITC proposed by Kennedy Administration:* 1961 HWM 20–48 (May 3, 1961); 1962 SFC 80–82, 87.

215–16   *Vanik on employment history of top 100 corporations (and lowest 100 corporations—see footnote):* 118 CR H6708 (Daily), July 19, 1972.

216   *Estimate of $6–$12,000 per job:* 1971 HWM 154–5.

216   *Two Senatorial critics:* Sens. Paul Douglas of Illinois and Albert Gore of Tennessee, 1962 SFC Report, p. 398.

216   *1971 ITC applied to motion pictures:* See Walt Disney Productions v. U.S., 327 F. Supp. 189 (1971).

218   *Tax benefits to utility companies from ITC:* 1962 SFC 87.

218–19   *Congress forbade "pass-through" of ITC benefits:* IRC Sec. 46(c) (3) and 46(e).

218   *$13 billion cost of 1962–69 ITC:* 1967 Corporate SOI 171; 1968 Source Book; 1969 Corporate SOI (Preliminary).

219   *Protest by Sens. Gore and Douglas:* 1962 SFC Report, p. 398.

219   *Statement by Hewlett-Packard secretary-treasurer: Business Week,* Apr. 29, 1961, p. 30.

219   *By James M. Roche:* Statement on New Economic Program of President Nixon, Aug. 31, 1971, quoted at JCER Hearing, Sept. 20, 1971, p. 523.

219   *Estimate of $500 million benefit to IBM:* Assumes that 30% of the approximately $2 billion of capital spending listed in the company's annual report qualifies for ADR treatment. Also assumes an annual growth rate of capital investment of 5%.

220   *Sen. Bible estimate:* 117 CR S5372, Apr. 22, 1971.

221   *Commerce Clearing House example:* 1971 Depreciation Guide, No. 40, Aug. 17, 1971, p. 58.

222   *Price, Waterhouse testimony re Reserve Ratio Test:* Testimony of J. D. Coughlan at Treasury hearing on ADR, May 3, 1971, typed transcript, p. 545.

223   *View espoused by Treasury Dept.:* 116 CR E6955, July 23, 1970.

223–4   *1962 Treasury Dept. survey, "guidelines" fixed at 70% level:* Described in Appendix 3, letter from Prof. Martin David to IRS Commissioner, Apr. 1, 1971.

224   *Administration admits variations in equipment replacement practices:* "Tax Depreciation Policy Options," in which the Treasury talked of the "admittedly great diversity of replacement policies among firms in the same industry and the still greater diversity between industries." See 116 CR E6966, July 23, 1970.

224   *Task Force on Business Taxation:* White House press release of Sept. 22, 1969, in which "the President today announced" the Task Force and its membership, noting that "the first meeting of the task force was held on Saturday, September 13"—nine days before the White House first made public the existence and the membership of the group. The former Nixon law partner chairing the group was John H. Alexander, of the firm of Mudge, Rose, Guthrie

Page

and Alexander (formerly Nixon, Mudge, Rose, etc.). The Connally law partner was Marvin K. Collie, of the firm of Vinson, Eklins, Searls and Connally of Houston, Texas.

225–6   *Arguments against ADR:* Letters to IRS Commissioner by Prof. Martin David, University of Wisconsin, Apr. 1, 1971; Prof. Robert Eisner of Northwestern University, Apr. 12, 1971; and Prof. Boris I. Bittker, Yale University. Released by Taxation with Representation, Arlington, Va.

225   *Assistant Treasury Secretary Cohen:* Press conference, Jan. 11, 1971, quoted by Prof. Eisner, p. 3.

226   *Prof. Robert Eisner:* Letter to IRS Commissioner, Apr. 12, 1971, p. 7 (released by Taxation with Representation, Arlington, Va.).

226   *John Connally quote:* 1971 HWM 10.

226–7   *Proportion of profits and sales going to largest corporations:* Rep. Charles Vanik of Ohio at 118 CR H6709 (Daily), July 19, 1972.

227   *Estimate re share of ADR benefits that will go to largest corporations:* Sen. Alan Bible, 117 CR S5372, Apr. 22, 1971.

11. Ah, To Be an Oilman

228   *H. L. Hunt income:* New York *Times Magazine,* Oct. 20, 1957, p. 38.

228   *Jean Paul Getty income:* Esquire, Oct. 1970, p. 146.

228   *Getty re "a billion dollars":* Newsweek, July 15, 1963, p. 48.

229   *Treasury Study of Mr. D and Mr. B:* 109 CR 24399, Dec. 12, 1963.

229–30   *Oil company profits and taxes:* Oil Week, Aug. 21, 1972, and Aug. 5, 1968. (*Footnote to second table, p. 230, re portion of taxes going to states and to foreign governments:* a study by the Petroleum Industry Foundation, Inc., covering the years 1967–70, said that the taxes by 18 U.S. oil corporations to states and localities amounted to $109 million, compared with "foreign income taxes" in those same years of $3.5 *billion.*)

231   *Total depletion cost of $140 billion:* Rep. Charles Vanik, cited at Dugger, p. 85.

231   *$1.6 billion revenue loss:* Press release re Federal subsidies by Joint Committee on the Economic Report, June 4, 1971, p. 2.

231   *Comparative spending for Head Start, etc.:* Special Analyses, Budget, FY 1973, pp. 118, 121, 134, 152.

232   *$5.5 billion of depletion deductions:* Preliminary Corporation SOI, 1968, p. 16, col. 1. Excludes depletion deductions listed for timber industry, which are almost entirely cost rather than percentage depletion.

232   *Depletion for 110 other minerals:* IRC Sec. 613.

233   *Hugh Roy Cullen:* New York *Times Magazine,* Oct. 20, 1957; Holiday, Feb. 1957, p. 55.

233–4   *Murchison, Richardson, Young:* Holiday, Feb. 1957, p. 56.

234   *Dr. Martin Miller, Michael Benedum:* Fortune, Nov. 1957, p. 176.

234   *Industrialist confides to* Wall Street Journal: Engler, p. 158.

234   *Tax joys summarized by Houston oil expert:* 105 CR 11915 (1959).

235   *Three advantages of oil:* Based on analysis by Louis Eisenstein. See Eisenstein, Ch. 6.

236   *"Intangibles" more powerful incentive than depletion:* J. P. Jackson, "Tax Planning Before Drilling," 27 *Tulane Law Review* 21 (1952).

236   *Corporation depletion and "intangible" deductions:* "Depletion Deductions" (1960 IRS publication), p. 16, col. 1.

237   *Depletion deductions as multiple of cost:* 118 CR S4288 (Daily), Mar. 21, 1972; 1 Compendium 296.

237–9   *Technical study commissioned by U.S. Treasury Dept.:* See note on p. 145, above. Study is summarized at Tr. 426–8.

238   *Depletion deductions by Aramco:* Engler, p. 225.

238   *$5.8 billion profits from Mid-East operations:* Washington *Post,* Feb. 20, 1972, p. G1.

239   *Jersey Standard, Gulf taxes to U.S., foreign governments:* Dugger, p. 84.

240   *Treasury would have been $4½ billion richer:* Based on what the two oil companies would have paid the U.S. if they had continued paying at the same rate of the late Forties and early Fifties, compared with what they *did* pay after the transformation of the "royalties" into "taxes."

240   *Sen. Mike Monroney:* 105 CR 11914 (1959).

240   (Footnote) *Special 33% tax rate:* IRC Sec. 632.

242   *Senate study revealed defects of "discovery depletion":* 67 CR 3768, 3772, 3777 (1926).

242   *History of 27½% depletion allowance:* 30 *Indiana Law Journal* 406; 67 CR 3762, 3776–8 (1926).

243   *Corporate depletion deductions:* 1946 Corporate SOI, p. 8; 1956–57 Corporate SOI, p. 6; 1968 Corporate SOI (Preliminary), p. 16.

243   *1945 court ruling on "capital outlays":* F.H.E. Oil Co. v. Commissioner, 150 F.2d 857 (1945).

243   *Congress directed IRS:* IRC Sec. 263(c).

243   *Congress bars depletion to "soil, sod, dirt", etc.:* IRC Sec. 613(b) (7).

243   *Depletion claimed on underground water and steam:* Marvin Shurbet v. U.S., 63-2 USTC, para. 9528 (1963). Courts granted depletion (on a par with natural gas) to geothermal steam, which a dissenting Tax Court judge labeled "depletion run riot." Reich v. Commissioner, 52 TC 700, at 716 (Raum, J. dissenting). Depletion for underground steam was upheld at 454 F.2d 1157 (1972).

245   *$1.18 per barrel v. 80 cents:* "The Oil Depletion Issue" (publication of the Petroleum Industry Research Foundation, Inc.), p. 96 (1959).

245–6   *Supreme Court rulings on depletion:* U.S. v. Dakota-Montana Oil Co., 288 U.S. 459, 462 (1933); F.H.E. Oil Co. v. Commissioner, 147 F.2d 1002, 1003 (1945) and 150 F.2d 857, 858 (5th Cir. 1945).

246   *Oil companies keep two sets of books:* 1953 HWM 11996.

246   *1964 discrepancy between "book" and "tax" profits:* Dugger, p. 85.

246   *1966 discrepancy:* 1966 Corporate SOI, p. 112, cols. 6, 11.

246   Dun's Review *on business failure rates:* from *Dun's Review and Modern Industry,* Mar. 1955, pp. 33–5.

248   *". . . one of your most ardent Senatorial supporters":* Sen. Monroney of Oklahoma, 97 CR 11726 (1951).

248   *Drilling record of five largest companies: Oil and Gas Journal,* Vol. 57, No. 16, cited at 2 Compendium 975.

265   *Proposal by some Congressional reformers:* Sec. 309 of H.R. 11058, by Rep. James C. Corman of California, 117 CR H9212, Oct. 5, 1971.

265   *Hammond Organ Co.:* Hammond Organ Western Export Corp., 327 F.2d 965 (1964).

267   *Pittsburgh Plate Glass Co.:* PPG Industries, 55 TC 928 (1971).

268   *Kennedy calls for end to tax havens:* "Public Papers of the Presidents," 1969, p. 296 (Apr. 20, 1961).

269   *70–30 method of "un-tainting" foreign profits:* IRC Sec. 954(b) (3).

269   *Explanation of "minimum distribution" formula:* If a company arranges the channeling of its overseas profits and the repatriation of a precisely calculated portion of those profits in such a way that the U.S.-plus-foreign taxes amount to 90% of what the full U.S. tax would have been, then no further tax is required on those profits. Result: the company has been able to realize, in effect, a 10% tax saving.

269   *$30 million saving to Standard of New Jersey:* Based on a *Fortune* estimate that 52% of the firm's profits that year were earned overseas.

269   (Footnote) Fortune *on obstacles to small-firm use of "minimum distribution" escape hatch:* Fortune, Feb. 1969, p. 96.

270   *Arrangement into "chains," "groups" and "single first-tiers":* IRC Sec. 963(c) (2); Regs. 1.963 1(a) (1).

270   *1969 provision to curb use of fictional depletion allowance:* IRC Sec. 901(e).

271   *Formal complaints lodged against DISC:* See Washington *Post,* July 4, 1972; also "Daily Executives' Report" of Bureau of National Affairs, July 5, 1972, pp. G1, G2.

271   *Treasury ruling on DISC as paper entity:* Rev. Rul. 72-166.

272   *After-the-fact adjustment of profit allocation:* Treasury Dept. booklet, "DISC: A Handbook for Exporters," Jan. 24, 1972, p. 25. Many observers have been struck by the vigor with which the Treasury Dept. (usually considered the protector and conserver of the taxpayers' dollars) actively promoted and encouraged business tax avoidance through the DISC. The above-mentioned "handbook" is replete with enticing invitations to make the most of the DISC; and in 1972 Treasury officials were on the speaking circuit, "selling" the DISC to business groups—a function ordinarily associated with "tax shelter" promoters who receive an 8% commission for arranging inroads into the U.S. Treasury by "shelter"-seeking taxpayers.

273   *Prediction of concentration of DISC benefits:* 117 CR S5377 (Daily), Apr. 22, 1971.

274   Wall Street Journal *labels DISC a "gimmick":* Editorial, Sept. 30, 1971, p. 22.

274   *Shipping company profits entirely "untainted":* IRC Sec. 955 (c) (2).

275   *Shipping companies exempt from U.S. taxes even if plying American ports:* IRC Sec. 872(b) (1).

275   *Financial saga of "John Smith":* "Tax Planning for a Foreign Flag Shipping Company," Prentice-Hall Report Bulletin No. 9, July 6, 1972.

13. Timber—Ideal for Your "Tax Shelter"

Page

289   *Increase of five companies' share from 51.3% to 57.3%:* Sunley, p. 327.

289   (Footnote) *Senator Barkley's complaint:* 90 CR 1950 (1944).

290   *Timber losses fully deductible:* IRC Sec. 1231(b)(2). The same "one-way street" provision applies to coal and iron ore royalties as well.

291   *Combined effects of timber preferences on taxes, rates of return:* Sunley, p. 323.

292   *Timber valuation problems:* For examples of such disputes, see Polson Logging Co., 12 TCM 664 (1953); Cascade Lumber Co. v. Squire et al., 57-2 USTC, para. 9841 (1957); and Deer Park Pine Industry, Inc. v. Squire et al., 60-2 USTC, para. 9608 (1960).

14. Old Loopholes Never Die, They Just Get Bigger

295   *Sen. La Follette on depletion:* 88 CR 8017 (1942).

295   (Footnote) *Sen. McKellar on ball and sagger clay:* 88 CR 8021–2 (1942).

296   *Sen. Humphrey, "How far shall we go?":* 97 CR 11812 (1951).

296   *1963 court ruling on depletion for water:* Marvin Shurbet v. U.S., 63-2 USTC, para. 9528 (1963).

296   *1969 Tax Court on underground steam: Wall Street Journal,* Aug. 6, 1969, quoted in Russkay and Osserman, p. 123. See *A. E. Reich,* 52 TC 700; *Rowan,* 28 TCM 797.

296   *Eisenstein quote:* p. 176.

297   *National Sand and Gravel Association:* 1951 HWM 1539.

297   *Sen. Douglas re "just as good a claim":* 97 CR 11811–2 (1951).

297   *1954 request of Sand and Gravel Association:* 1954 SFC 1267.

297   *Two Senators from Texas:* 100 CR 9043 and 9450 (Daily), July 1, 1954.

297   *Sen. Elmer Thomas on rock asphalt:* 88 CR 8022–3 (1942).

298   *Congress extended depletion list:* Sec. 15, H.R. 4069, 80–1; 93 CR 997–8, July 24, 1947.

298   (Footnote) *Medical expenses enacted "for the duration":* S. Rep. 1631, 77-2, p. 6 (1942).

298   (Footnote) *Sand and Gravel Association:* 1954 SFC 1267.

299   *Douglas-Thye exchange:* 97 CR 12336–7 (1951).

299   (Footnote) *Two tax experts on "one-way street" for banks:* Russkay and Osserman, p. 205.

300   *Sen. George on "chicken amendment":* 97 CR 12336–7 (1951).

300   *Capital gains for coal royalties:* Revenue Act of 1951, Sec. 325; S. Rep. 782, 82-1, p. 42 (1951).

301   *Kennedy Administration proposed repeal of capital gains for coal royalties:* 1963 HWM 151–2.

301   *Capital gains for iron ore royalties:* IRC Sec. 631.

301   *Alvord on justice of Mayer amendment:* 1951 SFC 1478.

302   *Treasury Department on rationale for DISC:* 1971 SFC 36.

303   *American Bar and other groups favoring retirement deductions for the self-employed:* 1959 SFC Hearings on H.R. 10.

303   *Sen. Smathers, "have not heard the last of this one":* 108 CR 17675 (Daily), Sept. 5, 1962.

305   *Sens. Long and McCarthy:* S. Rep. 1615, 86-2, p. 47 (1960).

Page

305   *Sen. Gore:* 108 CR 17716 (Daily), Sept. 6, 1962.
305   *Fred and Briedy Heisler:* New York *Times,* June 25, 1972.
305   *Gloria Swanson on depletion for actresses:* Washington *Post,* Mar. 28, 1972, p. B1.
305   *Jockeys' Guild of America on depletion for jockeys:* See Sen. Eugene McCarthy at 106 CR 13225 (1960).
305–6   *National Football League Players' Association; Douglas-Carlson interchange:* 1963 SFC 2495–6 (quoted in Russkay and Osserman, p. 93).
306   *Randolph Paul on "men who came to dinner":* 1955 JCER 309.

15. Tax Handouts Behind Closed Doors

309   *Background of Continental Oil–Consolidation Coal "ABC":* See Senate speeches by Sen. Albert Gore of Tennessee, 112 CR 12684–8, June 8, 1966, and at 112 CR 18979–80, Aug. 11, 1966.
310   *30,000 "letter rulings" per year:* In FY 1971, for example, IRS issued about 33,000. Letter from Assistant IRS Commissioner Swartz to Sen. Ribicoff, Aug. 15, 1971.
310   *14,000 request accounting changes:* Rulings Compendium, p. 72-117.
310   *Treble-damage ruling in electric company case:* Rev. Rul. 64-224. *$400 million cost estimate:* Rulings Compendium, p. 72-104; *$250 million for electric companies alone:* see Morton Mintz and Jerry S. Cohen, *America, Inc.: Who Owns and Operates the United States* (Dial, 1971), in which they say damage suits against electric companies were settled "for almost $500 million" (p. 71).
311   *Copper company rulings:* See Rulings Compendium, p. 72-103 and pp. 107–10. *Re "some stretching of past law and practice" by IRS:* This ruling centered on the question of whether the losses suffered by the copper companies when the Chilean government expropriated their assets in Chile should be immediately deductible for U.S. income tax purposes. This in turn involved, in essence, a question of fact: whether the loss was beyond any hope of recoupment (e.g., through a change in Chilean policy and the return of the assets to the companies). Ordinarily, in issuing ruling letters, the IRS steadfastly refuses to pass on such questions of fact. It was this usual policy from which critics say IRS departed in the case of the copper companies.
311   *U.S. Steel ruling:* The situation here was that the company had generated a large amount of "excess foreign tax credits" (see Chapter 12) from its subsidiary in Venezuela (Orinoco Mining). Those excess credits were about to expire, under the law, and thus, in effect, "go to waste." The only way that unhappy result could be avoided was to quickly generate some profits in the Venezuelan company, against which the about-to-expire credits could be applied. The solution: quickly to sell the right to *future* income from the Venezuelan mining operation, and apply the proceeds of the sale to use up the credits before they expired. But that had two distinct drawbacks. For one thing, to get anyone to buy those future rights—which was tantamount to borrowing money for

future repayment—U.S. Steel would have to pay what amounted to interest; second, since Orinoco's income for the next few years had already been committed to the "purchaser," it would be operating at a substantial loss during those years—and under the generally applicable law, those losses could not be deducted by U.S. Steel (because Orinoco was a *subsidiary*, not a *branch* of U.S. Steel). That was where the ruling saved the day. U.S. Steel asked—and received IRS assent—to have its cake and eat it too: to take in the immediate income and get the advantage of the about-to-expire credits and *then*, when Orinoco began to show losses, to get special permission to treat Orinoco *as if it were a branch*, so that it could combine its tax return with U.S. Steel's. Thus the American "parent" got the full advantage of the "loss" deductions.

312   *Only two independent coal companies in 1972:* Sen. Philip Hart of Michigan, Chairman of the Senate Antitrust Subcommittee, quoted in the Washington *Post*, Apr. 14, 1972, at p. A17.

312   *1969 Congressional reversal of "ABC" transactions:* IRC Sec. 636; *reversal of treble-damage ruling:* IRC Sec. 162(f) and (g).

313   (Footnote) *Closed-door meeting in office of IRS Commissioner Mortimer Caplin:* See Caplin testimony in Hearing before Senate Antitrust Subcommittee, July 27–29, 1966, at p. 89.

313–14   *IRS lawyer re "questionable chances" of success:* Antitrust Hearing (see above), p. 124.

314   (Footnote) *IRS attorneys convinced in 1961:* Acting IRS Commissioner Harding letter of Oct. 18, 1961, stating IRS's "opinion, after full study of the [judicial] decisions" that disallowance of a tax deduction for treble-damage claims was the proper interpretation of the law. Antitrust Hearing (see above), p. 124.

314   (Footnote) *Examples of IRS litigation on smaller questions: on elm disease damage*—see Appleman v. U.S., 338 F.2d 729 (1964); *on termite damage*—see Denton v. Bingler, 63-2 USTC, para. 9731 (1963).

314   *IRS directive to publish all rulings of "general interest":* Letter from IRS Commissioner Dunlap of May 28, 1952, cited at Rulings Compendium, p. 72-117.

315   *Only 480 rulings published a year:* Rulings Compendium, pp. 72–118.

315   *Three practicing attorneys:* George B. Javaras, Howard G. Krane and Jack S. Levin, in Rulings Compendium, pp. 138–40.

315   (Footnote) *Two Washington reporting services that summarize unpublished rulings:* "Shop Talk" in the *Journal of Taxation* and "Tidbits" in *Tax Management.*

315   *Enactment of Freedom of Information Act:* See U.S. Code 552(a) (2)(B), which required "interpretations [by Federal agencies] to be made available for public inspection and copying," together with "a current index" of those interpretations.

315   (Footnote) *One of the Congressional explanations of that law:* H. Rep. 1497, 89-2, p. 7.

315   *IRS change of "precedent" to "reference":* See para. 18 in the government's "Statement of Material Facts Not in Issue" in Civil Action 841–72 (the litigation described on p. 315).

after his death, an estate of $15 million would be required, involving an estate tax of $10 million. Thus the gift tax ($1.8 million) is less than one-fifth of the estate tax ($10 million).

332   *Treasury findings on lifetime gifts v. bequests:* Tr. 115, Table 7.

332–3   *Case of Oliver Johnson:* Estate of Oliver Johnson v. Commissioner, 10 TC 680 (1948).

333   *Congress acknowledging gift tax escapes:* H. Rep. 2319, 81-2, p. 62; S. Rep. 2375, 81-2, p. 57 (1950).

333   *DuPont gift of $36 million:* In re DuPont, 41 Del. Ch. 300, 194 A.2d 309 (1963), cited at Westfall, p. 988, note 10.

334   *John D. Rockefeller and 37 living descendants:* New York *Times*, May 24, 1937, p. 10.

334–7   *Devices for avoiding tax on political gifts:* Jerry Landauer, *Wall Street Journal*, Sept. 27, 1972, p. 1.

335   *Re "politicians running for office partly at Treasury expense":* They can already do that to a very minor extent, under a law enacted in 1971 permitting couples to take tax *credits* of half of political contributions up to $25 or *deductions* for contributions up to $100 (half that amount in each case for an unmarried person) —IRC Secs. 41 and 642(a) (3). As you can see, the tax advantages there are strictly limited; in the capital gains avoidance device, however, the donor can write his own ticket, limited only by his own wealth and generosity and the inventiveness of the recipient party in conjuring up special committees to cash in the stock in $3,000 units.

335   *Richard Mellon Scaife donation of $990,000 to Republicans:* Washington *Post*, Oct. 25, 1972, p. A1.

337   *Congressional explanation for $3,000 gift-tax exemption:* H. Rep. 708, 72-1, p. 29; S. Rep. 665, 72-1, p. 41 (1931).

337   *Louis Eisenstein estimate:* 1955 JCER 812; see also 94 CR 7908 (1948).

338   *Eisenhower Administration annoyed at insurance industry:* Wall Street Journal, Nov. 17, 1954.

339   *Ailsa Mellon Bruce:* See note re p. 325, above.

339   *Sen. McGovern proposal:* 118 CR S73–5 (Daily), Jan. 19, 1972.

340   *Pliny the Younger:* Schultz, *The Taxation of Inheritance* (1926), p. 6.

340   *Sen. William V. Allen:* 31 CR 5081 (1898).

340   *Andrew Mellon:* Mellon, *Taxation: The People's Business* (1924), p. 123.

340   *John Stuart Mill:* Mill, *Principles of Political Economy*, Book 2, Chapter 2, Section 4.

340   *Roger Babson:* Gustavus Myers, *The Ending of American Hereditary Fortunes* (Kelley, 1939), p. 255.

17. Some Moral Preachments of Our Tax Laws

343   *Nora Payne Hill:* Nora Payne Hill v. Commissioner, 13 TC 291 (1949); 181 F.2d 906 (1950).

346   *67% "tax" on welfare recipients; 30% "tax" on food-stamp users:* "Why Is Welfare So Hard to Reform?" by Henry Aaron (preliminary draft), 1972.

18. The Slightly-Privileged Many

351   *Share of benefits of personal exemption for the non-needy:* Paul M. Dodyk, "The Tax Reform Act of 1969 and the Poor," 71 *Columbia Law Review* 758 (May 1971), at 798, Table IX.

351   *$2 billion added revenue by replacing $750 exemption with $150 credit:* Sen. Gaylord Nelson estimated that such a step would raise an additional $1.9 billion. 118 CR S4289 (Daily), March 21, 1972.

351   *Congress on economic handicaps of the elderly:* H. Rep. 1274, 80-2, p. 20 (1948).

352   *Government study on living expenses of the elderly:* Social Security Administration Research Note 12, Sept. 27, 1961, p. 9.

353   *Kennedy proposal of flat $300 credit for the elderly:* 1963 HWM 44.

354   *Income tax "can't provide a shirt for the naked":* Groves, *Federal Tax Treatment of the Family* (Brookings Institution, 1963), p. 115 (preliminary manuscript).

354   *$13 billion cost of nontaxation of government benefit payments:* Pechman-Okner, Table A-3, col. 6.

355   *$15.5 billion of untaxed "rental" income:* Pechman-Okner data.

355–6   *Figures on tax savings and untaxed "rental" income for various priced houses:* based on Henry Aaron, "Income Taxes and Housing," American Economic Review, Dec. 1970, Table 1, p. 790.

356   *(Footnote) British abandonment of rental income tax: The Economist,* Apr. 6, 1953, p. 71.

357   *"Tax expenditures" for housing six times direct outlays:* See note re p. 144, above.

358   *Home ownership up 50% since 1940:* Richard Goode, "Imputed Rent of Owner-Occupied Dwellings Under the Income Tax" (Brookings Institution Reprint No. 50), pp. 509–10.

358   *66 cents v. $6,000 per year in housing "tax welfare":* Pechman-Okner, Table A-2, col. 5 divided by Table 8, col. 1.

361   *Dan Throop Smith re "sick pay" abuses: Federal Tax Reform,* p. 58 (1961).

362   *Nixon on expanded deductions for the self-employed:* Message to Congress on Pension Reform, Dec. 8, 1971.

363   *1948 Treasury survey on taxpayer errors:* C. H. Kahn, *Personal Deductions in the Federal Income Tax* (National Bureau of Economic Research), p. 169n.

364   *Volume of personal deductions, 1950–70:* IRS "Statistics of Income" for the respective years.

365   *Kennedy proposal for cutback on personal deductions:* 1963 HWM 47.

367   *1969 cutback in interest deductions:* IRC 163(d).

368   *Cat Lovers, Footprint Association, Genealogical Society as approved recipients of tax-deductible gifts:* IRS Cumulative List of Organizations, Dec. 31, 1970, pp. 28, 315, 242, respectively.

369   *Prediction of effect of standard deduction in 1942:* Speech by Stanley S. Surrey, 109 CR 3683 (Daily), Mar. 11, 1963.

369   *1970 percentages of income given to charity:* 1970 SOI (Preliminary), p. 40, cols. 3, 10.

369   *1968 percentages of income given to charity:* 1968 SOI, p. 75.

369   *Taxpayer who gave just $463 to charity:* Tr. 92.

Page

369   *Two oilmen with $4,500,000 who gave zero to charity:* Cases A ($2,110,060 income) and B ($2,271,723 income). 109 CR 24399–400, Dec. 12, 1963.

371   *Proposal to make fallout shelter expenses deductible:* H.R. 104, 88-1 (1963).

371   *1972 Presidential candidates endorsed tax credits for school tuition:* Nixon: Washington *Post,* Oct. 26, 1972; McGovern: "Aid to Parents of Children in Parochial and Bona Fide Public Schools," Statement in Chicago, Ill., Sept. 19, 1972.

19. Letter from an Indignant Taxpayer

372   *Irene Saunders' salary and taxes:* Potentially inquisitive Internal Revenue agents should be advised that some illustrative license has been taken here regarding Miss Saunders' salary, her taxes, and the moonlighting activities to which she refers on p. 379.

374   *Geneen:* 1972 ITT Proxy Statement.

374   *Roche:* GM Proxy Statement, Apr. 13, 1972.

374   *Shifting $100 million tax burden:* 1969 SFC Report, p. 333.

376   *Sen. Long's suggestion of fingerprinting welfare recipients:* The Washington *Post* of Mar. 4, 1972 (p. A1), in reporting that the Senate Finance Committee was "studying a plan for fingerprinting all applicants for Social Security cards in order to curb fraudulent acquisition of cards by illegal immigrants and welfare cheaters," quoted Sen. Long as follows: "We would only require fingerprints in 'high risk' cases, like a person who was over 30 and still doesn't have a card. If we ask for fingerprints [of children receiving Social Security cards in school] at age 6, it would be on a voluntary basis. I personally think that everyone ought to have fingerprints on file, but I don't think we should require it at age 6."

376   *Sen. Long on welfare recipients' "filthy" neighborhoods:* Washington *Post,* Dec. 19, 1971, p. C4.

376   *Banks getting quarter of a billion a year:* Tr. 102.

377   *Seventeen-year transition period for banks:* IRC Sec. 585.

377   *Korean war tax increase effected immediately; heavier on poor than on rich:* New York *Times,* Sept. 23, 1950, p. 1.

378   *John D. Rockefeller, III, about voluntarily paying 5% to 10% tax:* 1969 HWM 1567, Feb. 27, 1969.

378   *67% "tax" on welfare recipients; 30% "tax" on food-stamp users:* See note re p. 346, above.

380   *General Motors' three-and-a-half-billion-dollar profit:* 118 CR H6713 (Daily), July 19, 1972.

20. Why the Wealthy Few Win Out over the Un-Rich Many

381   *Roughly 60 million Americans who would benefit from $800 personal exemption:* 1970 SOI (Preliminary), p. 22, col. 6, listing 59.3 million *taxable* returns filed in 1970.

381   *30,000 who benefited from 50% top rate on salary income:* 1969 SFC Report, p. 333.

381   *Only 1 in 10 got any capital gains:* 1970 SOI (Preliminary), p. 38, col. 2, showing that 7.9 million returns (out of a total 74 million returns filed that year) listed any capital gain or loss transactions in 1970.

Page

381 *Only 1 in 100 got more than $1,500:* 1970 SOI (Preliminary), p. 38, cols. 2, 4, shows that only those with "adjusted gross incomes" of $30,000 or more listed more than $1,500 of *average* net capital gains in 1970.

382 *90% of political contributions come from 1% of the population:* Time, Nov. 23, 1970, p. 11.

383 (Table) *Political gifts by corporation executives and wealthy families:* Herbert E. Alexander, *Financing the 1968 Election* (Heath, 1971), p. 185 (25 largest corporations), p. 180 (prominent families), p. 184 (American Petroleum Institute), p. 188 (persons worth $150,000,000 or more).

383 *Contributions by bank officers:* Press statement by Rep. Henry Reuss of Wisconsin, Apr. 18, 1972.

383 *Portion of Humphrey campaign expenses from 50 individuals:* Alexander (see above), p. 152. Breakdown of their occupations is in Appendix J, pp. 341–4.

383 *Portion of Presidential funds from contributors of $500 or more:* Alexander (see above), p. 163.

384 *Account of Kleppe-Burdick campaign:* Washington *Post*, Nov. 22, 1970, p. A14.

385 *Contributions by officers of Litton Industries:* Congressional Quarterly, Sept. 18, 1970, p. 2292.

385 *White House pressure on behalf of Pew Foundation:* New York Times, Oct. 14, 1971.

385 *Harvey family generosity to Democratic party: special provision for Harvey Aluminum Co.:* Wall Street Journal, Apr. 26, 1967, p. 1.

386 *Contributions from the oil industry: Alexander* (see above), p. 184; Congressional Quarterly, Sept. 18, 1970, p. 2292; Washington *Post*, Jan. 31, 1971, p. A25.

386–7 *Richard Harris in* The New Yorker: Aug. 7, 1971, pp. 52–3.

388 *Sen. Long speech re "monetary bread cast upon the water":* Quoted in Harris *New Yorker* account (see above), p. 53.

390 *V. O. French on flexibility of seniority system re Finance Committee membership:* French, p. 32.

391 *Sen. Douglas on fate of loophole-closing amendments:* 105 CR 11910 (1959).

393 *Secrecy of Congressional tax-writing committees:* French, p. 33.

394 *Examples of complex sections of the Internal Revenue Code:* IRC Sec. 341 (e) (5) (A) and IRC Sec. 509 (a).

394 *Learned Hand on complexity of the tax laws:* quoted by Joseph Goulden, *The Superlawyers* (Weybright, 1972), p. 308.

396 *Clay Pipe Industry Depletion Committee, etc., as Congressional witnesses:* Index of 1969 SFC Hearings, Vol. 7, p. xxvi.

397 *Billion-dollar cost of oil shale amendment:* Joseph Goulden, *The Superlawyers*, p. 309.

21. What Should Be Done About Our Tax System?

398 *Lowering all tax rates by about two-fifths:* Pechman-Okner, Table 9, col. 3.

399 *Raising upwards of $77 billion:* Pechman-Okner, Table 8, col. 5.

404–5 *Rate schedule suggested by Pechman and Okner:* Pechman-Okner, Table 10, Rate Schedule 5.

Page

408 (Table) *Average family income:* Pechman-Okner, Table 2, col. 1 divided by Table 8, col. 1.

408 *Average tax under present law and no-loophole system:* Pechman-Okner, Table 6, cols. 2 and 1 are divided by Table 8, col. 1.

409 *Three families with $2.5 million of dividend income:* 1970 SOI (Preliminary), p. 36, cols. 11, 12 (comparing all returns with taxable returns).

409 *5 million taxpayers making less than $3,000 a year:* 1970 SOI (Preliminary), p. 22, col. 6, shows 5,013,966 *taxable* returns filed in 1970 with "adjusted gross incomes" of less than $3,000.

410 *Justice Holmes re "pay[ing] for civilized society":* Compañía General de Tabacos v. Collector, 275 U.S. 87, 100 (1927).

410 *Andrew Mellon taking Treasury official with him:* A. M. Schlesinger, Jr., *The Age of Roosevelt, Vol. I: Crisis of the Old Order: 1919–1933* (Houghton Mifflin, 1957), p. 63.

411 *Andrew Mellon on low tax rates as salvation of free enterprise:* Mellon, *Taxes: The People's Business,* pp. 17, 18, 69, 80.

411 *Top tax rate ranged from 82% to 94%:* Pechman, *Federal Tax Policy,* Table A-2, p. 256.

412 *Sen. McGovern capital gain proposal:* In speech to New York Society of Security Analysts, Aug. 29, 1972.

414 *George Meany opposition to ending "sick pay" provision:* 1963 HWM 1962.

414–16 *Plan for Federal financing of election campaigns:* This plan is embodied in a bill (S. 1039) introduced by Sen. George McGovern, Mar. 1, 1971 (117 CR 4396–403), which the author helped develop for the Senator.

417 *1968 figures on apportionment of before-tax privately earned income:* Roger A. Herriott and Herman P. Miller, "Who Paid the Taxes in 1968" (paper prepared for the National Industrial Conference Board meeting in New York, Mar. 18, 1971), p. 3. Cambridge Institute pamphlet, p. 17. These figures reflect "total income" (before taxes and before government benefit payments). This differs from "money income" (see note below) in that, in addition to "money income," it includes the following: income underreported in Census Bureau Surveys; "imputed" income (see Glossary) such as the rental value of owner-occupied homes; capital gains not reported in Census Bureau surveys; retained corporate earnings that under some analyses are attributed to the shareholders; and some indirect taxes less government benefit payments. For more detail, see Cambridge Institute pamphlet, p. 17, note 2.

417 *1962 figures on concentration of wealth: Inequality and Poverty,* ed. by Edward C. Budd (Norton, 1967), p. xxii. Cambridge Institute pamphlet, p. 22.

418 (Table) *Before- and after-tax apportionment of incomes: Inequality and Poverty* (see above), pp. xiii, xvi. Cambridge Institute pamphlet, p. 20.

418 *The view "from the bottom of the heap":* These figures, from the Herriott and Miller paper (see above note), list *money* income, as published by the Bureau of the Census.

419 *Distribution of income, 1947–70:* U.S. Bureau of the Census, Current Population Reports, Series P-60, No. 80, Oct. 4, 1971, Table

Page

14, p. 28. Cambridge Institute Pamphlet, p. 15. Figures show money income before deductions (for Federal and state income taxes, Social Security contributions and other taxes) and are for families (two or more people residing together who are related by blood, marriage or adoption).

420 *Professor James Tobin quote:* Tobin and W. A. Wallace, "Welfare Programs: An Economic Appraisal" (American Enterprise Institute for Public Policy Research, 1968), p. 2.

421 *Sen. McGovern proposal for merging welfare and tax systems:* 118 CR S73–5 (Daily), Jan. 19, 1972.

424 *Statement by Republican Ways and Means members:* H. Rep. 871, 78-1, Part 2, p. 7 (1943).

424 *Mills and Curtis statements:* Quoted in Scripps-Howard newspaper series on taxes by Jack Steele, Jan. 1958.

424 *Randolph Paul re "wasting asset":* 1955 JCER 307.

425 *James C. Carter before the Supreme Court:* Pollack v. Farmers' Loan and Trust Co., 157 U.S. 429, 516 (1895).

INDEX

473